Endorsements of *The Fulfillment of All Desire*

"Ralph Martin has produced a gem of a guidebook for those who would set out on the path to holiness in language that readily engages the modern reader. Martin's particular genius is to make the most profound spiritual treasures accessible to contemporary people. Like the masters whose wisdom he distills, he communicates a burning desire to respond to the Lord's call. The result is an inspiring work brimming with insight and practical help for people at every stage of the spiritual journey."

FATHER PETER RYAN, S.J.
Professor of Moral Theology,
Mount St. Mary's Seminary, Emmitsburg, MD.

"I am deeply moved by this work. There is a beauty in this book which draws the reader into intimate friendships with the saints and opens one to the Holy Spirit's presence, increasing our desire for nuptial union. This book, with its synthesis of the saints' teaching, is an extraordinary gift to the Church for the work of the new evangelization."

FATHER JOHN HORN, S.J.
Co-founder of the Institute for Priestly Formation,
Creighton University, Omaha, NE.

"Many Catholics leave the church and seek refuge in eastern religions and in cult movements because they are seeking a spirituality and prayer of greater depth than they find in their own tradition. But they need not seek elsewhere. Ralph Martin opens up the sources of the rich, Catholic, mystical tradition and makes it accessible to all, clergy and laity alike."

FATHER KILIAN MCDONNELL, O.S.B.
Founder and President of the Institute for Ecumenical and Cultural Research,
St. John's University, Collegeville, MN.

"This reliable and challenging synthesis, which is obviously the fruit of lots of prayerful reflection and study, abounds in wisdom, offers practical guidance, and deserves to be a classic."

FATHER PATRICK COLLINS, C.M.
Author of numerous books and lecturer in spirituality at
All Hallows College as well as at Milltown Institute, Dublin, Ireland.

"Ralph Martin has written an excellent book that gathers together the wisdom of Bernard of Clairvaux, Teresa of Avila and others as well who have left us with a great store of wisdom about how we can cooperate with the transforming work of the Spirit. Without watering down the depth of these writers Ralph has made their teachings understandable and accessible and given us a true "guidebook" for the journey to God. Men and women in all parts of the Body of Christ will find this book both inspiring and practically useful. A great help for our life of prayer."

PASTOR MIKE BICKLE
Founder of the International House of Prayer, Kansas City, MO.

"Ralph Martin transmits in an orderly and attractive manner the consensus teaching of some of the great representatives of the Western spiritual tradition. I would recommend this book particularly to young couples who wish to come to know God more deeply and allow him, with the help of genuine spiritual masters, to work a deep transformation in their lives, one that builds their family and endures for eternity."

FATHER FRANCIS MARTIN, SSD
Holder of the Adam Cardinal Maida Chair in Sacred Scripture,
Sacred Heart Major Seminary, Detroit, MI.

THE
FULFILLMENT
OF ALL
DESIRE

—⁄⁄⁄—

Other Books by Ralph Martin

Author
Hungry for God:
Practical Help in Personal Prayer
Ignatius Press, 2000

Called to Holiness:
What It Means to Encounter the Living God
Ignatius Press, 1999

Is Jesus Coming Soon?:
A Catholic Perspective on the Second Coming
Ignatius Press, 1997

The Catholic Church at the End of an Age:
What Is the Spirit Saying?
Ignatius Press, 1994

A Crisis of Truth:
The Attack on Faith, Morality and
Mission in the Catholic Church
Servant Press, 1983

Coeditor
John Paul II And the New Evangelization:
How You Can Bring the Good News to Others
Servant Press, 2006

Audio Albums by Ralph Martin
Available from Renewal Ministries
www.renewalministries.net

THE
FULFILLMENT
OF ALL
DESIRE

A Guidebook for the Journey to God
Based on the Wisdom of the Saints

—◆—

Ralph Martin

EMMAUS
ROAD
PUBLISHING

Steubenville, Ohio

♂

Emmaus Road Publishing
A Division of
Catholics United for the Faith
827 North Fourth Street
Steubenville, OH 43952

© 2006 by Ralph Martin
All rights reserved. Published 2006
Printed in the United States of America
10 09 08 07 06   1 2 3 4

Library of Congress Control Number: 2006928253
ISBN: 1-931018-38-3

Cover design and layout by
Beth Hart

Cover artwork:
Thomas Cole, *The Pilgrim of the Cross at the End of His Journey*
Smithsonian American Art Museum / Art Resources NY

*To Augustine, Bernard, Catherine,
Teresa, John, Francis and Thérèse,
in whom and through whom
God is greatly glorified.*

CONTENTS

Contents

—∿—

PART III
Transforming Union
(The Unitive Way)
371

—∿—

ACKNOWLEDGEMENTS

This book wouldn't have been possible without receiving permission to use the best contemporary English translations of the writings of the Doctors of the Church whose teachings we are drawing on in this book.

Excerpts from Catherine of Siena: *The Dialogue*, translation and introduction by Suzanne Noffke, O.P., from The Classics of Western Spirituality, © 1980 by Paulist Press, Inc., New York/Mahwah, NJ. Used with permission of Paulist Press. www.paulistpress.com

Excerpts from Bernard of Clairvaux: *On the Song of Songs, Volume One*, translation by Kilian Walsh OCSO, introduction by M. Corneille Halflants OCSO, ©1971 by Cistercian Publications, Inc., Kalamazoo, Michigan. Used with permission of Cistercian Publications.

Excerpts from Bernard of Clairvaux: *On the Song of Songs, Volume Two*, translation by Kilian Walsh OCSO, introduction by Jean Leclercq OSB, ©1976 by Cistercian Publications, Inc., Kalamazoo, Michigan. Used with permission of Cistercian Publications.

Excerpts from Bernard of Clairvaux: *On the Song of Songs, Volume Three*, translation by Kilian Walsh OCSO and Irene M. Edmonds, introduction by Emero Stiegman, © 1979 by Cistercian Publications, Inc., Kalamazoo, Michigan. Used with permission of Cistercian Publications.

Excerpts from Bernard of Clairvaux: *On the Song of Songs, Volume Four*, translation by Irene Edmonds, introduction by Jean Leclercq, © 1980, by Cistercian Publications Inc., Kalamazoo, Michigan. Used with permission of Cistercian Publications.

Excerpts from *The Collected Works of St. Teresa of Avila, Volume One*, translated by Kieran Kavanaugh and Otilio Rodriquez ©1976 by Washington Province of Discalced Carmelites, ICS Publications, 2131 Lincoln Road, N.E., Washington, DC 20002-1199 U.S.A. www.icspublications.org

Excerpts from *The Collected Works of St. Teresa of Avila, Volume Two*, translated by Kieran Kavanaugh and Otilio Rodriguez ©1980 by Washington Province of Discalced Carmelites, ICS Publications, 2131 Lincoln Road, N.E., Washington, DC 20002-1199 U.S.A. www.icspublications.org

Acknowledgements

Excerpts from *The Collected Works of St Teresa of Avila, Volume Three*, translated by Kieran Kavanaugh and Otilio Rodriguez ©1980 by Washington Province of Discalced Carmelites, ICS Publications, 2131 Lincoln Road, N.E., Washington, DC 20002-1199 U.S.A. www.icspublications.org

Excerpts from *The Collected Letters of St. Teresa of Avila, Volume One*, translated by Kieran Kavanaugh and Otilio Rodriguez © 2001 by Washington Province of Discalced Carmelites, ICS Publications, 2131 Lincoln Road, N.E., Washington, DC 20002-1199 U.S.A. www.icspublications.org

Excerpts from *The Collected Works of St. John of the Cross*, translated by Kieran Kavanaugh and Otilio Rodriguez ©1964, 1979, 1991 by Washington Province of Discalced Carmelites, ICS Publications, 2131 Lincoln Road, N.E., Washington, DC 20002-1199 U.S.A. www.icspublications.org

Excerpts from *Story of a Soul*, translated by John Clarke, O.C.D. ©1975, 1976, 1996 by Washington Province of Discalced Carmelites, ICS Publications, 2131 Lincoln Road, N.E., Washington, DC 20002-1199 U.S.A. www.icspublications.org

Excerpts from *St. Augustine: Confessions*, translated by Henry Chadwick ©1991 by Oxford University Press, Oxford, United Kingdom. Used by permission of Oxford University Press.

Excerpts from *St. Francis De Sales: Introduction to the Devout Life*, translated and edited by John K. Ryan, ©1950, 1952, 1966, published by Image Books/Doubleday, New York (1989 edition). Translation used by permission of the National Society for the Propagation of the Faith, New York.

―⁓―

I would also like to thank Dr. Patricia Cooney-Hathaway whose History of Spirituality class at Sacred Heart Major Seminary in Detroit helped me to rediscover the depth of spiritual insight found in the Doctors of the Church; Beth Hart and Regis Flaherty and their colleagues who have been a delight to work with at Emmaus Road Publishing and who have done such a fine job in the design, lay-out and shepherding of this book to publication; and the remarkable group of spiritual leaders and scholars who have taken the considerable time and trouble to read the book with a view towards writing an endorsement who have written more positively than I could have hoped for or imagined; and finally, my family and colleagues at Renewal Ministries and Sacred Heart Seminary who have been so consistently supportive and encouraging in both my work and journey.

ABBREVIATIONS

The Old Testament
Gen./Genesis
Ex./Exodus
Lev./Leviticus
Num./Numbers
Deut./Deuteronomy
Josh./Joshua
Judg./Judges
Ruth/Ruth
1 Sam./1 Samuel
2 Sam./2 Samuel
1 Kings/1 Kings
2 Kings/2 Kings
1 Chron./1 Chronicles
2 Chron./2 Chronicles
Ezra/Ezra
Neh./Nehemiah
Tob./Tobit
Jud./Judith
Esther/Esther
Job/Job
Ps./Psalms
Prov./Proverbs
Eccles./Ecclesiastes
Song/Song of Solomon
Wis./Wisdom
Sir./Sirach (Ecclesiasticus)
Is./Isaiah
Jer./Jeremiah
Lam./Lamentations
Bar./Baruch
Ezek./Ezekiel
Dan./Daniel
Hos./Hosea
Joel/Joel
Amos/Amos

Obad./Obadiah
Jon./Jonah
Mic./Micah
Nahum/Nahum
Hab./Habakkuk
Zeph./Zephaniah
Hag./Haggai
Zech./Zechariah
Mal./Malachi
1 Mac./1 Maccabees
2 Mac./2 Maccabees

The New Testament
Mt./Matthew
Mk./Mark
Lk./Luke
Jn./John
Acts/Acts of the Apostles
Rom./Romans
1 Cor./1 Corinthians
2 Cor./2 Corinthians
Gal./Galatians
Eph./Ephesians
Phil./Philippians
Col./Colossians
1 Thess./1 Thessalonians
2 Thess./2 Thessalonians
1 Tim./1 Timothy
2 Tim./2 Timothy
Tit./Titus
Philem./Philemon
Heb./Hebrews
Jas./James
1 Pet./1 Peter
2 Pet./2 Peter
1 Jn./1 John

2 Jn./2 John
3 Jn./3 John
Jude/Jude
Rev./Revelation (Apocalypse)

Church Documents and Writings
NMI   John Paul II, Apostolic Letter at the Close of the Jubilee Year,
      Novo Millennio Ineunte, January 6, 2001
LG   Second Vatican Council, Dogmatic Constitution on the Church
      Lumen Gentium, November 21, 1964

—〰—

INTRODUCTION

A FEW MONTHS BEFORE GRADUATING from the University of Notre Dame, I experienced a significant reawakening of my childhood faith that set me on a path I've been on now for more than forty years. After graduating from Notre Dame, I enrolled, as planned, in the graduate philosophy department at Princeton University, beginning studies towards a doctorate in philosophy. After my first year of graduate studies a friend and I spent a summer at a monastery seeking direction for our lives. We felt that the Lord was leading us to leave graduate school and become more directly involved in the work of evangelization. A short while later we were asked to take up research and training positions at the national office of the Cursillo Movement, positions we held for five years. At the same time we were engaged in campus ministry at the Catholic student parish at Michigan State University, and later at the student parish at the University of Michigan in Ann Arbor, Michigan, where I have mainly lived since then.

As the charismatic renewal unfolded in the Catholic Church in the late 1960's, we found ourselves in a leadership position and became very involved in writing and speaking as well as in directly evangelistic and pastoral work in this country and overseas. This included a four-year period during which my wife, my family, and I lived in Brussels, Belgium, working closely with Cardinal Suenens, who at that time was the primate of the Catholic Church in Belgium and had served as one of the four moderators of the Second Vatican Council.

It would truly take an entire book to recount the experiences of those years of life and service, but in the late 1980's and early 1990's there was a shift in our work of the sort that gave me the opportunity to take up graduate level theological studies, part-time, at the Sacred Heart School of Theology, the major seminary in Detroit. I eventually ended up getting an MA in theology in 1996.

In the spring of 1993 I was in an airport in Zurich, Switzerland, waiting for a plane back to the United States. I was using the layover as a chance to catch up with my reading for a History of Spirituality course I was taking at the time. The assignment was to read *The Spiritual Canticle* by Saint John of the Cross.

I had first tried to read Saint John of the Cross's *The Ascent of Mount Carmel* shortly after the spiritual awakening I had experienced at Notre Dame. After reading maybe less than a hundred pages or so, I remember putting it down because it seemed hard to understand and rather negative in its approach. It wasn't something I could relate to at the time.

Now, however, in an airport in Zurich in 1993, as I read *The Spiritual Canticle*, it was as if I was blinded by an excess of light and insight. As I read I felt that everything I had ever experienced, felt, desired, longed for, and strove to understand was being revealed to me in a depth of understanding and measure of beauty and meaning that literally took my breath away. It was the right book at the right time.

I had never flagged in my desire to follow the Lord or to grow in holiness through all these years but reading John reopened for me some of the absolute depths that I encountered in God during that awakening so many years ago, and gave me the hope that all I had hoped for then, in relationship to Him, was indeed possible. I was being called again to "launch out into the deep."

I found myself working through John's other writings, including *The Ascent of Mount Carmel* that I had found so unattractive and difficult years ago, and finding in them immense insight and great help in continuing the spiritual journey. Maybe a certain amount of life experience, at least in my case, was necessary before I could understand the truth and relevance of these works.

Even though I only had to read portions of these works in my theology class I found myself wanting to read the whole of these works and more besides. I worked through the writings of Saint Teresa of Avila, Saint Catherine of Siena, and Saint Thérèse of Lisieux and found in them immense depths of insight, encouragement, and practical wisdom. And then I studied Saint Bernard of Clairvaux, Saint Augustine's *Confessions*, the works of Saint Francis De Sales, and more. I couldn't get enough of these great Doctors of the Church and their teachings on the spiritual life.

Then, in 1997, Father Michael Scanlan, at that time president of Franciscan University of Steubenville, called me and asked if I would be interested in teaching a graduate level theology class on the "new evangelization." I told him I could do that if he wanted, but I'd rather teach a course on Saint Teresa of Avila and Saint John of the Cross. He knows me well and was a bit surprised at my request. He knew I was studying these Doctors but asked me: "Do you feel ready to teach them?" I did feel ready and answered yes. The student evaluations were very positive, and every summer since then I've been asked to teach in the graduate theology program at Franciscan University and have taught over a number of summers all seven of the Doctors of the Church that we are using as guides in this book.

Then I was asked to teach the Catholic Spirituality course at the relatively new Catholic college in my own area, Ave Maria, which I did for several years before it moved to Florida.

And then I was asked to teach the Introduction to Catholic Spirituality course and a graduate level course on Evangelization and Spirituality at Sacred Heart Major Seminary and School of Theology, in the Archdiocese of Detroit, which I've been doing the last several years as well. I am now a regular part of the faculty and Director of Graduate Theology Programs in the New Evangelization at the seminary.

When, on January 6, 2001, at the end of the Jubilee year 2000, Pope John Paul II published *Novo Millennio Ineunte*, his vision of dynamic Catholic life for the new millennium, I was amazed to see him call for the whole Church to reconnect with the mystical tradition, mentioning specifically Catherine of Siena, Teresa of Avila, John of the Cross and Thérèse of Lisieux, four of the saints I had been teaching for several years at various institutions. I felt a deep confirmation that I was on the right track in following the Spirit's lead.

I believe that the Lord has given me a deep desire to understand the writings of these great Doctors of the Church not just for myself but so I can share them with others. I know, from my own experience, that many people have tried to read these saints and Doctors and have found them difficult and stopped. There are many reasons why this is so. Some of the writings are poorly translated into English that is now somewhat archaic. Some "ramble," making it difficult at first to see the structure and clarity of their thought. Some of the writings are just plain difficult. For whatever reason, at this stage of my life and service, the Lord has given me a measure of understanding of these Doctors, and a desire and ability to communicate their teachings to others.

So far I have done this by direct teaching in many different settings, and by making audio albums available on each of these Doctors which attempt to communicate the integrity of their teachings in an understandable way.[1] As I have done this I have been very struck by the fundamental agreement of these Doctors in what they teach about the spiritual journey: they really are giving us a "roadmap" of the journey to God. Across so many centuries, languages, cultures, and different types of personalities, the Lord has infused a wisdom about the spiritual journey that is immensely inspiring and helpful, and remarkably harmonious.

I feel ready now, and led by the Lord as well, to attempt to put together in one book, a picture and explanation of this spiritual roadmap as it is found in the writings and lives of these Doctors of the Church. I have tried as much as possible to let these saints speak for themselves by a generous use of their own words, keeping my commentary to a minimum so as not to impede the flow of the "roadmap." I am very grateful to the copyright holders of the translations I have used for giving me permission to use the saints' words as much as I have. I hope you will find, as I have, that their words are irreplaceable—oftentimes for their literary brilliance, and always for their depth of insight and their practical relevance. I have also wanted to use their own words as much as possible so the remarkable harmony of their teachings with one another may stand out clearly. The reliability of the roadmap I am tracing is increased manyfold not just because of the eminence of a particular Doctor's teaching but also because of their remarkable harmony with one another on the essentials of the spiritual journey. I hope you will see that there is a multitude of highly authoritative, holy, and insightful witnesses pointing clearly to the road we must take to reach our goal of union with God, where we will find the fulfillment of all desire. I hope also that you will find the book useful as a "guidebook" or "map" that can be referred to repeatedly over the years when wisdom is needed about a particular aspect of the journey. The wisdom of these saints is that reliable and that useful!

I have restricted myself in this book just to those saints of the Western Church who have been recognized as Doctors by the Church and make a major contribution to our understanding of the spiritual journey. There are thirty-three Doctors of the Church in total. Some are recognized for their contribution to scriptural commentary; some for moral theology; some for defending against heresy; some for systematic theology; some for "spiritual theology" or wisdom about the way to union with God. Doctors of the Church have the highest level of authority and their teachings are recognized as being of universal value. There are of course Doctors of the Church from the East that have made important contributions in the area of spirituality, and many other saints and writers of the West as well, but in this book we will focus on only seven of these Doctors, all of whom made a major contribution to the understanding of the spiritual journey.

Bernard of Clairvaux, a twelfth-century Cistercian abbot whom we will learn more about later, asks where the teachers are who will help us make this awesome journey, and then answers:

> God will provide for this. Look, they are here already, they who are to instruct the new bride in the thing she needs to know, and prepare her for her marriage to the heavenly Bridegroom, and to teach her the faith and counsel her in the way of holiness.[2]

These seven Doctors of the Church whom we will be looking to for wisdom to guide us on this journey, including Bernard himself, are preeminent among those "instructors" Bernard promised the Lord would provide.

I have sought the Lord's help and the help of our friends and teachers, the Doctors and saints who form the substance of this book, so that this book will be useful in helping others to begin or continue or complete the journey to God, at the end of which we find the fulfillment of all desire. May we find in the voices of these saints, in the pages of this book, the voice of the Teacher Himself, guiding us on our journey to God. "And though the Lord give you the bread of adversity and the water of affliction, yet your Teacher will not hide himself any more, but your eyes shall see your Teacher. And your ears shall hear a word behind you, saying, 'This is the way, walk in it,' when you turn to the right or when you turn to the left" (Is. 30:20–21).

A highway will be there,
    called the holy way;
No one unclean may pass over it,
    nor fools go astray on it.
No lion will be there,
    nor beast of prey go up to be met upon it.
It is for those with a journey to make,
    and on it the redeemed will walk." (Is. 35:8–9, NAB)

CALLED TO HOLINESS

JESUS SUMMED UP HIS TEACHING in a startling and unambiguous call to His followers: "You, therefore, must be perfect, as your heavenly Father is perfect" (Mt. 5:48). Perfect in purity of heart, perfect in compassion and love, perfect in obedience, perfect in conformity to the will of the Father, perfect in holiness—when we hear these words we can be understandably tempted to discouragement, thinking that perfection for us is impossible. And indeed, left to our own resources, it certainly is—just as impossible as it is for rich people to enter heaven, or for a man and a woman to remain faithful their whole lives in marriage. But with God, all things are possible, even our transformation.

John Paul II—and he himself may be among those recognized as a Doctor one day—in his prophetic interpretation of the events of the second half of the twentieth century and the beginning of the twenty-first, *Novo Millennio Ineunte*, points out that the Holy Spirit is again bringing to the forefront of the Church's consciousness the conviction that these words of Jesus are indeed meant for every single one of us. He points out that the Jubilee of the year 2000 was simply the last phase of a period of preparation and renewal that had been going on for forty years, in order to equip the Church for the challenges of the new millennium.[1]

Pope John Paul II speaks of three rediscoveries to which the Holy Spirit has led the Church beginning with the Second Vatican Council, which concluded in 1965. One of these rediscoveries is the rediscovery of the "universal call to holiness."[2]

> All the Christian faithful, of whatever state or rank, are called to the fullness of the Christian life and to the perfection of charity. (NMI 30; cf. LG 40)

John Paul further emphasizes that this call to the fullness of holiness is an essential part of being a Christian.

> To ask catechumens: "Do you wish to receive Baptism?" means at the same time to ask them: "Do you wish to become holy?" It means to set before them the radical nature of the Sermon on the Mount: "Be perfect as your heavenly Father is perfect" (Mt. 5:48). . . . The time has come to repropose wholeheartedly to everyone this *high standard of ordinary Christian living*: the whole life of the Christian community and of Christian families must lead in this direction. (NMI 30, 31)

Before we go much further in our examination of the spiritual journey, let's take an initial look at what "holiness" really means. In the Book of Ephesians we read, "He chose us in him before the foundation of the world, that we should be holy and blameless before him" (Eph. 1:4). To be holy is not primarily a matter of how many Rosaries we say or how much Christian activity we're engaged in; it's a matter of having our heart transformed into a heart of love. It is a matter of fulfilling the great commandments which sum up the whole law and the prophets: to love God and our neighbor, wholeheartedly. Or as Teresa of Avila puts it, holiness is a matter of bringing our wills into union with God's will.

Thérèse of Lisieux expresses it very similarly: "Perfection consists in doing His will, in being what He wills us to be . . . who resists His grace in nothing."[3] As she said towards the very end of her life: "I do not desire to die more than to live; it is what He does that I love."[4]

John Paul II goes on to call the parishes of the third millennium to become schools of prayer and places where "training in holiness" is given.

> Our Christian communities must become *genuine "schools" of prayer,* where the meeting with Christ is expressed not just in imploring help but also in thanksgiving, praise, adoration, contemplation, listening and ardent devotion, until the heart truly "falls in love." . . . It would be wrong to think that ordinary Christians can be content with a shallow prayer that is unable to fill their whole life." (NMI 33)

John Paul cites several reasons why this turn to holiness of life and depth in prayer is important. Besides the fact that it is quite simply part and parcel of the Gospel message, he points out that the supportive culture of "Christendom" has virtually disappeared and that Christian life today has to be lived deeply, or else it may not be possible to live it at all. He also points out that in the midst of this world-wide secularization process there is still a hunger for meaning, for spirituality, which is sometimes met by turning to non-Christian religions. It is especially important now for Christian believers to be able to respond to this hunger and "show to what depths the relationship with Christ can lead" (NMI 33, 40).

Recognizing how challenging this call is, John Paul makes clear that it will be difficult to respond adequately without availing ourselves of the wisdom of the mystical tradition of the Church—that body of writings and witness of life that focuses on the process of prayer and stages of growth in the spiritual life. He tells us why the mystical tradition is important and what we can expect it to provide for us.

> This great mystical tradition . . . shows how prayer can
> progress, as a genuine dialogue of love, to the point of
> rendering the person wholly possessed by the divine
> Beloved, vibrating at the Spirit's touch, resting filially
> within the Father's heart. (NMI 33)

These are truly extraordinary words that John Paul uses here, words to which we will need to return in the course of this book. How is this extraordinary depth of union with the Trinity possible? It is indeed the answer to this question that the mystical tradition gives us and that this book will attempt to clearly communicate. John Paul makes clear that this depth of union isn't just for a few unusual people ("mystics") but is a call that every Christian receives from Christ Himself. "This is the lived experience of Christ's promise: 'He who loves me will be loved by my Father, and I will love him and manifest myself to him' (Jn. 14:21)." (NMI 32)

Then John Paul summarizes some of the main wisdom taught by the mystical tradition about the spiritual journey, wisdom that we will pay close attention to in the course of this book.

> It is a journey totally sustained by grace, which nonethe-
> less demands an intense spiritual commitment and is
> no stranger to painful purifications (the "dark night").
> But it leads, in various possible ways, to the ineffable joy
> experienced by the mystics as "nuptial union." How can
> we forget here, among the many shining examples, the
> teachings of Saint John of the Cross and Saint Teresa of
> Avila? (NMI 32)

These four principles that John Paul identifies are basic to a proper understanding of the spiritual journey.

1. Union with God of this depth is totally unattainable by our own efforts; it is a gift that only God can give; we are totally dependent on His grace for progress in the spiritual life. Yet we know also that God is eager to give this grace and bring us to deep union.

Without Him, we can do nothing, but with Him all things are possible (cf. Jn. 14:4–5, Lk. 18:27, Phil. 4:13). Without God, successfully completing the journey is impossible, but with Him, in a sense, we are already there. He is truly both the Way and the destination; and our lives are right now, hidden with Christ, in God (Col. 3:3).

2. At the same time our effort is indispensable. Our effort is not sufficient to bring about such union, but it is necessary. The saints speak of disposing ourselves for union. The efforts we make help dispose us to receive the gifts of God. If we really value something we must be willing to focus on doing those things that will help us reach the goal. And yet without God's grace we cannot even know what's possible, or desire it, or have the strength to make any efforts towards it. It's God's grace that enables us to live the necessary "intense spiritual commitment."

"You will seek the LORD your God and you will find him, if you search after him with all your heart and with all your soul" (Deut. 4:29).

3. As the Gospel tells us, it's important to assess what's required before undertaking a task (before starting to build a tower, or entering into a battle in war) if we want to successfully complete it. Much has to change in us in order to make us capable of deep union with God. The wounds of both original sin and our personal sins are deep and need to be healed and transformed in a process that has its necessarily painful moments. The pain of purification is called by John of the Cross the "dark night." It is important not to be surprised by the painful moments of our transformation but to know that they're a necessary and blessed part of the whole process.

"Through many tribulations we must enter the kingdom of God" (Acts 14:22).

4. And finally, we need to know that all the effort and pain is worth it! *Infinitely* worth it. The pain of the journey will appear in ret-

rospect to have been light, compared to the weight of glory that we were being prepared for (see 2 Cor. 4:16–18).

Deep union (the "nuptial union" or "spiritual marriage" or "transforming union") is possible even in this life. Teresa of Avila tells us that there's no reason that someone who reaches a basic stability in living a Catholic life ("mansion" three in her classification system) can't proceed all the way to "spiritual marriage" in this life ("mansion" seven).[5]

All of these principles will be explored in-depth in later chapters. Now we need to recognize the significance of the "rediscovery" of the universal call to holiness and determine our own response to the call.

We all probably know in some way that we're called to holiness but perhaps struggle to respond. Feeling the challenge of the call and yet seeing the obstacles, it is easy to rationalize delaying or compromising and avoid a wholehearted and immediate response.

It is not uncommon, for example, to "pass the buck" to others whom we deem in a better position to respond wholeheartedly. Those of us who are Catholic lay people often look at our busy lives and sluggish hearts and suppose that priests and nuns are in a better position to respond to the call. After all, we may think to ourselves, that's what we pay them for! We may think that when our kids are grown, or when we retire, or after a business crisis passes, or when we don't have to care for ailing parents, or when we get a better job, or when we get married, or . . . that *then* we'll be in a better position to respond.

Unfortunately, being a priest or nun doesn't eliminate temptations to also "pass the buck." With the reduction in numbers, it is understandably easy for priests and nuns to feel overwhelmed by their responsibilities and have such a busy pace of life that they might suppose that it's the cloistered orders who are truly in a good position to respond wholeheartedly to the call to holiness.

But even in cloistered orders, it's possible to rationalize and "pass the buck." What with caring for guests, overseeing building renovations, attending monastic conferences, or making cheese, bread, or jams, it's possible to suppose that it's the hermit who really can respond wholeheartedly.

But even being a hermit doesn't guarantee such a response. After all, hermits need to work out a rule of life, have meetings with superiors to review it, make sure their medical insurance is covering them properly, deal with internal and external distractions and temptations, and maybe even contribute to a newsletter for hermits!

What really holds us back from a wholehearted response to the call of Jesus, of Vatican II, of the repeated urgings of the Spirit, is not really the external circumstances of our lives, but the interior sluggishness of our hearts. We need to be clear that there will never be a better time or a better set of circumstances than now to respond wholeheartedly to the call to holiness. Who knows how much longer we'll be alive on this earth? We don't know how long we'll live or what the future holds. Now is the acceptable time. The very things we think are obstacles are the very means God is giving us to draw us to depend more deeply on Him.

Or sometimes what holds us back from responding wholeheartedly in our present circumstances is believing that we don't have to focus too much on that right now, because sooner or later any purification needed will be taken care of in purgatory. There are a few problems with this way of thinking.

It's true that sometimes we don't hit the goal we're aiming at, and it's good to have a backup. If we aim for heaven at the moment of our death, and indeed die in friendship with Christ but haven't been transformed enough to be ready for the sight of God, purgatory is a wonderful blessing. But if we aim for purgatory and miss, there really isn't a good backup available.

The source of all our unhappiness and misery is sin and its effects, and the sooner the purification of sin and its effects can take place in our life, the happier we will be and the better able to truly love others. Only then will we be able to enter into the purpose God has for our life. Truly, in this case, better sooner than later.

And finally, it's important to realize that there is only one choice; either to undergo complete transformation and enter heaven, or be eternally separated from God in hell. There are only two ultimate destinations, and if we want to enter heaven we must be made ready for the sight of God. Holiness isn't an "option." There are only saints in heaven; total transformation is not an "option" for those interested in that sort of thing, but is essential for those who want to spend eternity with God.

> Strive for peace with all men, and for the holiness without which no one will see the Lord. (Heb. 12:14)

The whole purpose of our creation, the whole purpose of our redemption is so that we may be fully united with God in every aspect of our being. We exist for union; we were created for union; we were redeemed for eternal union. The sooner we're transformed the happier and the more "fulfilled" we'll be. The only way to the fulfillment of all desire is to undertake and complete the journey to God.

In the Old Testament it was clear that to actually see God in our untransformed human condition was to be destroyed.

> Then Moses said, "Do let me see your glory!" He answered, "I will make all my beauty pass before you, and in your presence I will pronounce my name, "LORD"; I who show favors to whom I will, I who grant mercy to whom I will. But my face you cannot see, for no man sees me and still lives." (Ex. 33:18–20, NAB)

It is only Jesus who sees the face of the Father, and it is through Jesus that we can be made ready to share in His vision of the Father. It is through our union with Jesus, our contemplation of His "face," that we are, little by little, transformed and made ready for the beatific vision, which is so much more than what we commonly understand as "seeing"; it is indeed a participation in the ecstatic knowing and loving of the Trinity, a participation in Love itself.

When Pope John Paul considered what was the most important legacy of the Jubilee year 2000 that should be carried forward into the new millennium, this is what he said: "But if we ask what is the core of the great legacy it leaves us, I would not hesitate to describe it as the *contemplation of the face of Christ*" (NMI 15).

Bernard of Clairvaux expands our vision of what it means to contemplate the face of Christ by pointing out that we "look upon the Son in the Father and the Father in the Son."[6] Bernard also wholeheartedly encourages us to undertake the journey.

> Come then, follow, seek him; do not let that unapproachable brightness and glory hold you back from seeking him or make you despair of finding him. "If you can believe all things are possible to him who believes" (Mk. 9:22). "The Word is near you, in your mouth and in your heart" (Rom. 10:8). Believe, and you have found him. Believing is having found. The faithful know that Christ dwells in their hearts by faith (Eph. 3:17). What could be nearer? Therefore seek him confidently, seek him faithfully, "The Lord is good to the soul who seeks him" (Lam. 3:25). Seek him in your prayers, follow him in your actions, find him in faith.[7]

And, of course, this wholehearted seeking of the Lord, this contemplation of Christ, is a central part of the message of Scripture.

> And we all, with unveiled face, beholding the glory of the Lord, are being changed into his likeness from one degree of glory to another; for this comes from the Lord who is the Spirit. (2 Cor. 3:18)

This Scripture text is a powerful summary of the process of transformation, which we will now begin to examine in some detail.

AN OVERVIEW OF THE JOURNEY

VARIOUS ATTEMPTS TO CLASSIFY THE STAGES of spiritual growth have been made over the centuries. The predominant classification, used by a number of the Doctors we are drawing from and many other writers as well, is the three-stage division of purgative, illuminative, and unitive. (Another major attempt at delineating the stages of growth is that of Saint Teresa of Avila, who divides the journey into seven "mansions" or stages.)

In brief, the *purgative* stage or way includes the initial phases of the spiritual life, including coming to conversion, turning away from sin, bringing one's life into conformity with the moral law, initiating the habit of prayer and the practices of piety, and maintaining a relatively stable life in the Church. (The first three mansions of Teresa deal with issues connected with the purgative stage.)

The *illuminative* stage is one of continuing growth. It is characterized by deeper prayer, growth in the virtues, deepening love of neighbor, greater moral stability, more complete surrender to the lordship of Christ, greater detachment from all that is not God, and increasing desire for full union. It is accompanied by various kinds of trials and purifications and sometimes by great consolations and blessings, including what are commonly referred to as "mystical phenomena." (Teresa's fourth, fifth, and sixth mansions deal with issues connected with this stage.)

The *unitive* stage is one of deep, habitual union with God, characterized by deep joy, profound humility, freedom from fears of suffering or trials, great desire to serve God, and apostolic fruitfulness. The experience of the presence of God is almost continual; great insight into the things of God is experienced; and while not without suffering, suffering now becomes primarily the grace of sharing in the redeeming suffering of Christ rather than the suffering of purification. This deep, habitual union is variously described as a "spiritual marriage" or "transforming union." (Teresa describes the unitive stage in the seventh mansion.)

This three-stage division is a useful way of broadly characterizing the different aspects of the spiritual journey, and so we will be using it as an organizing principle for our study of the journey. But since many people experience the traditional terminology as a bit obscure and abstract, we will often use alternative descriptions in ordinary language.

At this point I'd like to present a chart that attempts to broadly correlate the terminology that several of the doctors we will be drawing on use, and relate it to the traditional three stages of the spiritual life. This chart is simply a point of reference and an attempt to give a simplified overview of the journey in schematic form. All of the concepts will be explained in the appropriate chapters. Also, it's important to bear in mind that in practice no one's life perfectly matches any of the stages described by the various saints. They themselves note how different aspects of these stages can be present in one's life simultaneously, although the direction of our lives, if we are making progress, should increasingly mirror the characteristics the saints point out as indicators of spiritual progress. As Catherine puts it, "These are three stages for which many have the capacity, and all three can be present in one and the same person."[1]

	Purgative way	Illuminative way	Unitive way	Beatific vision
Teresa of Avila	Mansions one to three; turning away from sin; praying; growing in stable, well ordered, Catholic life.	Mansions four to six; recollection; prayer of quiet, prayer of union; union of wills; preparation for union by gifts and graces, interior and exterior trials.	Mansion seven; "spiritual marriage;" "perfect" but still faults and inadvertent venial sins are possible; great fruitfulness in prayer and action.	Knowing
John of the Cross	"Beginners"; meditation; "active night of the senses" (*Ascent* I); "passive night of the senses" (*Dark Night* I).	"Proficients"; contemplation; "active night of the spirit" (*Ascent* II, III) (*Spiritual Canticle* 1-21); "passive night of the spirit"; "spiritual betrothal" (*Dark Night* II).	"Perfect," habitual, contemplative union; "spiritual marriage" "transforming union" *Living Flame*; *Spiritual Canticle* 22-40).	and loving
Catherine of Siena	"Slavish fear" (fear based turning to God); embrace of the feet of Christ (conversion).	"Mercenary love" (service of God motivated by reward); growing in prayer, virtue, stability (patience, obedience, humility); contemplating the wounded side of Christ.	"Filial love"; "love as a very dear friend" (love for the sake of the other); kiss of the mouth of Christ; union of contemplation and action.	as we
Bernard of Clairvaux	"Natural affection" (loving those who love us); prostrate at the feet of Christ (repentance from sins, conversion).	"Liberty of spirit" (loving others as one loves oneself; hoping for gain); kissing the hands of Christ, (virtue, prayer, the fruits of repentance).	"Spousal love"; "friends of the Bridegroom" (universal love, even of enemies).	are known
Francis De Sales	Turning away from mortal sin, venial sin, and the affection for sin; establishing ordered pattern of prayer; servile fear of hell.	Growing in virtue: humility, obedience, patience, poverty of spirit, detachment, stability of prayer, and love of neighbor; mercenary love, a servant looking for payment.	Ruled by love; spousal love; perfect union of wills, in the following of the commandments, counsels, and inspirations of the Holy Spirit; Jesus living in and through us; perfect love casts out fear but servile and mercenary motives still help in time of temptation.	and loved.

Having an overall view of how the various saints classify the stages of the process of transformation can be helpful as we examine in detail the particular elements of the journey to God.

PART I

TRANSFORMATION BEGINS

(The Purgative Way)

AWAKENING AND CONVERSION

SOMETIMES PEOPLE WHO ARE BAPTIZED AS INFANTS simply grow up in an atmosphere of faith, gradually maturing into a life of deep holiness and mission. While healing and purification are often still needed for people in this situation to make progress (sometimes quite a bit), there is no marked experience of an awakening or conversion from a life apart from God. Such was the case with Thérèse of Lisieux and Francis de Sales, two of the great Doctors of spirituality to whom we will refer frequently in this book. They were blessed with family environments of faith and solid instruction, and simply matured (in Thérèse's case not without significant trauma) into the life of holiness and the special missions God gave them.

On the other hand, there are others who, while they may be living some measure of Catholic life, often do so with lukewarmness or significant compromise. We know that lukewarmness is not a state pleasing to the Lord (see Rev. 3:15–16). People in this situation seem to be stuck "serving two masters" or simply blind or unaware of what the call to holiness really involves, and don't make much (if any) progress on the spiritual journey. The Lord often gives grace to people in this situation to awaken them to a fervent Christian life. Teresa of Avila testifies that she was among the lukewarm whom the Lord needed to awaken in order for her to begin again to make significant progress on the spiritual journey.[1]

There are others living further away from the Lord who need more than an awakening, or reawakening. Some of these may be living in the depths of unbelief or in deep bondage to serious sin. Some may have practiced their faith at one time to some degree but for various reasons have turned away. Some may have never heard the Gospel or been baptized or embarked on the spiritual journey. For people in these situations, God in His mercy gives grace sufficient to bring about conversion or reconversion. Saint Augustine testifies that such was his situation.

Beginnings and rebeginnings are important in the spiritual life. Lessons are learned about sin and grace, about our efforts and God's mercy, that are valuable not just at the beginning but all along the way to full union. In just this way, the lessons learned in the "purgative stage" of the journey continue to shape and mold the soul.

In this chapter we will examine some of the lessons we can learn from the testimony that Teresa and Augustine give about, respectively, their awakening and conversion to a life of holiness and mission.

Awakening to God: Teresa's Testimony

Teresa was born on March 28, 1515, in Avila, Spain, to a devout Catholic family. Teresa had eleven siblings. Her father had remarried after his first wife died. When Teresa was thirteen, her mother (the second wife) also died. Teresa then asked Mary, the Mother of Jesus, to be her mother also.

As Teresa grew older, her father felt his high-spirited and attractive daughter needed a more protective environment, and sent her to a convent school when she was sixteen years old. Teresa, later reflecting on her own experience, even has some advice for parents in similar situations:

> If I should have to give advice, I would tell parents that
> when their children are this age they ought to be very
> careful about whom their children associate with. For
> here lies the root of great evil since our natural bent is
> toward the worst rather than toward the best.[2]

Impressed with one of the nuns there, Teresa reasoned that the best way to save her soul was probably to enter a convent, which she did when she was about twenty years old. She entered the Carmelite Convent of the Incarnation in Avila, which was large, and not particularly strict. There was a lot of coming and going of both nuns and visitors; social and economic distinctions were carefully preserved. Some nuns had suites of rooms, with servants and pets, while others had simple cells. Teresa started her time in the convent with reasonable fervor; she occasionally even experienced the prayer of union, which she describes as characteristic of the fifth mansion. But after a few years she settled into a routine that contained within it many compromises with worldliness and vanity, which blocked further progress. Only when she was almost forty years old was she awakened again to a fervent life, and she began again to make progress on the journey.

The means that God used to call her to Himself again was a small statue that showed His sufferings as He approached crucifixion. As she meditated on what Christ had suffered for her, she fervently asked for and experienced the grace of deeper conversion, which relaunched her on the spiritual journey. Shortly afterwards she read Augustine's *Confessions*, which had just recently been translated into Spanish. God used Augustine's testimony to consolidate the awakening that was occurring in Teresa. This awakening occurred in 1554, when Teresa was almost forty years old. She began to single-heartedly focus on loving and serving the Lord and, eight years later, in 1562, experienced the "spiritual betrothal" she speaks of in her description of the sixth mansion. Ten years after that, in 1572, after receiving Communion from John of the Cross, she experienced the "spiritual marriage" she describes in the seventh mansion. She was fifty-seven years old. In 1582, at the age of sixty-seven, she died, worn out from her labors. Along with John of the Cross, she had carried out a very difficult reform of the Carmelite order, and by the time of her death there were seventeen reformed monasteries with over two hundred nuns and ten monasteries containing approximately three hundred friars.

What Blocked Teresa's Progress?

Teresa, at the request of her spiritual director, wrote an account of her life, an actual autobiography, entitled *Her Life*. In this work, as in all her writings, Teresa is very honest in speaking of her weaknesses and mistakes. She clearly identifies a number of things that blocked her progress after an initially promising start in her early twenties during her first few years in the monastery.

Carelessness about Sin

Teresa makes a very striking statement about how carelessness about sin seriously blocked her progress.

> As for venial sins, I paid little attention; and that is what destroyed me.[3]

She points out that this was partly the case because of "liberal and permissive" advice given to her by priests.

> What was venial sin they said was no sin at all, and what was serious mortal sin they said was venial. This did me so much harm. . . . I went on in this blindness for I believe more than seventeen years until a Dominican Father, a very learned man, enlightened me about many things.[4]

Yet at the same time, Teresa acknowledges that she probably should have known instinctively what was really right and wrong, and that there may have been something in her that too easily accepted such advice.

There is indeed an inclination in all of us to look for advice that will let us follow our selfish desires.

> For the time is coming when people will not endure sound teaching, but having itching ears they will accumulate for themselves teachers to suit their own likings, and will turn away from listening to the truth and wander into myths. (2 Tim. 4:3–4)

Teresa makes a very important distinction between deliberate, freely chosen venial sin (advertent) and venial sin that is not deliberately and freely chosen (inadvertent). She gives a very clear description of what she means:

> Be careful and attentive—this is very important—until you see that you are strongly determined not to offend the Lord, that you would lose a thousand lives rather than commit venial sins—that is, advertently; for otherwise, who can go without committing many?

When Scripture comments that "a righteous man falls seven times and rises again" (Prov. 24:16), Teresa understands this as referring to a basically righteous person inadvertently committing small—venial—sins. Teresa thinks that these inadvertent faults may be with us throughout our life to some degree even though we are progressing on the spiritual journey.

Teresa comments that, sometimes, committing a small sin and becoming aware of it happen almost simultaneously and that such "inadvertent" venial sins, although unfortunately common, don't impede the spiritual journey nearly as much as freely choosing to commit "small" sins. Her definition of "advertent" venial sin is clear.

> It seems to me a sin is very deliberate when, for example, one says: "Lord, You see it, and I know You do not want

it, and I understand this; but I want to follow my whim and appetite more than Your will." It doesn't seem to me possible that something like this can be called little, however light the fault; but it's serious, very serious.[5]

Making a decision never to freely choose to commit even a small sin is an important turning point in the spiritual journey. As Teresa points out, freely choosing to commit a "small" sin isn't really a little thing if we are trying to live a life pleasing to God.

Not Avoiding the Near Occasions of Sin

One of the most common reasons why people fail to make progress in the spiritual journey, frequently falling back into the same sins, is a lack of wisdom about avoiding those occasions that usually contribute to our sinning. This was true for Teresa during those many years during which she "spun her wheels" not making progress on the journey.

She alludes to some problems to which she was vulnerable when engaged in conversations with certain persons, and expresses her frustration about being sorry but not able to change.

> And seeing my lack of amendment, I became extremely vexed about the many tears I was shedding over my faults, for neither were my resolutions nor were the hardships I suffered enough to keep me from placing myself in the occasion and falling again. They seemed fraudulent tears to me. . . . The whole trouble lay in not getting at the root of the occasions and with my confessors who were of little help. For had they told me of the danger I was in and that I had the obligation to avoid those friendships, without a doubt I believe I would have remedied the matter. For in no way would I have endured being in mortal sin even for a day should I have understood that to be the case.[6]

Even those who have come to the second dwelling places (the second mansion) in the early stages of the journey are still in danger of turning back and giving up because "they don't avoid the occasions of sin."[7]

Not avoiding people, places, or situations associated with sinning may in turn weaken our resolve to avoid sin, and is a reason why many people don't make progress in the spiritual life. We need to ask God for the wisdom to identify those situations that weaken our resolve to resist sins and avoid them as much as possible.

Self-Reliance

Teresa makes another very strong statement, virtually identical to what she said about carelessness about sin, identifying a false understanding and attitude that very seriously blocked her progress:

This self-reliance was what destroyed me.[8]

One of the most common reasons why people begin the spiritual journey but then turn back is because they find themselves failing, wearing out, or getting tired or discouraged as a result of relying on their own strength or intellect rather than on the Lord. In the course of this book we will see that this is a point virtually all of these Doctors of the Church make in one way or another. Teresa's testimony about how significantly this problem impeded her progress is very clear, and she has advice about what to do about it.

> I give you one counsel; that you don't think that through your own strength or efforts you can arrive, for reaching this stage is beyond our power; if you try to reach it, the devotion you have will grow cold. But with simplicity and humility, which will achieve everything, say: *fiat voluntas tua (your will be done).*[9]

Teresa points out the discernible difference between the demeanor of someone who is approaching the spiritual journey as a matter of one's own effort, and that of someone approaching it as a matter of trusting in the mercy of God.

> When we are more determined we are less confident of ourselves, for confidence must be placed in God. When we understand this . . . there will be no need to go about so tense and constrained. . . . [We will] go about with a holy freedom.[10]

Teresa urges us to trust in the blood of Christ and the mercy of God to lead us in the spiritual journey, confident that we will make progress.

> Through the blood He shed for us I ask those who have not begun to enter within themselves to do so; and those who have begun, not to let the war make them turn back. . . . Let them trust in the mercy of God and not at all in themselves, and they will see how His Majesty brings them from the dwelling places of one stage to those of another . . . and they shall enjoy many more blessings than one can desire—blessings even in this life, I mean.[11]

Eventually, little by little, even if it may not be soon, Teresa promises that if we keep trying and trusting we will become saints.

> Have great confidence, for it is necessary not to hold back one's desires, but to believe in God that if we try we shall little by little, even though it may not be soon, reach the state the saints did with His help.[12]

Not Valuing the Graces of God

One of the characteristics we find in many saints is their promptness in responding to the inspirations of the Spirit. When Francis of

Assisi was moved to pray, he would often start praying immediately, wherever he was, even if it was in the middle of a crowded street. Catherine of Siena was known for the same promptness in responding to the inspirations of the Lord wherever she was and whatever she was doing. Francis de Sales defines the nature of the "devout" life as being characterized by a frequent, careful, and prompt response to the will of God and to His inspirations.

Teresa of Avila points out that not valuing the graces God grants us, such as when He gives us a sense of His presence in prayer, keeps many people from making progress.

> A soul to whom God grants such pledges has a sign that He wants to give it a great deal; if not impeded through its own fault, it will advance very far. But if the Lord sees that after He places the kingdom of heaven in the soul's house this soul turns to earthly things, He will not only fail to show it the secrets there are in His kingdom but will seldom grant it this favor, and then for just a short space of time.

Teresa gives us direction about how to respond appropriately when the Lord gives tokens of His presence.

> Now it could be that I am mistaken in this matter, but I see and know that this is what happens, and in my opinion this is why there are not many more spiritual persons. When individuals do not respond by service that is in conformity with so great a favor, when they do not prepare themselves to receive it again, but take back their wills from the hands of the Lord who already possesses these wills as His own, and set them upon base things, the Lord goes in search of those who do love Him so as to give more to them. Yet He doesn't take away entirely what He has given, when one lives with a pure conscience. But there are persons—and I have been one of them—who make themselves deaf when the Lord, taking pity on them, gives them holy inspirations and light

concerning the nature of things, and, in sum, gives this
kingdom and places them in this prayer of quiet.[13]

Bernard also realizes that not many of us in the beginning are as
attentive as we should be to these visits of the Lord.

> Who among us, do you think, is so vigilant, so attentive
> to the time of his visitation and the Bridegroom's coming
> that he every moment scans every detail of his approach,
> so that when He comes and knocks, he opens the door
> to Him right away? (Lk. 12:36)[14]

And yet Bernard encourages us to grow in such attentiveness
to the sometimes barely perceptible "lights" and "nudges" that the
Holy Spirit wishes to give us.

> If he can say with the psalmist: "My eyes are ever on the
> Lord," and "I keep the Lord always before me" (Ps. 23:
> 5), shall that person not receive a blessing from the Lord
> and mercy from God his saviour? (Ps. 23:5) He will be
> visited often, and never be unaware of the time of the
> visit (Lk. 19:44), even though he who visits in spirit
> comes secretly and stealthily like a shy lover.[15]

I believe it's quite possible that, as one reads this book, the Lord
will give tokens of His presence, insight into His workings, invitations to come closer; it would be worth implementing this practice
of immediately responding to the Lord by that attentiveness in
prayer and action of which Teresa and Bernard speak.

It's also possible that certain teachings of the saints in this
book will initially strike one as impossible, disturbing, unreason-
able, imbalanced, unrealistic, or even untrue—very much like the
response of many to some of the teachings of Jesus. I would ask
you please to hang in there and travel the whole journey. It may
take some time to understand what a particular saint may mean by

something they express in a strong way; it may take a while for our defensiveness, fears, and misconceptions to give way to a broader and deeper view of reality, including our own reality. I can promise you that the struggle is worth it.

We'll be returning to the wisdom of Teresa and Bernard at later stages of the journey, but now let's consider the insight into conversion that Augustine provides.

Dynamics of Conversion: Augustine's Testimony

Augustine was born on November 13, 354, in a town that is now a part of eastern Algeria, forty-five miles inland from the Mediterranean. His parents, Patricius and Monica, had a comfortable living from the small farm they managed. Monica came from a Christian family and was very devout. Patricius was not a Christian, but was baptized on his deathbed in 372.

A good student, Augustine excelled at the Latin classics. At the age of seventeen, he took as a mistress a girl from Carthage with whom he lived for fifteen years, until, in Milan, she became an obstacle to his social advancement. They had a son, Adeodatus, who was converted along with Augustine. Adeodatus died in 389 at the age of seventeen, a year after he and Augustine had returned to Africa from Italy.

Although Augustine was very interested in money and in worldly success as a teacher, he also had a very genuine desire to know the truth. But he was also very desirous of having a regular sexual relationship.

He eventually became an adherent of the Manichean version of Christianity and stayed with this belief system for ten years. Mani's answer to the problem of evil was to declare God good but not all-powerful. He also had a very negative view of the material world and of procreation, although members of the "Hearers" category of believers could have wives or mistresses as long as they avoided procreation by contraception or periodic abstinence.

Eventually, Augustine's knowledge of astronomy caused him to question the various cosmic myths that were part of the Manichean explanation of reality, and in his later years he even wrote a defense of Christianity against the Manicheans. Centuries later Bernard was to call Augustine "that mighty hammer of heretics."[16]

Bernard also had to combat a reappearance of the Manichean errors in the Cathari heresy of his time.

> But if you limit the goodness of God after the insane manner of the Manichaean, so that what he has created and given to be received with thankfulness, you, ungrateful, thoughtless and censorious, judge to be unclean and shun like the plague, then I certainly do not commend your abstinence.[17]

After teaching for seven years in Carthage, a major North African city in proximity to Italy, Augustine moved to Rome, hoping for better-behaved students and for opportunities for greater advancement in his career.

After a year in Rome, disillusioned with the behavior of the students who often switched teachers just before payment was due, Augustine moved to Milan in 384. Here he came into contact with philosophers influenced by Plato, whose writings eventually helped lead him to Christianity. These philosophers helped him solve some conceptual problems he had in coming to an intellectually convincing idea of God. He still had moral issues to deal with, though, as well as various fears.

Seven hundred years later, Bernard of Clairvaux also noted how an incorrect image of God can hold someone back from faith and conversion:

> My opinion is that all those who lack knowledge of God are those who refuse to turn to him. I am certain that they refuse because they imagine this kindly disposed God to be harsh and severe, this merciful God to

be callous and inflexible, this lovable God to be cruel and oppressive. So it is that wickedness plays false to itself, setting up for itself an image that does not represent him.[18]

Bernard then goes on to counter false conceptions of God that hold people back from surrendering to Him.

What are you afraid of, you men of little faith? That he will not pardon your sins? But with his own hands he has nailed them to the cross. That you are used to soft living and your tastes are fastidious? But he is aware of our weakness. That a prolonged habit of sinning binds you like a chain? But the Lord loosens the shackles of prisoners. Or perhaps angered by the enormity and frequency of your sins he is slow to extend a helping hand? But where sin abounded, grace became superabundant. Are you worried about clothing and food and other bodily necessities so that you hesitate to give up your possessions? But he knows that you need all these things. What more can you wish? What else is there to hold you back from the way of salvation?[19]

In July of 386, Augustine experienced conversion, to the joy of his mother, and was baptized in Milan by Saint Ambrose during the Easter Vigil of 387.

In 388, while Monica, Augustine, and Adeodatus were in the Roman seaport of Ostia, Monica died and was buried there. Augustine's account of their final days together, their common experience of God, and his grief is very moving. He then returned to Africa where he formed a lay community of Christian friends. In 391 he was "drafted" as a priest in the diocese of Hippo Regius,[20] on the coast, and about four years later was made bishop.

Augustine died on August 28, 430, at the age of seventy-five, as the Vandals were attacking Hippo and the Roman Empire was collapsing. Along with Thomas Aquinas, he is considered one of the two greatest theologians the Church has known. Along with Bernard of Clairvaux, he is considered one of the two greatest Christian writers in Latin.

During his lifetime, Augustine was a tremendous defender of the faith against various heresies and published a huge amount of material. It is said that even Augustine scholars aren't able to study it all. One of his most influential books was his account of his conversion, which he called the *Confessions*. Written in the form of an address or prayer to God that is obviously meant for others to hear, the *Confessions* is considered one of the greatest masterpieces of Latin Christian literature. They are confessions in the two-fold sense: confessions of sin as well as confessions of the mercy, goodness, beauty, and greatness of God. While telling his own story, Augustine communicates great insight into the process of conversion, which will help us greatly in understanding some of the most important principles of the spiritual journey. We have already noted how Augustine's confessions, more than a thousand years after he wrote them, profoundly impacted Teresa of Avila in solidifying her own reawakening to a fervent following of the Lord.

One of the most striking things in reading Augustine's account is how gradually, over many years and using many different means, God prepared Augustine for conversion.

In first place, perhaps, is the well-known prayer of his mother, Monica, for his conversion. Monica didn't just pray, but tried to encourage Augustine in the faith, with no immediate success. Augustine gives the impression, despite his great respect for Monica, that as a younger man he wasn't very interested in listening to her exhortations about becoming a Catholic. But there are many other influences as well.

While still in his late teens he read a book of the Roman philosopher Cicero, called *Hortensius*, which gave him a conviction that happiness was found in the truth rather than in physical pleasures. And even though many years passed before Augustine had the motivation and strength to act on this insight, a seed was planted which prepared the way.

Another experience God used to prepare the way was to allow Augustine to experience firsthand the tawdry side of the world. His experience of the noble career of a teacher of literature was marred by the politics involved in getting good appointments, the difficulty in earning a living, and the less than sincere and serious behavior of his students.

And then God used the great "pagan" Greek philosopher Plato and his teachings, which were being developed at the time by philosophers in the Roman Empire, to bring Augustine to a closer perception of the truth, enabling him to move beyond the myths of the Manichees.

Besides these important but more distant or indirect preparations for conversion, there were some very striking proximate and explicitly Christian means that God used to impact Augustine. These are recounted primarily in books VIII and IX of the *Confessions.*

> All doubt had been taken from me that there is indestructible substance from which comes all substance. My desire was not to be more certain of you but to be more stable in you. But in my temporal life everything was in a state of uncertainty, and my heart needed to be purified from the old leaven (1 Cor. 5:7f). I was attracted by the way, the Saviour himself, but was still reluctant to go along its narrow paths. And you put into my heart . . . that I should visit Simplicianus. It was evident to me that he was a good servant of yours; your grace shone in him. . . . I wanted to consult with him about my troubles, so that he could propose a method fitted for someone in my disturbed condition, whereby I could learn to walk in your way. . . .
>
> My secular activity I held in disgust, and now that I was not burning with my old ambitions in hope of honor and money it was burdensome to me to tolerate so heavy a servitude. By now those prizes gave me no pleasure in comparison with your gentleness and "the beauty of your

house which I loved" (Ps. 25:8). But I was still firmly
tied by woman . . . and because of this one factor I was
inconstant in other respects and was wasting away with
nagging anxieties. . . . And now I had discovered the
good pearl. To buy it I had to sell all that I had; and I
hesitated (Matt. 13:46).[21]

Augustine, although attracted by Christianity, was nevertheless
reluctant to follow what he perceived as its "narrow" paths, particularly in the area of sexual morality. He was eventually led to talk to
Simplicianus, a priest mature in the faith who knew exactly how to
talk to Augustine. (Simplicianus had actually baptized Ambrose and
was later to succeed him as bishop of Milan.) He told Augustine of
another conversion, that of Victorinus.

Victorinus was a very famous Roman teacher, a Platonist who
also defended the traditional Roman gods. In fact, the Romans held
him in such high esteem that they offered to erect his statue in the
Roman forum.

Victorinus became a secret believer. Yet, out of fear for his
reputation, he didn't want to declare himself publicly by getting
baptized and joining the Christian community; it was Simplicianus
who eventually convinced him to do so. Augustine relates in the
Confessions:

He [Victorinus] was afraid to offend his friends, proud
devil-worshippers. . . . But after his reading [of scripture],
he began to feel a longing and drank in courage. He was
afraid he would be "denied" by Christ "before the holy
angels" (Luke 12:9). . . . He gave in his name for baptism
that he might be reborn, to the amazement of Rome and
the joy of the Church.[22]

Throughout the *Confessions*, Augustine makes constant reference to Scripture to illuminate and interpret the experience he is
recounting.

> You, also, merciful Father, rejoice "more over one
> penitent than over ninety-nine just persons who need
> no penitence" (Lk. 15:4). . . . Tears flow at the joy of
> the solemnities of your house (Ps. 25:8) when in your
> house the story is read of your younger son "who was
> dead and is alive again, was lost and has been found"
> (Lk. 15:32).[23]

The effect on Augustine of hearing Simplicianus's account of the conversion of Victorinus was immediate.

> As soon as your servant Simplicianus told me this story
> about Victorinus, I was ardent to follow his example. He
> had indeed told it to me with this object in view.[24]

Augustine gives witness many times to the power of personal testimony in drawing people to Christ, and we will again have occasion to see its role in Augustine's own life. But one very large problem still stood in Augustine's way to conversion: he was deeply in bondage to sin and felt himself unable to break with it. Here we come to the nub of what often holds people back from conversion: deep bondage to habitual sin.

> I sighed after such freedom [the freedom of Victorinus
> to turn away from it all] but was bound not by an iron
> imposed by anyone else but by the iron of my own
> choice. The enemy had a grip on my will and so made
> a chain for me to hold me a prisoner. The consequence
> of a distorted will is passion. By servitude to passion,
> habit is formed, and habit to which there is no resistance
> becomes necessity. . . . But I was responsible for the fact
> that habit had become so embattled against me, for it was
> with my consent that I came to the place in which I did
> not wish to be.[25]

Bernard of Clairvaux makes a similar observation:

For although the soul fell of itself, it cannot rise of itself, because the will lies weak and powerless through the vitiated and depraved love of a corrupt body, yet is at the same time capable of a love of justice. So, in some strange and twisted way the will deteriorates and brings about a state of compulsion where bondage cannot excuse the will, because the action was voluntary, nor can the will, being fettered, free itself from bondage. For this bondage is in some sense voluntary. . . . For it is the will which, although free, by consenting to sin became slave to sin; and it is the will which puts itself in subjection to sin by its willing servitude.[26]

Bernard's analysis of the downward spiral from occasional sin into habitual sin is intended to function not only as an insight into such slavery but also as a guard against it.

But is there anyone like Paul, anyone who does not consent at times to this sensual desire and so submits to sin? Let him who yields to sin take note that he has raised another wall against himself by that wicked and unlawful consent. A man of this kind cannot boast that for him the Bridegroom stands behind the wall, because not one wall but walls now intervene. . . . But what if the repetition of sins becomes a habit, or the habit induces contempt, as Scripture says: "When wickedness comes, contempt comes also"? (Prov. 18:3). If you die like this, will you not be devoured a thousand times by those that roar as they await their food, before you can reach the Bridegroom now shut off from you not merely by one, but a succession of walls? The first is sensual desire; the second, consent; the third, the action; the fourth, habit; the fifth, contempt. Take care then to resist with all your strength the first movements of sensual desire lest they lure you to consent, and then the whole fabric of wickedness will vanish.[27]

In our desire to understand the dynamics of sin and conversion, we should take careful note of the insight and honesty of Augustine and Bernard. Augustine found himself in a situation of very real slavery. He was locked in a deep habit of serious sin. But he clearly acknowledges that it was he who made the series of decisions that little by little brought him to this point of slavery. Even though there was a real sense in which he was no longer free to stop sinning—he was truly a slave to sin—he was responsible for having come to that place by a series of prior decisions in which he chose, little by little, to place himself into slavery to sin. What a predicament! Yet this is the very predicament in which, apart from Christ, the whole human race finds itself. This brings us to the heart of the drama of salvation (cf. Rom. 6–8).

At this point in his *Confessions*, Augustine acknowledges that his uncertainty about the truth was no longer a valid excuse for the way he was living. He admits that he now knows the truth of Christ and the Church, but is torn apart by being unable to decisively respond. In fact, he is plunged into the agony of being pulled in two opposite directions. He wants to repent, but then again, he doesn't!

> In this way I understood through my own experience what I had read, how "the flesh lusts against the spirit and the spirit against the flesh" (Gal. 5:17). I was split between them, but more of me was in that which I approved in myself than in that which I disapproved. . . .
>
> Though at every point you showed that what you were saying was true, yet I, convinced by that truth, had no answer to give you except merely slow and sleepy words: "At once"—"But presently"—"Just a little longer, please." But "At once, at once" never came to the point of decision, and "Just a little longer, please" went on and on for a long while. . . .
>
> The law of sin is the violence of habit by which even the unwilling mind is dragged down and held, as it deserves to be, since by its own choice it slipped into the habit. "Wretched man that I was, who would deliver me from this body of death other than your grace through Jesus Christ our Lord?" (Rom. 7:24-5).[28]

Augustine now tells us how God's grace gratuitously came to him in his genuine helplessness, and describes the means that God used to bring him to these final steps of conversion and liberation.

> Lord, my helper and redeemer, I will now tell the story, and confess to your name, of the way in which you delivered me from the chain of sexual desire, by which I was tightly bound, and from the slavery of worldly affairs. I went about my usual routine in a state of mental anxiety.[29]

It was an unexpected visit from Ponticianus, a fellow African holding a high position in the Roman Imperial court, which was then located in Milan, that triggered a chain of events that culminated in Augustine's deliverance from satanic bondage to habitual sin.

During a visit, Ponticianus noticed that Augustine and his friends had a copy of Saint Paul's epistles in their house and volunteered that he was a baptized Christian. Augustine acknowledged that indeed he and his friends were seeking to understand the truth, at which point Ponticianus began to tell them about what was happening in the Egyptian deserts as a result of the example of a desert monk, Anthony. He told them of the amazing life of Anthony, which inspired thousands of young people to flock to the desert to embrace the Christian, monastic way of life. Augustine and his friends had not even heard of Anthony and the monastic "revival," and "listened with rapt silence."[30]

Then Ponticianus told of how God had used Anthony and the monastic revival as a means to his own conversion and the conversion of several of his friends. One day, while walking in a garden, waiting for the Emperor to return from the spectacle of the circus, they encountered some Christians who introduced them to Athanasius's *Life of Anthony*.

> One of them began to read it. He was amazed and set on fire, and during his reading began to think of taking up

this way of life and of leaving his secular post in the civil service to be your servant. For they were agents in the special branch. Suddenly he was filled with holy love and sobering shame. Angry with himself, he turned his eyes on his friend and said to him: "Tell me, I beg of you, what do we hope to achieve with all our labors? What is our aim in life? What is the motive of our service to the state? Can we hope for any higher office in the palace than to be Friends of the Emperor? And in that position what is not fragile and full of dangers? How many hazards must one risk to attain to a position of even greater danger? And when will we arrive there? Whereas, if I wish to become God's friend, in an instant I may become that now." So he spoke, and in pain at the coming to birth of new life, he returned his eyes to the book's pages. He read on and experienced a conversion inwardly where you alone could see and, as was soon evident, his mind rid itself of the world. . . . As for myself, I have broken away from our ambition, and have decided to serve God, and I propose to start doing that from this hour in this place.[31]

After this event, two of Ponticianus's friends left their careers, and they and their fiancées decided to pursue the monastic life. Another friend and Ponticianus decided to continue their careers, but now, as Christians.

As Ponticianus was speaking, Augustine experienced a very strong conviction of the depth and ugliness of his own sin.

This was the story Ponticianus told. But while he was speaking, Lord, you turned my attention back to myself. . . . And I looked and was appalled. . . . You thrust me before my own eyes so that I should discover my iniquity and hate it. I had known it, but deceived myself, refused to admit it, and pushed it out of my mind. But at that moment the more ardent my affection for those young men of whom I was hearing, who for the soul's health had given themselves wholly to you for healing, the more was the detestation and hatred I felt for myself in comparison with them. Many years of my life had passed by—about twelve—since in my nineteenth year I had read Cicero's Hortensius, and had been stirred to a zeal for wisdom. . . . But I was an unhappy young man, wretched as at the beginning of my adolescence when I prayed you for chastity and said: "Grant me chastity and continence, but not yet." I was afraid you might hear my prayer quickly, and that you might too rapidly heal me of the disease of lust which I preferred to satisfy rather than suppress.[32]

Augustine was also coming to the disturbing realization that he perhaps loved the search for truth more than the finding; perhaps he came to certain intellectual judgments as a way of avoiding the challenge to his way of life that the actual truth would bring. As Ponticianus, the unexpected visitor, left, Augustine was in turmoil. He was chagrined to hear of how readily so many others were accepting the truth, a truth he put off accepting for at least twelve years. He was ashamed ("violently overcome by a fearful sense of shame") of the perhaps manufactured complexity of his search, faced with the pure-hearted surrender to truth on the part of those following Anthony. He had run out of excuses, run out of intellectual objections, and he was finally brought face-to-face with his own perverse clinging to sin—leaving him with a "mute trembling," a "sickness unto death (Jn. 11:4)."

Extremely agitated, "distressed not only in mind but in appearance," Augustine turned to the friend with him in the house, Alypius, and cried out: "'What is wrong with us? What is this that you have heard? Uneducated people are rising up and capturing heaven (Matt. 11:12), and we with our high culture without any heart—see where we roll in the mud of flesh and blood.' . . . He contemplated my condition in astonished silence. For I sounded very strange. My uttered words said less about the state of my mind than my forehead, cheeks, eyes, color, and tone of voice."[33]

Augustine rushed out into the garden of the house with Alypius following, worried, as Augustine "made many physical gestures" as he experienced the "agony of hesitation" and great internal conflict.

> Such was my sickness and my torture, as I accused myself even more bitterly than usual. I was twisting and turning in my chain until it would break completely: I was now only a little bit held by it, but I was still held. You, Lord, put pressure on me in my hidden depths with a severe mercy wielding the double whip of fear and shame. . . . Inwardly I said to myself: Let it be now, let it be now. And by this phrase I was already moving towards a decision; I had almost taken it, and then I did not do so. . . . The nearer approached the moment of time when I would become different, the greater the horror of it struck me. But it did not thrust me back nor turn me away, but left me in a state of suspense.
>
> Vain trifles and the triviality of the empty-headed, my old loves, held me back. They tugged at the garment of my flesh and whispered: "Are you getting rid of us?" And "from this moment we shall never be with you again, not for ever and ever." . . . What filth, what disgraceful things they were suggesting! . . . Meanwhile the overwhelming force of habit was saying to me: "Do you think you can live without them?"[34]

Then Augustine remembered the example of the many who had embraced chastity, even celibacy, for the sake of the kingdom, and that gave him strength.

> Are you incapable of doing what these men and women have done? Do you think them capable of achieving this by their own resources and not by the Lord their God? . . . Why are you relying on yourself, only to find yourself unreliable? Cast yourself upon him, do not be afraid. He will not withdraw himself so that you fall. Make the leap without anxiety, he will catch you and heal you.[35]

Here we meet again, as we did with Teresa of Avila, the foundational truth of the utter primacy of the grace of God and the utter impossibility of proceeding on the spiritual journey without God's grace.

Augustine moved deeper into the garden, away from Alypius, so his groans and weeping would not be inhibited by another's presence, and prayed:

> Why not now? Why not an end to my impure life in this very hour?[36]

And now, the decisive grace arrives.

> As I was saying this and weeping in the bitter agony of my heart, suddenly I heard a voice from the nearby house chanting as if it might be a boy or a girl (I do not know which) saying and repeating over and over again "Pick up and read, pick up and read." . . . I checked the flood of tears and stood up. I interpreted it solely as a divine command to me to open the book and read the first chapter I might find. For I had heard how Anthony happened to be present at the gospel reading . . . [and was immediately converted]. . . . So I hurried back to the place where Alypius was sitting. There I had put down the book of the apostle when I got up. I seized it, opened it and in silence read the first passage on which my eyes lit: "Not in riots and drunken parties, not in eroticism and indecencies, not in strife and rivalry, but put on the Lord Jesus Christ and make no provision for the flesh in its lusts" (Rom. 13:13-14). I neither wished nor needed to read further. At once, with the last words of this sentence, it was as if a light of relief from all anxiety flooded into my heart. All the shadows of doubt were dispelled.[37]

Augustine went and told Alypius, who himself was struck by the passage following Augustine's and decided to convert also. They then went into the house to tell Monica, who was filled with joy. After many years of struggle, Augustine was free.

As we examine the story of Augustine's conversion it is quite striking to see the powerful means through which God can work—through books, providential encounters, disillusionment with the things of the world, intercessory prayer, the power of other people's decisions and example, and, especially, the power of the Word, in verbal testimony and in the written Scriptures. And through it all we see the merciful, wise, patient, and powerful hand of the Lord, guiding Augustine, as He guides us, to the freedom and peace that can only be found in Him.

Sometimes when we read a conversion testimony like Augustine's, from such a life of immorality, those of us who have always been relatively "good" may feel left out—not in the sense of missing the sin, but rather in missing the fervor and passion of love that often seems to accompany such conversions. Thérèse of Lisieux—who, while she certainly needed to undergo purification in her life to reach the fullness of holiness, was thought by one of her confessors to have never committed a mortal sin—offers a solution to this issue.

Meditating on the penitent woman whose story is recounted in Luke 7:36–50 (traditionally identified with Mary Magdalene), Thérèse received light on how she could qualify for the passionate response of love that seems particularly characteristic of those "forgiven much."

> I know that without Him, I could have fallen as low as Saint Mary Magdalene, . . . but I also know that Jesus *has forgiven me more* than *Saint Mary Magdalene* since He forgave me *in advance* by preventing me from falling. Ah! I wish I could explain what I feel.[38]

With a depth of accurate insight, Thérèse perceives that, truly, "there but for the grace of God go I." If we have not sinned as seriously it is because of God's grace preventing and protecting us, which gives us the right and duty of being as deeply grateful and passionately loving as the greatest of forgiven sinners.

Now that we've examined the story of Teresa of Avila's awakening and Augustine's conversion we need to reflect, before going on, to understand clearly the testimony they both give to the utter priority of the grace of God. This is essential not just at the beginning of the spiritual life, but at every stage along the way.

The Primacy of Grace

John Paul II spoke quite clearly of the crucial role of grace when he shared his dynamic vision for Catholic life in the new millennium.

> If in the planning that awaits us we commit ourselves more confidently to a pastoral activity that gives personal and communal prayer its proper place, we shall be observing an essential principle of the Christian view of life: *the primacy of grace.* There is a temptation which perennially besets every spiritual journey and pastoral work: that of thinking that the results depend on our ability to act and to plan. God of course asks us really to cooperate with his grace, and therefore invites us to invest all our resources of intelligence and energy in serving the cause of the Kingdom. But it is fatal to forget that "without Christ we can do nothing" (cf. Jn. 15:5). It is prayer which roots us in this truth. It constantly reminds us of the primacy of Christ and, in union with him, the primacy of the interior life and of holiness. When this principle is not respected, is it any wonder that pastoral plans come to nothing and leave us with a disheartening sense of frustration? (NMI 38)

John Paul II points out that to neglect to put in first place the power of Christ and His grace, and to neglect to express this practically by opening ourselves to interior transformation through prayer, is a constant temptation. There is a powerful tendency in fallen human nature to drift from God-reliance to self-reliance, with the woeful results to which Teresa of Avila testified. At the very heart of the biblical revelation is a profound insight into the incapacity of the human being, apart from Christ, to live the Christian life. The primacy of grace, and our response in faith to this gift, is the clear biblical witness and an absolutely foundational element of the spiritual life. We have to be very clear on this as we proceed in exploring the elements of the spiritual journey. To neglect the very foundation, the primacy of grace, is to build a shaky structure that won't stand. Let's consider one key biblical text that makes this point clearly before we continue.

> And you he made alive, when you were dead through the trespasses and sins in which you once walked, following the course of this world, following the prince of the power of the air, the spirit that is now at work in the sons of disobedience. Among these we all once lived in the passions of our flesh, following the desires of body and mind, and so we were by nature children of wrath, like the rest of mankind. But God, who is rich in mercy, out of the great love with which he loved us, even when we were dead through our trespasses, made us alive together with Christ (by grace you have been saved), and raised us up with him, and made us sit with him in the heavenly places in Christ Jesus, that in the coming ages he might show the immeasurable riches of his grace in kindness toward us in Christ Jesus. *For by grace you have been saved through faith; and this is not your own doing, it is the gift of God—not because of works, lest any man should boast. For we are his workmanship, created in Christ Jesus for good works, which God prepared beforehand, that we should walk in them.* (Eph. 2:1–10, emphasis added)

Apart from Christ we are spiritually dead, slaves to sin, deserving of God's wrath, even hell. But simply because of the gratuitous choice, the gift, of God, mercy is extended to us and heaven is offered. Paul repeats the absolutely fundamental point: salvation, in its first moments, is purely a gift of God, which can only be received with gratitude and faith. It is neither a reward for any of our accomplishments nor the result of any of our efforts. And the reason that God structured salvation in this particular manner is to remove absolutely any possibility of human pride claiming salvation as its own doing. Human pride and self-reliance must be broken for salvation to break in.

After the initial acknowledgement of our own incapacity and desperate need (repentance) and our acceptance of the gift of mercy, pardon, and new life (faith), then, indeed, it is important to live in accordance with the gift. But even the good deeds of the Christian life that we have an obligation to live out—the life of prayer, of holiness, of compassion, of mercy, of forgiveness, of service and mission—were "prepared for us in advance" by God. The Christian journey begins with accepting the grace of God in faith, but it continues in the same way. That's why John Paul II speaks so strongly of the need to recognize and accept the reality of the "primacy of grace." It is this very primacy to which Teresa of Avila and Augustine testify so clearly in the stories of their journeys.

Francis de Sales also testifies to the priority of this truth:

> The works of good Christians are of such worth that heaven is given us for them; but it is not because they proceed from us and are the wool of our hearts but because they are dyed with the blood of the Son of God. . . . So our souls, which of themselves are not able to produce one single good thought towards God's service, being steeped in sacred love by the Holy Spirit who dwells within us, produce sacred actions, which tend towards and carry us to immortal glory . . . by reason of the Holy Spirit, who, by charity dwelling in our hearts, works in us with so exquisite an art, that the same works which are wholly ours are still more wholly his, since he produces them in us as we again produce them in him, he does them for us as we do them for him, he operates them with us as we cooperate with him. . . . He leaves for our part all the merit and profit of our services and good works, and we again leave him all the honor and praise thereof, acknowledg-

ing that the commencement, the progress, and the end of all the good we do depends on his mercy, by which he has come unto us and prevented us, has come into us and assisted us, has come with us and conducted us, finishing what he had begun.[39]

Thérèse, at the very beginning of her autobiography, states emphatically that her whole story from start to finish is not about her willing or trying, but about grace, about the "mercies of the Lord."[40]

Later in her life, almost incapacitated in an emotional and spiritual crisis brought on by the death of her mother and the subsequent departure of her "second Mother" Pauline for the convent, it was only the "ineffable" grace of the "miracle" of Mary's smile that rescued Thérèse from such darkness. (A family statue of Mary in her room appeared to her to smile, imparting such love and tenderness that it brought about her healing.) In her helplessness God's grace made it possible for her "to be born again to life" and to continue to grow because of God's continuing grace.[41]

She knew that her only hope of being a saint was if God chose to make her one, granting her continuing grace to grow and progress.

> This desire [to be a great saint] could certainly appear daring if one were to consider how weak and imperfect I was, and how, after seven years in the religious life, I still am weak and imperfect. I always feel, however, the same bold confidence of becoming a great saint because I don't count on my merits since I have *none*, but I trust in Him who is Virtue and Holiness. God alone, content with my weak efforts, will raise me to Himself and make me a *saint*, clothing me in His infinite merits.[42]

Bernard also consistently witnesses to the primacy of grace. He speaks about the confusion and anguish of being a slave to sin, yet at the same time desiring righteousness. He speaks of being simultaneously repelled by the evil and drawn to the good we see in ourselves, but at the same time being unable to respond by turning towards the good.

> But I must insist that we can only dare to undertake either of these things by grace, not by nature, nor even by effort. It is wisdom which overcomes malice, not effort or nature. There is no difficulty in finding grounds for hope: the soul must turn to the Word.[43]

Bernard also warns of the continual danger of turning the greatest good we have received—the gratuitous grace of God—into the greatest evil, the deluded pride that thinks God's gifts are our own doing or are deserved.

> Surely so that every soul among you who is seeking God may know that she has been forestalled, and that she was found before she was sought. This will avoid distorting her greatest good into a great evil; for this is what we do when we receive favors from God and treat his gifts as though they were ours by right, and do not give glory to God. . . . For if a man who is very good takes the credit for his goodness he becomes correspondingly evil. For this is a very evil thing. If anyone says "Far be it from me! I know that it is by the grace of God I am what I am," and then is careful to take a little of the glory for the favor he has received, is he not a thief and a robber? Such a man will hear these words: "Out of your own mouth I judge you, wicked servant." What is more wicked than for a servant to usurp the glory due his master?[44]

Now that we have recognized the foundation of the spiritual life—the primacy of grace and faith—we need also to take note of the whole biblical framework in which these great Doctors of the Church and teachers of the spiritual life view their lives and the whole spiritual journey. It is the key to understanding much of what they say.

Chapter Four

THE BIBLICAL WORLDVIEW OF THE SAINTS

IT'S POSSIBLE TO FOCUS ON THE PARTICULAR TEACHINGS of these Doctors of the Church and yet not notice the powerful vision of reality—the biblical worldview—that forms the framework of their teaching. Yet it's almost impossible to understand the sense of a particular teaching unless one understands the larger framework, which is nothing less than the fundamental structure of reality—past, present, and future—that is unfolded to us in biblical revelation. In this chapter I'd like to show what the most important elements of this framework are, how it shapes the spiritual journey, and how similarly it is understood throughout the spiritual tradition we are studying. What we're considering here is an important aspect of that "renewal of the mind" or "putting on of the mind of Christ" urged by the apostles:

> Do not be conformed to this world but be transformed
> by the renewal of your mind, that you may prove what is
> the will of God, what is good and acceptable and perfect.
> (Rom. 12:2)

As we begin, it's time to meet some new saints. One of the saints chosen by God to make this biblical framework of the Christian journey especially clear is Saint Catherine of Siena.[1]

The Father's Gift to Catherine: A Vision of Reality

Catherine was born in Siena, Italy, in 1347, the twenty-fourth of twenty-five children. Her father was a prosperous wool-dyer, and the family home is largely preserved for visitors to see today.

Like another saint who was to die young, Thérèse of Lisieux, the process of transformation began for Catherine at a remarkably young age. When she was six years old, a vision of Christ the King appeared to Catherine over the Dominican Church in Siena, blessing her. She felt personally called by the Lord to Himself, and made a promise of virginity at the age of seven. At fifteen, she cut off her hair as a way of resisting her parents' efforts to give her in marriage. At eighteen, she convinced the leaders of a local Dominican third order, intended primarily for widows, to accept her as a member. For three years she lived a life of solitude and prayer, leaving her bedroom in her family's home only for Mass. At twenty-one, having experienced the "spiritual marriage" that many of the Doctors we are studying speak of, she emerged from her room and began a life of service to her family and to the poor and sick in Siena. When the plague broke out in Siena in 1374, Catherine, at the age of twenty-seven, took the lead in ministering to the plague victims.

It soon became evident that Catherine possessed an extraordinary combination of contemplative and charismatic gifts: knowledge and wisdom, healing, deliverance, and prophecy. People recognized that God was working in her and began to seek her out for advice. She ate very little yet lived a very active life. On one occasion, she even tried to mediate between warring parties in Italy, with mixed results. She also traveled to Avignon, where the pope, Gregory XI, was living, to urge him to overcome his fears and return to his rightful place in Rome. The pope did return, and most scholars think that Catherine's prophetic intervention was a factor in his decision.

Her spiritual director, Blessed Raymond of Capua, who later became the general of the Dominican order, wrote a wonderful first-hand account of Catherine's life.[2] Catherine herself didn't know how to read or write until well into her twenties and never received any formal theological training, but, like Teresa of Avila, learned much through conversations with trained theologians, and received a great deal of wisdom directly from God.

Catherine dictated many letters, over four hundred of which survive. Her main work, which was a significant basis for her recognition as a Doctor of the Church, is simply called *The Dialogue*. As the title implies, the book is in the form of a dialogue between Catherine and God the Father. Catherine asks the Father four questions, and the book contains what God the Father communicated to Catherine in response. Many witnesses testify that she received almost the entire book directly in prayer, dictating it as she received it.

She and her little community of men and women moved to Rome at the request of Pope Urban VI, Gregory's successor. For the last few years of her life, she ministered to the pope and various cardinals, while continuing to teach her disciples. She walked from her lodgings in Rome to Saint Peter's Basilica to attend Mass each day, until in February of 1380 she was no longer able to walk. On April 29, 1380, she died, at the age of thirty-three.

Pope Paul VI declared her a Doctor of the Church on October 4, 1970, one week after Teresa of Avila. Pope John Paul II named her Patroness of Europe in 1999.

Jesus: The Bridge over Troubled Waters

One of the primary images that God the Father gave Catherine to explain the "structure of reality" was the image of Jesus as the bridge between heaven and earth. Beneath the bridge flow dark and troubled waters, sweeping human beings to destruction. The only way over these satanically ruled waters is to take the path of the bridge that is Jesus.

The Father communicates to Catherine that Jesus is the only hope for the human race to escape destruction and that all those who know of the bridge must take it in order to be saved. The

Father also tells Catherine that there really is a heaven and a hell, and that the consequences of rejecting the salvation offered in Jesus are horrifying. Human life is continually evaluated in the light of eternity. What we believe and how we behave in this life determine our eternal destinies.

Bernard, like Catherine, vividly expresses the deep and significant reality of our fallen condition due to the original sin.

> In this day we are all born. All of us bear branded upon us the mark of this conspiring, burnt into us; Eve still lives in our flesh, and because of our inborn lust the serpent schemes ceaselessly to win our consent to his rebellion.[3]

He then spells out some of the implications:

> If I were not born a child of wrath, I should not have needed to be re-born in baptism (Jn. 3:7). . . . Woe to the children of disobedience (Eph. 5:6), to those descended from Adam, who were born of wrath (Eph. 2:3), but turned it into fury against themselves by their fiendish obstinacy, turning as it were a switch into a rod—or rather into a hammer! For they store up wrath for themselves in the day of wrath (Rom. 2:5). But what is stored-up wrath but fury? They have committed the devil's sin, and incur the same punishment as the devil.[4]

The Horror of Hell

Catherine continues to fill in the picture as she shares more of what she understands the Father to be communicating to her.

> But those who do not keep to this way [the bridge which is Christ] travel below through the river. . . . No one can cross through it without drowning. . . . Such as these are following a lie by going the way of falsehood. They are children of the devil, who is the father of lies (Jn. 8:44). And because they pass through the gate of falsehood they are eternally damned. Thus will those miserably come to their end who travel by the way beneath the bridge,

through the river. They never turn back to admit their sins or to ask for my mercy, so they come to the gate of falsehood because they follow the teaching of the devil, who is the father of lies. And this devil is their gateway through which they come to eternal damnation.[5]

Bernard too spells out the consequences of rejecting the mercy of Christ and the awful finality of hell. Now is the time of mercy; but with death or the return of the Lord, the time of mercy, the time to freely respond to the offer of salvation in Jesus, will have come to an end.

Go then, wait in the midst of hell for the salvation which has already been worked in the midst of the earth. What use to dream of obtaining pardon among the everlasting fires, when the time for mercy has already passed? No victim will be left to atone for your sins (Heb. 10:26), you will be dead in your sins (Jn. 8:24). The son of God is not crucified again (Heb. 6:6). He died once, he dies no more (Rom. 6:10, 9). His blood which was poured out over the earth, does not go down to hell (his was one visit there) (1 Pet. 3:19). All the sinners on earth will drink of it, but it is not for demons to claim for putting out their flames, nor for men who have allied themselves with demons.[6]

Bernard doesn't hesitate to identify some likely historical examples of those who have met the fate of eternal damnation.

David rightly mourned for his parricidal son, because he knew all exit from the pit of death was denied to him forever by the greatness of his sin. Rightly he mourned over Saul and Jonathan, for whom, once engulfed by death, there seemed no hope of deliverance (2 Sam. 1:17-27). They will rise indeed, but not to life: or if to life, only to die more miserably in a living death, though one must reasonably hesitate to apply this judgment to Jonathan.[7]

He also links the hellish existence of both the demons and the damned humans, describing them both as "shadows."

Shadows refer to those hostile powers which the Apostle Paul called not merely shadows or darkness but even the princes of darkness (Eph. 6:12) and that this includes also those from our race who consent with them, children of night, not of light or day (1 Thess. 5:5), and when the day breathes forth life these shadows will not be annihilated like natural shadows, which we see not only fading away but completely disappearing; they will not be utterly destroyed but they will be utterly wretched. They will still exist, but cowering and subdued. . . . They are not blotted out, that they may burn forever.[8]

The Four Torments of Hell

The Father gave Catherine a vivid understanding of the reality of hell and the four principal torments that are suffered there.

The first is that these souls are deprived of seeing me. This is so painful for them that if they could they would choose the sight of me along with the fire and excruciating torments, rather than freedom from their pains without seeing me.

The second torment is ceaseless regret and agonizing about what has been lost. For when they see that their sinfulness has deprived them of me and of the company of the angels and made them worthy instead of seeing the demons and sharing their fellowship, conscience gnaws away at them constantly.

Just as theologians sometimes refer to the state of heavenly bliss as the "beatific vision," God the Father indicates to Catherine that the third torment of hell will be its opposite, the demonic vision of the source of evil itself, which intensifies all the torments. The Father indicates that the lost souls, in seeing the horrifying sight of the devil, come to know better what they have become through their unrepented sin. Just as in life all knowledge of the supernatural realities is significantly veiled, after death, the veil is removed; both evil and good are seen for what they really are. By turning to Christ we gradually become more like Him in His great beauty; by turning to sin and the devil we become more like him in his extreme horror and ugliness. What we have become through the beliefs and actions we have given ourselves to in this life is revealed with utter clarity after death.

> Their suffering is even worse because they see the devil as he really is—more horrible than the human heart can imagine.

Then, the Father reminds Catherine of an experience she once had.

> You will recall that when I once let you see him for a tiny while, hardly a moment, as he really is, you said (after coming to your senses again) that you would rather walk on a road of fire even till the final judgment day than see him again. But even with all you have seen you do not really know how horrible he is.

The fourth torment is the ceaseless burning of an immaterial fire that has as many forms as the forms of the sins that were committed, and is more or less severe in proportion to their seriousness.[9]

> For on their bodies will appear the mark of their evil deeds, with pain and excruciating torment. And when they hear with terror those words, "Depart, you cursed ones, into the everlasting fire!" (Mt. 25:41) soul and body will enter the company of the demons with no hope of return. They will be engulfed in all the filth of the earth, in as many different ways as their evil deeds were different. The misers will be plunged in the filth of avarice, engulfed at once in the burning fire and in the goods of the world that they loved inordinately. The violent will be engulfed in cruelty, the indecent in indecency and wretched lust, the unjust in their own injustice, the envious in envy, and those who were hateful and bitter toward their neighbors

will be engulfed in hate. Their disordered love for themselves, out of which grew all their wickedness, will burn
and torture them intolerably, for along with pride it is the
head and source of all evil. So will they all be differently
punished soul and body together.[10]

Bernard points out that many do not grasp these truths due to
a lack of contemplative insight, or by failing to invite the action of
the Holy Spirit in bringing Sacred Scripture to life.

There is another place from which God, the just Judge
(Ps. 7:12), "so much to be feared for his deeds among
mankind" (Ps. 65:5), watches ceaselessly with an attention that is rigorous yet hidden, over the world of fallen
man. The awe-struck contemplative sees how, in this
place, God's just but hidden judgment neither washes
away the evil deeds of the wicked nor is placated by their
good deeds. He even hardens their hearts lest they should
repent, take stock of themselves, and be converted and he
would heal them (Jn. 12:40). And he does this in virtue
of a certain and eternal decree, all the more frightening
from its being unchangeably and eternally determined.
The contemplative's fears are intensified if he recalls
God's words to the angels as recorded in the Prophet:
"Shall we show favor to the wicked?" And when they ask
with dismay: "Will he not, then, learn to do justice?"
God answers: "No," and gives the reason: "He does evil
in the land of the upright, and he will not see the glory
of the Lord" (Is. 26:10).[11]

The Fear of the Lord

The "fear of the Lord" as it is spoken of in the Bible is not just a
concept, but an experience that predisposes us to wisdom. In fact,
"The fear of the LORD is the beginning of wisdom; a good understanding have all those who practice it" (Ps. 111:10; Sir. 1:14).[12]

This fear is not the fear of a tyrannical God who impetuously and
arbitrarily inflicts punishment, but the proper respect, and fear, of a

God who administers just punishment for those who deserve it. The biblical fear of the Lord is an intelligent fear, based on a deep perception of the holiness and majesty of God, which rightly recognizes the possibility of violating the law of God, despising His love, rejecting His mercy, and meriting eternal separation from Him. While the fear of the Lord is simply the beginning of wisdom, and the end of wisdom is love (1 Jn. 4:17), one doesn't jump into love without a deep and ongoing experience of biblical, Spirit-inspired fear. The Scripture tells us in fact that "blessed is the man who fears the LORD" and that, indeed, this God-given fear of the Lord frees us from other fears: "He is not afraid of evil news; his heart is firm, trusting in the Lord. His heart is steady, he will not be afraid" (Ps. 112:1, 7–8).

> The fear of the Lord is glory and exaltation,
>   and gladness and a crown of rejoicing.
> The fear of the Lord delights the heart,
>   and gives gladness and joy and long life.
> With him who fears the Lord it will go well at the end;
>   on the day of his death he will be blessed. (Sir. 1:11–13)

Today, there is a great aversion to an appropriate fear of the Lord. And consequently, there is a great trivialization of love and a great foolishness as regards relationship with God. Fear of the Lord is a gift of God; it is not opposed to love, but prepares for it. Fear of the Lord and love of the Lord go together. One of the reasons why there has been so much foolishness in the Church and in the world is because there has been so much lack of fear of the Lord.

Bernard tells us that we don't learn wisdom in a lecture hall, but in an encounter with the Lord which produces appropriate fear.

> For there we listen to Wisdom as a teacher in a lecture hall, delivering an all embracing discourse, here we receive it within us; there our minds are enlightened, here our wills are moved to decision. Instruction makes us learned, experience makes us wise. . . . Though Wisdom

gives light to many to see what they should do, it does not immediately spur them on to action. . . . And so with God: to know him is one thing, to fear him is another, not does knowledge make a man wise, but the fear that motivates him. . . . How truly is the fear of the Lord the beginning of wisdom, because the soul begins to experience God for the first time when fear of him takes hold of it, not when knowledge enlightens it. . . . Fear of him is itself an experience. . . . From the beginning it is a barrier to foolishness.[13]

The Glory of Heaven

One of the most striking things that Catherine relays from God the Father is how much more "depth" there is to reality than many commonly suppose. Sin and evil are far more ugly and more horrendous than most of us can imagine; but so too are the beauty, glory, and goodness of heaven greater than we can comprehend.

> The good of these souls is beyond what your mind's eye can see or your ear hear or your tongue describe or your heart imagine. What joy they have in seeing me who am all good! What joy they will yet have when their bodies are glorified! . . . You will all be made like him in joy and gladness; eye for eye, hand for hand, your whole bodies will be made like the body of the Word my Son. . . . These souls wait for divine judgment with gladness, not fear. And the face of my Son will appear to them neither terrifying nor hateful, because they have finished their lives in charity, delighting in me and filled with good will toward their neighbors.[14]

Bernard describes the difference in the ultimate destinations of human beings:

> Those who are in darkness will be in darkness still, and those who see will see more and more . . . and this is the last day of both, complete blindness and perfect sight. Then nothing remains to be taken from those who are

completely emptied, nor is there anything more to be given to those who are filled, unless they may expect to receive more than fullness, according to the promise made to them. . . . "They shall put into your arms full measure pressed down and overflowing . . ." (Lk. 6:38) "a weight of glory" (2 Cor. 4:17) exalted above measure, so that the super abundant outpouring of light should reflect upon bodies also. . . . Those whom he enlightens within he adorns also without, and clothes them with a robe of glory (Sir. 6:32).[15]

The union with and love of God that begin in this life and grow as the spiritual journey progresses will be gloriously manifested and perfected in heaven. But so also will the union and love that we have had with one another in this life be gloriously manifested and perfected in heaven. The Father tells Catherine that the particular relationships we had on earth, insofar as they were in the Lord, will actually increase in depth of intimacy and love in heaven. Friendships and marriages that were lived in and with Jesus will be "saved" and indeed prove to be a love that is truly "forever." The time for biological procreation will have come to an end—our bodies now transformed in glory, made ready for an eternity of celebration—but the love, in Christ, that was built up in true Christian relationships will last forever. We will not only know and recognize one another in heaven, but know and love each other even more!

They are hungry and satisfied, satisfied yet hungry—but they are far from bored with satiety or pained in their hunger. . . . They are established in love for me and for their neighbors. And they are all united in general and special love, both of which come from one and the same charity. They rejoice and exult, sharing each other's goodness with loving affection, besides that universal good which they all possess together. They rejoice and exult with the angels, and they find their places among the saints according to the different virtues in which they excelled in the world.

And though they are all joined in the bond of charity, they know a special kind of sharing with those whom they loved most closely with a special love in the world, a love through which they grew in grace and virtue. They helped each other proclaim the glory and praise of my name in themselves and in their neighbors, So now in everlasting life they have not lost that love; no, they still love and share with each other even more closely and fully, adding their love to the good of all. . . . When a soul reaches eternal life, all share in her good and she in theirs.[16]

Not only do souls know and love each other even more fully in heaven, but they don't stop knowing and loving people that are still on the journey on earth. We are not alone. We are known. We are loved.

Their desires are a continual cry to me for the salvation of others, for they finished their lives loving their neighbors, and they did not leave that love behind but brought it with them when they passed through that gate which is my only-begotten Son. So you see that in whatever bond of love they finish their lives, that bond is theirs forever and lasts eternally. . . . What these blessed ones want is to see me honored in you who are still on the way, pilgrims running ever nearer your end in death. Because they seek my honor they desire your salvation, and so they are constantly praying to me for you. I do my part to fulfill their desire provided only that you do not foolishly resist my mercy.[17]

Because there has been so much silence, or outright skepticism, in the Church in recent decades concerning heaven and hell, the horror of sin and the glory of heaven,[18] it may be that confronting the vision of Catherine—which is absolutely scripturally based and firmly embedded in the Tradition of the Church—may cause us to struggle with issues of "fairness" or to ask the famous question "how could a good God send someone to hell?" It's interesting to note how the Father shows Catherine that as each person dies he or she actually rushes to where they *want* to be. In a very real way each person chooses their own destiny over the course of their lifetime and, at the moment of death, embraces what has truly become their choice.

We Choose Our Own Destiny

> How great is the stupidity of those who make themselves weak in spite of my strengthening, and put themselves into the devil's hands! I want you to know, then, that at the moment of death, because they have put themselves during life under the devil's rule (not by force, because they cannot be forced, as I told you; but they put themselves voluntarily into his hands), and because they come to the point of death under this perverse rule, they can expect no other judgment but that of their own conscience. They come without hope to eternal damnation. In hate they grasp at hell in the moment of their death, and even before they possess it, they take hell as their prize along with their lords the demons.

As horrible as the final moments of unrepentant sinners are, so wonderful are the final moments of those who die trusting in the mercy of the Lord.

> The just, on the other hand, have lived in charity and die in love. If they have lived perfectly in virtue, enlightened by faith, seeing with faith and trusting completely in the blood of the Lamb, when they come to the point of death they see the good I have prepared for them. They embrace it with the arms of love, reaching out with the grasp of love to me, the supreme and eternal Good, at the very edge of death. And so they taste eternal life even before they have left their mortal bodies.

Even purgatory makes perfect sense as a marvelous provision of God's mercy, a wonderful part of the Good News.

There are others who have passed through life and arrive at the end point of death with only a commonplace love, and were never very perfect. These embrace my mercy with the same light of faith and hope as those who were perfect. But these have this light imperfectly, and because they are imperfect they reach out for mercy, considering my mercy greater than their own guilt.

Catherine summarizes the Father's words:

So no one waits to be judged. All receive their appointed place as they leave this life. They taste it and possess it even before they leave their bodies at the moment of death: the damned in hate and despair; the perfect in love, with the light of faith and trusting in the blood. And the imperfect, in mercy and with the same faith, come to that place called purgatory.[19]

The state of our soul even determines how the Lord "appears" to us and what emotion the encounter with Him instills in us. As Bernard puts it:

You see, the gaze of the Lord, though ever in itself unchanged, does not always produce the same effect. It conforms to each person's deserts, inspiring some with fear but bringing solace and security to others.[20]

The Father reveals to Catherine a very similar insight:

These souls [those who die in friendship with the Lord] wait for divine judgment with gladness, not fear. And the face of my Son will appear to them neither terrifying nor hateful, because they have finished their lives in charity, delighting in me and filled with good will toward their neighbors. The different appearances of his face when he comes in my majesty for judgment will not be in him but in those who are to be judged by him. To the damned he will appear with just hatred, but to the saved, with mercy and love.[21]

Even in this life, the condition of our soul will color how we think of and perceive God.

Part of Catherine's special mission as a Doctor in the Church is to teach the biblical worldview that is found in the Scripture, augmented by the particular insights that the Father gives her for this purpose. But all the Doctors of the Church that we are considering share this worldview, in all its essentials. All of them write in light of the seriousness of the situation of the human race apart from Christ, the reality of heaven and hell, and the urgent necessity to order one's life as much as possible to the following of Jesus—right *now*. As Bernard bluntly puts it:

> Lord Jesus, whoever refuses to live for you is clearly worthy of death, and is in fact dead already. Whoever does not know you is a fool. And whoever wants to become something without you, without doubt that man is considered nothing and is just that. . . . You have made all things for yourself, O God, and whoever wants to live for himself and not for you, in all that he does, is nothing. "Fear God, and keep his commandments," it is said, "for this is the whole duty of man (Eccles. 12:13)."[22]

Some of these saints' teachings can only be fully understood when we see what they see about the true shape of reality. Catherine helps us to enter into that reality, but so do many others. It's time to meet Saint John of the Cross.

Keep Your Eyes on the Goal:
The Brilliant Vision of Saint John of the Cross

John of the Cross was born in 1542 in central Spain. With the death of his father when he was only three years old, his mother and two brothers struggled to survive. An uncle who was a priest looked after him, helping him to get a job as an orderly and also to begin his studies. Perhaps as a result of these early experiences, all through his life John had a special sensitivity to the poor and the sick. John was a very good student and was admitted to the university where he pursued liberal studies and eventually theology. He felt called to the priesthood and planned to become a Carmelite friar, but was uneasy with what he perceived as laxity in the order. A year before his ordination, while he was thinking of perhaps leaving the Carmelites and joining the Carthusians, he met Teresa of Avila. He was about twenty-five and she was fifty-two. Teresa and John had a "meeting of the minds," and Teresa convinced John to work with her for the reform of their order. While Teresa led the reform of the women Carmelites, John worked in establishing reformed monasteries for men. They were able at different points in their journeys to spend considerable periods of time with one another, and it is clear that their writings, although quite different in tone and style, are fundamentally teaching the same approach to the spiritual life. They even refer to each other occasionally in their writings.

Teresa and John met many obstacles in their attempt to reform their order. The order as a whole didn't appreciate their efforts, and resisted them rather vigorously at times. A confusing overlap of state and church authority, local and universal, further caused difficulties. The Catholic king of Spain, the papal nuncio, the general of the order, various papal legates, various councils of the order, local superiors—all added to a mix that was often confused and filled with conflict. At one point John's own order abducted him from where he was serving, blindfolded him, and brought him to one of their monasteries where he was placed in solitary confinement in a cell, with little light, no change of clothing for many months, and poor food. For periods of time he was brought before the other monks and pressured into denying his efforts at reform, which he refused to do. He was falsely told that everyone else had abandoned the reform effort, including Teresa, and was regularly whipped by each of the monks in turn in an effort to break him down. Upon his abduction Teresa appealed to the king for help, but received none.

After about nine months of this confinement, John, who was in very poor condition, felt that he received both a heavenly invitation and the practical wisdom needed to escape, which he did.

It was in prison that John composed in his head and on scraps of paper his great poem *The Spiritual Canticle*, to which he later wrote a commentary. Eventually the pope allowed the reformed Carmelites (called the "discalced" since they wore sandals or bare feet rather than shoes) to form an autonomous province. It was only after the deaths of both Teresa and John that full independence was granted. For a number of years John was part of the central government of the reformed Carmelites in Spain and helped to form many monasteries. But when a new head of the reformed Carmelites who didn't favor John's influence was elected, John wasn't re-elected to the government of the order. When John's friends expressed consternation at this, he wrote to one of them:

> Do not let what is happening to me, daughter, cause you any grief, for it does not cause me any. What greatly grieves me is that one who is not at fault is blamed. Men do not do these things, but God, who knows what is suitable for us and arranges things for our own good. Think nothing else but that God ordains all, and where there is no love, put love, and you will draw out love.[23]

In these remarkable few sentences John communicates his strong faith in the overriding providence of God in all the events of life—even those that seem to be a personal setback or a setback for the kingdom. He also gives practical advice on how to deal with situations that seem "imperfect," motivated by something other than love: When God the Father didn't find love in the human race, He put love in the human race, in the Incarnation of His Son. Then, He found love, in His Son Jesus and in all who had become a part of His Body. John counsels us to go and do the same. When we don't find love in a situation, we can put love in the situation, and then we will find it!

Bernard, with considerable wit, says something very similar:

> If he [Jesus] had not loved his enemies, he could not have
> had any friends, just as he would have had no one to love
> if he had not loved those who were not.[24]

As the government in the order changed and John was excluded from leadership, a friar who had once been corrected by John launched a campaign to have him expelled from the order. Although he tried to find information about John that would give grounds for the expulsion, he found none. There was some talk of sending John to Mexico when he took ill with a serious infection (erysypilis) in his leg. The prior of the monastery where John traveled for medical attention gave him little welcome, worried about the burden John would be as another mouth to feed. Eventually, this critical prior was so touched by John's humility and patience that he repented of his harsh attitude and went on to grow significantly in holiness. There were no antibiotics in those days, and the infection spread through John's whole system. As he lay dying, the friars reminded him of all he had suffered for God and of all the good work he had done, but his reply silenced them.

> Father, this is not the time to be thinking of that; it is by
> the merits of the blood of our Lord Jesus Christ that I
> hope to be saved.[25]

John continues in a long line of vivid witness which we have already seen in Teresa of Avila and Catherine of Siena—that all our hope is in the blood Christ shed for us.

John asked the friars not to recite the traditional prayers for the dying, but rather to read to him from the biblical Song of Songs, which speaks so movingly of the love between Christ and the soul, and which had been so influential in John's own life and writings. By the time John died he had written four major works on the spiritual journey, now considered by many to be the greatest works on the spiritual life ever written. We will have ample opportunity to learn from them in the chapters that lie ahead. But he too, just as Catherine did, operated within the framework of a very clear grasp of the vision of reality God reveals to us in the Scripture.

The Presuppositions of John's Teaching: The Biblical Worldview

For the most part, John presumes that those to whom he's writing have already experienced a spiritual awakening or conversion; in fact, his primary audience is those who are in Carmelite monasteries. For this reason, he doesn't spend a lot of time on the most basic steps of the spiritual life. But as he begins his *Spiritual Canticle*, he does lay out what he presumes we have come to understand as we begin the journey.

> The soul . . . has grown aware of her obligations and observed that life is short (Job 14:5), the path leading to eternal life constricted (Mt. 7:14), the just one scarcely saved (1 Pet. 4:18), the things of the world vain and deceitful (Eccles. 1:2), that all comes to an end and fails like falling water (2 Sam. 14:14), and that the time is uncertain, the accounting strict, perdition very easy, and salvation very difficult. She knows on the other hand of her immense indebtedness to God for having created her solely for himself, and that for this she owes him the service of her whole life; and because he redeemed her solely for himself she owes him every response of love. She knows, too, of the thousand other benefits by which she has been obligated to God from before the time of her birth, and that a good part of her life has vanished, that she must render an account of everything—of the beginning of her life as well as the later part—unto the last penny (Mt. 5:26), when God will search Jerusalem with lighted candles (Zeph. 1:12), and that it is already late—and the day far spent (Lk. 24:29)—to remedy so

much evil and harm. She feels on the other hand that God is angry and hidden because she desired to forget him so in the midst of creatures. Touched with dread and interior sorrow of heart over so much loss and danger, renouncing all things, leaving aside all business, and not delaying a day or an hour, with desires and sighs pouring from her heart, wounded now with love for God, she begins to call her Beloved and say:

> Where have you hidden,
> Beloved, and left me moaning?
> You fled like the stag
> After wounding me;
> I went out calling you, but you were gone.[26]

What John says here is so direct and so intense that it is easy to be startled. Or we might be tempted to pretend that we haven't just read it, and move on. Maybe our emotional reaction will incline us to say, "I can't deal with that!" Hopefully we'll resist the temptation and attempt to understand!

And it is not only John, of course, who communicates to us this awesome vision of the need for men and women to be accountable before God. Bernard does so in an equally vivid fashion. In the text that follows, "Jerusalem" refers to those living devout lives, and "Babylon" to those living apart from God.

> "On that day I will search Jerusalem with lamps" (Zeph. 1:12). . . . He will scrutinize minds and hearts (Ps. 7:10), man's very thought will open up to him (Ps. 75:11). If Jerusalem is to be scrutinized, what is safe in Babylon? . . . But I, a monk and a Jerusalemite, have sins that are definitely hidden, overshadowed by the name and habit of a monk; and consequently it is necessary to probe them with an exacting investigation, and bring them from darkness to light, as it were by the aid of lamps. . . . We must be very much afraid that, when that time comes, under so exacting scrutiny much of

our righteousness may show up as sin. There is only one thing to do: if we shall have judged ourselves we shall not be judged (1 Cor. 11:31).

Genuine fear of the Lord, and the repentant and careful life that it produces, leads to a growing confidence in God's love. Fear of the Lord and love of the Lord are not enemies, but friends. The gift of fear of the Lord prepares the way for the gift of love.

> The bride fears nothing, because she is not aware of anything against herself (1 Cor. 4:4). What should she, his friend, his dove, his beautiful one, be afraid of?[27]

Bernard is trying to prepare us for the spiritual journey. He is trying to help us understand how very much we need mercy and grace. He wants us to begin to desire to pass through the purgative stage to the illuminative stage and, eventually, to reach the unitive stage. Only then can we live in the freedom of the "bride," where fear is replaced by love, joy, and confidence.

We may not be used to hearing sermons from the contemporary pulpit on the passages that John and Bernard reference, and yet they are some of the most important in the Bible. For what they do is bring out the seriousness of the task in which we are engaged, strip off the illusions that we construct to avoid facing difficult truths, and give us the chance to base our life decisions on truth rather than on illusion, the chance to be saved rather than die in our sin.

Each of the passages that John and Bernard reference would bear careful reflection, but that will have to be left to a time of spiritual reading and prayerful reflection if we are to accomplish the goal of this book. I would, however, like to highlight one of the texts that John cites, as it is one that he and others return to over and over again throughout their writings. It is perhaps the Scripture passage that John quotes most often:

> Enter through the narrow gate; for the gate is wide and
> the road broad that leads to destruction, and those who
> enter through it are many. How narrow the gate and con-
> stricted the road that leads to life. And those who find it
> are few. (Mt. 7:13–14, NAB)

In these words, Jesus gives us absolutely essential information, which we neglect at our considerable peril. He makes clear that drifting along with contemporary culture will not lead us to heaven, but rather, to hell. He clearly teaches that if we want to arrive at happiness—the fulfillment of all desire—rather than destruction (which is perpetual frustration) we need to take the road and enter through the gate that leads to heaven. Jesus makes clear that He is the way to heaven and the gateway to eternal life.

It is very sad, but true, that as I talk to Catholics all over the world in my travels, many have come to view reality in a way that is almost directly opposite to that which Jesus indicates is the case. If I were to articulate the worldview of many Catholics today I would state it something like this: "Broad and wide is the way that leads to heaven and many are traveling that road. Narrow is the path that leads to hell and hardly anyone is traveling that path."

It is absolutely shocking and tragic that in a matter of such critical importance as this, so many Catholics have come to believe the exact opposite of what Jesus tells us is the case. Indeed, it verifies the truth of what Jesus teaches: drifting along with contemporary culture, with contemporary "thinking," leads us away from truth and happiness into falsehood and destruction.

John of the Cross knows that we need to be clear on the basic shape of reality, the biblical revelation of what really goes on in life, in order to make wise decisions as we undertake the spiritual journey. To focus on "improving our prayer time," for example, is to focus too narrowly when we think about the spiritual journey as a whole. We need to have the "big picture," as it were, in order to understand how each element of the spiritual life plays its role and why certain decisions must be made, and why these decisions make so much sense.

But it is not just in Bernard, Catherine, and John that we find this startlingly clear grasp of the biblical worldview. We find it throughout the writings of all the saints we are considering. For example, throughout the writings of Teresa of Avila, we find continual references to the "big picture" that she is presupposing we all understand: the reality of the devil, the horror of sin, the price paid for our salvation, the shortness of life, the consequences of our choices, and the reality of judgment, heaven or hell.

> What would it matter were I to remain in purgatory until judgment day if through my prayer I could save even one soul. . . . Pay no attention to sufferings that come to an end if through them some greater service is rendered to Him who endured so many for us. . . .
>
> For even if you may not have so many sins, seldom is there anyone who hasn't done something by which he has merited hell.[28]

Teresa understands that having a clear vision of the "big picture" will change how we live and what we choose, because we will see what really matters.

> Now it seems to me that those whom God brings to a certain clear knowledge love very differently than do those who have not reached it. This clear knowledge is about the nature of the world, that there is another world, about the difference between the one and the other, that the one is eternal and the other a dream.[29]

Understanding what Catherine understood about how human love, in the Lord, can continue into eternity, Teresa draws out the implication about what happens when human love isn't in the Lord, when one party wants to love according to the mind of Christ and the other doesn't.

They see that they are not at one with the other. For it is a love that must end when they die if the other is not keeping the law of God, and these persons understand that the other does not love God and that the two must then go to their different destinies.[30]

Teresa knows that there's a spiritual battle going on for the souls of human beings and that dependence on the Lord is the key to victory.

Doing little by little what we can, we will have hardly anything else to fight against; it is the Lord who in our defense takes up the battle against the demons and against the world. . . . The only concern is to give ourselves entirely to Him.[31]

Spiritually sensitive people like Teresa have an acute awareness of what is true for everyone, and a firm grasp of the logical implications of such truth.

All life is short, and the life of some extremely short. And how do we know if ours won't be so short that at the very hour or moment we determine to serve God completely it will come to an end? This is possible. In sum, there is no reason to give importance to anything that will come to an end. And who will not work hard if he thinks that each hour is the last? Well, believe me, thinking this is the safest course.[32]

And Bernard too, profoundly steeped in the worldview of Scripture, is acutely aware of the shortness of life and the "one thing necessary" as well.

Let us then make haste to respire, to come to life out of that ancient disobedience, that conspiring, for the days of men are brief (Job 14:5). May the day come and breath upon us before we are devoured by the sighing horror of the night and overwhelmed by the everlasting shadows of outer darkness (Mt. 8:12).[33]

Chapter Five

THE TRANSFORMATION OF THOUGHT, DESIRE, AND ACTION

As THE TRUTH ABOUT REALITY—ABOUT GOD, the world, and ourselves—is communicated to us in a wide variety of ways, we experience a progressive transformation. We not only think differently and act differently, but we actually begin to desire and feel differently. As we take on the "mind of Christ" we also take on His desires and participate in the dynamics of His active love.

And now, it is time to meet another of the saints who are teaching us, Thérèse of Lisieux. Thérèse gives us a remarkably detailed picture of the different ways in which God communicated Himself to her, and the subsequent transformation she experienced.

Thérèse: The Desire for Heaven

Thérèse is the youngest of our teachers in two senses: she lived and died just before the beginning of the twentieth century, and when she died she was only twenty-four years old. We have already had the benefit of some of Thérèse's insights, and there are many more yet to come. But now it is time to "meet" her and have her share with us some of the great desire for heaven that God gave her. Her keen perception about how everything needs to be ordered to obtain such a great gift gives us another witness to the "biblical worldview."

Thérèse was born on January 2, 1873, in the Normandy region of France, the youngest of the five surviving Martin girls. As with Catherine, because of how short Thérèse's life was to be, God began the process of drawing her to Himself at a very early age, in a very intense way. She was born into an extraordinarily devout, warm, and wise Catholic family and had some of the best family instruction in the faith that one can imagine. Sensitive by nature, the beauty of nature and of human relationships profoundly struck her, and God used all of these to reveal His own beauty to Thérèse from an early age. Eager to follow her two older sisters into the Carmelite monastery of Lisieux, she was finally able to enter at the age of fifteen. She didn't seem to be anything "special" in the convent, but interiorly the Lord was bringing about a great purification in order to unite her to Himself. He was also teaching her deep insights into the spiritual journey. In the last few years of her life she was asked to write down some of her life story, which was published after her death under the title *The Story of a Soul.* In it, Thérèse shared the story of her own journey in a way that has inspired millions.

Thérèse divides the story of her journey into three stages. The first stage was from birth to the age of four, which she describes as a time filled with happiness and love. The second stage was from the death of her mother at the age of four and a half to that of fourteen, which she describes as the most painful of the three stages. The third stage began with an intervention of God's purifying, healing grace. It enabled her to find healing for the crippling, emotional wounds that the death of her mother and the departure of her "second mother,"(her sister Pauline), for the convent, had inflicted on her soul. Thérèse acknowledges that how she responded to these losses was also rooted to some degree in her own self-will as well as attacks of the devil. This third stage was comprised mostly of her life in the Carmelite monastery until her death at the age of twenty-four.[1] Thérèse realized that her purification had to be intense and begin early "in order to be offered earlier to Jesus."[2]

Although without the great activity of Teresa of Avila or the acute theological understanding of John of the Cross, Thérèse really was their "daughter" in the Carmelite spiritual tradition. In simple language, she has communicated the very same truths of Teresa and John, indeed, of the Gospel itself. Perhaps because she is nearest to us in time and has been so popular in recent Catholicism, it is easy to sentimentalize Thérèse and miss the great depths of the story of her life and wisdom, but Thérèse's witness is no less challenging, and no less helpful, than that of the other saints who are teaching us. We will try not to do so!

During the last few years of her life she suffered from advancing tuberculosis and, for the last year and a half, a great and unrelenting temptation against faith. But more about that later.

On September 30, 1897, at the age of twenty-four, she died. A year after, her autobiography was published and pilgrims began coming to her grave, testifying to the power of her intercessory prayer. By 1914, her convent was receiving two hundred letters a day attesting to the power of her intercession. By 1923 almost a thousand letters a day were being received. She was canonized a saint in 1925 and named a Doctor of the Church in 1997 by Pope John Paul II.

Life in the Splendid Light of Eternity

Thérèse saw with a startling clarity from the earliest age that if heaven existed, all of life on earth had to be evaluated in its light. Life on earth is passing, heaven is eternal; this has consequences for how we believe and make choices now. Thérèse saw, with the astounding logic of divine revelation, that the greatest good we could wish for any human being we love is to wish them heaven.

A great longing for God was birthed in Thérèse's heart by the Spirit, echoing the profound desires for God expressed by the Spirit in the Psalms.

As a hart longs for flowing streams,
  so longs my soul for thee, O God.
My soul thirsts for God,
  for the living God;
When shall I come and behold
  the face of God? (Ps. 42:1–2)

Thérèse's mother, Zélie, told this story in one of her letters to her daughter Pauline:

> Baby [Thérèse] is a little imp; she'll kiss me and at the same time wish me to die. "Oh, how I wish you would die, dear little Mother!" When I scold her she answers: "It is because I want you to go to heaven and you say we must die to get there!" She wishes the same for her Father in her outbursts of affection for him.[3]

Thérèse shares that even when she was a little girl the Lord used the simplest of occasions to deeply impress on Thérèse the reality of the shortness of life and the joy of eternity. She writes to an older sister of one time in particular when her father took her on a fishing outing:

> Sometimes I would try to fish with my little line, but I preferred to go *alone* and sit down on the grass bedecked with flowers, and then my thoughts became very profound indeed! Without knowing what it was to meditate, my soul was absorbed in real prayer. . . . I listened to distant sounds, the murmuring of the wind, etc. At times, the indistinct notes of some military music reached me where I was, filling my heart with a sweet melancholy. Earth then seemed to be a place of exile and I could dream only of heaven. . . . The *beautiful* bread and jam you had prepared had changed its appearance: instead of the lively colors it had earlier, I now saw only a light rosy tint and the bread had become old and crumbled. Earth again seemed a sad place and I understood that in heaven alone joy will be without any clouds.[4]

Even as a little girl, Thérèse had an acute insight into the significance of things. And she is not the only child who has seen and felt things with such clarity. She saw the inner heart of the fallen creation, slowly crumbling into decay. The wisps of beauty that surround us stirred up in her a longing for the greater Beauty that doesn't pass, that truly remains forever. Thinking about these things of ordinary life became for her meditation and contemplative prayer, without knowing the terminology of spiritual theology. Nature, relationships, loneliness, the longing of her heart for completion, in all these she perceived the invitation present, placed there by the Creator, illumined in her mind and heart by the Spirit: to lift up her mind and heart to God, to pray.

Nature

Everything in nature, just as the Psalms say, spoke to Thérèse of the glory of God. The universe exists to speak of God's glory and it does so with astounding power and eloquence, for those who have eyes to see and ears to hear.

> I was six or seven years old when Papa brought me to Trouville. Never will I forget the impression the sea made upon me. I couldn't take my eyes off it since its majesty, the roaring of its waves, everything spoke to my soul of God's grandeur and power.[5]

At another time, seeing the sunset reflecting on the ocean, she understood it to be an image of God's grace shedding its light across the path she had to travel from earth to heaven:

> And near Pauline, I made the resolution never to wander far away from the glance of Jesus in order to travel peacefully toward the eternal shore![6]

She tells of remembering the smallest details of the family's Sunday walks before her mother died: the fields full of wildflowers,

wide-open spaces, huge fir trees.[7] She speaks fondly of her canary
and the other birds she had for pets.[8]

She gives breathtaking descriptions of the Swiss Alps, recounting her pilgrimage to Rome to appeal to the pope to admit her to
the monastery earlier than the normal sixteen-year age limit. She
wanted to be on both sides of the train at the same time (typical of
Thérèse to "choose all") and could hardly keep up with the onrush-
ing spectacle of the mountains, villages, ravines, peaks, forests,
clouds, waterfalls, rushing streams, snow-capped peaks, lakes, and
brilliant sun. She comments,

> When I saw all these beauties very profound thoughts
> came to life in my soul. I seemed to understand already
> the grandeur of God and the marvels of heaven. . . . I
> understood how easy it is to become all wrapped up in self,
> forgetting entirely the sublime goal of one's calling.[9]

She thought about the time when she would be in the convent and would only be able to glimpse a small portion of the
starry sky. Thérèse resolved that the memory of these wonders
would help her to forget "my own little interests". . . . "now that
*my HEART HAS AN IDEA of what Jesus has reserved for those who
love him*" (1 Cor. 2:9).

At another time she even makes a point of saying how much she
loves snow.[10]

Thérèse knew though that there was something even greater than
nature: the God who created nature.

> Ah! what poetry flooded my soul at the sight of all these
> things I was seeing for the first and last time in my life!
> It was without regret I saw them disappear, for my heart
> longed for other marvels. It had contemplated *earthly
> beauties* long enough; *those of heaven* were the object of its
> desires and to win them for *souls* I was willing to become
> a *prisoner!*[11]

But it wasn't just nature that called forth a longing for heaven in Thérèse; it was also the love and affection she found in human relationships.

Friends and Family: Wounds of Love

Thérèse had a deep love for her family, and her family a deep love for her. Apart from the early death of her mother, which was indeed traumatic for Thérèse, she had what she would consider an almost ideal upbringing. Being the youngest of the five living Martin girls (four other Martin children had died in infancy) she was doted on, spoiled even. At the age of eleven, while away for a pre-first Communion retreat she was embarrassed to admit to the teacher in charge that she didn't know how to comb or curl her hair herself as her sisters always did it for her. Even though she was only away for a few days, her father and sisters visited her daily and brought her pastries.[12] (When she was dying, knowing there was no danger of "inordinate attachment," she asked one of her sisters to kiss her in a way that made a big noise and asked also for a chocolate éclair! She loved chocolate.) But the "spoiling" was balanced with a firm but loving communication of the truths of the faith, along with correction when needed.[13] Thérèse knew that the "soil" she was planted in was ideal for knowing the love of the Father. Indeed, her father and mother are in the process of being considered for canonization, and may one day be recognized as saints themselves.

Thérèse adored her father. She saw in him an image of God the Father. She called him her "king" and he called her his "queen."[14] She thought he was becoming a saint and compared him to Saint Francis de Sales whom she understood, like her father, to have overcome an impetuous personality and reached a point of mature virtue. His wife and his daughter both claim that he never said an unkind word in his life.[15] It was on their afternoon walks to visit different churches in the towns in which they lived that they first visited the chapel of the Lisieux Carmel, which was to eventually receive four of the five Martin girls.

When Thérèse saw her father praying her heart was lifted to heaven.

> During his daily visits to the Blessed Sacrament his eyes were often filled with tears and his face breathed forth a heavenly beatitude.[16]

Or on another occasion Thérèse remarked that while the sermon at Mass was very good the sermon of watching her father pray was better.

> I looked more frequently at Papa than at the preacher, for his *handsome* face said so much to me! His eyes, at times, were filled with *tears* which he tried in vain to stop; he seemed no longer held by earth, so much did his soul love to lose itself in the eternal truths. His earthly course, however, was far from completed; long years had to pass by before heaven opened his enraptured eyes and the Lord would wipe the *tears* from the eyes of His good and faithful servant![17]

While the life of the Martin family was centered on God, it was also very human. Thérèse's father played games with her, sang to her both secular and spiritual songs, told her stories (some scary)—the family shared a lot of joy and many "good times" together.

Thérèse was very close to her sisters and loved them deeply. Lots of "tender caresses" and "kisses and embraces" characterized their relationships.[18] Outsiders noticed and sometimes exclaimed: "How they love one another! Ah! nothing will be able to separate them!"[19]

She and Céline, the one closest to her in age, were often described by Thérèse and others as "inseparable."[20] Thérèse spoke of herself and Celine as "spiritual sisters" called by the Lord "to advance together" with bonds of love in Christ stronger than blood. As she did so often, she cited a passage from John of the Cross to explain what she was experiencing.[21]

> Following Your footprints
> Maidens run lightly along the way;
> The touch of a spark,
> The special wine,
> Cause flowings in them from the balsam of God.[22]

When Pauline, her "second mother," became the first of the Martin girls to enter Carmel, Marie, the oldest sister, lovingly cared for Thérèse. When it came time for Marie to enter, Thérèse describes her response.

> *Each time* I passed in front of the door of her room I knocked until she opened it and I embraced her with all my heart. I wanted to get a supply of kisses to make up for all the time I was to be deprived of them.[23]

In speaking about her great desire to join her sister Pauline in the convent, Thérèse understood the significance of being there was not just to be with her sister, but "to await *heaven* with her!"[24]

The human and spiritual solidarity that we can experience with one another on the journey to God is expressed poignantly by Thérèse, as she recalls how she and her sisters shared deeply in the profound suffering of their father's physical and mental deterioration. At this time Thérèse, Pauline, and Marie were in the convent and Céline and Léonie were at home taking care of their father.

> We were no longer walking in the way of perfection, we were flying, all five of us. . . . Ah! far from separating us, Carmel's grilles united our souls more strongly; we had the same thoughts, the same desires, the same *love for Jesus* and *for souls.*[25]

Ultimately, Thérèse knew that the tenderness she experienced in the love of her family wasn't supposed to diminish as they grew in holiness, but rather, increase.

> When the human heart gives itself to God, it loses nothing of its innate tenderness; in fact, this tenderness grows when it becomes more pure and more divine.[26]

How similar to the words that the Father spoke to Catherine about the intensification of interpersonal love in heaven![27]

Thérèse had a vivid sense of how human love is not diminished in heaven but intensified, and she looked forward to being able to love her sisters even more in the glorified life of heaven.

> I was like an idiot. . . . No one ever caused you as much *trouble* as I, and no one ever received as much *love* as you bestowed on me. Happily, I shall have heaven to avenge myself, for my Spouse is very rich and I shall draw from His treasures of *love* to repay you a hundredfold for all you suffered on my account.[28]

So often, when we read these writings, phrases of Scripture come to mind. These saints are living, experiencing, teaching, what is revealed to us in Scripture but which we seldom fathom in its depth of insight or present applicability.

> If then you have been raised with Christ, seek the things that are above, where Christ is, seated at the right hand of God. Set your minds on things that are above, not on things that are on earth. For you have died, and your life is hid with Christ in God. When Christ who is our life appears, then you also will appear with him in glory. (Col. 3:1–4)

> I consider that the sufferings of this present time are not
> worth comparing with the glory that is to be revealed to
> us. (Rom. 8:18)

> What else have I in heaven but you?
> Apart from you I want nothing on earth.
> My body and my heart faint for joy;
> God is my possession for ever. . .
> To be near God is my happiness." (Ps. 73:25–28)[29]

Thérèse herself was attracted to Saint Joan of Arc, another young, French saint, who, externally at least, lived a life so different from the cloistered Thérèse—leading the French armies in battle against the English! But internally, their fierce love for God was the same and the spiritual battle they were engaged in was the same. Thérèse in fact wrote two plays about Joan which she and her fellow nuns performed in the convent, with Thérèse playing the role of Joan. In reflecting on her attraction to Joan, Thérèse shares some very important insights.

> Then I received a grace which I have always looked
> upon as one of the greatest in my life because at that
> age I wasn't receiving the *lights* I'm now receiving when
> I am flooded with them. I considered that I was born
> for *glory*. . . . After seven years in the religious life, I still
> am weak and imperfect. I always feel, however, the same
> bold confidence of becoming a great saint because I don't
> count on my merits since I have *none,* but I trust in Him
> who is Virtue and Holiness. God alone, content with my
> weak efforts, will raise me to Himself and make me a
> *saint,* clothing me in His infinite merits.[30]

The purpose of each one of our lives is to reach the state of glory, to be saints. Either we become saints and reach heaven, or become conformed to the image of the demons, in hell. God helped Thérèse to understand this and also gave her a great awareness that it wasn't by her merits or strength or virtue that this would happen but by trust in God alone. Remember the stark words of Teresa of Avila (whom, incidentally, Thérèse was named after): "This self-reliance was what destroyed me."[31]

All the saints have come to know this profound and fundamental truth: that the purpose of our life is the glory of heaven, and the only way to reach the goal is by absolute confidence in God.

God allowed Thérèse the ability to see the lack of true discernment and truly logical thinking that permeates the atmosphere of the world, especially in comparison to the penetrating clarity and crystalline logic of the biblical worldview.

> God gave me the grace of knowing the *world* just enough to despise it and separate myself from it. . . . I must admit this type of life had its charms for me. . . . The friends we had there [at Alencon] were too worldly; they knew too well how to ally the joys of this earth to the service of God. They didn't think about *death* enough, and yet *death* had paid its visit to a great number of those whom I knew, the young, the rich, the happy! . . . And I see that all is vanity and vexation of spirit under the sun, that the *only good* is to love God with all one's heart and to be *poor in spirit* here on earth. Perhaps Jesus wanted to show me the world before His *first visit* [her upcoming first Communion] to me in order that I may choose freely the way I was to follow.[32]

Thérèse had a similar experience on her pilgrimage to Rome. She traveled in comfort with well-off Catholics, some of whom were nobility and had titles, some of whom were priests. They stayed in the finest of hotels. She admits that she was a little dazzled at first by traveling in such company. As the trip went on, however, she could see the foolishness and vanity in being attached to titles, wealth, and social position, impressing upon her that the only true nobility and dignity comes from our relationship with the Lord. In particular, witnessing the weakness and frailty of the priests in her company helped her understand one of the principal missions of Carmel: to pray for priests.[33]

For Thérèse, this "first class" pilgrimage became an opportunity to see firsthand the vanity and emptiness of everything that is not God.

> During the course of the whole trip, we were lodged in princely hotels; never had I been surrounded with so much luxury. . . marble staircases, and silk tapestries. . . Ah! I really felt it: joy isn't found in the material objects surrounding us but in the inner recesses of the soul. One can possess joy in a prison cell as well as in a palace. The proof of this: I am happier in Carmel even in the midst of interior and exterior trials than in the world surrounded by the comforts of life, and even the sweetness of the paternal hearth![34]

Thérèse's sensitivity extended not only to the worldliness and lack of discernment so common in society but also to the positive dimensions of the "forms of this world," in so far as they participated in and pointed to the great mystery of Christ and the Church. As her cousin, Jeanne, prepared for her wedding, Thérèse was eagerly attentive to see what she could learn about being a better spouse of Jesus.

> Jeanne's wedding took place eight days after I received the Veil. It would be impossible, dear Mother, for me to tell you how much I learned from her example concerning the delicate attentions a bride can bestow upon her bridegroom. I listened eagerly to what she was saying so that I would learn all I could since I didn't want to do less for my beloved Jesus than Jeanne did for her Francis; true, he was a perfect creature, but he was still only a *creature*![35]

And yet as much as God used human relationships to help Thérèse on the journey, at times the absence of these relationships was also permitted by God for Thérèse's good. On the day of her profession and also when she took the veil, neither the bishop nor her spiritual director nor her father, who was in severely declining health, were able to be present.

> On the day of my wedding I was really an orphan, no longer having a Father on this earth and being able to look to heaven with confidence, saying in all truth: "Our *Father* who art in Heaven . . ."[36]

The one spiritual director she felt connected to was transferred to Canada, and to every twelve letters that Thérèse wrote she received one from him. Thérèse knew though that Jesus Himself was her Director.[37]

She also notes that even though the superiors in the convent were for the most part admirable women, they were often harsh with her. She recognized in this a grace from the Lord that helped her not to have become "humanly attached" to them, helping her love remain pure and non-possessive.[38]

Like Thérèse there's much we can learn from human friendship, love, and marriage (or their absence!) that can help us in understanding and living our relationship with the Father, Son, and Holy Spirit. Teresa of Avila summed up her whole spiritual teaching by exhorting us to be a good friend to Jesus.

The Call of the Liturgy

The spirit of the liturgy permeated the life of the Martin family. Thérèse frequently noted the importance of the Mass and receiving communion. So too, the importance of the sacrament of Reconciliation. Her descriptions of the care with which she prepared for her first Confession and first Communion are truly inspiring. And it is clear that Thérèse was very aware of the interpersonal core of the sacraments—the encounter with the love of God and its expression in love of neighbor.

She speaks of making a general Confession the night before her First Communion.

> On the evening of the great day, I received absolution for the second time. My general confession left a great peace in my soul and God did not permit the lightest cloud to come and trouble me. In the afternoon, I begged pardon from the *whole family* who came to see me, but I wasn't able to speak except through my tears so much was I moved.[39]

She also describes her first Communion:

> Ah! how sweet was that first kiss of Jesus! It was a kiss of *love;* I *felt,* that *I was loved,* and I said: "I love You, and I give myself to You forever!" There were no demands made, no struggles, no sacrifices; for a long time now Jesus and poor little Thérèse *looked at* and understood each other. That day, it was no longer simply a *look,* it was a fusion; they were no longer two, Thérèse had vanished as a drop of water is lost in the immensity of the ocean. Jesus alone remained; He was the Master, the King. Had not Thérèse asked Him to take away her *liberty,* for her *liberty* frightened her? She felt so feeble and fragile that she wanted to be united forever to the Divine Strength![40]

The Lord gave to Thérèse a vivid understanding and experience of the reality of the communion of saints and the interpenetration of heaven and earth, especially in the liturgy. Even though her mother had died and Pauline was in the convent, she knew they were present as she received Communion.

> Oh! no, the absence of Mama didn't cause me any sorrow on the day of my First Communion. Wasn't Heaven itself

in my soul, and hadn't Mama taken her place there a long time ago? Thus in receiving Jesus' visit, I received also Mama's. She blessed me and rejoiced at my happiness.[41]

She would have preferred to have Pauline there "in person" but knew she was united to Pauline in Communion also.

On that day, joy alone filled my heart and I united myself to her [Pauline] who gave herself irrevocably to Him who gave Himself so lovingly to me![42]

Thérèse knew, though, that this communion of love, this inter-penetration of heaven and earth, wasn't restricted to these special sacramental encounters but extended to all of life. When she was still suffering from excessive scrupulosity and nothing seemed to be helping, she decided to ask her deceased brothers and sisters to win for her the grace of a healing. She wanted them to "show me that in heaven they still knew how to love! The answer was not long in coming, for soon peace came to inundate my soul with its delightful waves, and I knew then that if I was loved on earth, I was also loved in heaven. Since that moment, my devotion for my little brothers and sisters has grown and I love to hold dialogues with them fre-quently, to speak with them about the sadness of our exile, about my desire to join them soon in the Fatherland!"[43]

Thérèse also had a remarkable insight into the sacrament of Confirmation.

I was prepared with great care to receive the visit of the Holy Spirit, and I did not understand why greater atten-tion was not paid to the reception of this sacrament of *Love.* . . . Like the Apostles I awaited the Holy Spirit's visit with great happiness in my soul. . . . Finally the happy moment arrived, and I did not experience an impetuous wind at the moment of the Holy Spirit's descent but rather this *light breeze* which the prophet Elias heard on

> Mount Horeb. On that day, I received the strength to
> *suffer*, for soon afterward the martyrdom of my soul was
> about to commence.[44]

But it wasn't just the sacraments and special feast days that imparted grace and increased desire for God in Thérèse—it was the whole life of the Catholic family and parish in which she was raised. She loved the processions of the Blessed Sacrament, where she threw her rose petals high enough to hopefully touch the monstrance. She loved the daily visits to pray before the Blessed Sacrament in the various area churches. She loved the pilgrimages to shrines both near and far. Her family and her parish and the whole Catholic environment of her town were truly a "school of prayer" for Thérèse in which she received "training in holiness" (see NMI 31–33).

Thérèse knew that these visible signs point to greater and presently invisible realities, which the visible draws us towards. When speaking of her pilgrimage to Rome with her father, she testifies that her "soul grew through contact with holy things."[45] But she also knew that these holy things fell far short of the realities that await us in heaven.

Speaking of her visit to Loreto, Italy, where the Holy Family's house was said to have been transported, she witnesses to her thirst for the "thing in itself."

Even though the others on the pilgrimage were content to have Mass in the general church building that was built over the Holy House, Thérèse and Céline wanted to attend Mass right within the "house," and found a priest who had special permission to say Mass there. She comments,

> And what shall our happiness be when we receive
> Communion in the eternal abode of the King of heaven?
> Then we shall see our joy never coming to an end; there
> will no longer be the sadness of departings, and it will be
> no longer necessary to have some souvenir, *to dig furtively*

into the walls sanctified by His divine presence, for His *home* will be ours for all eternity. He doesn't want to give us His earthly home, but is content to show it to us so as to make us love poverty and the hidden life. What He does reserve for us is His Palace of glory where we shall see Him no longer hidden under the appearance of a child or a white host, but such as He really is, in the brightness of His infinite splendor![46]

Whether it was sneaking past the guards into the Coliseum and taking a stone hallowed by the deaths of the martyrs or taking a piece of the House of Loreto,[47] Thérèse tells us that she always had to "touch everything"—knowing that what she really wanted to touch was the Lord Himself.

And she loved Sundays.

What a day Sunday was for me! It was God's feast day, and feast of *rest*. First, I stayed in *bed* longer than on the other days; then Pauline spoiled her little girl by bringing her some chocolate to drink while still in *bed* and then she dressed her up like a little Queen. Marie came to curl her hair and Thérèse was not always nice when Marie pulled her hair. Afterward she was very happy to take the hand of her *King* who on that day kissed her more tenderly than usual. The whole family then went off to Mass.[48]

Amazing Catechetics

One of the amazing things to see in Thérèse's "formation" was the significant transmission of faith through those who were her teachers. While she learned much in her short years of schooling and benefited a great deal from pre-sacramental retreats, the preaching in her parish, and the books she read, it was her family that had the main role in communicating the faith to her. Through her family she experienced faith as a living reality, accurately and insightfully communicated in an atmosphere of faith, love, and

personal witness. While the role of her father was extremely important, both by way of teaching through words and activities as well
as by example, her sisters played an important role as well.

Pauline, while she was still at home, cleared up many questions
that Thérèse had about the ways of God.[49] And when Pauline was
later in Carmel, Thérèse credits her sister's letters as instrumental in
preparing her for her first sacraments.

> Oh! dear Mother, with what care you prepared me for
> my first confession, telling me it was not to a man but to
> God I was about to tell my sins. I was very much con-
> vinced of this truth.[50]

But it was Marie who, still living at home, perhaps did the most
for Thérèse.

> I sat on her [Marie's] lap and listened *eagerly* to every-
> thing she said to me. It seemed to me her *large and gen-
> erous* heart passed into my own. Just as famous warriors
> taught their children the art of war, so Marie spoke to me
> about life's *struggles* and of the palm given to the victors.
> She spoke also about the eternal riches that one can so
> easily amass each day, and what a misfortune it was to
> pass by without so much as stretching forth one's hand
> to take them. She explained the way of becoming *holy*
> through fidelity in little things; furthermore, she gave me
> a little leaflet called "Renunciation" and I meditated on
> this with delight.[51]

Wisdom from Above

Even people who have never heard of "meditation" or "contemplation" can find themselves meditating and contemplating as God
draws their thoughts to Him and infuses in them light and love from
above. Thérèse witnesses to this uncomplicated, non-analytic infusion
of grace, which she would often experience in her free moments.

> I think about God, about life, about ETERNITY . . . I
> *think*! . . . I understand now that I was making mental
> prayer without knowing it and that God was already
> instructing me in secret.[52]

Despite the great lights that Thérèse had been receiving since the age of four, after her mother died, and until the age of fourteen, she also struggled greatly with her self-will and with anguish over the loss of her mother. She acknowledged that she was "really unbearable" because of her "extreme touchiness"[53]; hypersensitivity, fears, and possibly psychosomatic illnesses plagued her. Thérèse's anguish only intensified when her "second mother," Pauline, entered the convent and left her as well. Her struggle became so intense she could only believe that the devil had been permitted to afflict her in these ways.

It wasn't until Christmas Eve when she was fourteen years old that the Lord delivered her from this ongoing struggle and affliction. Being attached to a certain Christmas custom of the Martin family, Thérèse was devastated when she overheard her father tell one of her sisters that he was glad that this was the last year they would do this. Heroically, for her, Thérèse overcame her devastation and walked bravely downstairs to continue the celebration. Her effort to overcome her hurt and woundedness was met by an infusion of God's grace, a moment she considered a very significant turning point. She received in this mercy of God "the grace of . . . complete conversion" and the strength and courage to leave her "childhood" behind.[54] What blossomed then in Thérèse was a great desire to work for the conversion of sinners.

> On that *night of light* began the third period of my life,
> the most beautiful and the most filled with graces from
> heaven. The work I had been unable to do in ten years
> was done by Jesus in one instant, contenting himself
> with my *good will* which was never lacking. . . . He made
> me a fisher of *souls*. I experienced a great desire to work

for the conversion of sinners, a desire I hadn't felt so intensely before. I felt *charity* enter into my soul, and the need to forget myself and to please others; since then I've been happy. . . . The cry of Jesus on the Cross sounded continually in my heart: "*I thirst!*" These words ignited within me an unknown and very living fire. I wanted to give my Beloved to drink and I felt myself consumed with a *thirst for souls.* As yet, it was not the souls of priests that attracted me, but those of *great sinners;* I *burned* with the desire to snatch them from the eternal flames.[55]

God infused into the mind and heart of Thérèse a clear understanding of the urgency of bringing others to conversion, and a burning desire to help them avoid the "eternal flames."

When Thérèse happened to read a famous book at the time about the "end of the present world and the mysteries of the future life," her longing for heaven and her desire to participate in the saving mission of Jesus increased.

This reading was one of the greatest graces in my life . . . the impressions I received are too deep to express in human words. All the great truths of religion, the mysteries of eternity, plunged my soul into a state of joy not of this earth. I experienced already what God reserved for those who love Him (not with the eye but with the heart), and seeing the eternal rewards had no proportion to life's small sacrifices, I wanted *to love, to love Jesus with a passion,* giving Him a thousand proofs of my love while it was possible.[56]

What we have seen in Thérèse's narrative of her life is a transformation of mind, heart, and deeds, and we will see more in later chapters. We are witnessing the Word of God and the Spirit of God "in action."

This transformation, which Thérèse narrates, is analyzed in remarkable detail by John of the Cross. Let's now take a look at

John's analysis of the transformation of emotions, as an aid to our understanding of the process of transformation of our desires. Let's begin with some words of Jesus about the emotions of fear and joy, words that are foundational for the experience of transformation.

The Transformation of Desire

We begin the spiritual journey with all kinds of conflicting desires. As we are formed by the Word of God and take on the mind of Christ, we also find our desires beginning to change or reconfigure themselves. Things we greatly desired at one point are now less important; things we had a positive distaste for we may now find ourselves desiring more strongly. The value we place on things begins to change and our emotions share in the transformation.

Jesus points out the importance of allowing our emotions to come into harmony with our more profound appreciation of the biblical worldview. He speaks specifically of how what we fear and what we take joy in will begin to change.

The Transformation of Fear

> I tell you, my friends do not fear those who kill the body, and after that have no more that they can do. But I will warn you whom to fear: fear him who, after he has killed, has power to cast into hell; yes, I tell you, fear him! (Lk. 12:4–5)

Jesus is clearly telling us that fear of the Lord in light of the eternal consequences of our actions is much more important than fearing those who merely can kill the body, but not affect us eternally.

But then Jesus goes on immediately to say:

> Are not five sparrows sold for two pennies? And not one of them is forgotten before God. Why, even the hairs of your head are all numbered. Fear not; you are of more value than many sparrows. (Lk. 12:6–7)

Here we see Jesus speak of the progressive transformation of our fearful emotions as we grow in the truth and love of the Lord. The truth leads us to redirect our fear from a shortsighted fear of merely temporary loss to a much more wisely placed fear of eternal loss. But as we grow in relationship with the Lord, progressing on the spiritual journey, we come to a confidence in his love and in the harmony of our life with His will, and fear is gradually dissipated by a loving confidence in God's care, now and for eternity. The deep abiding reverence for the holiness of God remains, and the horror of offending Him, but the previously predominant fear of punishment is replaced by confidence in His love.

> In this is love perfected with us, that we may have confidence for the day of judgment, because as he is so are we in this world. There is no fear in love, but perfect love casts out fear. For fear has to do with punishment, and he who fears is not perfected in love. (1 Jn. 4:17–18)

The Transformation of Joy

Jesus also taught about the transformation of the emotion of joy as we are formed in the truth of things by the Word of God.

When the disciples returned from a mission they excitedly rejoiced that they were successful in casting out demons. Jesus exhorted them rather to rejoice in what was of eternal significance.

> Do not rejoice in this, that the spirits are subject to you; but rejoice that your names are written in heaven. (Lk. 10:20)

As the truth the Lord reveals to us permeates our being, our emotions will begin to reflect the logic of this truth.

John of the Cross explains that we can become accustomed to respond emotionally to various things in a way that is not really in harmony with the truth of things. Understanding the ways in which our emotional responses don't really correspond with reality can be an important step in opening to the Spirit's work of transformation.

John, following scholastic theology, talks about the primary emotions of joy, hope, sorrow, and fear. He provides a lengthy analysis of how the emotion of joy, when it foolishly responds to things in a way that is not in harmony with the actual truth, can damage the soul and slow down our progress on the journey to God.[57] He doesn't provide such an analysis for the other primary emotions, but indicates that when one emotion comes into harmony with the truth, the others often follow. This "death" to disordered rejoicing is an aspect of what John talks about as the "dark night of the will." It is another way in which John helps us come to love more completely what God loves, and to hate more completely what God hates.

John identifies six classes of goods in which we should rejoice: temporal, natural, sensory, moral, supernatural, and spiritual. By temporal goods he means things like money, reputation, position, and relationships. By natural goods he means things like beauty, gracefulness, elegance, and bodily configuration, as well as qualities of the soul such as intelligence, discretion, and other talents. By sensory goods he means that which gives delight to the senses, exterior and interior, such as delight in what we see, hear, smell, taste, touch, and imagine. By moral goods he means the virtues, works of mercy, obeying the commandments, good judgment, and manners. By supernatural goods John means things like the charismatic gifts of the Spirit, which are given to build up the Body of Christ and benefit others. By spiritual goods John means the infused gifts of God, both delightful and painful, which prepare us for union.

In order not to get bogged down at this point in our account of the journey, I'd like to summarize some of John's teaching about how we tend to rejoice inappropriately in the first class of goods, temporal goods, and the damage that this causes to the soul. Seeing how he analyzes this first class will give us a good feel for how he treats the other classes of goods as well. We will have occasion also to draw on some additional insights of John in this area in later chapters.

Temporal Goods

John of the Cross defines temporal goods as, specifically, "riches, status, positions, and other things claiming prestige; and children, relatives, marriages, and so on."[58] While he clearly states that nothing in these goods is necessarily sinful or the cause of sin, he warns that because of our weakened human natures we tend to become attached to them, looking to them for satisfaction that only God can give. John claims that he would never finish quoting Scripture if he gave references for how each of these goods can become an obstacle in our journey to God. His basic principle is that we should rejoice in these goods to the extent that we are coming closer to God, fulfilling His will, and giving Him honor and glory through them. As he puts it:

> People should not rejoice over riches, neither when they possess them nor when their neighbor possesses them, unless God is served through them. . . .
>
> The same holds true for other temporal goods, titles and positions and so on. It is vain for people to rejoice in these goods if they do not serve God by them and walk more securely on the road of eternal life. . . . As for children, there is no reason to rejoice in them because they are many, or rich, or endowed with natural talents and gifts, or because they are wealthy. One should rejoice in them if they are serving God. . . . It would also be vanity for a husband and wife to rejoice in their marriage when they are uncertain whether God is being better served by it. . . .
>
> Nothing but what belongs to the service of God should be the object of our joy. Any other joy would be vain and worthless, for joy that is out of harmony with God is of no value to the soul.[59]

John points out, in some detail, the considerable damage inflicted on the soul when we rejoice inappropriately in these temporal goods. He even claims that he would run out of "ink, paper, and time" if he were to describe all the harm that happens!

His basic point is that to the extent that we take an inordinate joy in things that are less than God we withdraw ourselves from God, and this damages the soul. He further defines four degrees of harm.

The first degree of harm is a clouding of the intellect to the things of God, which causes a certain "backsliding."

> The first degree of harm to spring from this joy is backsliding: a blunting of the mind in relation to God by which God's goods become dark to it, just as a cloud darkens the air and prevents the sun from illumining it.
>
> By the very fact that spiritual persons rejoice in something and give reign to the appetite in frivolous things, their relationship with God is darkened and their intellect clouded. . . . Even though the intellect is without the thought of any malice, joy in these vanities and concupiscence for them is alone sufficient to produce the first degree of this harm: dullness of mind and darkness of judgment in understanding truth and judging well of each thing as it is in itself.[60]

The second degree of harm from an inappropriate joy in temporal goods is an increasingly lenient attitude toward the passing things of this world. John speaks of it as a certain "spreading out of the will in temporal things . . . in making little of joy and pleasure in creatures, in not being afflicted about it nor considering it to be so serious a matter." This harm "causes one to withdraw from spiritual exercises and the things of God, to lack satisfaction in these exercises because of the pleasure found in other things, and to give oneself over to many imperfections, frivolities, joys, and vain pleasures." Persons at this stage of deterioration are not without culpability and even malice, because "they gradually turn from justice and virtue because their will reaches out more and more into affection for creatures. The trait of those in this second degree is extreme lukewarmness—as well as carelessness—in spiritual matters, observing them through mere formality, force, or habit, rather than through love."[61]

The third degree of harm is "the complete abandoning of God." Carelessness and lukewarmness now lead to falling into "mortal sins through covetousness." Greediness for temporal goods has become the controlling motivation of their lives and as "their appetite and thirst increase more as they regress further from God, the fount that alone can satisfy them. . . . The reason for this dissatisfaction is that creatures do not slake the thirst of the avaricious but rather intensify it. These greedy persons fall into thousands of kinds of sins out of love for temporal goods, and the harm they suffer is indeterminable."[62]

The fourth degree of harm, according to John, is the very forgetting of God. These people now have a new god, money. Greed itself has become a form of idolatry (cf. Col. 3:5).

We will soon consider—in the next chapter—the advice of Saint Francis de Sales: the best moment to defeat temptation is the first moment we become aware of it. John of the Cross has similar advice concerning dealing with small, inordinate attachments to temporal things.

> Spiritual persons must exercise care that in their heart and joy they do not become attached to temporal goods. They must fear lest, through a gradual increase, their small attachments become great. . . what is small in the beginning can be immense in the end. . . And they should never assure themselves that, since their attachment is small, they will break away from it in the future even if they do not do so immediately. If they do not have the courage to uproot it when it is small and in its first stage, how do they think and presume they will have the ability to do so when it becomes greater and more deeply rooted?[63]

All the saints, including John, speak of the wonderful results that come from embracing the disciplines and practical wisdom of the spiritual journey. Paradoxically, the one who "loses" his inordinate joy in temporal goods gains a greater and purer joy in them. It's the paradox of the Gospel. He who denies himself—indeed, loses himself (i.e., his disordered self)—finds himself.

Those who "deny" themselves inordinate joy in temporal things will amazingly discover a *greater* joy in temporal things, as well as

> liberty of spirit, clarity of reason, rest, tranquility, peaceful confidence in God . . .
>
> [They will] obtain more joy and recreation in creatures through the dispossession of them. They cannot rejoice in them if they behold them with possessiveness, for this is a care that, like a trap, holds the spirit to earth and does not allow wideness of heart (2 Cor. 6:11). . . .
>
> Those, then, whose joy is unpossessive of things rejoice in them all as though they possessed them all; those others, beholding them with a possessive mind, lose all the delight of them all in general.
>
> The former, as Saint Paul states, though they have nothing in their heart, possess everything with greater liberty (2 Cor. 6:10); the others, insofar as they possess things with attachment, neither have nor possess anything. Rather their heart is held by things and they suffer as a captive . . . and spend all their time going to and fro about the snare to which their heart is tied.[64]

John tells us that the Lord oftentimes mercifully turns our vain rejoicing in temporal goods into sadness and bitterness as an invitation to return to our senses and worship Him alone. If we only can hear the message!

Often John states his insights so directly and uncompromisingly that we can feel overwhelmed or discouraged. Yet if we read carefully and prayerfully, we will find him encouraging us as well. He acknowledges that despite our best efforts our emotions will not be completely transformed until we reach the point of the "spiritual marriage," in which God Himself completes the purification that we could only lean in the direction of, as it were.

Prior to the "spiritual marriage"—the seventh mansion in Teresa's classification, and the unitive way in Catherine and Bernard's—John states:

> In the memory there are usually many wanderings, cares, and useless imaginings after which she [the soul] follows.

Regarding, too, the four passions of the soul, there are many useless hopes, joys, sorrows, and fears that she follows (referred to as a "herd" by John).

> Some have more and others less of this herd, and they follow until having entered the interior wine cellar to drink, all transformed in love, they lose it entirely. In this wine cellar these herds of imperfections are more easily consumed than are the rust and tarnish of metal consumed by fire. Thus the soul now feels free of all the childish likes and trifles she pursued; and she can say: "And lost the herd which I was following."[65]

It's the biblical worldview—the truth of God's Word—that enables our minds to be renewed, our emotions rightly ordered, and our actions made righteous.

It's the same Word of God, as explained to us by the saints, that can help us win the important battle against sin. And to that we now turn.

Chapter Six

THE STRUGGLE AGAINST SIN

AS WE BEGIN THE SPIRITUAL JOURNEY, the struggle against sin may be particularly intense. Ignorance about what's right and wrong needs to give way to true understanding. Conversion has to deepen. Deeply ingrained habits have to be exposed to the light and the power of grace.

Bernard gives a striking summary:

> We have seen how every soul—even if burdened with sin (2 Tim. 3:6), enmeshed in vice, ensnared by the allurements of pleasure, a captive in exile, imprisoned in the body, caught in mud (Ps. 68:3), fixed in mire, bound to its members, a slave to care, distracted by business, afflicted with sorrow, wandering and straying, filled with anxious forebodings and uneasy suspicions, a stranger in a hostile land (Ex. 2:22), and, according to the Prophet, sharing the defilement of the dead and counted with those who go down into hell (Bar. 3:11)—every soul, I say, standing thus under condemnation and without hope, has the power to turn and find it can not only breathe the fresh air of the hope of pardon and mercy, but also dare to aspire to the nuptials of the Word, not fearing to enter into alliance with God or to bear the sweet yoke of love (Mt. 11:30) with the King of angels."[1]

Bernard, excruciatingly aware of the condition of the soul apart from God, nevertheless knows that every soul, without exception, however deeply mired in the mud of sin and disordered lives, is called not only to begin the journey to union with God, but to complete it successfully by attaining spiritual marriage.

It's time now for us to meet another teacher who can help us a great deal in making progress on this noble journey, Saint Francis de Sales.

Everyday Holiness: The Wisdom of Francis de Sales

Francis was born on August 21, 1567, in France, near the present-day Swiss border. He was the firstborn of thirteen children, five of whom died in infancy, and was named after Francis of Assisi. His father, also named Francis, at the age of forty-three married a young girl named Frances, who was fourteen years old at the time. Unlike Augustine, Francis grew up in the faith, and when he was twelve years old he felt strongly called to serve the Lord as a priest. He was well educated, and studied at the Jesuit College in Paris, and was fluent in both Latin and French. He was accomplished in the "arts of the nobility" (horsemanship, fencing, dancing). He pursued higher studies in law and theology at the University of Padua and received a doctorate at the age of twenty-four.

The University of Padua was a large, cosmopolitan university with over twenty thousand students. It was there that Francis learned the wisdom that enabled him to live a life of holiness in the midst of the world, wisdom which he later developed in detail in his famous work, *Introduction to the Devout Life*. His other major work is the *Treatise on the Love of God*, which presents a detailed account of the more advanced stages of the spiritual journey.

After completing his studies he was given a title of nobility and offered a senatorship in the senate of Chamberey. Francis's father, now seventy years old, had picked out a fourteen-year-old girl for him to marry, an offer that he declined. He finally told his father of his vocation to the priesthood.

After ordination, he was assigned to try to re-establish the Catholic Church in a region near Geneva, which had come under Calvinist domination. Geneva was the diocese in which Francis was born and in which he served as a priest, but during his lifetime it remained firmly in the hands of the Calvinists and the Catholic bishop resided in exile in Annecy, France, not a great distance to the south.

During this time, when passions were running strong between Catholics and Protestant reformers, Francis carried out his mission in a way that showed considerable respect for the Protestants while firmly holding to Catholic truth. In this regard, as in so many others, he anticipated the ecumenical spirit and policy of the Second Vatican Council. He declared that prayer, alms, and fasting would be the spiritual means used in re-establishing the Church in the region. While firmly resolved to win back Geneva to the Catholic Church, Francis declared that it must be done with charity, and that he and his collaborators should suffer deprivation rather than their adversaries. He received special permission to read Calvin's major works so he could have a firsthand acquaintance with their thought. He also made private visits to the successor of Calvin in Geneva in an attempt to win him over, efforts that appeared to be unsuccessful but were cordial and established mutual respect.

The years spent in this early mission were difficult. Because of the great hostility to his work, Francis often had to flee in order to avoid being beaten, or worse. He did convince some of the Calvinist pastors to engage him in public debate, however, and also posted hand-copied pamphlets in public places or slipped them under the doors of homes as a way of sharing the Catholic truth. Eventually, he did achieve considerable success. Many Catholic parishes were re-established, and much of the population reconciled with the Church.

At a certain point Pope Clement VIII invited Francis to Rome to engage in theological debate with the theologians of Rome. He did so well that he was named the coadjutor bishop of Geneva and eventually succeeded to the See of Geneva when the former bishop died. Still unable to reside in Geneva itself, he continued the Catholic exile in Annecy.

On a mission to Paris he came in contact with the writings of Teresa of Avila, who had died only twenty years before and whose reformed Carmelites were establishing a convent in France. He also had occasion to make the Spiritual Exercises of Saint Ignatius several times, which confirmed his belief that all Catholics are called to holiness. As a bishop he placed great emphasis on the recruitment and formation of priests, ordaining nine hundred priests in his twenty-two years as bishop. He always encouraged his priests to look for lay people called to "devotion" and work with them, giving them formation.

In 1604 he met a married woman with children, Jeanne Francoise de Chantal, who upon the death of her husband worked with Francis in establishing a new religious order called the Visitation. Francis and Jeanne wanted the nuns to be able to visit people in their homes, but the rules for religious life at the time required that they be cloistered.

In 1609 he published *Introduction to a Devout Life*, which has been in print ever since.

Experiencing a variety of health problems, Francis died of a stroke on December 28, 1622, at the age of fifty-five. He was canonized a saint in 1665, and declared a Doctor of the Universal Church in 1877.

Up until the time of Francis, priests, nuns, or monks wrote almost all of the books on the spiritual life. Although these works contained much that was useful for lay people, and oftentimes their writers did attempt to relate what they were writing to lay life, they were nonetheless particular to religious life. Francis set out to write a book specifically for people living in the "world."

Spirituality for Lay people: The "Devout Life"

Francis states his purpose very clearly:

> Almost all those who have hitherto written about devotion have been concerned with instructing persons wholly withdrawn from the world or have at least taught a kind of devotion that leads to such complete retirement. My purpose is to instruct those who live in town, within families, or at court, and by their state of life are obliged to live an ordinary life as to outward appearances.[2]

What does Francis mean by devotion? In effect, when he speaks about the "devout" life he is speaking about the fervent, committed life, a life ordered towards growing in holiness. Let's consider his definitions.

First, he takes pains to show what true devotion is not. He is concerned that popular understandings of the devout life contain many distortions, and even promote false spirituality.

> Everyone paints devotion according to his own passions and fancies. A man given to fasting thinks himself very devout if he fasts, although his heart may be filled with hatred. Much concerned with sobriety, he doesn't dare to wet his tongue with wine or even water but won't hesitate to drink deep of his neighbor's blood by detraction and calumny. Another man thinks himself devout because he daily recites a vast number of prayers, but after saying them he utters the most disagreeable, arrogant and harmful words at home and among the neighbors.

Francis goes on to describe how someone else may give money to the poor but not forgive his enemies. Or another may forgive his enemies but not pay his bills unless compelled to do so by law. The point he's making is that "devotion" or holiness doesn't consist primarily in external practices of piety but in a heart transformed in love and justice.[3]

Bernard was similarly aware that the outward appearances of devotion can hide inward disorder, even in the life of religious orders.

> We do sometimes hear men who have committed themselves to religious life and wear the religious habit, shamelessly boasting as they recall their past misdeeds: the duels they fought, their cunning in literary debate or other kinds of vain display. . . . Some recount past vices as though to express sorrow and repentance for them, but their minds thrill with a secret pleasure . . . about how, even after receiving the holy habit, they craftily outwitted their neighbor, how they cheated a brother in a business deal (1 Thess. 4:6), how they recklessly retaliated on those who insulted or reproached them, returning evil for evil, a curse for a curse (1 Pt. 3: 9).[4]

Francis insists that true devotion must touch every area of our life. True devotion is not just a matter of spiritual practices but of bringing all our life under the lordship of Christ. Francis is known for his slogan: "Live, Jesus! Live, Jesus!" What he means by this is an invitation to Jesus to "live and reign in our hearts forever and ever."[5]

As we will see later on, the Scripture, and all our writers, make clear that true spirituality or devotion is characterized by both love of God and love of neighbor. The two cannot be separated without serious distortion.

One of the greatest challenges facing the Church today, as Vatican Council II pointed out, is the split between faith and daily life. Or, as Pope Paul VI put it, the split between faith and culture.

After establishing what true devotion is not, Francis gives his own unique definition.

> When it [divine love] has reached a degree of perfection at which it not only makes us do good but also do this carefully, frequently, and promptly, it is called devotion. . . . In short, devotion is simply that spiritual agility and vivacity by which charity works in us or by aid of which we work

quickly and lovingly. . . . He must have great ardor and
readiness in performing charitable actions. . . .

It arouses us to do quickly and lovingly as many good
works as possible, both those commanded and those
merely counseled or inspired. . . . Like a man in sound
health he not only walks but runs and leaps forward
"on the way of God's commandments" (Ps. 119:32).
Furthermore, he moves and runs in the paths of his heavenly counsels and inspirations.[6]

In other words, for Francis, to live the devout life is to reach the
point in our love for God and neighbor that we eagerly ("carefully,
frequently, and promptly") desire to do His will in all the various
ways in which it is communicated to us: in the duties of our state in
life, in the objective teaching of God's Word, in opportunities and
occasions presented to us, in response to interior inspirations.

Francis is well aware that reaching this level of devotion is no small
thing, and so proceeds to give instruction about how to make progress on the spiritual journey in order to reach this point. As we have
already seen in considering the testimonies of Teresa and Augustine,
turning from sin is a very important part of the process.

As the psalm puts it:

> Who shall ascend the hill of the LORD?
> And who shall stand in his holy place?
> He who has clean hands and a pure heart,
>   who does not lift up his soul to what is false,
>   and does not swear deceitfully. (Ps. 24:3–4)

The First Purgation: Mortal Sin

Obviously, turning away from serious sin is one of the first things
that needs to happen in true conversion. As Francis writes:

What is your state of soul with respect to mortal sin? Are
you firmly resolved never to commit it for any reason

whatsoever? . . . In this resolution consists the foundation
of the spiritual life.[7]

Francis recommends that a person in such a situation—coming
back to the Lord from a life that included serious sin—consider the
possibility of making a "general confession." This entails making an
appointment with a trusted confessor and going over one's whole
life as a way of making a fresh start. Francis acknowledges that this
is not absolutely necessary, but he strongly advises it.

He also points out how important the regular practice of the sacrament of Reconciliation can be in making a real change in our lives.
He points out, though, that for the sacrament to be really efficacious
it is important that we prepare for going to confession and be sincere
and serious about wanting to turn away from sin.

> Often they make little or even no preparation and do not
> have sufficient contrition. Too often it happens that they
> go to confession with a tacit intention of returning to sin,
> since they are unwilling to avoid its occasions or use the
> means necessary for amendment of life.[8]

Francis recommends weekly confession, although other spiritual writers recommend other frequencies, such as monthly. Even
when we don't have mortal sins to confess, Francis points out the
advantage of confessing venial sins, even though we don't have an
obligation to do so, as it brings them into focus so we can work on
them more intently, as well as benefiting from the grace given in the
sacrament. Francis emphasizes that we really need to be sorry for our
sins in order to make their reappearance less likely.

> Many who confess their venial sins out of custom and
> concern for order but without thought of amendment
> remain burdened with them for their whole life and
> thus lose many spiritual benefits and advantages. . . . It
> is an abuse to confess any kind of sin, whether mortal or

venial, without a will to be rid of it since confession was instituted for no other purpose.[9]

He also recommends that we be as specific as possible in our confession and not just confess generalities. For example, he encourages us not to confess in such general terms such as we didn't love God or our neighbor enough, or pray devoutly enough, since "Every saint in heaven and every man on earth might say the same thing if they went to confession."[10]

The Second Purgation: The Affection for Sin

One of Francis's most helpful insights is his teaching on the affection for sin. He points out that oftentimes we might turn away from serious sins in our life and try hard not to commit them, but still nurture affection for such sin, which greatly slows down our spiritual progress and disposes us to future falls.

He points out that although the Israelites left Egypt in effect, many did not leave it in affection; and the same is true for many of us. We leave sin in effect, but reluctantly, and look back at it fondly, as did Lot's wife when she looked back on the doomed city of Sodom.

Francis gives an amusing but telling example of how a doctor, for the purpose of health, might forbid a patient to eat melons lest he die. The patient therefore abstains from eating them, but "they begrudge giving them up, talk about them, would eat them if they could, want to smell them at least, and envy those who can eat them. In such a way weak, lazy penitents abstain regretfully for a while from sin. They would like very much to commit sins if they could do so without being damned. They speak about sin with a certain petulance and with liking for it and think those who commit sins are at peace with themselves."[11]

Francis says this is like the person who would like to take revenge on someone "if only he could" or a woman who doesn't intend to commit adultery but still wishes to flirt. Such souls are in danger. Besides the real danger of falling into serious sin again, having such a "divided heart" makes the spiritual life wearisome and the "devout" life of prompt, diligent, and frequent response to God's will and inspirations virtually impossible.

Bernard similarly reminds us that feeling such affection for sin is not necessarily a sin in itself. To feel jealousy without yielding to it is no sin, but "a passion that time will heal." He warns us though that if we "nurture" such affections or disordered passions we are heading in the wrong direction. He also tells us we should strive to eliminate or reduce such affection for sin by confession, tears, and prayer. Even if we should not prove successful, at least we can grow in gentleness and humility as we bear the burden of such a continuing struggle.[12]

What does Francis propose as the remedy for such remaining attachment to the affection for sin? A recovery of the biblical worldview!

Francis himself leads the reader of the *Introduction to the Devout Life* through ten such meditations on these basic truths, focusing on all we have been given by God and the debt of gratitude we owe Him, the ugliness and horror of sin, the reality of judgment and hell, the great mercy and goodness of Jesus' work of redemption, the shortness of life, and the great beauty and glory of heaven.[13] Francis and all the saints we are considering believe that there truly is power in the Word of God, and that meditating on the truth can progressively free us from remaining affection for sin.

The Scripture is clear:

> How can young people keep their way pure?
>> By guarding it according to your word.
> With my whole heart I seek you;
>> do not let me stray from your commandments.
> I treasure your word in my heart,
>> so that I might not sin against you. . . .

I will meditate on your precepts,
    and fix my eyes on your ways.
I will delight in your statutes;
    I will not forget your word. (Ps. 119:9–16, NRSV)

The saints have a wonderful way of bringing the insight of Scripture into contact with the circumstances of our lives. Teresa of Avila puts it this way:

> A great aid to going against your will is to bear in mind continually how all is vanity and how quickly everything comes to an end. This helps to remove our attachment to trivia and center it on what will never end. Even though this practice seems to be a weak means, it will strengthen the soul greatly and the soul will be most careful in very little things. When we begin to become attached to something, we should strive to turn our thoughts from it and bring them back to God—and His majesty helps.[14]

We need to make the prayer of Scripture our own:

> So teach us to number our days
>   that we may gain wisdom of heart. (Ps. 90:12)

Meditating on the passion of Christ is often recommended as being of special value. Bernard puts it like this:

> What greater cure for the wounds of conscience and for purifying the mind's acuity than to persevere in meditation on the wounds of Christ?[15]

Francis knows that as long as we're alive in this body the wounds of original sin and our past actual sins will cause affection for sin to spring up again and again. But it's our response to this bent of our nature towards sin that is determinative of the progress we make on the spiritual journey. We need to grow in our hatred for sin so we can resist it when it makes its appeals. Catherine of Siena talks of the two-edged sword with which we fight the spiritual battle: one side is hatred for sin, the other is love for virtue.

Bernard speaks of how miserable it is to turn back to the slavery of our disordered passions once having tasted the grace of God. Such a person is doomed to continual frustration, as the things of the world simply can't satisfy our hunger and "ravenous curiosity" since the forms of this world are passing away. He bemoans the fate of the soul "who once fed so delicately now lies groveling on the dunghill (Lam. 4:5)."[16]

The vigorous effort that the saints urge us to make in the struggle against sin is firmly grounded in the Scriptures.

> Submit yourselves therefore to God. Resist the devil and he will flee from you. Draw near to God and he will draw near to you. Cleanse your hands, you sinners, and purify your hearts, you men of double mind. . . . Humble yourselves before the Lord and he will exalt you. (Jas. 4:7–10)

We need to determine, with the help of God's grace, never to freely choose to offend Him. Francis makes clear that such purification of the affection for sin must extend to venial sins also.

Venial Sin

Teresa, Bernard, and Francis all acknowledge that there will probably always be some inadvertent venial sins that we commit, without full reflection or choice. As Bernard puts it:

> Which of us can live uprightly and perfectly even for one hour, an hour free from fruitless talk and careless work?[17]

They all also teach, though, very clearly and strongly, that in so far as it lies in our power, we need to resolve never to freely choose to offend God, even in a small matter, if we are to make progress in the spiritual life.

Both Francis and Teresa point out that to fall into same involuntary lie, out of embarrassment, for example, is one thing; but to maintain an affection for telling little lies, or to freely choose to do so, is a significant obstacle to making progress, and truly offensive to the Lord.[18]

Affection for venial sin, just as affection for mortal sin, needs to progressively disappear from our lives as we make progress on the spiritual journey.

> We can never be completely free of venial sins, at least so as to continue for long in such purity, yet we can avoid all affection for venial sins. . . . We must not voluntarily nourish a desire to continue and persevere in venial sin of any kind. It would be an extremely base thing to wish deliberately to retain in our heart anything so displeasing to God as a will to offend him. No matter how small it is, a venial sin offends God.[19]

Living in the close quarters of a community of monks, Bernard is particularly sensitive to how unkindness in speech and attitude can damage relationships and wound souls.

> It is not enough, I say, to guard one's tongue from these and similar kinds of nastiness [public insult and abuse, venomous slander in secret]; even slight offences must be avoided, if anything may be termed slight that is directed against a brother for the purpose of hurting him, since merely to be angry with one's brother makes one liable to the judgment of God.[20]

Bernard also counsels us to be careful how we respond when a wrong has been done to us.

So when an offence is committed against you, a thing hard to avoid at times in communities like ours, do not immediately rush, as a worldly person may do, to retaliate dishonorably against your brother; nor, under the guise of administering correction, should you dare to pierce with sharp and searing words one for whom Christ was pleased to be crucified; nor make grunting, resentful noises at him, nor mutter and murmur complaints, nor adopt a sneering air, nor indulge the loud laugh of contempt, nor knit the brow in menacing anger. Let your passion die within, where it was born; a carrier of death, it must be allowed no exit or it will cause destruction, and then you can say with the Prophet: "I was troubled and I spoke not."[21]

To nourish affection for venial sin, Francis points out, weakens the powers of our spirit, stands in the way of God's consolations, and opens the door to temptations. At the same time Francis doesn't want to engender a morbid scrupulosity about the myriad temptations and sometimes inadvertent venial sins that are part of life in this world. He assures us that inadvertent venial sins and faults are "not a matter of any great moment" if as soon as they occur we reject them, and refuse to entertain any affection for them.[22]

Francis makes clear that the process of purification will continue throughout our life, and so "we must not be disturbed at our imperfections, since for us perfection consists in fighting against them."[23]

Hatred for sin is important. Confidence in the mercy of God is even more important.

> May the LORD, who is good, grant pardon to everyone who has resolved to seek God, the LORD, the God of his fathers, though he be not clean as holiness requires. (2 Chron. 30:18b–19)

Thérèse makes clear that growth in the spiritual life is usually a gradual process; Jesus is patient with us, "for He doesn't like pointing everything out at once to souls. He generally gives His light little by little."[24]

Thérèse also speaks of a "joyful resignation" to the lifetime struggle with faults.

> At the beginning of my spiritual life when I was thirteen or fourteen, I used to ask myself what I would have to strive for later on because I believed it was quite impossible for me to understand perfection better. I learned very quickly since then that the more one advances, the more one sees the goal is still far off. And now I am simply resigned to see myself always imperfect and in this I find my joy.[25]

Thérèse's resignation was not one of despair, discouragement, passivity, or lack of effort, but a humble acceptance of her creaturely imperfection despite her efforts, infused with joy by her hope in God's transforming love eventually bringing her to perfection.

In the last days of her life, when she was virtually suffocating from the tuberculosis, Thérèse was corrected for an impatient remark to a sister whom she found "tiresome." Her response?

> Oh! how happy I am to see myself imperfect and to be in need of God's mercy so much even at the moment of my death.[26]

Realistically, Francis says, there will probably be falls along the way, but God can use even these to deepen our humility.

> Imperfections and venial sins cannot deprive us of spiritual life; it is lost only by mortal sin. Fortunately for us, in this war we are always victorious provided that we are willing to fight.[27]

Francis, like many of the saints, wants to encourage us on the spiritual journey. This is a journey on which we are all called to embark; and God will give us the grace to make progress on this journey, if only we are willing to persevere, to fight the good fight.

> As for the seed that fell on rich soil, they are the ones who, when they have heard the word, embrace it with a generous and good heart, and bear fruit through perseverance. (Lk. 8:15, NAB)

Bernard wants us to know that even in the midst of the struggle—whether it be with mortal sin or venial sin, worldliness or temptation, perseverance in prayer or growth in virtue, loving or forgiving—we profoundly need to "lean on the Beloved."

Bernard knows that to "fight against yourself without respite in a continual and hard struggle, and renounce your inveterate habits and inborn inclinations" is very hard, impossible really, without the help of the Lord.

> But this is a hard thing. If you attempt it in your own strength, it will be as though you were trying to stop the raging of a torrent, or to make the Jordan run backwards (Ps. 113:3). What can you do then? You must seek the Word. . . . You have need of strength, and not simply strength, but strength drawn from above (Lk. 24:49).[28]

The words from Hebrews come to mind:

> Therefore, since we are surrounded by so great a cloud of witnesses, let us also lay aside every weight, and sin which clings so closely, and let us run with perseverance the race that is set before us, looking to Jesus the pioneer and perfecter of our faith, who for the joy that was set before him endured the cross, despising the shame, and is seated at the right hand of the throne of God. (12:1–2)

The journey up to the summit of the mountain of God (or Mount Carmel, as John of the Cross calls it) is difficult. And John, Bernard, Catherine, Thérèse, Teresa, Augustine, and Francis know that it's impossible to attain the summit—spiritual marriage in this life, beatific vision in the next, without leaning heavily on the Beloved.

As Bernard, in accord with his fellow Doctors, explains:

> "Who shall ascend the mountain of the Lord?" (Ps. 23:3) If anyone aspires to climb to the summit of that mountain (Ex. 24:17), that is to the perfection of virtue, he will know how hard the climb is, and how the attempt is doomed to failure without the help of the Word. Happy the soul which causes the angels to look at her with joy and wonder and hears them saying, "Who is this coming up from the wilderness, rich in grace and beauty, leaning upon her beloved?" (Song 8:5). Otherwise, unless it leans on him, its struggle is in vain. But it will gain force by struggling with itself and, becoming stronger, will impel all things towards reason . . . bringing every carnal affect into captivity (2 Cor. 10:5), and every sense under the control of reason in accordance with virtue. Surely all things are possible to someone who leans upon him who can do all things? What confidence there is in the cry, "I can do all things in him who strengthens me!" (Phil. 4:13). . . . "Thus if the mind does not rely upon itself, but is strengthened by the Word, it can gain such command over itself that no unrighteousness will have power over it" (Ps. 118:133).[29]

The Good News is that the Beloved loves to be leaned on!

Chapter Seven

THE IMPORTANCE OF PRAYER

JOHN OF THE CROSS MAKES THE POINT that sensual attractions are so strong and so rooted in our nature that efforts of renunciation by themselves will not be totally successful. A greater attraction, a greater love has to inflame us in order to enable us to let go of lesser, disordered loves.

> A love of pleasure, and attachment to it, usually fires the will toward the enjoyment of things that give pleasure. A more intense enkindling of another, better love (love of the soul's Bridegroom) is necessary for the vanquishing of the appetites and the denial of this pleasure. By finding satisfaction and strength in this love, it will have the courage and constancy to readily deny all other appetites. The love of its Bridegroom is not the only requisite for conquering the strength of the sensitive appetites; an enkindling with urgent longings of love is also necessary. For the sensory appetites are moved and attracted toward sensory objects with such cravings that if the spiritual part of the soul is not fired with other, more urgent longings for spiritual things, the soul will be able neither to overcome the yoke of nature nor to enter the night of sense; nor will it have the courage to live in the darkness of all things by denying its appetites for them. . . .

How easy, sweet, and delightful these longings for their Bridegroom make all the trials and dangers of this night seem.[1]

Bernard of Clairvaux makes the same point. He speaks of a depth of prayer that can properly be called a "sleep" or "death"—not a death to life, but a death to what holds us back from true life and union.

> How I long often to be the victim of this death that I may escape the snares of death, that I may not feel the deadening blandishments of a sensual life, that I may be steeled against evil desire, against the surge of cupidity, against the goads of anger and impatience, against the anguish of worry and the miseries of care. . . . How good the death that does not take away life but makes it better; good in that the body does not perish but the soul is exalted.[2]

Bernard calls this deeper prayer of "sleep" or "death" contemplation.

> This kind of ecstasy, in my opinion, is alone or principally called contemplation. Not to be gripped during life by material desires is a mark of human virtue; but to gaze without the use of bodily likenesses is the sign of angelic purity. Each, however, is a divine gift, each is a going out of oneself, each a transcending of self, but in one one goes much farther than in the other.[3]

One of the main ways we open ourselves for this greater love to possess us is through prayer. We need to remember though that the spiritual life is not primarily about certain practices of piety and techniques of prayer, but about a relationship. It's about responding to the One who has created and redeemed us, and who loves us with a love stronger than death, a love that desires to raise us from the dead. Much that is true of human relationships is also true of our relationship with God. Human relationships of friendship or marriage need time, attention, and care for them to continue and to grow. The same is true of our relationship with God. We have been called to union but we need to respond. As we turn to God in conversion or in a deeper awakening, besides turning away from deliberate sin—which deforms the soul, blocks the relationship and offends the Person who has sacrificed His life for us—we need to positively build the relationship by paying attention to the One who loves us. Prayer is at root simply paying attention to God. All the saints speak of its importance.

Thérèse speaks of the power and simplicity of prayer.

> How great is the power of *Prayer*! . . . I say very simply to God what I wish to say, without composing beautiful sentences, and He always understands me.
>
> For me, *prayer* is an aspiration of the heart, it is a simple glance directed to heaven, it is a cry of gratitude and love in the midst of trial as well as joy; finally, it is something great, supernatural, which expands my soul and unites me to Jesus.[4]

Teresa of Avila tells us that the entrance into the mansions (or stages) of the spiritual journey begins with prayer. Francis de Sales tells us that while the struggle against sin is crucial, even more so is prayer.

> Since prayer places our intellect in the brilliance of God's light and exposes our will to the warmth of his heavenly love, nothing else so effectively purifies our intellect of ignorance and our will of depraved affections. . . . I especially counsel you to practice mental prayer, the prayer of the heart, and particularly that which centers on the life and passion of our Lord. By often turning your eyes on him in meditation, your whole soul will be filled with him. You will learn his ways and form your actions after the pattern of his.[5]

Bernard concurs:

> But I must insist that we can only dare to undertake
> either of these things [turning from sin, turning to God]
> by grace, not by nature, nor even by effort. It is wisdom
> which overcomes malice, not effort or nature. There is
> no difficulty in finding grounds for hope: the soul must
> turn to the Word.[6]

In Teresa's and also in Francis's time there was a great deal of discussion about vocal versus mental prayer, in a way that is not of as
great interest today. Vocal prayer—prayer said out loud—was usually understood to be a matter of reciting the memorized prayers such
as the "Our Father" or the "Hail Mary." Mental prayer was generally understood to be prayer that was said with the attention of the
mind, the words formed interiorly and not spoken out loud. Mental
prayer also could be understood as "contemplative" prayer—prayer
that consists in being aware of the presence of the Lord, understanding truths, or inflaming the will with love. Yet because of a concern
that people could get into spiritual trouble and possibly be deceived
if they practiced mental prayer, the spiritual advice commonly given
at the time was that most people should stick with vocal prayer.
Teresa, Francis, and many of the saints had to fight against this
overly cautious approach in order to free people to respond to the
way the Holy Spirit works in our lives by a communication of His
presence apart from (or along with) words.

Teresa of Avila makes the point that it isn't whether the prayers
are memorized or not or said out loud or not that determines their
value, but whether we pay attention to what we're saying and to
whom we're speaking.

Bernard addresses his brothers in a similar vein, exhorting them to
pay attention to what they are saying when they chant the Psalms.

> So, dearest brothers, I exhort you to participate always
> in the divine praises correctly and vigorously: vigorously,

that you may stand before God with as much zest as reverence, not sluggish, not drowsy, not yawning, not sparing
your voices, not leaving words half-said or skipping them,
not wheezing through the nose with an effeminate stam-
mering, in a weak and broken tone, but pronouncing the
words of the Holy Spirit with becoming manliness and
resonance and affection; and correctly, that while you
chant you ponder on nothing but what you chant.[7]

Methods of Prayer

Many spiritual writers, including some of the saints, offer suggestions concerning methods in prayer. Francis de Sales, very
much influenced by his own experience of Saint Ignatius's Spiritual
Exercises, offers some suggested structures and formats for the practice of meditation and prayer. He suggests six steps as a guide to
moving through a time of prayer.

1. Place yourself in the presence of God. Remember that God is
   near, not far away. He is in the very depth of your heart, your
   spirit. "Begin all your prayers, whether mental or vocal, in the
   presence of God. Keep to this rule without any exception and you
   will quickly see how helpful it will be."[8]
2. Ask the Lord to help you pay attention to Him, to open yourself
   up to His Word and presence.
3. Pick out a passage from Scripture, a scene from the Gospel, a
   mystery of the Faith, or a passage from some spiritual reading. If
   the subject matter you have chosen lends itself to it, picture yourself in the same place as the action or event that is happening. Use
   your imagination to place yourself in the midst of the scene near
   Jesus, with the disciples.
4. Think about what you've chosen to meditate on in such a way as
   to increase your love for the Lord or for virtue. The purpose is
   not primarily to study or know more, but to increase your love
   for God and the life of discipleship.

5. If good affections should rise up—gratitude for God's mercy, awe at His majesty, sorrow for sin, desire to be more faithful, for example—yield to them.

6. Come to some practical resolutions concerning changes you would like to make as a response to these affections. For example, resolve to be more faithful in prayer, or more ready to forgive, or more eager to share the faith with others, or more determined to resist sin, in as practical and concrete a way as you can determine.

> Most of all, after you rise from meditation you must remember the resolutions and decisions you have made and carefully put them into effect on that very day. This is the great fruit of meditation and without it meditation is often not only useless but even harmful. Virtues meditated on but not practiced sometimes inflate our minds and courage and we think that we are really such as we have thought and resolved to be.[9]

Francis recommends that we end the time of meditation-prayer with expressions of gratitude to God for the light and affections He has given us in our time of prayer; then, an offering of ourselves to the Lord in union with the offering of Jesus; and thirdly, a time of intercession for our self and others.

At the same time, Francis doesn't intend that the structure or method he proposes be followed mechanically if the Holy Spirit draws us to something different.

> It may sometimes happen that immediately after the preparation you will feel that your affections are drawn wholly towards God. In this case, you must give them free rein and not follow the method I have shown you. Ordinarily, consideration must precede affections and resolutions. However, when the Holy Spirit gives you the affections before the consideration, you must not look for the consideration since it is used only to arouse the

affections. In a word, whenever affections present themselves you must accept them and make room for them
whether they come before or after the considerations.[10]

While Francis acknowledges the usefulness of praying the Rosary,
various litanies, and fixed, written prayers, he advises us to always give
the priority to mental prayer and the leading of the Holy Spirit.

> However, if you have the gift of mental prayer, you should
> always give it first place. Afterwards if you cannot say your
> vocal prayers because of your many duties or for some other
> reason don't be disturbed on that account. . . . During
> vocal prayer if you find your heart drawn and invited
> to interior or mental prayer, don't refuse to take it up.
> Let your mind turn very gently in that direction and
> don't be concerned at not finishing the vocal prayers
> you intended to say. The mental prayer you substitute
> for them is more pleasing to God and more profitable
> for your soul.[11]

Francis makes an exception in his general advice regarding flex-
ibility in prayer, as does Catherine of Siena: those in Holy Orders or
by virtue of a rule of religious life are obligated to pray the Divine
Office must keep their commitment.

The Simplicity of Prayer

Teresa of Avila points out on more than one occasion how some
very simple nuns in her own convent had reached the highest state
of union by reciting devoutly the "Our Father" with attention and
openness to the Spirit's presence. She tells us that the same can happen to us.

> It is very possible that while you are reciting the Our
> Father or some other vocal prayer, the Lord may raise you
> to perfect contemplation.[12]

125

Francis gives similar advice about how to say the common memorized prayers.

> They must be said with strict attention of mind and with affections aroused by the meaning of the words. Do not hurry along and say many things but try to speak from your heart. A single *Our Father* said with feeling has greater value than many said quickly and hurriedly.[13]

Teresa of Avila likewise has much helpful advice on prayer. She acknowledges how important meditation and prayer are to growth in the spiritual life, but also acknowledges how difficult it can be to concentrate. In her own case, she couldn't meditate without the help of a book for more than fourteen years.

> For meditation is the basis for acquiring all the virtues, and to undertake it is a matter of life and death for all Christians. . . . I spent 14 years never being able to practice meditation without reading. There will be many persons of this sort, and others who will be unable to meditate even with the reading but able only to pray vocally, and in this vocal prayer they will spend most of their time. There are minds so active they cannot dwell on one thing but are always restless, and to such an extreme that if they want to pause to think of God, a thousand absurdities, scruples, and doubts come to mind. . . . There are some souls and minds so scattered they are like wild horses no one can stop. . . . This restlessness is either caused by the soul's nature or permitted by God.[14]

Teresa's comments resonate with the traditional method of prayer called *lectio divina* (sacred reading), a method of alternating prayer and reading that is common in the monastic life but has been found useful by many lay people as well. It's simply a matter of taking up the Scriptures or some spiritual book, reading until our mind and heart are lifted to the Lord, and then prayerfully reflecting on what we've read, speaking to the Lord about it, or simply being in His presence. Once our mind starts to wander again, we then return to the reading until we're once again recollected, and then put the book down and turn to the Lord in any of a number of ways, from meditation to contemplation. Bernard warns us not to underestimate the degree to which God is at work in what may appear to us to be simply our own "good thoughts" as a result of our meditation, prayer, or reflection.

> For our meditations on the Word who is the Bridegroom, on his glory, his elegance, power and majesty, become in a sense his way of speaking to us. And not only that, but when with eager minds we examine his rulings, the decrees from his own mouth (Ps. 118:13); when we meditate on his law day and night (Ps. 1:2), let us be assured that the Bridegroom is present, and that he speaks his message of happiness to us lest our trials should prove more than we can bear. . . . Without grace man's heart is incapable of thinking good thoughts, that its capacity to do so comes from God (2 Cor. 3:5): the good thought is God's inspiration, not the heart's offspring.[15]

At the same time Bernard notes that wicked thoughts either come from us or from the devil.

Neither Teresa nor Francis wants to unduly complicate the approach to prayer, and so they offer their suggestions as helps, not as rigid rules. Teresa in particular keeps reminding us that in prayer we're primarily involved in a *relationship*, not an exercise of technique or the following of a method. Keeping in mind that it's a relationship that we're trying to respond to and nurture can oftentimes be guidance enough.

> For mental prayer in my opinion is nothing else than an intimate sharing between friends; it means taking time frequently to be alone with Him who we know loves us.[16]

Speak with him as a father, or a brother, or a lord, or as with a spouse; sometimes in one way, at other times in another. . . . The intellect is recollected much more quickly with this kind of prayer even though it may be vocal; it is a prayer that brings with it many blessings. This prayer is called "recollection," because the soul collects its faculties together and enters within itself to be with its God. And its divine Master comes more quickly to teach it and give it the prayer of quiet than He would through any other method it might use.[17]

Teresa places a great emphasis on remembering the personal nature of what we are doing in prayer and the value of simply being aware of whom we're speaking to, namely, praying with attention. Teresa's sharp wit and sly humor are frequently manifested in the advice she gives.

The nature of mental prayer isn't determined by whether or not the mouth is closed. If while speaking I thoroughly understand and know that I am speaking with God and I have greater awareness of this than I do of the words I'm saying, mental and vocal prayer are joined. If, however, others tell you that you are speaking with God while you are reciting the Our Father and at the same time in fact thinking of the world, then I have nothing to say. But if you are to be speaking, as is right, with so great a Lord it is good that you consider whom you are speaking with as well as who you are, at least if you want to be polite. . . .

Refuse to be satisfied with merely pronouncing the words. . . .

It is even an obligation that we strive to pray with attention. Please God that with these remedies we shall recite the Our Father well and not end up in some other irrelevant thing. I have experienced this sometimes, and the best remedy I find is to strive to center the mind upon the One to whom the words are addressed. . . .

We should see and be present to the One with whom we speak without turning our backs on Him, for I don't think speaking with God while thinking of a thousand other vanities would amount to anything else but turning our backs on Him. All the harm comes from not truly understanding that He is near, but in imagining Him as far away . . . even in the midst of occupations.[18]

Much of what Teresa says resonates with the strong exhortation that Pope John Paul II gave to the whole Church as we began the journey of the third millennium: to contemplate the face of Christ.

> All harm comes to us from not keeping our eyes fixed on You; if we were to look at nothing else but the way, we would soon arrive. . . .
> Remember Jesus, close to your side. . . . Get used to this practice! Get used to it! I'm not asking you to do anything more than look at Him.[19]

Teresa, knowing our—and her own—humanity, encourages us to a truly human prayer to a God who is fully human as well as fully divine!

> The soul can place itself in the presence of Christ and grow accustomed to being inflamed with love for His sacred humanity. It can keep Him ever present and speak with Him, asking for its needs and complaining of its labors, being glad with Him in its enjoyments and not forgetting Him because of them, trying to speak to Him, not through written prayers but with words that conform to its desires and needs. This is an excellent way of making progress, and in a very short time. I consider that soul advanced who strives to remain in this precious company and to profit very much by it, and who truly comes to love this Lord to whom we owe so much. [20]

As much as Teresa makes it clear that we must try our best to pay attention to the One to whom we are speaking, she realizes that there are times and circumstances when that is very hard to do. Her advice on making progress in the spiritual life is completely informed by a good knowledge of human weakness, and is very realistic.

> There can be exceptions at times either because of bad humors—especially if the person is melancholic—or because of faint feelings in the head so that all efforts become useless. Or it can happen that God will permit days of severe temptation in his servants for their greater good. And though in their affliction they are striving to be quiet, they cannot even be attentive to what they are saying, no matter how hard they try; nor will the intellect settle down in anything, but by the disordered way it goes about, it will seem to be in a frenzy.[21]

Teresa has advice for how to handle situations like these:

> Whoever experiences the affliction these distractions cause will see that they are not his fault; he should not grow anxious, which makes things worse, or tire himself trying to put order into something that at the time doesn't have any, that is, his mind. He should just pray as best he can; or even not pray but like a sick person strive to bring some relief to his soul; let him occupy himself in other works of virtue. This advice now is for persons who are careful and who have understood that they must not speak simultaneously to both God and the world.[22]

Teresa is concerned that her advice not be misconstrued as toleration for laxity. She makes clear that she intends this advice for people who have not brought their distracted state upon themselves through carelessness in prayer or in dallying with temptation. In other places Teresa makes clear that among the "other works of virtue" besides prayer are acts of charity or helpfulness to others. It sounds like what my mom used to say: "Get out of yourself. Stop moping around. Stop thinking about yourself. Stop complaining. Do something good for someone else!"

It's entirely appropriate, for many reasons, that the Carmelites refer to Teresa of Avila as "holy mother."

Time and Place

What advice do the saints have regarding how much time we should spend in prayer? The goal, as Scripture indicates, is to pray always!

> Rejoice always, pray constantly, give thanks in all circumstances; for this is the will of God in Christ Jesus for you. (1 Thess. 5:16–18)

To be in such a state of union with God that even in the midst of activities there is a current of thanks, praise, adoration, and intercession rising from our hearts is indeed our call. But the saints also indicate that to reach such a state of prayerfulness in our life definite times of prayer are necessary.

The Catechism of the Catholic Church, incorporating as it does the wisdom of the saints and Doctors in its beautiful sections on prayer, echoes this advice of Teresa.

> But we cannot pray "at all times" if we do not pray at specific times, consciously willing it. (CCC 2697)

Teresa, at various points, indicates that unless one spends sufficient time in prayer, progress will definitely be slowed. A sufficient amount of time needs to be devoted to prayer just to withdraw from the busyness of life. In Teresa's reformed Carmelite convents, the nuns participated in the Liturgy of the Hours and in Mass, and had an hour of meditation and prayer in the morning and another hour before the evening meal.

But what about the overwhelming majority of the Church that doesn't live in cloistered monasteries? Francis de Sales has very specific advice for people involved in the world of work and family—advice that may surprise us.

Set aside an hour every day before the mid-day meal, if possible early in the morning, when your mind is less distracted and fresher after the night's rest. Don't extend it for more than an hour unless your spiritual director expressly tells you to do so.[23]

Francis is writing for business people, laborers, soldiers, government administrators, housewives—people with the whole range of worldly responsibilities. What are we to make of his advice?

I think it's good advice, and, like him, I think it's possible for virtually all of us. How? If we're not used to praying an hour a day we should perhaps begin with a shorter period of time. Like Teresa, we should probably utilize an approach that alternates prayerful spiritual reading and times of prayer, drawing on the suggestions about how to structure a time of meditation and prayer. Just as with physical exercise—in the beginning it may be hard and we're not capable of much—with practice our capacity increases and it becomes easier; so too with prayer.

Francis advises not to pray longer than an hour a day (in addition to Mass) without the advice of a spiritual director, as a safeguard against the possible neglect of the responsibilities of our state in life and the possible danger of spiritual deception, pride, or imbalance in our life. There are perhaps many people who at some point in their spiritual journey will be called to longer or more frequent times of prayer. At these points seeking wise spiritual counsel would be a very good idea.

Determining how much time we should be spending in a time of personal prayer each day is an important decision, but so also is the decision about when and where. Francis recommends taking the time of personal prayer as early in the day as possible, before the busyness of life begins to fill our consciousness and the inevitable distractions, interruptions, and demands begin to accelerate. For some this may mean immediately upon arising. For some it might mean after breakfast. Each of us knows our own situation best. Also, as our situation changes, we may need to change the time we dedicate to personal prayer. Some people have found it practicable to pray during the lunch break in a nearby park or church. Some people have found it workable to pray right before the evening meal. Bernard recommends the advantages of praying in the silence of the night when others are asleep, when we can pour out our heart freely.[24]

For example, now that we have no small children at home and no school carpools, my wife and I try to attend the 7:00 a.m. Mass in a local parish church each weekday and spend time in the church afterwards taking a time of prayer. We also look for an opportunity to return to prayer at some point later in the day. This works very well right now, but in earlier years we couldn't have done it this way.

I must say, from my own experience, that the longer in the day I put off having the initial prayer time, the more likely it is for it not to happen at all or to happen in a very ragged way.

Francis recommends praying in a church, as this may be the best place to avoid interruptions and have the atmosphere most conducive to prayer. On the other hand, a church may not be convenient to our home or work; or if it is, it may not be open for prayer during times that we can pray, or there may be activities happening in the church after Mass that make praying difficult. If there is a church in the area that has an adoration chapel, this can be a wonderful place to pray.

Prayerfulness throughout the Day

Francis is very clear about the need to take a personal prayer time each day, but he also communicates a vision of prayerfulness throughout the day and offers some suggestions about how this can happen. He actually proposes a pattern for our day which will help us to "remember" the Lord at various points. Here are his suggestions.

- As soon as we wake up turn to the Lord, thank Him for another day, dedicate it to Him and ask His help for living it in a way pleasing to Him.
- Take a substantial time for personal prayer (including spiritual reading) as early in the morning as feasible.
- Attend daily Mass as often as possible.
- As far as circumstances permit, pray the Liturgy of the Hours.[25]
- Withdraw into the cell of our souls periodically during the day to remember the Lord, to be aware of His presence and speak to Him. We can do this even in the midst of activities.

> Always remember to retire at various times into the solitude of your own heart even while outwardly engaged in discussions or transactions with others.[26]

Bernard also has tremendous insight into how solitude is possible in the midst of the world.

> Therefore you must withdraw, mentally rather than physically, in your intention, in your devotion, in your spirit. For Christ the Lord is a spirit before your face (Lam. 4:20), and he demands solitude of the spirit more than of the body, although physical withdrawal can be of benefit when the opportunity offers, especially in time of prayer. . . . Apart from that the only solitude prescribed for you is that of the mind and spirit. You enjoy this solitude if you refuse to share in the common gossip, if you shun involvement in the problems of the hour and set no store by the fancies that attract the masses; if you reject what everybody covets, avoid disputes, make light of losses, and pay no heed to injuries. Otherwise you are not alone even when alone. Do you not see that you can be alone when in company and in company when alone? However great the crowds that surround you, you can enjoy the benefits of solitude if you refrain from curiosity about other people's conduct and shun rash judgment.

Even if you should see your neighbor doing what is wrong, refuse to pass judgment on him, excuse him instead. Excuse his intention even if you cannot excuse his act, which may be the fruit of ignorance or surprise or chance.[27]

- Shortly before the evening meal, draw aside for a few minutes of prayer and an examination of conscience. Thank God for the blessings of the day, for any faults or sins ask His forgiveness, and renew your dedication to live for Him.

Looking at the list of all the spiritual practices that Francis recommends can be overwhelming. Francis anticipates this objection. In reply he points out that very busy men, like King David and Saint Louis, king of France, by putting the Lord and devotion to Him before all else, were able to accomplish a great deal. Francis assures that the same will be true for us.

Perform these exercises confidently, as I have marked them out for you, and God will give you sufficient leisure and strength to perform all your other duties.[28]

Little by little, we can make our daily life more and more prayerful, as we are able, over time, to incorporate those suggestions that work with our schedule and that we are ready for spiritually. There is a particular spiritual practice that Francis highly recommends that is possible for all of us: even on those "impossible" days when we are perhaps unable to undertake our normal spiritual practices, we can stay rooted in prayer by constantly addressing brief prayers to the Lord. These can be acts of love, of adoration, of faith, of hope, of petition, or simply of saying the name of Jesus—throughout the course of the day. Francis places a very high value on these simple utterances, traditionally called ejaculatory prayers or aspirations.

Since the great work of devotion consists in such use of spiritual recollection and ejaculatory prayers, it can supply the lack of all other prayers, but its loss can hardly be repaired by other means. Without this exercise we cannot properly lead the contemplative life, and we can but poorly lead the active life. Without it rest is mere idleness, and labor is drudgery. Hence I exhort you to take up this practice with all your heart and never give it up.[29]

The short prayer that Bernard most strongly recommends is simply saying the name of Jesus. He writes in a very moving away about the power of the name of Jesus in our prayer.

The name of Jesus is more than light; it is also food. Do you not feel increase of strength as often as you remember it? What other name can so enrich the man who meditates? What can equal its power to refresh the harassed senses, to buttress the virtues, to add vigor to good and upright habits, to foster chaste affections? . . . Write what you will, I shall not relish it unless it tells of Jesus. Talk or argue about what you will, I shall not relish it if you exclude the name of Jesus. Jesus to me is honey in the mouth, music in the ear, a song in the heart.[30]

Prayer is essential for the spiritual journey. But so is learning how to respond to temptations and trials, and to this we now turn.

TEMPTATIONS AND TRIALS

GOD, IN HIS WISDOM, has ordained that the very temptations and tribulations that are a result of our fallen condition can become very important means to bringing about our transformation into His image, which is our destiny and calling. One of the most important things to realize about the spiritual journey is that encountering temptations and trials is a necessary condition for making progress.

> Through many tribulations we must enter the kingdom of God. (Acts 14:22)

These trials aren't pleasant. Indeed, they're often outright painful. Yet they can lead, if we respond in the right way, to the deep peace of holiness (cf. Heb. 12:11).

Even though it may appear at times that everything around us is falling apart, including ourselves, in retrospect we will be able to see how "light" this affliction was, compared to the "eternal weight of glory" that was being prepared for us and in us (cf. 2 Cor. 4:16–18).

Unfortunately, not understanding how to identify and deal with temptations and trials can often bring confusion and lead to unwise decisions, blocking us from making progress. One of the great contributions of the saints is their remarkable insight into the nature of the temptations and trials that we will encounter on the journey and their advice on how to deal with them successfully.

Teresa of Avila, for example, identifies certain temptations that commonly face those in the earlier stages of the journey, in the times right after conversion or awakening. These same temptations can appear later in the journey as well, but learning how to deal with them at the beginning is a great help.

Teresa indicates that some of the temptations are primarily rooted in our own fallen human nature, with its disordered desires bent and blinded by sin; others are rooted in the "conventional wisdom" of the world, which is often inimical to the ways of God; and others still are instigated by demons. Teresa identifies the devil as a "noiseless file" that quietly works to lead us into unwise decisions and cause us harm. Progress in the spiritual life means being progressively freed from being subject to these influences and becoming more and more subject to the Spirit of God.[1] Understanding what's happening to us greatly helps in becoming free. The truth will, indeed, make us free.

Common Temptations
in the Early Stages of the Journey

Immature Zeal

In her systematic treatment of the stages of the spiritual journey, Teresa identifies some of the common temptations in the early stages.

Teresa identifies "indiscreet zeal" as a significant danger.[2] Bernard uses the exact same phrase, "indiscreet zeal," and adds to it "incredibly obstinate intemperance."[3] Sometimes the devil can work to cause someone to overdo it when it comes to sacrifice or commitment or zeal. If someone in the earlier stages of spiritual growth attempts to take on too much prayer or fasting or service they can quickly burn out and become discouraged as they are not able to sustain such commitments at this point of their development.

Sometimes, Bernard points out, the devil takes advantage of the pride and vanity that may coexist with genuine fervor in order to tempt to imprudence or excess. He gives as examples people tempted to pray more by getting up earlier, and then falling asleep at the regular time of prayer; or people pursuing "stricter" vocations and finding that they've gone beyond the grace God was giving them; or people fasting more than they should and ending up being useless for the service to which God has called them.[4]

Bernard also notes the strange obstinacy or stubbornness that sometimes characterizes "spiritual" people who are "wise in their own eyes." He points out the seriousness of such obstinacy and underlying rebelliousness by quoting a startling passage from Scripture.

> Rebellion is as the sin of witchcraft, and stubbornness like the crime of idolatry. (1 Sam. 15:23)[5]

Bernard points out that even those at later stages of the spiritual journey—"proficients" at the illuminative stage—can become vulnerable to temptations rooted in indiscreet zeal, which are more subtle and harder to detect than outright temptations to mortal sin.

> How many fervent souls have been drawn from their monasteries by the attraction of the solitary life (Rom. 12:11), and have then become lukewarm and have been spewed forth (Rev. 3:16), or if they have remained, have become slack and dissolute, violating the law of the hermit. . . . He supposed that the solitary life would produce the fruits of the Spirit in much greater abundance than the common life, where he had experienced, so he thought, only ordinary grace. The idea seemed to him a good one, but the outcome showed that it was more like a destructive fox.[6]

Immature zeal can also lead to becoming critical of others—examining the speck in our neighbor's eyes and missing the log in our own—and undermining the very love of neighbor toward which the spiritual journey is leading us. Teresa, Bernard, and many of the saints point out the importance of seeking out wise and balanced spiritual counsel as we make decisions along the way.

Misplaced Priorities

An opposite danger of "indiscreet zeal," Teresa tells us, is the distractedness that comes from over-involvement in worldly affairs. Teresa makes clear that a certain reordering of our priorities is necessary if we are to make progress. Giving the Lord the time and attention He is asking for is essential.

> His mercy and goodness are so bountiful; whereas we are occupied in our pastimes, business affairs, pleasures, and worldly buying and selling, and still falling into sin and rising again.[7]

Even though a soul at this stage may not be in a state of habitual mortal sin there is still a darkness in a soul filled with the things of this world.

> Even though it may not be in a bad state, it is so involved in worldly things and so absorbed with its possessions, honor, or business affairs. . . . If a person is to enter the second dwelling places, it is important that he strive to give up unnecessary things and business affairs. Each one should do this in conformity with his state in life . . . if he doesn't begin doing this I hold that it will be impossible for him to get there. And it will be even impossible for him to stay where he is without danger.[8]

> How the whole world's habit of getting involved in vanities vitiates everything! Our faith is so dead that we desire

what we see more than what faith tells us . . . clearly many remedies are necessary to cure us.[9]

Teresa is clearly speaking to people who are living ordinary lives in the world. She strongly advises that in so far as it is compatible with our state in life we should eliminate the nonessentials and make room for ordering our life more and more to God.

Teresa recognizes that for some there may be a certain distractedness or even lukewarmness in the early stages of the journey, but counsels us not to become discouraged.

> Nor should you become disconsolate if you don't respond at once to the Lord. His Majesty knows well how to wait many days and years, especially when he sees perseverance and good desires.[10]

Of course, the sooner we can respond, the better!

As the soul confronts the need to reorder its life more around God, strong temptations may arise that make the things and pleasures of this world appear very attractive, almost "eternal," and the things of God appear abstract and distant, even fearful. Bernard reminds us that such temptations and fears are normal, but they must be fought.

> Our common experience tells us that it is fear which disturbs us at the beginning of our conversion, fear of that dismaying picture we form for ourselves of the strict life and unwonted austerities we are about to embrace. . . . [But] if we could see the dawn of that day in whose light we should perceive the rewards as well as the trials, our desire of the rewards would entirely obliterate fear, since in the clear light it would be apparent that "the sufferings we now endure bear no comparison with the splendor, as yet unrevealed, which is in store for us" (Rom. 8:18). . . . Beginners on the way to God, therefore, must in particular watch and pray against this first temptation.[11]

Teresa's advice is similar: to fight with the capacities of our mind and the gift of faith that God has given us.

> Memory shows it [the soul] where all these things end, holding before it the death of those who found great joy in them. Through the memory it sees how some have suffered sudden death, how quickly they are forgotten by all. Some whom it had known in great prosperity are under the ground, and their graves are walked upon. This soul itself has often passed by these graves. It reflects that many worms are swarming over the corpses and thinks about numerous other things. The will is inclined to love after seeing such countless signs of love; it would want to repay something; it especially keeps in mind how this true Lover never leaves it, accompanying it and giving it life and being. Then the intellect helps it realize that it couldn't find a better friend, even were it to live for many years, that the whole world is filled with falsehood, and that so too these joys the devil gives it are filled with trials, cares, and contradictions.[12]

Remembering the eternal perspective, recalling the basic truths, remembering the biblical worldview, is key to the entire journey and a real "secret" of the saints' progress.

Is God Fair?

One temptation that can afflict people at all stages of the spiritual journey is to look at the "wicked" and wonder why they seem to be doing so well, while the "righteous" wonder why things are going so badly for them. Again, the solution is to look at all of reality in the light of eternity, revealed to us in God's Word. How well or how badly things seem to be going for people in this life can't really be accurately judged except in the light of how it all ends—in the light of eternity.

> But, as for me, I lost my balance;
> my feet all but slipped,

Because I was envious of the arrogant
    when I saw the prosperity of the wicked.
For they suffer no pain;
    their bodies are healthy and sleek.
They are free of the burdens of life;
    they are not afflicted like others. . . .
They say, "Does God really know?" . . .
Is it in vain that I have kept my heart clean,
    washed my hands in innocence?
For I am afflicted day after day,
    chastised every morning. . . .
Though I tried to understand all this,
    it was too difficult for me,
Till I entered the sanctuary of God
    and came to understand their
    end. (Ps. 73:2–5, 11, 13–14, 16–17, NAB)

The same eternal perspective is needed in order to "understand" why the righteous may be suffering or have died.

In the eyes of the foolish they seemed to have died,
and their departure was thought to be an affliction,
and their going from us to be their destruction;
but they are at peace.
For though in the sight of men they were punished,
their hope is full of immortality.
Having been disciplined a little, they will receive great
good, because God tested them and found them
worthy of himself;
like gold in the furnace he tried them,
and like a sacrificial burnt offering he accepted them.
In the time of their visitation they will shine forth,
and will run like sparks through the stubble.
They will govern nations and rule over peoples, and
the Lord will reign over them forever. (Wis. 3:2–8)

Resisting temptations to turn back to the things and pleasures of the world or to people who tempt us to sin can truly be agonizing for the soul in these early stages. The soul, having conformed itself to these things, will experience a deprivation and emptying that is truly painful. John of the Cross calls this purification the dark night of the senses. Francis de Sales describes aspects of this initial purifying agony:

> It may well turn out that this change in your way of life will cause you many problems. You have bid a great, general farewell to the world's follies and vanities and this may bring on a feeling of sadness and discouragement. If this should be the case, have a little patience, I beg of you, for it will come to nothing. Things will seem a little strange because they are new, but when such feelings pass you will receive countless blessings.[13]

And yet enduring these temptations and trials is precisely the remedy that the Lord utilizes to cure us. As the senses are being withdrawn from an inordinate attachment to the things and pleasures of the world or from disordered attachments to others, an agony may be experienced in the soul. Eventually, if the soul perseveres, a stability and peace will ensue, for a positive infilling of the presence and gifts of God will fill the emptiness. It's in this regard that John speaks so often of persevering in the darkness of faith as the most valuable and proximate means of union with God. When we are obedient to what we know by faith rather than to the longings of our sin-wounded flesh, it is the time when—in the darkness of faith—we are most effectively being prepared for the light of God's gifts and presence.

Teresa also speaks about the importance of reaching the right balance in the knowledge of our sins and our weaknesses and the knowledge of the mercy of God. The correct perspective will produce a true humility, which is the foundation of spiritual growth.

Teresa herself had to struggle to understand how it was possible that God could actually be working in her life while she at the same time still had obvious weaknesses and imperfections. She recounts how the devil used her awareness of her "vanities and weaknesses" to discourage her and tempt her to give up or deny the action of God in her life. Sometimes, even though she was receiving graces and favors from God, she felt that the "vanities and weaknesses of the past were again awakening." She had to struggle to cast herself upon the Lord's mercy. God helped her on this occasion through advice from her confessor, which gave her perspective and put her at peace.

Many of the saints talk about the importance of self-knowledge regarding our own sinfulness, but never apart from knowledge of the mercy of God. If we aren't sufficiently aware of our sins and weaknesses, presumption and pride may dominate; if we aren't sufficiently aware of the mercy of God, discouragement, fear, and despair are dangers. Here, too, being in contact with a mature spiritual friend or director is very helpful.

> Ah, my Lord! Your help is necessary here; without it one can do nothing. In Your mercy do not consent to allow this soul to suffer deception and give up what was begun . . . that it may turn away from bad companions. It's a wonderful thing for a person to talk to those who speak about this interior castle, to draw near not only to those seen to be in these rooms where he is but to those known to have entered the ones closer to the center. Conversation with these latter will be a great help to him, and he can converse so much with them that they will bring him to where they are.[14]

And Teresa loses no time in sounding a central Carmelite warning: Don't seek feelings of consolations in prayer. Seek the Lord, seek to conform your will to His!

If the Lord chooses to give delights and consolations, be grateful, she advises, but let them accomplish the purpose for which they were given: to encourage us to persevere in daily taking up our cross and following Him.

Thérèse's Little Way: Daily Self-Denial in the Service of Love

Teresa of Avila's namesake, Thérèse, understood this very well. She knew she was neither capable of nor called to "great feats" of public witness or service. But she resolved to be no less generous in taking advantage of the little things of daily life to deny herself and take up her cross out of love for God and others. Her little "mortifications"—death to self-love and selfish preference—lie within reach of each of us in our everyday lives as well. She called this her "little way," for it is a path to holiness open to everyone.

Waiting Purifies

When Thérèse finally received permission to enter Carmel at the age of fifteen, she had to wait an additional three months. This was hard for her, but she knew that "waiting" was helping her to grow in "abandonment and in the other virtues."[15]

In fact, God frequently made Thérèse "wait" as a means to help her overcome her self-will. She wanted God's will, but often in her own way and in her own time. And so the Lord helped her to overcome this conflict of wills: she had to wait to enter Carmel, and she had to wait to make her profession. She tells us of how she began to understand how God used these times as a means of purification in her life.

> One day, during my prayer, I understood that my intense desire to make Profession was mixed with a great self-love. Since I had *given* myself to Jesus to please and console Him, I had no right to oblige Him to do *my will* instead of His own.[16]

When she had to wait another three months to enter Carmel she at first entertained the notion of "goofing off" a little, but decided against it.

> At first the thought came into my mind not to lead a life as well regulated as had been my custom, but soon I

understood the value of the time I was being offered. I
made a resolution to give myself up more than ever to a
serious and *mortified* life.[17]

Thérèse hastens to explain that she had "no attraction" for the
great mortifications of the saints and "never" made any acts of penance, because of her "cowardliness." She acknowledges she had been
coddled in various ways but recognizes a special way of mortification that the Lord had showed her.

My mortifications consisted in breaking my will, always
so ready to impose itself on others, in holding back a
reply, in rendering little services without any recognition,
in not leaning my back against a support when seated,
etc., etc. It was through the practice of these *nothings* that
I prepared myself to become the fiancée of Jesus.[18]

Daily Self-Denial

Thérèse's life in the convent continued along these lines, taking
advantage of opportunities to deny her self-will or self-love in the
little challenges of daily life with others. She gives us many examples
of how she applied this self-denial in the circumstances of her daily
life in the convent.

Somebody, by mistake, had taken her lamp after night prayers,
when the sisters were no longer permitted to speak. "Instead of feeling annoyed at being thus deprived of it, I was really happy, feeling
that Poverty consists in being deprived not only of agreeable things
but of indispensable things too. And so in this *exterior darkness*, I
was interiorly illumined!"[19]

She tells of a similar joy she experienced when the pretty little jug
she had in her cell was replaced with a large, ugly one, "all chipped."

Yet what was most difficult for Thérèse was to not make excuses
when she was blamed for something that wasn't her fault. Unjustly
blamed for breaking a vase, she decided to remain silent and accept
the correction without excusing herself, but this took much effort.

Because of my lack of virtue these little practices cost me very much and I had to console myself with the thought that at the last Judgment everything would be revealed.[20]

Thérèse, in her striving for perfection, wanted to appear perfect in her own eyes and in the eyes of others. This effort at humbling herself, while hard, was necessary.

Once in the convent, her effort at not leaning against the back of her chair was forbidden to her because of her tendency to stoop. But Thérèse acknowledged that "her ardor for penances would not have lasted long had the Superiors allowed them. The penances they did allow me consisted in mortifying my self-love, which did me much more good than corporeal penances."[21]

She singles out her assignment to kitchen duty as a good means of "putting my self-love in its proper place, i.e., under my feet."[22] Not only did she experience the ordinary annoyances of working with others on a common task, but because one of her sisters was assigned to the same duty she had to deny her great desire to chat freely as they used to do, in light of the rule of silence. She speaks of countless other opportunities for small mortifications: of trying to please an elderly sister to whom she was assigned who was virtually impossible to please, of having dirty laundry water splashed on her and trying not to react, of having her painting supplies moved out of place, of bearing patiently the clicking noises that a nun made at community prayer which she was eventually able to offer to the Lord, remarking that this prayer of offering "was not the *Prayer of Quiet*," of refraining, in her duties in the formation of the novices, of asking questions to satisfy her curiosity that had no bearing on her duties, and not trying "to attract their hearts to me."[23] All of these, and more, she was able eventually to offer to the Lord.

At another time two sisters were given the opportunity to go on an errand that Thérèse would have enjoyed. She responded slowly in order to give the other sister the first chance at it. Her slowness was interpreted as a sign of a selfish reluctance to serve, and she was corrected.

Don't Waste Any Opportunity

As her spiritual journey continued Thérèse grew in confidence that she was on the right track.

> Yes, my Beloved, this is how my life will be consumed. I have no other means of proving my love for you other than that of strewing flowers, that is, not allowing one little sacrifice to escape, not one look, one word, profiting by all the smallest things and doing them through love.[24]

She recognizes that she has made progress in loving since the days of her novitiate.

> Alas! When I think of the time of my novitiate I see how imperfect I was. I made so much fuss over such little things that it makes me laugh now. Ah! how good the Lord is in having matured my soul, and in having given it wings.

But she also realizes that she is probably still filled with imperfections, and that at some time in the future the present time that now seems so "mature" will also be seen as being full of imperfections.

> Later on, no doubt, the time in which I am now will appear filled with imperfections, but now I am astonished at nothing. I am not disturbed at seeing myself *weakness* itself. On the contrary, it is in my weakness that I glory, (2 Cor. 12:5) and I expect each day to discover new imperfections in myself.[25]

Thérèse wasn't discouraged by this weakness, but saw it as another opportunity to avail herself of the rich treasure of God's mercy and love, a sign that He wanted to live more deeply in her.

She speaks of some "big victories" that functioned as turning points in her efforts to grow in charity. She describes one of them like this:

> There is in the Community a Sister who has the faculty of displeasing me in everything, in her ways, her words, her character, everything seems *very disagreeable* to me. And still, she is a holy religious who must be very pleasing to God. Not wishing to give in to the natural antipathy I was experiencing I told myself that charity must not consist in feelings but in works; then I set myself to doing for this Sister what I would do for the person I loved the most.[26]

Thérèse prayed for this sister, thanked God for creating her, and tried to express friendliness to her in her manner and in small services she did for her.

Eventually this pattern of thinking and acting in love became easier for Thérèse. In writing to her superior at the time she says:

> Mother, when reading what I have just written, you could believe that the practice of charity is not difficult for me. It is true; for several months now I no longer have to struggle to practice this beautiful virtue. I don't mean by this that I no longer have any faults; ah! I am too imperfect for that. But I mean that I don't have any trouble in rising when I have fallen.[27]

This didn't mean, Thérèse tells us, that there weren't times when the situation she encountered seemed to be beyond her level of virtue. In situations like that Thérèse tells us "my *last means* of not being defeated in combats is desertion."[28] She would, if possible, try to avoid the troubling situation, aware that in her weakness she might fail the test of charity.

Loving with His Love

What enabled Thérèse to make progress was not only understanding more clearly what the Lord is calling us to as regards love, but also understanding that the Lord puts His own love within us, enabling us to love as He loves.

> When meditating upon these words of Jesus [Jn. 15:13], I understood how imperfect was my love for my Sisters. I saw I didn't love them as God loves them. Ah! I understand now that charity consists in bearing with the faults of others, in not being surprised at their weakness, in being edified by the smallest acts of virtue we see them practice. . . . It is no longer a question of loving one's neighbor as oneself but of loving him as *He, Jesus, has loved him,* and will love him to the consummation of the ages.
>   Ah! Lord, I know you don't command the impossible. You know better than I do my weakness and imperfection; You know very well that never would I be able to love my Sisters as You love them, unless *You,* O my Jesus, *loved them in me. . . .* Yes, I feel it, when I am charitable, it is Jesus alone who is acting in me, and the more united I am to Him, the more also do I love my Sisters.[29]

Thérèse is living what Teresa of Avila continually emphasizes: the centrality of the Cross in making spiritual progress and love as the mark of holiness, all the while drawing strength from God.

> It's an amusing thing that even though we still have a thousand impediments and imperfections and our virtues have hardly begun to grow—and please God they may have begun—we are yet not ashamed to seek spiritual delights in prayer or to complain about dryness. May this never happen to you. . . . Embrace the cross your Spouse has carried and understand that this must be your task.[30]

John of the Cross similarly points out the danger of seeking pleasure in prayer rather than union with God, identifying it as spiritual gluttony.

> Once they do not find delight in prayer, or in any other spiritual exercise, they feel extreme reluctance and repugnance in returning to it and sometimes even give it up. . . . They are like children who are prompted to act not by reason but by pleasure.
>
> All their time is spent looking for satisfaction and spiritual consolation; they can never read enough spiritual books, and one minute they are meditating on one subject and the next on another, always hunting for some gratification in the things of God.[31]

Francis also has some important things to say about this.

> I hold that devotion does not consist in the sweetness, delight, consolation, and sensible tenderness of heart that move us to tears and sighs and bring us a certain pleasant, relishful satisfaction when we perform various spiritual exercises. . . . Many souls experience these tender, consoling feelings but still remain very vicious. Consequently, they do not have true love of God, much less true devotion.[32]

Francis illustrates his point by drawing our attention to the effusive sentiments of affection that Saul expressed towards David (1 Kings 24)—while still wanting to kill him!

> In spite of all this show of devotion such unfortunate people will not part with a single penny of their ill-gotten riches; they will not give up one of their perverse affections; they will not endure the least temporal inconvenience for the service of that Savior over whose sufferings they have just been weeping. The good feelings they experience are no better than spiritual mushrooms. Not

only are they not true devotion but very often they are tricks played by the enemy. He charms such souls with these trifling consolations to make them content and satisfied with such things, and keep them from further search for true, solid devotion. True devotion consists in a constant, resolute, prompt, and active will to do whatever we know is pleasing to God.[33]

Or, as Thérèse puts it:

I do not hold in contempt beautiful thoughts which nourish the soul and unite it with God; but for a long time I have understood that we must not depend on them and even make perfection consist in receiving many spiritual lights. The most beautiful thoughts are nothing without good works.[34]

Teresa, like Bernard and John, is extremely clear in identifying the essence of holiness and the spiritual life: what the spiritual journey is all about is uniting our will with God's will, wanting what He wants, loving what He loves, living a life that in all its aspects honors Him and gives Him glory. Although the spiritual life can sometimes appear to be shrouded in mystery and somewhat esoteric, Teresa clearly reassures us that profound simplicity lies at the heart of the journey; it's all about uniting our will with God's will.

Don't think that in what concerns perfection there is some mystery or things unknown or still to be understood, for in perfect conformity to God's will lies all our good.[35]

If we keep this clear in our minds, Teresa indicates, we'll avoid many pitfalls.

The whole aim of any person who is beginning prayer—and don't forget this, because it's very important—should be that he work and prepare himself with determination and every possible effort to bring his will into conformity with God's will. Be certain that . . . the greatest perfection attainable along the spiritual path lies in this conformity.[36]

As Thérèse grew in the simplicity of her relationship with God, she found it increasingly difficult to speak about what was going on inside her soul even to her wise and kind superiors. One day an elderly nun spoke to her about why this was the case.

> "[It is] because your soul is extremely *simple*, but when you will be perfect, you will be even *more simple*; the closer one approaches to God, the simpler one becomes." The good Mother was right.[37]

Thérèse spoke often of the importance of being a child, in all simplicity and dependence on the Father, as a key to making progress on the spiritual journey.[38]

As with so much of the wisdom of the Doctors of the Church, what we find here is an ability to articulate and apply to various situations the clear teaching of the Scripture.

> If you love me, you will keep my commandments.
> (Jn. 14:15)

> Unless you become like a little child you will not enter the kingdom of heaven. (Mt. 18:3)

Dealing with Temptation

Teresa has helped identify for us certain possible deceptions, imbalances, and misunderstandings that can divert us from the true path to union. Francis de Sales, who has helped us in identifying the way in which affection for sin can block us from making progress, also helps us identify exactly how temptations to particular sins work and how to successfully resist them.

Francis identifies three steps in the process of temptation. First, sin is proposed to the soul. Then, we are either pleased or displeased by the proposal. Finally, we consent to or reject the temptation to sin.[39]

While we are all familiar with the basic concept of being tempted and giving into it or not, Francis points out that a crucial decision is actually made right after the temptation presents itself, at the stage where we are either initially pleased or displeased by it. He points out that even if we have no intention of giving in to the temptation the decision to take pleasure in thinking about it for a while before rejecting it is both dangerous and damaging in itself. Although we may sometimes find ourselves taking an almost involuntary pleasure or delight in a temptation, as soon as we become aware of it we need to immediately reject both the pleasure and the temptation. For example, while we may feel an almost automatic pleasure when a temptation to revenge or lust presents itself, it is very important that we immediately reject any voluntary delight in it. To linger over the temptation, to voluntarily take pleasure in it, even if we don't intend to do the sinful action, may in itself be sinful, and certainly muddies the spiritual waters of our soul.

To dally over a temptation is to run the risk of weakening our resolve and makes it more likely that at that time or at a future time we will consent to it. Also, it damages the "purity of heart" that is necessary both to "see God" and to make steady progress on the journey to union.

Catherine of Siena talks about fighting the spiritual battle with a two-edged sword in our hands, with hatred of sin as one edge of the blade and love of virtue as the other. It's right and necessary to hate sin. Sin is ugly. Sin always hurts ourselves and others. Sin is offensive to God. To grow not just in our intellectual understanding of the ugliness of sin but in our emotional reaction to it is helpful for resisting temptation.

Hate what is evil, hold fast to what is good. (Rom. 12:9)

You loved justice and hated wickedness;
    therefore God, your God, anointed you
    with the oil of gladness above your companions.
    (Heb. 1:9)[40]

Of course, both Francis and Teresa concur in emphasizing the importance of avoiding the occasions that may lead us into sin. They both point out how important it is to avoid those people, places, situations, activities, and thought processes that will lead us to be tempted to a particular sin. If we see that there is a connection between getting drunk, for example, and stopping at a bar after work, the first step in avoiding the sin is to avoid the occasion for temptation, the stopping at the bar. If we see that watching a certain television program or a certain movie stirs up lust in ourselves we need to avoid those programs and movies.

To voluntarily put ourselves into situations where we know we will experience pleasurable temptations—even if we don't intend to yield to the actions proposed—may even in itself be sinful.

> Similarly, it sometimes happens that the temptation itself involves us in sin because we are ourselves its cause. . . . If I know that certain associations will expose me to temptation and to giving way and yet willingly go there, I am undoubtedly guilty of all the temptations I encounter there.
>
> At times the pleasure proceeding from the temptation can be avoided. Hence it is always a greater or less sin to permit the temptation in proportion as the pleasure taken or the consent given is great or small or long or short in duration. . . . When pleasure follows the temptation and could have been avoided but was not, there is always some kind of sin according to the amount of time it is dwelt on and the pleasure taken in it.[41]

Even if we are vigilant about avoiding near occasions of temptation and sin, we will nevertheless run into temptations at times, and may feel pleasure when we do. Francis talks about how sometimes the "lower" part of the soul involuntarily may feel pleasure while the "higher" part of the soul rejects the temptation.

> Hence, even though it surrounds the will, it is not inside it. By this we see that such delight is involuntary and as such it cannot be sinful.[42]

Many of the Doctors of the Church base their vision of the nature of the human soul and its connection to the body ("Christian anthropology") on the broad biblical categories that the apostle Paul uses to describe the human person. They deduce from this, with some variations, that there is a "higher" part of the soul that is more identified with the true self and endures as a spirit after death, and a "lower" part of the soul that is more intimately bound up with the life of the body. We will find this language in many of the saints' writings. As Bernard puts it, interpreting Paul in harmony with Francis de Sales:

> "When I say me," he [Paul] said, "understand it to mean what is most excellent in me, that in which I exist by favor of God, my mind and reason. When I speak of my soul, think of that lower principle whose purpose as you see is to animate the body, and even share in its concupiscence. . . . Not in the flesh but in this spirit is my true self to be found. What if the soul still experiences carnal lusts? "The thing behaving that way is not my true self but sin living in me. (Rom. 7:17)." And therefore I do not regard this carnal instinct as my real self, but as something possessed by my self; in other words, my sensitive soul.[43]

Even though we have little or no control over the "involuntary" urges of our sinful nature, we do have control over whether we "dally" with them or not.

> Sometimes we are caught off guard by certain symptoms of pleasure immediately following a temptation. At most this

can be only a very slight venial sin. However, it becomes greater if after we perceived the evil that has befallen us we carelessly delay for some time and dally with the pleasure to decide whether we ought to allow or reject it. The sin becomes still greater if after becoming aware of the pleasure we dwell on it for some time through downright negligence and without any determination to reject it. When we voluntarily and with full deliberation resolve to take pleasure in such delights, this deliberate purpose is of itself a great sin if the object in which we take delight is also very evil.[44]

Francis points out that temptation is quite simply a fact of life that we will have to face. He points out that great saints were often tempted violently, and sometimes had to fight certain temptations their whole lives. He mentions the apostle Paul, Angela of Foligno, Francis of Assisi, Benedict, and Catherine of Siena as among the great saints who had to fight violent temptations.

Catherine herself gives a sobering account of how on one occasion the most awful temptations to sexual sin buffeted her. When they were over she complained to God about Him apparently being absent during the time of this temptation. The Lord's reply was that even though Catherine was only aware of the ferocious temptations at the time, He was indeed there right in the midst of them, giving her the strength to make it through.

Francis reminds us that to be greatly tempted while refusing to yield in no way makes us displeasing to God, but rather, just the contrary. God is delighted when we resist temptations, even though we may feel "slimed" after enduring them.

Temptation to a certain sin, to any sin whatsoever, might last throughout our whole life, yet it can never make us displeasing to God's Majesty provided we do not take pleasure in it and give consent to it. . . . You must have great courage in the midst of temptation. Never think yourself overcome as long as they are displeasing to you, keeping clearly in mind the difference between feeling temptation and consenting to it.[45]

Resisting Temptation: A Means to Growth

As a matter of fact, in addition to the basic practices of a fervent Christian life, resisting temptations and enduring trials is one of the primary means of spiritual growth. God uses the unavoidable realities of the world, the flesh, and even the devil as means to propel us to union with Him, if we grow in determination to resist them. The very attacks intended to defeat us in fact become the means to victory if we apply the wisdom of the saints in dealing with them.

> I tell you this so that if you ever happen to be attacked by strong temptations you can know that God confers an extraordinary favor on you. By it he declares that he wants to make you great in his sight but that you must always be humble and self-fearful. Your only assurance that you will be able to overcome little temptations even after you have prevailed over great ones is by constant fidelity to his majesty. No matter what temptations may come to you and no matter what pleasure accompanies them, as long as your will refuses consent not only to the temptation but also to the pleasure, they should not disturb you since God is not offended by them.[46]

Thérèse tells us about how helpful it is when beset by a great temptation to bring it into the light by seeking help and counsel from a spiritual director, confessor, or mature spiritual friend. She tells of how the night before her profession, which she had longed for so greatly, "a storm arose within my soul the like of which I'd never seen before." Never having had a doubt about her vocation before, she was suddenly assaulted by the feeling that this wasn't the right path for her and she had deceived her superiors into thinking that it was. She speaks of great darkness and anguish in her soul. When she pulled the novice mistress out of community prayer to confide her great distress, the novice mistress reassured her about her vocation, and the darkness lifted. As Thérèse explains,

> The act of humility I had just performed put the devil to flight since he had perhaps thought that I would not dare admit my temptation. My doubts left me completely as soon as I finished speaking.

The next morning she was "flooded with a river of peace."[47]

Blessed Raymond of Capua, Catherine of Siena's spiritual director and biographer, tells of the violent temptations—to impurity, to abandon her vocation, to pride, to despair—that assailed Catherine until late in her life, even on her death bed, and how important her openness with her spiritual director was and frequent Confession was in resisting them.[48]

John of the Cross points out that enduring through temptation is an essential part of the purification that God is bringing about in us. He speaks of this as the "passive night of the senses." For those who want to continue all the way to full union this dark night of the senses "is ordinarily accompanied by burdensome trials and sensory temptations that last a long time, and with some longer than with others." He indicates, as does Catherine, that temptations of the most distressing kinds may plague us, such as strong temptations to sexual immorality, shocking and disturbing temptations to blasphemy, or to the anguish of scrupulosity. He reminds us though that "by these trials it [the soul] is truly humbled in preparation for its coming exaltation."[49]

How Long Will the Purification Last?

It's normal to wonder how long the various phases or stages of the spiritual journey may last. Both John and Teresa frequently point out that the journey is normally a long one; the purification is gradual and each stage may take years. They also remind us though that God is sovereign, and guides each soul in the way that's best for it. John's answer to the question of how long the temptations and aridity in prayer in the "passive night of the senses" lasts is very useful.

> Yet we cannot say certainly how long the soul will be kept in this fast and penance of the senses. Not everyone undergoes this in the same way, neither are the temptations identical. All is meted out according to God's will and the greater or lesser amount of imperfection that must be purged from each one. In the measure of the degree of love to which God wishes to raise a soul, he humbles it with greater or less intensity, or for a longer or shorter period of time.
>
> Those who have more considerable capacity and strength for suffering, God purges more intensely and quickly. But those who are very weak he keeps in this night for a long time. Their purgation is less intense and their temptations abated, and he frequently refreshes their senses to keep them from backsliding. They arrive at the purity of perfection late in life. . . . Yet, as is evident through experience, souls who will pass on to so happy and lofty a state as is the union of love must usually remain in these aridities and temptations for a long while no matter how quickly God leads them.[50]

Our level of cooperation also determines how long different stages of the journey may take. John makes the serious but humorous observation that we often pray for God to make us holy and then run away from the answer when it arrives in the form of trials and ordinary suffering.

> And here it ought to be pointed out why so few reach this high state of perfect union with God. It should be known that the reason is not that God wishes only a few of these spirits to be so elevated; he would rather want all to be perfect, but he finds few vessels that will endure so lofty

and sublime a work. Since he tries them in little things and finds them so weak that they immediately flee from work, unwilling to be subject to the least discomfort and mortification, it follows that not finding them strong and faithful in that little (Mt. 25:21, 23), in which he favored them by beginning to hew and polish them, he realizes that they will be much less strong in these greater trials. As a result he proceeds no further in purifying them and raising them from the dust of the earth through the toil of mortification. They are in need of greater constancy and fortitude than they showed.

There are many who desire to advance and persistently beseech God to bring them to this state of perfection. Yet when God wills to conduct them through the initial trials and mortifications, as is necessary, they are unwilling to suffer them and they shun them, flee from the narrow road of life (Mt. 7:14) and seek the broad road of their own consolation, which is that of their own perdition (Mt. 7:13); thus they do not allow God to begin to grant their petition. . . . They hardly even begin to walk along this road by submitting to what is least, that is, to ordinary sufferings.[51]

Overcoming Temptation: More Helpful Advice

Before moving on I'd like to summarize some additional advice from the saints that is both helpful and inspiring.

- Resist the small, petty temptations as well as the big ones. Temptations to anger, suspicion, jealousy, envy, flirtatious behavior, frivolity, vanity, inappropriate affection, craftiness, and evil thoughts attack everyone, "even the most devout and resolute."[52] They must be resisted.
- Don't "dialogue" with the temptation but perform some contrary act of virtue. "So also when a devout soul sees itself attacked by temptation, it must not lose time in argument or discussion but with all simplicity turn toward Jesus Christ, its spouse, and

affirm again its fidelity to him and its desire to be solely and entirely his forever."[53]

- Bring the temptation out into the light with your spiritual director or mature spiritual friend. "The sovereign remedy against all temptation, whether great or small, is to open your heart and express its suggestions, feelings, and affections to your director."[54]

- Just say no! "If temptation continues to harass and persecute us after all this, there is nothing further to do on our part but to remain steadfast in our protestations never to consent to it. Just as girls can never be married as long as they say no, so too a soul though tempted can never sin as long as it says no."[55]

- The best remedy when being tempted after we reject it is to run to the Cross of Christ and ask for help. "Moreover, this is so terrifying to the evil spirit that as soon as he sees that his temptations urge us on to God's love he ceases to tempt us."[56]

Bernard has some wonderful words about invoking the name—and presence—of Jesus when faced not only with temptation but with all manner of difficulties.

> It is a medicine. Does one of us feel sad? Let the name of Jesus come into his heart. . . . Does someone fall into sin? Does his despair even urge him to suicide? Let him but invoke this life-giving name and his will to live will be at once renewed. The hardness of heart that is our common experience, the apathy that bred of indolence, bitterness of mind, repugnance for the things of the spirit—have they ever failed to yield in presence of that saving name? The tears dammed up by the barrier of our pride—how have they not burst forth again with sweeter abundance at the thought of Jesus' name? And where is the man, who terrified and trembling before impending peril, has not been suddenly filled with courage and rid of fear by calling on the strength of that name? Where is the man who tossed on the rolling seas of doubt, did not quickly find certitude

by recourse to the clarity of Jesus' name? Was ever a man so discouraged, so beaten down by afflictions, to whom the sound of this name did not bring new resolve? In short, for all the ills and disorders to which flesh is heir, this name is medicine. For proof we have no less than his own promise: "Call upon me in the day of trouble; I will deliver you, and you shall glorify me" (Ps. 49:15).[57]

The Positive Power of Trials: Dryness in Prayer

In addition to learning how to combat temptations, learning how to deal with other kinds of trials is also important for progress in the spiritual life. There are many types of trials that challenge us on our journey to God. They all can be used to propel us faster into the heart of God if we relate to them with faith and wisdom. There are all kinds of exterior trials: criticism, difficult relationships, setbacks in all areas of life, illness, failures of various kinds, financial stress, rejection by others, etc. There are also various kinds of interior trials: temptation to particular sins, dryness in prayer, experiences of desolation and abandonment, agony over the sufferings of others, assaults on faith, hope, and love, etc. One of the trials virtually everyone encounters on the spiritual journey is that of experiencing dryness or aridity in prayer. Not feeling the presence of God, not experiencing His love, feeling distant, empty, cut off, are all possible aspects of the experience of dryness. Francis describes this trial of deprivation:

> Sometimes you will find yourself deprived and destitute of all feelings of devotion and your soul will seem like barren, sterile desert where there is no path or road leading to God, nor any water of grace to refresh you because of the aridity that now seems to threaten it with complete and absolute desolation[58]

Teresa, Francis de Sales, John of the Cross, Bernard, and Catherine of Siena all frequently speak of the important role this encounter with dryness plays in our spiritual development. As John explains,

Yet until a soul is placed by God in the passive purgation of that dark night, which we will soon explain, it cannot purify itself completely of these imperfections or others. But people should insofar as possible strive to do their part in purifying and perfecting themselves and thereby merit God's divine cure. In this cure God will heal them of what through their own efforts they were unable to remedy. No matter how much individuals do through their own efforts, they cannot actively purify themselves enough to be disposed in the least degree for the divine union of the perfection of love. God must take over and purge them in that fire that is dark for them as we will explain.[59]

What's the Cause of the Dryness We Experience?

These saints teach that there may be a variety of causes for the experience of dryness in our prayer and that it is important to ascertain what the root cause of the dryness is in order to know how we should respond. They pick out three main reasons why dryness may be experienced in prayer.

Lukewarmness and Infidelity

We may experience dryness in our prayer because we have become negligent in our spiritual practices. Francis describes it like this:

> It is ourselves who are often the cause of our own sterile, arid state. . . . God holds back consolations from us when we have a foolish complacence in them and are subject to the worms of presumption. . . . When we neglect to gather the dear delights of God's love at the proper season, he takes them from us in punishment for our sloth. . . . The duplicity and subtlety that we use in our confessions and spiritual communications with our director may also produce spiritual aridity and sterility. . . . You have glutted yourself with worldly pleasures and it is no wonder that spiritual delights disgust you. . . . Those who are rich with the world's pleasures are incapable of spiritual delights.[60]

We may have become careless in being faithful to our spiritual commitments such as attendance at daily Mass, our daily time of prayer, spiritual reading, and so on. Or we may have become careless in valuing the gifts God gives us, or in rejecting or dallying with temptation. Or we may have begun to allow distractions, entertainments, and engagement in worldly activities to deaden our hunger for God.

Bernard sketches a powerful picture of the downward spiral that can be set in motion by such little infidelities:

> If this cold once penetrates the soul when (as so often happens) the soul is neglectful and the spirit asleep and if no one (God forbid) is there to curb it, then it reaches into the soul's interior, descends to the depths of the heart and the recesses of the mind, paralyses the affections, obstructs the paths of counsel, unsteadies the light of judgment, fetters the liberty of the spirit, and soon—as appears to bodies sick with fever—a rigor of the mind takes over: vigor slackens, energies grow languid, repugnance for austerity increases, fear of poverty disquiets, the soul shrivels, grace is withdrawn, time means boredom, reason is lulled to sleep, the spirit is quenched (1 Thess. 5:19), the fresh fervor wanes away, a fastidious lukewarmness weighs down, brotherly love grows cold (Mt. 24: 12), pleasure attracts, security is a trap, old habits return. Can I say more? The law is cheated, justice is rejected, what is right is outlawed, the fear of the Lord is abandoned (Job 6:14). Shamelessness finally gets free rein. There comes that rash leap, so dishonorable, so disgraceful, so full of ignominy and confusion; a leap from the heights into the abyss, from the court-yard, to the dung-heap, from the throne to the sewer, from heaven to the mud, from the cloister to the world, from paradise to hell.[61]

Dryness experienced as a result of such negligence, lukewarmness, and infidelity—and whatever stage of the downward spiral it may have led to—has only one solution: repentance. This dryness is self-induced; the solution to it is to return to fidelity in our spiritual practices. The difficulty is that once we get "out of shape" in the spiritual life the effort required to reestablish good spiritual "tone" can become distasteful or repugnant. Just as with physical exercise, when we're used to "working out" regularly it's not so difficult, even though it still requires effort. But when we neglect our physical exercise and then start again it takes special effort. We get out of breath and our muscles hurt much more readily than they did before. As Teresa of Avila puts it, with her characteristic straight talk and realism, the only solution for having stopped praying is to start again! Teresa also points out that sometimes this dryness is caused by a refusal to respond to an invitation the Lord is giving to deeper surrender.[62]

Bernard singles out the role of pride in producing such dryness and aridity.

> Even now I pay the penalty [for pride]. I am bitterly flogged. It is not without reason that this languor of soul, this dullness of mind has laid hold of me. . . . Pride was discovered in me. . . . Hence the barrenness of my spirit and the resourcelessness of devotion that I suffer. . . . That sorrow from which tears spring I cannot find, such is my heart's hardness (Mk. 16:14). The psalms are stale, reading is disagreeable, prayer is devoid of joy, the accustomed meditations irretrievable. Where now that intoxication of the Spirit (Eph. 5:18)? Where that serenity of mind, and peace, and joy in the Holy Spirit (Rom. 14:17)? This is the reason for repugnance for work, drowsiness at vigils, quickness to anger, obduracy in hatred, over-indulgence of tongue and appetite, greater indifference and dullness in preaching.[63]

Again, repentance, humbling ourselves, is the proper response.

> But I want you not to spare yourselves, but to accuse yourselves as often as you discern, even slightly, that grace is getting lukewarm, that virtue is languishing, even as I, too, accuse myself of such things. This is how a man

acts who cautiously assesses himself, who examines his tendencies and desires and in everything watches relentlessly for the vice of arrogance, lest it take him by stealth. In very truth, I have learned nothing is so efficacious for the gaining, the retention, and the recovery of grace as to discover that in God's presence you must always stand in awe rather than yield to pride (Rom. 11:20).[64]

Bernard also makes the interesting observation that an experience of presence, or of grace or consolation, may be withdrawn "in advance," not because pride currently is a problem but because it would be in the future if the experience of consolation was allowed to continue! Bernard interprets Paul's "thorn in the flesh" (2 Cor. 12:7) as just such a preemptive protection against pride.

There are times though when it is withdrawn, not because of pride already present, but because of pride that will occur unless it is withdrawn.[65]

Fatigue and Illness

A second cause for the experience of dryness in prayer may be physical or emotional fatigue or illness. Francis de Sales comments on these situations:

It sometimes happens that distaste, aridity, and sterility come from some bodily indisposition, as when we are overcome by fatigue, drowsiness, indifference, and the like because of protracted vigils, work, or fasting. Although they affect our body, they are such that they also affect our mind because of the close connection between the two. At such times we must not forget to perform various acts of virtue with all the power of our spirit and with our highest will. Although our whole soul seems to be asleep and overcome by drowsiness and fatigue, yet the actions of the superior part do not cease to be most acceptable to God. At the same time we may say with the sacred Spouse, "I was sleeping but my heart kept vigil" (Song 5:2). As I have observed before, there is less satisfaction in such activity, but there is greater merit and virtue in it. At such times the remedy is to build up strength and vigor by some kind of lawful relief and recreation.[66]

The condition of our body and mind definitely impacts the ability of our soul to focus on God. We are not angels, or pure spiritual beings; we're embodied, and the condition of our bodies affects our ability to focus on the life of prayer. Teresa and John counsel us to persevere as best we can in prayer during times of illness and not to be distressed at the dryness that is rooted in the illness of our bodies. They both also say that as we grow in union with God, at the higher stages of growth, the depth of purification can sometimes take away these illnesses. Francis counsels us to get help for our illness and try to get better through medical care, but then to accept the results—cure or no cure—as the current will of God for us, and to offer our illness to the Lord, uniting it with the offering of Jesus in His sufferings.

> When you are sick offer up all your grief, pain and weakness as a service to our Lord and beseech him to join them to the torments he suffered for you. Obey your physician, take your medicine, food, and other remedies out of love of God. . . . Desire to get well so that you may serve him, but do not refuse to lie ill so that thus too you may obey him and prepare for death, if that is his will, so that you may praise him and be happy with him forever.

One of the remarkable points of convergence we find in the writings of many of the saints is the high value they put on meditating on the sufferings of Christ as an inexhaustible source of insight, consolation, motivation, and strength.

Francis comments:

> Look often with your inward eyes on Christ Jesus, cruci-
> fied, naked, blasphemed, slandered, forsaken, and over-
> whelmed by every kind of weariness, sorrow, and labor.
> Remember that your sufferings are not comparable to
> his either in quality or quantity and that you can never
> suffer for his sake anything equal to what he has suffered
> for you.

Francis then counsels us to reflect also on the sufferings of those
who have suffered much more than we have—and not only the
martyrs, but also those living today who are enduring suffering,
handicaps, and severe afflictions.

> Think of the torments the martyrs endured and those
> so many people now endure that are incomparably more
> grievous than yours. Then say: "Alas! Are not my hard-
> ships consolations and my thorns roses in comparison
> with those who without help, assistance, or relief, live a
> continual death under the burden of afflictions infinitely
> greater than mine?"[67]

Dark Night

A third reason why we may be experiencing dryness in prayer is
because God is purposely removing the experience of His presence
so as to give us an opportunity to mature in faith, hope, and love.
Faith, in its essence, is believing without seeing. As Bernard puts it,

> "Blessed are they who have not seen, yet have believed.
> (Jn. 20:29)" So, giving room for virtue, he withdraws
> himself from her sight, that she may not be robbed of
> the merit of faith.[68]

When we continually "see" the work of God in our life, there is
less need for faith. When the perception of blessing or presence is
removed, there is an opportunity to exercise faith on a deeper and
purer level, which is very pleasing to God and unites us in a deep

way with Him, even when His closeness to us might not be felt. John of the Cross tells us that it is this ever-increasing purification of faith that most directly and immediately unites us to God. The act of deep trust and abandonment and fidelity that faith entails is very pleasing to God and brings us very close to Him.

The same is true of hope. Hope is expecting to receive something that is not yet in our possession. The more we "possess" of God in an experiential way, the less our hope is challenged to deepen and grow. Sometimes God removes what we "possess" of Him by way of perception of His presence, love, and providential care so as to give us a chance to mature and deepen in hope, by more purely hoping without possessing.

And the same is also true with love. When we are experiencing the love of God in a perceptible manner it is relatively easy to love Him in return. But the question can legitimately be raised: are we loving God for Himself or for what we are receiving from Him? When we're not receiving anything perceptible in return for our prayer by way of consolation, we can better determine the purity of our intentions and have a chance to grow in a more true and unselfish love of Him.

The same is true of love of neighbor. When we are being loved in return it is easy to keep on loving. But sometimes the Lord allows us to experience the lack of reciprocal love in relationships in order to give us the opportunity to love others in our life more purely and unselfishly.

But how do we know if the dryness we are experiencing is dryness ordained by God—a truly "purgative" dryness—or rather the result of lukewarmness or carelessness, or as the result of illness? Sometimes the cause is easy to discern. Obvious carelessness or infidelity in our relationship with the Lord could certainly be a cause of dryness, and the solution to this, as we know, is repentance. If we're going through an obvious physical or emotional illness, that could also be the cause, and we have seen the various advice that Teresa and Francis give for those in these situations. But sometimes the cause of the dryness is not obvious, and here John gives us three indicators to help us discern the nature of the dryness we are experiencing.

Advice for Discerning the Cause of the Dryness

Sometimes, as we have noted, dryness and distaste for spiritual things may be the result of our own lukewarmness, carelessness, or unfaithfulness, which is not what John of the Cross identifies as the "dark night." In cases like these consolations may be found in things other than God, in indulging the flesh in the things, comforts, entertainments, and pleasures of this world, further deadening our taste for spiritual things. In a "dark night" permitted by God we are not able to find consolation in things less than God; even in the dryness of our prayer, our yearning for Him increases.

> Since God puts a soul in this dark night in order to dry up and purge its sensory appetite, he does not allow it to find sweetness or delight in anything. Through this sign it can in all likelihood be inferred that this dryness and distaste is not the outcome of newly committed sins and imperfections.

In other words, the dryness is a purgative dryness if we have not found something else to give us consolation instead of prayer. Not that we should try to!

> There is a notable difference between dryness and luke-warmness. The lukewarm are very lax and remiss in their will and spirit, and have no solicitude about serving God. Those suffering from the purgative dryness are ordinarily solicitous, concerned, and pained about not serving God. Even though the dryness may be furthered by melancholia [emotional difficulties such as depression] or some other humor—as it often is—it does not thereby fail to produce its purgative effect in the appetite, for the

soul will be deprived of every satisfaction and concerned
only about God. If this humor [emotional difficulty] is
the entire cause, everything ends in displeasure and does
harm to one's nature, and there are none of these desires
to serve God that accompany the purgative dryness. Even
though in this purgative dryness the sensory part of the
soul is very cast down, slack, and feeble, in its actions
because of the little satisfaction it finds, the spirit is ready
and strong.

Here John very helpfully, and very realistically, explains that a
genuine purifying dryness may coexist with some elements of emotional problems, such as depression; nevertheless, if the concern to
serve and please God persists in the midst of the difficulty, it is a sign
of God's purifying work. If it were just a matter of emotional or physical illness, the desire to serve God might not be there so clearly.

The third sign for the discernment of this purgation of
the senses is the powerlessness, in spite of one's efforts, to
meditate and make use of the imagination, the interior
senses, as was one's previous custom. . . . God begins to
communicate himself through pure spirit by an act of
simple contemplation in which there is no discursive succession of thought.[69]

Here John refers to the early stages of purification, where prayer
that may have been in the beginning predominantly meditative
or reflective is becoming more contemplative. Efforts to continue to pray meditatively or reflectively when God is starting to
communicate Himself directly to us in some measure of infused
contemplation, even though it may be barely perceptible, will not
be successful. In the midst of the dryness the soul is being invited
to a new dimension of prayer, a "being still" and simply knowing
that He is God.

The Dark Night as an Important Means of Growth

Many of the saints tell us that these times of God-ordained "desolation" or dryness are very important times of growth if we persevere through them by exercising a deeper faith, hope, and love. It is particularly important, they tell us, not to give up our spiritual practices but to remain faithful. God in His wisdom knows how long and how deeply we must be tried in order to come closer to Him, and we should patiently trust Him during the trial while persevering in our practices.

In these times of dryness Thérèse responded in her own simple way.

> Sometimes when my mind is in such a great aridity that it is impossible to draw forth one single thought to unite me with God, I *very slowly* recite an "Our Father" and then the angelic salutation [the "Hail Mary"]; then these prayers give me great delight; they nourish my soul much more than if I had recited them precipitately a hundred times.[70]

Thérèse was always aware that the "great saints" of the Church seemed to embody a level of virtue and greatness of soul that was beyond her. In comparison to these "eagles" she felt herself a fledgling bird who was not strong enough to fly to the Sun of Love but could simply point in the Lord's direction and occasionally flap its underdeveloped wings. The Lord imparts to Thérèse an immense confidence in the power of His love to take even weak souls like hers and bring them to the heart of Love. In her writing and through her prayer, Thérèse imparts the same confidence to us.

> What then will become of it? Will it die of sorrow at seeing itself so weak? Oh no! the little bird will not even be troubled. With bold surrender, it wishes to remain gazing upon its Divine Sun. Nothing will frighten it, neither wind nor rain and if dark clouds come and hide the Star of Love, the

little bird will not change its place because it knows that beyond the clouds its bright Sun still shines on and that its brightness is not eclipsed for a single instant.[71]

If a soul truly desires the fullness of union, then God desires to impart the great fortitude and deep faith needed to "stand fast" in the midst of what appears to be utter darkness.

> At times the little bird's heart is assailed by the storm, and it seems it should believe in the existence of no other thing except the clouds surrounding it; this is the moment of *perfect joy* for the *poor little weak creature.* And what joy it experiences when remaining there just the same! And gazing at the Invisible Light which remains hidden from its faith![72]

With wet wings, in the midst of the storm, numb from cold and overcome with sleep, the "little bird" receives the grace to rejoice in its suffering, never losing hope in God's mercy. It always takes up, again and again, that loving prayer and faith that is its "work of love."

> When it awakens, it doesn't feel desolate; its little heart is at peace and it begins once again its work of *love.*[73]

It calls upon the saints and the angels to carry it to the consuming Fire and to protect it from demonic attack, in hope of heaven.

> As long as You desire it, O my Beloved, Your little bird will remain without strength and without wings and will always stay with its gaze fixed upon You. It wants to be *fascinated* by Your divine glance. It wants to become the *prey* of Your Love. One day I hope that You, the Adorable Eagle, will come to fetch me, Your little bird; and ascending with it to the Furnace of Love, You will plunge it for all eternity into the burning Abyss of this Love to which it has offered itself as victim.[74]

On a very deep level, we are dealing with the realization of profoundly rooted biblical themes, in this case an inspired song of Moses.

> He found him in a desert land
>   and in the howling waste of the wilderness;
> he encircled him, he cared for him,
>   he kept him as the apple of his eye.
> Like an eagle that stirs up its nest,
>   that flutters over its young,
> spreading out its wings, catching them,
>   bearing them on its pinions,
> the LORD alone did lead him,
>   and there was no foreign god with him.
> He made him ride on the high places of the earth,
>   and he ate the produce of the field;
> and he made him suck honey out of the rock,
>   and oil out of the flinty rock . . .
> with the finest of the wheat—
>   and of the blood of the grape
>   you drank wine. (Deut. 32:10–14)

God the Father communicates to Catherine of Siena the reason for these times of dryness and desolation.

> So I tell you, it is to make the soul rise from imperfection
> that I withdraw from her feelings and deprive her of the
> comfort she had known. . . . I withdraw from her feelings
> only, not withdrawing my grace.[75]

The Father makes clear that it's out of love that these withdrawals of felt presence occur. He tells Catherine that these alternations of presence and absence are "lover's games."

> When they reach perfection I relieve them of this lover's
> game of going and coming back. I call it a "lover's game"
> because I go away for love and I come back for love—no,

not really I, for I am your unchanging and unchangeable God; what goes and comes back is the feeling my charity creates in the soul.[76]

Bernard also attests to the Love that guides the experience of absence.

Indeed, he sometimes, by a loving arrangement, withdraws far from his saints for a time, not entirely but in part.[77]

In the early stages, this withdrawal helps center the soul properly on God and not on His consolations and gives an opportunity for deeper and truer decisions of commitment to God to be made. Also called the "dark night of the senses," the soul is purified of gross attachments to the delights of the senses and the things of this world, thus increasing its desire for God.

Bernard gives testimony to his own experience of this purification.

I am not ashamed to admit that very often I myself, especially in the early days of my conversion, experienced coldness and hardness of heart, while deep in my being I sought for him whom I longed to love (Song 3:1). I could not yet love him since I had not yet really found him; at best my love was less than it should have been, and for that very reason I sought to increase it, for I would not have sought him if I did not already love him in some degree. I sought him therefore that in him my numbed and languid spirit might find warmth and repose, for nowhere could I find a friend to help me, whose love would thaw the wintry cold that chilled my inward being, and bring back again the feeling of spring—like bliss and spiritual delight. But my languor and weariness only increased, my soul melted way for sorrow (Ps. 118:28), even to the verge of despair. All I could do was repeat softly to myself: "Who can stand before his cold (Ps. 147:17)?" Then, at times when I least expected, at the word or even the sight of a good and holy man, at the memory of a dead or absent friend, he set his wind blowing and the waters flowing (Ps. 147:18).[78]

In later stages, God leads the soul from the dark night of the senses through the "dark night of the spirit." By passing through these various types of dryness, the very roots of selfishness and sin deep in the human spirit are reached in the faculties of the soul—the intellect, memory, and will.

The saints tell us that usually, even in the very midst of exterior and interior trials, a deep-seated peace is felt. Persevering in the midst of these trials is a very important part of uniting our will to God's—and in His will is our peace.

Thérèse testifies to this reality in her own life especially as she approached its end.

> For seven years and a half that inner peace has remained my lot, and has not abandoned me in the midst of the greatest trials.[79]

Indeed, in His will is our peace.

PART II

REACHING STABILITY BUT MOVING ON

(The Illuminative Way)

Chapter Nine

A CERTAIN STABILITY

AS WE COOPERATE WITH GRACE and make efforts to center our life on God—praying, resisting temptations, enduring trials, using wisdom in the choices we make—a certain peace and stability become characteristic of our lives. Teresa of Avila describes this as the third stage (mansion) of the seven stages (mansions) of the spiritual journey.

> I believe that through the goodness of God there are many of these souls in the world. They long not to offend His Majesty, even guarding themselves against venial sins; they are fond of doing penance and setting aside periods of recollection; they spend their time well, practicing works of charity toward their neighbors; and are very balanced in their use of speech and dress and in the governing of their households—those who have them. Certainly, this is a state to be desired. And, in my opinion, there is no reason why entrance even into the final dwelling place should be denied these souls, nor will the Lord deny them this entrance if they desire it; for such a desire is an excellent way to prepare oneself so that every favor may be granted.[1]

There are a number of things to note about Teresa's comments. First of all, the description she gives of the relative stability and peace of this third stage can seem daunting. Even though she indicates that many reach this stage, the description she gives can seem challenging. After all, to try to avoid venial sins and have a disciplined pattern of life that includes prayer, fasting, almsgiving, and moderation in speech and dress is no small accomplishment in today's world! As Teresa will go on to point out, however, this portrait of the "good Catholic," as admirable as it is, can often coexist with a mixture of motives and compromises that lacks a complete abandonment to the Lord. And it helps to remember that not all saints—Thérèse of Lisieux, for one—were "fond" of doing penance.

Notice too that Teresa explicitly extends her comments to those who have households. While primarily writing for her fellow Carmelite religious, she is very much aware that there are many lay people who want to give themselves completely to God and are making progress on the spiritual journey. Teresa knew many such lay people personally, and was spiritual director for a number of them. In fact, at one point in her spiritual journey, it was a married man who was able to help her most in making progress. Teresa explains that the fundamental laws of spiritual progress are the same for religious and lay people, since, as Vatican II put it, "the classes and duties of life are many, but holiness is one—that sanctity which is cultivated by all who are moved by the Spirit of God, and who obey the voice of the Father and worship God the Father in spirit and in truth" (LG 41).

A third thing to notice, and we will have occasion to return to this point, is that Teresa doesn't see any reason why people who reach this stage in the spiritual journey—and, as she indicates, many do—can't proceed all the way to the fullest union possible with God in this life, the spiritual marriage that Teresa talks about in the seventh mansion (stage).

Even though Teresa sees no reason why people who fight through the initial battles, temptations, and trials of the beginning stages of the journey to a place of relative stability and peace can't proceed all the way to the spiritual marriage, she knows that many in fact don't. So do the other saints.

As Bernard puts it: "For the popular trend is not to seek first the kingdom of God and his righteousness (Mt 6:33), but, as the apostle says, to be concerned about worldly affairs. . . . (1 Cor. 7:38)."[2]

And even though all Christians, in the words of John Paul II, are called to "contemplate the face of Christ," Bernard again reminds us that relatively few do.

> How few there are who can say: "But we all, with unveiled face, beholding the glory of the Lord, are being changed into his likeness from glory into glory, even by the Spirit of the Lord" (2 Cor. 3:18).[3]

The saints speak of two main obstacles that hold us back from making progress on the journey: a lack of knowledge and a lack of desire.

Lack of Knowledge

The saints speak of a twofold knowledge that is essential for making progress in the spiritual life: self-knowledge and knowledge of God.

Bernard speaks in a particularly striking way of the dire consequences that flow from a lack of true knowledge of self and of God, a lack which both in this life and in the next can cause man to become lower than beasts.

> Because men, unaccepted or reprobated on account of their ignorance, have to stand before the dreaded judgment seat and be committed to the unquenchable fire, but not so the beasts. . . . It will not have their company in its endurance of hell's torments. . . . It is demonstrably clear therefore, that man is inferior to the herds, in this life by the depravity of his nature, in the next by the severity of the punishment. That is how a man becomes

accursed when he is found to be ignorant of God. Or should I say ignorant of self? I must include both: the two kinds of ignorance are damnable, either is enough to incur damnation.[4]

Self-knowledge involves both knowledge of the great dignity and beauty of the human soul in its exalted destiny as well as a profound understanding of the wounds and darkness that sin inflicts on it.

Teresa compares the soul to a beautiful crystal castle that is brilliantly illuminated by the Lord who dwells within it. She then tells of how horrible it is to see sin darken the soul and make it ugly.

> Mortal sin: there's no darker darkness nor anything more obscure and black. . . . I know a person to whom our Lord wanted to show what a soul in mortal sin was like. That person says that in her opinion if this were understood it would be impossible to sin, even though a soul would have to undergo the greatest trials imaginable in order to flee the occasions. So the Lord gave her a strong desire that all might understand this. . . . O souls redeemed by the blood of Jesus Christ! Understand and take pity on yourselves. How is it possible that in realizing these things you don't strive to remove the pitch from this crystal? See that if your life comes to an end you will never again enjoy this light. . . . There is nothing, while we are living, that deserves this name "evil," except mortal sin, for such sin carries in its wake everlasting evils.[5]

Bernard also speaks of the darkening of the soul by sin, drawing on the image used by Paul in Romans 1:21, "their senseless minds were darkened."

> It's attachment to earthly things—which all tend to destruction—makes the darkness deeper, until a soul which lives this way has only a pallid appearance, the very image of death.[6]

There are many, many biblical descriptions of the sickness of the untransformed soul. Here, the apostle James powerfully addresses Christians:

> What causes wars, and what causes fighting among you? Is it not your passions that are at war in your members? You desire and do not have; so you kill. And you covet and cannot obtain; so you fight and wage war. You do not have, because you do not ask. You ask and do not receive because you ask wrongly to spend it on your passions. Unfaithful creatures! Do you not know that friendship with the world is enmity with God? Therefore whoever wishes to be a friend of the world makes himself an enemy of God. (Jas. 4:1–4)

Paul also issues this urgent warning to the Galatians:

> But I say, walk by the Spirit, and do not gratify the desires of the flesh. . . . Now the works of the flesh are plain: immorality, impurity, licentiousness, idolatry, sorcery, enmity, strife, jealousy, anger, selfishness, dissension, party spirit, envy, drunkenness, carousing, and the like. I warn you, as I warned you before, that those who do such things shall not inherit the kingdom of God. (Gal. 5:16, 19–21)

John of the Cross speaks of the great beauty of the soul that, having heeded these scriptural prescriptions, has the inestimable dignity of having God dwell within it.

> Oh, then, soul, most beautiful among all creatures, so anxious to know the dwelling place of your Beloved so you may go in search of him and be united with him, now we are telling you that you yourself are his dwelling and his secret inner room and hiding place. There is reason for you to be elated and joyful in seeing that all your good and hope is so close as to be within you, or better, that you cannot be without him.[7]

Bernard emphasizes that the true home of God is not in the physical universe, in the "heaven" of stars and galaxies, but in the human soul, where "Christ dwells by faith" (cf. Eph. 3:17), a soul which must be purified of its attachment to worldly cares, gluttony, sensual pleasures, the ambition to rule, pride in possessions or power, hatred, envy and bitterness, and widen and grow in its capacity so that it may be "roomy enough for God (2 Cor. 6:13)."[8]

Bernard appeals to the fact that we have been created in the glorious image of God as the grounds for confidence in our approach to Him.

> Why should it not venture with confidence into the presence of him by whose image it sees itself honored, and in whose likeness it knows itself made glorious? Why should it fear a majesty when its very origin gives it ground for confidence? . . . Why then does it not set to work?[9]

And yet self-knowledge can never have a completely good effect unless it's experienced in relationship with knowledge of God. Perceiving the ugliness and selfishness of the soul marred by sin and the effects of sin can produce scrupulosity or despair if the mercy and goodness of God is not seen in close proximity. Bernard describes well the despair that can result from a partial knowledge of self, aware only of areas of sin, isolated from knowledge of God.

> If he does not know how good God is (Ps. 72:1), how kind and gentle (Ps. 85:5), how willing to pardon (Is. 55:7), will not his sensually-inspired reason argue with him and say: "What are you doing? Do you want to lose this life and the next? Your sins are too grave and too many; nothing that you do even to stripping the skin from your flesh, can make satisfaction for them. Your constitution is delicate, you have lived softly, a lifetime's habits are not easily conquered."

Such painful awareness of one's sin easily tempts one to despair, discouragement, and deep "depression"; thinking reform is hopeless, one may "surrender irrevocably to the world." Bernard calls this despair the greatest evil of all, and insists that God's mercy is always available whenever a sinner turns to Him.

> My opinion is that all those who lack knowledge of God are those who refuse to turn to him.[10]

And why is self-knowledge and knowledge of God so important? It produces humility, which John of the Cross as well as countless other saints tells us is foundational to making progress in the spiritual life.

> While we are on this earth nothing is more important to us than humility. . . . In my opinion we shall never completely know ourselves if we don't strive to know God. By gazing at His grandeur, we get in touch with our own lowliness; by looking at His purity, we shall see our own filth; by pondering His humility, we shall see how far we are from being humble.[11]

Teresa is blunt in her belief that self-knowledge in relationship to the knowledge of God's mercy is absolutely essential for the spiritual journey.

> Well now, it is foolish to think that we will enter heaven without entering into ourselves, coming to know ourselves, reflecting on our misery and what we owe God, and begging him often for mercy.[12]

Bernard explicates the relationship between self-knowledge and knowledge of God in his usual striking manner.

> How can he escape being genuinely humbled on acquiring this true self-knowledge, on seeing the burden of sin

that he carries (2 Tim 3:6), the oppressive weight of his mortal body, the complexities of earthly cares, the corrupting influence of sensual desires; on seeing his blindness, his worldliness, his weakness, his embroilment in repeated errors . . . one to whom vice is welcome, virtue repugnant? Can this man afford the haughty eyes, the proud lift of the head (Sir. 23:5)? With the thorns of his misery pricking him, will he not rather be changed for the better? (Ps. 31:4) . . . changed to acceptance of the Lord, to whom in his lowliness he will say: "Heal me because I have sinned against you" (Ps. 40:5). . . . In this way your self-knowledge will be a step to the knowledge of God. . . . You can see now how each of these kinds of knowledge is so necessary for your salvation, that you cannot be saved if you lack either of them. If you lack self-knowledge you will possess neither the fear of God nor humility.[13]

Catherine of Siena particularly insists on the integration of self-knowledge and knowledge of God. Catherine reports what she senses the Father showing her.

Now I do not want her [the soul] to think about her sins individually, lest her mind be contaminated by the memory of specific ugly sins. I mean that I do not want her to, nor should she, think about her sins either in general or specifically without calling to mind the blood and the greatness of my mercy. Otherwise she will only be confounded. For if self-knowledge and the thought of sin are not seasoned with remembrance of the blood and hope for mercy, the result is bound to be confusion.[14]

The Father points out to Catherine how the devil will take advantage of self-knowledge and awareness of our sinfulness to drive us to despair and discouragement and lead us to give up the journey, unless we immediately turn to the Lord and remember the power of His blood and the depth of His mercy.

The Father reminds Catherine of how she herself, empowered by His goodness, handled situations like this. At one time the devil tried to tempt Catherine to despair by getting her to believe that her whole life was a delusion and that she was doing her own will, not God's will. She replied, "I confess to my Creator that my life has been spent wholly in darkness. But I will hide myself in the wounds of Christ crucified and bathe in his blood, and so my wickedness will be consumed and I will rejoice with desire in my Creator." At this the devil fled, but returned at another time, wanting to tempt her to pride.

This time the devil attempted to communicate to Catherine that since she had reached such a high stage of union with God and was so perfect and pleasing to Him that she no longer needed to make efforts to be mindful of her sins and practice self-denial. God gave Catherine light to respond, and she answered the devil effectively.

> How wretched I am! John the Baptist never sinned. He was made holy in his mother's womb, yet he did such great penance. But I have committed so many sins and have not yet even begun to acknowledge it with tears and true contrition, seeing who God is who is offended by me and who I am who offend him![15]

Catherine's humbling of herself, casting herself on the mercy of God and trusting in the blood of Christ, provoked the devil to swear.

> Damnable woman! There is no getting at you! If I throw you down in confusion you lift yourself up to mercy. If I exalt you you throw yourself down.[16]

The Father then advises souls to season self-knowledge with knowledge of the Father, and knowledge of the Father with self-knowledge.

Bernard expresses the same truth:

> As for me, as long as I look at myself, my eye is filled with bitterness (Job 17:2). But if I look up and fix my eyes on the aid of the divine mercy, this happy vision of God soon tempers the bitter vision of myself.[17]

Progress Is Both Possible and Necessary

John Paul II urged the whole Church to reconnect with the mystical tradition of the Church because this tradition shows us that progress in the spiritual life is possible.

> This great mystical tradition . . . shows how prayer can progress, as a genuine dialogue of love, to the point of rendering the person wholly possessed by the divine Beloved, vibrating at the Spirit's touch, resting filially within the Father's heart. (NMI 33)

We know that the tradition, basing itself upon Scripture, asserts that progress is not only possible but also that it is necessary. No one can see God without being holy (cf. Heb. 12:14). A lack of knowledge concerning how much progress is possible and how necessary it is holds many people back from the spiritual journey.

The life of God that is born in us through faith and Baptism has to grow and be "perfected" in order for us to reach our heavenly destiny. The seed that is planted in our souls has to grow, develop, and mature. The saints' frequent talk of "perfection" is deeply rooted in the teaching of Jesus and the apostles, and we need to be deeply convinced of this in order to persevere to journey's end.

The fear of the Lord, as we have seen, is the beginning of wisdom—or "the first stage" as one translation has it—but the perfection of love is its end. Holiness begins in the fear of the Lord and ends in a love without fear.

> Beloved, if God so loved us, we also ought to love one another. No man has ever seen God; if we love one anoth-

er, God abides in us and his love is perfected in us. . . . In this is love perfected with us, that we may have confidence for the day of judgment, because as he is so are we in this world. There is no fear in love, but perfect love casts out fear. For fear has to do with punishment, and he who fears is not perfected in love. (1 Jn. 4:11–12, 17–18)

I am sure that he who began a good work in you will bring it to completion at the day of Jesus Christ. . . . And it is my prayer that your love may abound more and more, with knowledge and all discernment, so that you may approve what is excellent, and may be pure and blameless for the day of Christ, filled with the fruits of righteousness which come through Jesus Christ, to the glory and praise of God. (Phil. 1: 6, 9–11)

May the God of peace himself sanctify you wholly; and may your spirit and soul and body be kept sound and blameless at the coming of our Lord Jesus Christ. He who calls you is faithful, and he will do it. (1 Thess. 5:23)

May the Lord make you increase and abound in love to one another and to all men, as we do to you, so that he may establish your hearts unblamable in holiness before our God and Father, at the coming of our Lord Jesus with all his saints. (1 Thess. 3:12–13)

Again, the call to holiness, to progress, to growth, to "perfection," is rooted in the biblical worldview. What begins in this life ends before the judgment seat of Christ in the next, in an eternity of love or sorrow. To use the biblical language: we first are justified through faith and Baptism; then sanctified through the work of the Holy Spirit over a lifetime of growth; and finally glorified in the blessed vision of heaven. Knowing what we are called to is important, but so is desiring it with all our heart.

Bernard of Clairvaux:
The Role of Desire in the Spiritual Journey

Before we consider the role of desire and longing in the spiritual journey we need to meet the last of the seven Doctors of the Church that we are drawing on in our attempt to provide a map of the journey to full union with God. We've met him already through his writings, but let's make it "official."

Bernard was born of an aristocratic family near Dijon, France, in 1090. Once he determined as a young man that he wanted to become a monk, he convinced many of his relatives and friends to join him. At the age of twenty-two he and about thirty of his friends and relatives entered the monastery at Citeaux and became Cistercian monks. (The Cistercians are a reformed branch of the Benedictines, of which the Trappists also are a branch.) In the threefold path of recognition by the Church of sanctity through canonization, Bernard's father is "venerable" and his mother and five of his siblings are "blessed."

In 1115, at the age of twenty-five, he founded one of the original four "daughter" monasteries of Citeaux at Clairvaux.

Studying on his own, with no formal theological training except a good classical education (he and Augustine are considered to be the two great masters of Christian Latin), in the mid 1120s Bernard began to write some of the most influential works of spiritual theology in the history of the Church. His writings, like many of Augustine's, are overflowing with references to Scripture. He lived and breathed and communicated the Word of God. In fact, looking up his frequent references to Scripture would be a wonderful way to deepen the impact of his teaching, and this book. Those who do so will be astounded to see the spiritual depth of the Scripture, a depth which perhaps they've never seen before, now opened to us through the spiritual eyes and ears of Bernard and the other saints who are teaching us.

The work of spiritual theology for which Bernard is most known is his commentary on the Song of Songs. He managed to give eighty-six sermons on the Song of Songs over a period of eighteen years. Unfinished at his death (he had only covered about a third of the Song), they nevertheless contain great insight into the spiritual journey. Besides writing and governing his own monastery and founding others, he was also asked by the popes, one of whom was formerly one of his monks, to work on various projects for the good of the Church. He traveled a great deal in his service to the papacy, and wrote numerous letters of spiritual advice and counsel to ordinary people as well as to leaders of church and state. He was one of the most influential men of his age.

At his death in 1153, at the age of sixty-three, seventy daughter communities of Clairvaux had been established and ninety-four affiliated communities had joined Clairvaux.

Let's return now to our consideration of what holds us back from making progress beyond the relative stability and respectability of the "good Catholic life" of Teresa's third mansion.

Lack of Desire

If lack of knowledge of self and of God is an obstacle frequently cited by the saints; so also is the lack of desire for God. Teresa counsels us to let our desire for union with God grow.

> Have great confidence, for it is necessary not to hold back one's desires, but to believe in God that if we try we shall little by little, even though it may not be soon, reach the state the saints did with His help.[18]

Catherine of Siena frequently stresses the need for desire or thirst for God to grow.

> If you would make progress, then, you must be thirsty, because only those who are thirsty are called: "Let anyone who is thirsty come to me and drink." Those who are not thirsty will never persevere in their journey. Either weariness or pleasure will make them stop.[19]

And Augustine's famous words come to mind:

> You stir man to take pleasure in praising you, because you
> have made us for yourself, and our heart is restless until
> it rests in you.[20]

The whole Bible is full of expressions of desire for God. The
Psalms in particular give voice to our profound need for God.

> My soul longs, yea, faints,
>   for the courts of the Lord.
> my heart and flesh sing for joy
>   to God, the living God. (Ps. 84:2)

> O God, you are my God, I seek you;
>   my soul thirsts for you;
> my flesh faints for you,
>   as in a dry and weary land where there is no water. . . .
> Because your steadfast love is better than life . . .
> My soul clings to you . . . . (Ps. 63:1–3, 8, NRSV)

Not only is desire important for our own spiritual journey but
also for true reform and renewal of the Church.

> Not by the sword or by war or by violence will she regain
> her beauty, but through peace and through the constant
> and humble prayers and sweat and tears poured out by
> my servants with eager desire.[21]

The alternating experience of both the presence and absence of
God is intended to increase our desire for God.

> Unless we use the utmost vigilance in attending to these
> gift-laden visits of the Holy Spirit, we shall neither desire
> him when he seems absent nor respond to him when
> present. If he withdraws from us to stimulate us to a
> more eager search for him, how shall we seek for him

if we do not perceive his absence? Or when he comes to animate us, how shall we give him the welcome due his majesty if his visit passes unnoticed? The man who is indifferent to his absence will be led astray by other influences; the man who is blind to his coming cannot offer thanks for the visit.[22]

Bernard states that the Bridegroom will not long delay His return "when summoned by desires so great."[23] The wordless longing for God is itself a powerful prayer:

> Thus the Word is recalled—recalled by the longing of the soul (Is. 26:8) who has once enjoyed his sweetness. Is longing not a voice? It is indeed, and a very powerful one. Then the Psalmist says, "The Lord has heard the longing of the poor" (Ps. 9:38). When the Word departs therefore, the one unceasing cry of the soul, its one unceasing desire, is "return"—until he comes (1 Cor. 11:26).[24]

John of the Cross and Teresa of Avila both speak frequently of the "wounds of love" which God inflicts on the soul to increase the soul's desire for Him.

The more the soul knows of God the more the desire and anxiety to see Him increase.[25]

Sometimes the experience of the Lord's "delay" or "absence" can be frustrating. Bernard offers insightful commentary.

> Oh little while, little while! How long a little while! Dear Lord, you say it is for a little while that we do not see you. The word of my Lord may not be doubted, but it is a long while, far too long. Yet both are true: it is a little while compared to what we deserve, but a long while to what we desire. You have each meaning expressed by the prophet Habakuk: "If he delays, wait for him, for he will come, and will not delay" (Hab. 2:3). How is it that he will not delay if he does delay, unless it is that he comes sooner than we deserve but not as soon as we desire?[26]

Bernard also gives witness to the way that desire for God never ends and is present at the end of the spiritual journey as well as at its beginning.

> The psalmist says: "Seek his face always" (Ps. 104:4). Nor, I think, will a soul cease to seek him even when it has found him. It is not with steps of the feet that God is sought but with the heart's desire; and when the soul happily finds him its desire is not quenched but kindled. Does the consummation of joy bring about the consuming of desire? Rather it is oil poured upon the flames. So it is. Joy will be fulfilled, but there will be no end to desire, and therefore no end to the search. Think, if you can, of this eagerness to see God as not caused by his absence, for he is always present; and think of the desire for God as without fear of failure, for grace is abundantly present.[27]

Francis De Sales uses several vivid examples and images to speak about the depth of human desire and its only true fulfillment in union with God. He tells the story of Alexander the Great who, after having conquered so much of the known world, upon being informed that there was more to conquer, sat down and wept, knowing that he would never conquer all. Francis speaks of the deer, perishing for lack of water, driven on by great thirst, seeking desperately the water that will quench its thirst and save its life, an image vividly conveyed in the Psalms. He speaks also of the desperately feeding child burrowing into its mother's breast as if to enter into the breast or bring the whole breast into itself. He concludes:

> Our hearts have a thirst which cannot be quenched by the pleasures of this mortal life, whereof the most esteemed and highest prized if moderate do not satisfy us, and if extreme suffocate us. Yet we desire them always to be extreme, and they are never such without being excessive, insupportable, hurtful. . . . O wonderful yet dear

unrest of man's heart! . . . Ah! what a union of our hearts shall there be with God there above in heaven, where, after these infinite desires of the true good never assuaged in this world, we shall find the living and powerful source thereof . . . what a holy and sweet ardour to be united and joined to the plentiful breasts of the All-goodness, either to be altogether absorbed in it, or to have it come entirely into us![28]

What if we don't have a strong desire for God? What if we only half-heartedly desire to make progress on the path to full union with God?

The Scripture and the teaching of the saints makes clear that when we lack something essential for the spiritual journey—such as a strong desire for God—then we are to ask for it, and it will be given. Not all at once necessarily, but gradually, over time, as we persevere in asking.

Time after time Teresa makes a strong statement that we can't expect to make progress without courage, or strong determination, or great desire—and then acknowledges that if we lack these essential qualities we should ask God for them and He will give them. One of the fundamentally important verses in the scripture for this area is the truth of how very much we need the Father himself to draw us into union with Jesus.

> No one can come to me unless the Father who sent me draws him; and I will raise him up at the last day. (Jn. 6:44)

And is there a more frequently commented upon verse in this regard than the line from the Song of Songs?

> Draw me after you, let us make haste. (Song 1:4)

As Bernard comments,

> She who asks to be drawn wills to be drawn; she would
> not have asked if she possessed the power to follow her
> loved one of her own free will. . . . For no matter how
> great the perfection to which one attains, as long as one
> is burdened with this mortal body, as long as one is con-
> fined in the prison of this evil world, cramped by neces-
> sities and tormented by sinful urges, the contemplation
> of sublime truths can be achieved only little by little and
> in weariness of spirit; one is certainly not free to follow
> the bridegroom wherever he goes.[29]

And Bernard tells us that the Lord, in response to our request to
be "drawn," will give us a desire for Him that is "vehement . . . an
instilled eagerness to advance in holiness."[30]

In our inarticulate, poorly expressed longings, Bernard detects, in
keeping with the Scripture, the work of the Spirit.

> "The Spirit himself intercedes for us with sighs too deep
> for words" (Rom. 8:26). . . . By the light that he gives
> us, by a sure experience day after day, we are convinced
> that our desires and groanings come from him and go to
> God, to find mercy there in the eyes of God. For when
> did God make the voice of his owns Spirit ineffectual?
> He "knows what is the mind of the Spirit, because the
> Spirit intercedes for the saints according to the will of
> God" (Rom. 8:27).[31]

All of us need to pray for an increase in our desire for God, asking the Father to draw us to Him by wounding us with love and
purifying our desire through affliction. But we also need to be com-
forted and encouraged that even to be concerned with God at all is
a sign that He is at work in our life. As Bernard explains,

> The soul seeks the Word, but has been first sought by
> the Word. . . . Let her seek him as she can, provided
> she remembers that she was first sought, as she was first
> loved; and it is because of this that she herself both seeks
> and loves.[32]

God Will Draw Us:
The Work of the Holy Spirit on the Spiritual Journey

It is important to realize how active the Lord is as we struggle along the road to full union with Him. It is He who "draws us." It is He who gives us the desire to pursue Him. It is He who enables us to see the glory and treasures of Jesus. It is He who "touches" us and gives us freedom from habits of sin. It is He who gives the grace to humble ourselves, to love more faithfully and generously, and to overcome fear. He does this particularly through the agency of the Holy Spirit.

> It is within you, deep within, that the Spirit's unction is poured out: open and be anointed. . . . We must first invoke the Holy Spirit that he may be pleased to reveal to us that one name above all others. . . . And since I may not trust in my own powers for what I am to say, prayers must be offered that the Bridegroom himself, Jesus Christ, our Lord, may reveal it to us by his Spirit (1 Cor. 2:10).[33]

As we embrace the Lord, Bernard tells us, we share in His anointing by the Spirit.

> What wonder if she [the Bride/Church] be anointed, since she embraces him who is the Anointed One?[34]

Bernard knows that everyone, including him, is dependent on the Holy Spirit for any real insight or experience of the things of God. He continues his commentary on the Song of Songs:

> Today I shall speak no more to you about this kiss, I shall detain you no longer, but tomorrow you will hear from me whatever your prayers may win from him whose anointing teaches about all things (1 Jn. 2:27). For flesh and blood do not reveal such a secret (Mt. 16:17), but only he who searches the depths of God (1 Cor. 2: 10), the Holy Spirit

who, proceeding from the Father and the Son (Jn. 15:26),
lives and reigns equally with them for ever. Amen.[35]

The saints we are learning from in this book, while warning
against focusing on experience as an end in itself, nevertheless regularly witness to the importance of the experience of God for the
spiritual journey. It is through the Holy Spirit that the Father and
the Son are revealed to the soul.

> Are there not surely some among you who at certain times
> perceive deep within their hearts the Spirit of the Son
> exclaiming: "Abba, Father" (Gal. 4:6)? Let that man who
> feels that he is moved by the same Spirit as the Son, let him
> know that he too is loved by the Father. Whoever he be let
> him be of good heart, let his confidence never waver (Jas.
> 1:6). Living in the Spirit of the Son, let such a soul recog-
> nize herself as a daughter of the Father, a bride or even a
> sister of the Son. . . . For if marriage according to the flesh
> constitutes two in one body (Gen. 2:24), why should not
> a spiritual union be even more efficacious in joining two in
> one spirit (1 Cor. 6:16)? And hence anyone who is joined
> to the Lord is one spirit with him.[36]

Bernard sees the giving of the Holy Spirit to the Church and to the
individual Christian as the "kiss" spoken of in the Song of Songs.

> And hence the bride, although otherwise so audacious,
> does not dare to say: "Let him kiss me with his mouth,"
> for she knows that this is the prerogative of the Father
> alone. What she does ask for is something less: "Let him
> kiss me with the kiss of his mouth."

If we wish to see the bride receiving this kiss, Bernard explains,
then we must look at Jesus in the presence of His apostles at His
post-Resurrection appearance, breathing on them and saying,
"Receive the Holy Spirit" (Jn. 20:22). The Holy Spirit is the kiss

in common both to Him who kisses (the Father) and to Him who is kissed (the Son).

> For her it is no mean or contemptible thing to be kissed by the kiss, because it is nothing less than the gift of the Holy Spirit. If, as is properly understood, the Father is he who kisses, the Son he who is kissed, then it cannot be wrong to see in the kiss the Holy Spirit, for he is the imperturbable peace of the Father and the Son, their unshakable bond, their undivided love, their indivisible unity.

Bernard displays a remarkable awareness of the multitude of Scripture passages that indicate that knowledge of God is something given supernaturally, through the action of the Holy Spirit.

> For when the Son said: "No one knows the Son except the Father, just as no one knows the Father except the Son," he added: "and those to whom the Son chooses to reveal him" (Mt. 11:27). . . . Therefore, she dares to ask for this kiss, actually for that Spirit in whom both the Father and the Son will reveal themselves to her.[37]

Bernard then points out that the "kiss," the giving of the Spirit, contains within it light for the mind and fervor for the will. Both knowledge and love are increased by the action of the Spirit.[38]

John of the Cross, and other saints as well, speak also of the twofold dimension of contemplation: contemplation that imparts understanding to the mind, and contemplation that inflames the will with love. One or the other may predominate at any given time or in any given individual, but the two must be there together in some reasonable balance for progress in the spiritual life to proceed soundly. As Bernard tells us,

> Knowledge which leads to self-importance (1 Cor. 8:1), since it is devoid of love, cannot be the fruit of the kiss. Even those who have a zeal for God, but not according

to knowledge (Rom. 10:2), may not for any reason lay claim to that kiss. For the favor of the kiss bears with it a twofold gift, the light of knowledge and the fervor of devotion. . . . Two kinds of people therefore may not consider themselves to have been gifted with the kiss, those who know the truth without loving it, and those who love it without understanding it; from which we conclude that this kiss leaves room neither for ignorance nor for lukewarmness.[39]

Bernard urges us to call on the Spirit unceasingly, to be attentive to His presence and work and responsive to His inspirations and gifts.

Let us invoke the Spirit of truth (Jn. 14:17), let us call to him from the deep into which he has led us, because he leads us on the way by which we discover ourselves, and without him we can do nothing (Jn. 15:5). Nor should we be afraid that he will disdain to come down to us, for the contrary is true: he is displeased if we attempt even the least thing without him.[40]

And when the Spirit does "come," sometimes in barely perceptible stirrings, at other times in more manifest visitations, Bernard urges us to be alert.

Unless we use the utmost vigilance in attending to these gift-laden visits of the Holy Spirit, we shall neither desire him when he seems absent nor respond to him when present. . . . [We must be] vigilant and careful about the work of salvation ceaselessly performed in our inmost being with all the skill and sweetness of the Holy Spirit's artistry. If we do not wish to be deprived of a two-fold gift, let us make sure that this heaven-sent Director, who can teach us all things (1 Jn. 2:27), is never taken away from us without our knowledge. Let him never find us unprepared when he comes, but always with faces uplifted and hearts expanded to receive the copious blessing of the Lord.[41]

And wasn't this, remarkably, a central part of John Paul II's prophetic teaching as he led the Church into the third millennium?

In the Bull of Indiction that officially proclaimed the Jubilee Year 2000, John Paul II made the remarkable statement that since the very beginning of his pontificate he had "looked towards this occasion with the sole purpose of preparing everyone to be docile to the working of the Spirit."[42]

Again, in preparation for the Great Jubilee, the pope fervently exhorted all Christians to open themselves unreservedly to the gifts of the Holy Spirit.

> Today, I would like to cry out to all of you gathered here in Saint Peter's Square and to all Christians: Open yourselves docilely to the gifts of the Spirit! Accept gratefully and obediently the charisms which the Spirit never ceases to bestow on us![43]

Can we help but ardently pray? Come, Holy Spirit, come. Come, Holy Spirit, come!

Now, with the help of the Holy Spirit, with our knowledge of ourselves and God deepened, and our desire for union increased, we need to consider some important truths about what the spiritual tradition calls "detachment."

While the lack of knowledge of self and of God as well as the lack of desire for God can hinder us on the spiritual journey, keeping us from moving on from the third stage or mansion, so too can a lack of detachment. In order to make room for more of God in our life, we need to let go of things that are currently filling our heart and reorder the things that are not ordered properly in Him. The importance of an appropriate detachment from the things of this world—or as they sometimes speak of it, the putting of our loves into right order—is stressed by all the spiritual writers we are studying.

Chapter Ten

GROWING IN FREEDOM

EVERYTHING THAT EXISTS IS A GIFT FROM GOD. Yet oftentimes we look to the things and creatures created by God for a satisfaction and fulfillment that only God Himself can provide. When the soul wraps itself around the things and the people of this world, looking for a satisfaction or fulfillment that only God can give, it produces a distortion in itself, and in others as well. Many spiritual writers call the process of unwinding this possessive, self-centered, clinging, and disordered seeking of things and persons "detachment." The goal of the process of detachment is not to stop loving the things and people of this world, but, quite to the contrary, to love them even more truly in God, under the reign of Christ, in the power of the Holy Spirit. Things and people become even more beautiful and delightful when we see them in this light. There are almost always painful dimensions to this process of "letting go" in order to love more, but it's the pain of true healing and liberation. Christian detachment is an important part of the process by which we enter into a realm of great freedom and joy.

Bernard gives us an inspiring picture of what a life of such detachment is like.

Certainly there are within the Church of God spiritual persons who serve him faithfully and with confidence, speaking with him as a man speaks with his friend, and whose consciences bear witness to his glory. But who these are is known only to God, and if you desire to be among them, then hear what sort of people you should be. I say this, not as one who knows it by experience, but as one who desires to do so. Show me a soul which loves nothing but God and what is to be loved for God's sake, to whom to live is Christ, and of whom this has been true for a long time now; who in work and leisure alike endeavors to keep God before his eyes, and walks humbly with the Lord his God, who desires that his will may be one with the will of God, and who has been given the grace to do these things.[1]

The Father communicates to Catherine of Siena some striking insights on why detachment is needed.

For created things are less than the human person. They were made for you, not you for them, and so they can never satisfy you. Only I can satisfy you. . . . Do you want me to tell you why they suffer? You know that love always brings suffering if what a person has identified with is lost. These souls in one way or another have identified with the earth in their love, and so they have in fact become earth themselves. Some have identified with their wealth, some with their status, some with their children. Some lose me in their slavery to creatures. Some in their great indecency make brute beasts of their bodies. . . . They would like to be stable but are not. Indeed they are as passing as the wind, for either they themselves fail through death or my will deprives them of the very things they loved. They suffer unbearable pain in their loss. And the more disordered their love in possessing, the greater is their grief in loss. Had they held these things as lent to them rather than as their own, they could let them go without pain. They suffer because they do not have what they long for. For, as

I told you, the world cannot satisfy them, and not being satisfied, they suffer.[2]

Bernard also points out the deformity of soul that comes from being a friend of the world in such a way as to be an enemy of God.

> Those whose souls are warped in this fashion cannot love the Bridegroom, because they are not friends of the Bridegroom, they belong to this world. Scripture says: "Whoever wishes to be a friend of the world makes himself an enemy of God" (Jas. 4:4). Therefore to pursue and enjoy the worldly warps the soul, while, on the contrary, to meditate on or desire the things that are above (Col. 3:2) constitutes its uprightness.[3]

The Book of Wisdom has a beautiful passage about how the beautiful things of creation are intended to lead us to the beauty of the Creator, and how tragic it is when they don't.

> If through delight in the beauty of these things
>   men assumed them to be gods,
> let them know how much better than these is their Lord,
> for the author of beauty created them. . . .
> For from the greatness and beauty of created things
> comes a corresponding perception of their Creator. . .
> and they trust in what they see,
>   because the things that are seen are beautiful.
> Yet again, not even they are to be excused;
> for if they had the power to know so much
> that they could investigate the world,
> how did they fail to find sooner the Lord of these things?
> (Wis. 13:3, 5, 7b–9, NRSV)

Catherine of Siena points out that even in this life the greedy, the envious, the revengeful, and the lustful are tortured by their disordered desires. They suffer through their own sinfulness, meriting nothing by it and refusing to heed the message of this suffering: to repent and return to the Father. Christians, in taking up the Cross of Christ, can taste something of the joy of heaven in this life; so too, those who choose to follow their sinful desires take up "the devil's cross, and taste the pledge of hell even in this life. Unless they reform they go through life weakened in all sorts of ways, and in the end receive eternal death. They pass in hate through the gate of the devil and receive eternal damnation. . . . How deluded these souls are, and how painfully they make their way to hell—like martyrs of the devil!"[4]

What are some of the areas where detachment is important?

Money and Possessions

John of the Cross gives King David as an illustration of the freedom of heart in relationship to money and possessions that is necessary for spiritual progress.

> Even though he [David] was manifestly rich, he says he was poor because his will was not fixed on riches; and he thereby lived as though really poor. On the other hand, had he been actually poor, without his will being so, there would have been no true poverty, because the appetite of his soul would have been rich and full.
>
> Hence, we call this nakedness a night for the soul, for we are not discussing the mere lack of things; this lack will not divest the soul if it craves for all these objects. We are dealing with the denudation of the soul's appetites and gratifications. This is what leaves it free and empty of all things, even though it possesses them. Since the things of the world cannot enter the soul, they are not in themselves an encumbrance or harm to it; rather, it is the will and appetite dwelling within that cause the damage when set on these things.[5]

John states a very important principle: it is neither the presence nor the absence of things that indicate true detachment, but rather, the interior freedom of heart that puts its trust not in things—possessing or keeping what we already have, or longing for what we don't have—but rather in the Father's care.

Bernard also talks about this poverty of spirit, which is possible even in the midst of wealth. Speaking of wealthy disciples of the Lord, Bernard comments:

> They do possess earthly things, but with the spirit of men who possess nothing (2 Cor. 6:10); in reality they possess all things, not like unhappy beggars who get what they beg for, but as masters, masters in the best sense because devoid of avarice. To the man of faith the whole world is a treasure-house of riches: the whole world, because all things, whether adverse or favorable, are of service to him; they all contribute to his good. . . .
>
> The miser hungers like a beggar for earthly possessions, the man of faith has a lordly independence of them. The first is a beggar no matter what he owns, the latter by his very independence is a true owner.[6]

This basic principle of living in faith and trusting in God's care, so important to the entire spiritual journey, is clearly a central teaching of Jesus.

In addressing the anxiety He perceived in His disciples about having enough of the basic necessities for life in this world, He said:

> For all the nations of the world seek these things; and your Father knows that you need them. Instead, seek his kingdom and these things shall be yours as well. (Lk. 12:30–31)

The life of a Christian is to be different than the life of the unbeliever. Like all human beings, Christians need certain things of this world to live, but Jesus calls us to be primarily occupied with living for the kingdom. If we do this, He promises that the things we need for life on this earth will be given as well.

This poverty or detachment of spirit from material things has often been expressed in the life of the Christian people by an actual giving up of material goods in the context of religious life, where the vow of poverty is taken. In fact, Jesus goes on following the verse we have just considered to invite His disciples to an actual renunciation of material goods.

Francis acknowledges the great value of making solemn vows of poverty, as is done in religious life, but also points out that it is possible to reach perfection in this area without making such a vow. He makes the important distinction between the technical "state of perfection," religious life, and the reality of perfection, available to everyone.

> There is still a difference between the state of perfection and perfection itself. All bishops and religious are in the state of perfection, yet not all of them have arrived at perfection itself, as is only too plainly to be seen. Let us try then to practice these virtues well, each of us according to his vocation. Although they do not place us in the state of perfection, yet they will bring us perfection itself.[7]

Practical Advice on Detachment

It is clear that the principles of detachment and poverty of spirit are absolutely essential for making progress in the spiritual life. Francis de Sales gives some good advice to those not in formal religious life about how to approach this area. Although a true poverty of spirit can exist in the midst of wealth, the capacity for self-delusion is great. Francis gives us some indicators so we can discern whether we truly have a spirit of detachment or poverty or just think we do.

First of all, Francis acknowledges the positive advantage of wealth, and even acknowledges the right to increase it, if done in a proper manner.

> So also you can possess riches without being poisoned by them if you merely keep them in your home and purse

and not in your heart. To be rich in effect and poor in affection is a great happiness for a Christian. By this means he has the advantages of riches for this world and the merit of poverty for the world to come. . . . I willingly grant that you may take care to increase your wealth and resources, provided this is done not only justly but properly and charitably.[8]

At the same time Francis is very aware that avariciousness and greed often cloak themselves in various rationalizations. He gives the example of a person who claims that responsibility for his children demands that he increase and hold on to his wealth, but never thinks he has enough and always finds need for more. The more powerful the avarice and greed are, the more they may hide, and the more the reality of the situation may even be eventually hidden from the person's own conscience.

Little noticed in the list of sins that exclude people from the kingdom of God is that of greed (or "miserliness" in some translations).

Do you not know that the unrighteous will not inherit the kingdom of God? Do not be deceived; neither the immoral, nor idolaters, nor adulterers nor homosexuals, nor thieves, nor the greedy, nor drunkards, nor revilers, nor robbers will inherit the kingdom of God. (1 Cor. 6:9–19)

In fact, Paul indicates that greed can actually become idolatrous and warns against that "covetousness which is idolatry" (Col. 3:5, Eph. 5:3–6). When we give time, attention, effort, and affection to amassing and keeping the things of this world that we should give to God Himself, we have become idolaters. We have also, almost certainly, produced in ourselves a self-centered life, a dullness of spirit and blindness to spiritual realities that subject us to the "wrath of God" (Col. 3:6). The wrath of God is the experience which comes from turning away from His love.

How can we test our hearts to discover greed or avariciousness? Francis tells us,

> You are truly avaricious if you longingly, ardently, anxiously desire to possess goods that you do not have, even though you say that you would not want to acquire them by unjust means.[9]

Another indicator that Francis gives is noting our reaction when we lose some of our wealth or property.

> If you find your heart very desolated and afflicted at the loss of property, believe me, you love it too much. The strongest proof of love for a lost object is suffering over its loss.[10]

The wealth we have doesn't belong to us, but has been given to us by the Lord, in trust, to be utilized under His rule. Part of the vocation of those who have money is using it well—even increasing it if just opportunity presents itself—under the guidance of the Holy Spirit. A gift or ministry of the Holy Spirit is "giving in liberality" (Rom. 12:8). This must mean regularly giving part of our wealth away for the service of the Lord and the relief of the poor, and by personally serving them.

Francis points out, paradoxically, that those who give generously are often blessed with greater prosperity.

> Nothing makes us so prosperous in this world as to give alms, but until such time as God shall restore it to us we remain the poorer in the amount we have given.[11]

Yet we must also come to see "reverses of fortune" as opportunities to demonstrate true detachment and grow in humility and holiness.

> If you meet with losses that impoverish you either very much or a little, as in the case of tempests, fires, floods,

droughts, thefts, or lawsuits, that is the proper time to
practice poverty by accepting your losses meekly and
patiently and by courageously submitting to such impov-
erishment.[12]

Those who are materially poor can also transform necessity into
virtue, becoming truly poor in spirit as well as in material things.
Since our material poverty has come not by our own choice, but
has at least been permitted by God, it presents an opportunity to
eliminate self-will from such poverty and to more purely accept it
as God's will. Acceptance for the sake of God makes our suffering
very valuable. Secondly, while the voluntary poverty that is chosen in the religious life is praised and esteemed, pride and mixed
motives may easily be involved; actual "poverty" may in fact not be
so poor after all.

I am reminded of a story that Father Benedict Groeschel, the
American spiritual writer, tells occasionally about his visit to a very
impressive house of a religious order. Upon marveling at the rich
furnishings and materials used in construction Father Groeschel
remarked, "If this is poverty I'd hate to see what celibacy is like."

Since the involuntary poverty of lay people is not highly praised,
it can in fact even be poorer than the voluntary poverty of religious,
whose life is often praised. Not to complain about being poor in
actual fact reveals true poverty of spirit and the absence of that
"greedy desire" that John of the Cross talked about in his comments
regarding King David.

There is a Scripture passage that sheds much light on this matter.

> Keep your life free from love of money, and be content
> with what you have; for he has said, "I will never fail you
> nor forsake you." Hence we can confidently say,
> "The Lord is my helper,
> I will not be afraid;
> what can man do to me?" (Heb. 13:5–6)

It's not money itself—but the love of money—that Scripture describes as the "root of all evil."

> But those who desire to be rich fall into temptation, into a snare, into many senseless and hurtful desires that plunge men into ruin and destruction. For the love of money is the root of all evils; it is through this craving that some have wandered away from the faith and pierced their hearts with many pangs. (1 Tim. 6:7–10)

True contentment comes, as it came for Paul, in knowing how to abase and abound (cf. Phil. 4:12), trusting in God's care and providential rule over the circumstances of our life. The "contentment" that the Scriptures talk about is dependent not on how much or how little money we have but on knowing who is caring for us—God Himself!

I've known people who are very wealthy and have millions of dollars and are not content. They think they don't have enough and are afraid of losing what they have. And I've known literally the poorest of the poor, who have virtually nothing but are filled with joy and give generously from their nothing!

I remember one time visiting a small Christian village in India where the people seemed quite literally to have nothing. When they saw me coming they held a quick little meeting, and then someone went running off and came back later with a bottle of soda pop and gave it to me. They all had huge grins on their faces and were absolutely delighted to be able to give this to me. I felt like King David, who was so touched by the sacrifice of those who brought his favorite spring water to him through enemy lines at risk of their lives (2 Sam. 23:15–17) that he refused to drink it and poured it out as an offering to the Lord. I knew they truly wanted me to drink it, and so I did, as they all stood around and watched with great delight. At that moment, I understood even more what Jesus must have felt when people were praising those who gave large contributions to the temple, and He praised the poor widow who gave a small coin out of her nothing! Such freedom, detachment, and trust make room for God to enter more deeply into our lives. Teresa of Avila says such detachment is essential.

> But believe me in one thing: if there is any vain esteem of honor or wealth (and this can be had inside monasteries as well as outside, although inside the occasions for it are more removed and the fault would be greater), you will never grow very much or come to enjoy the true fruit of prayer. And this is so even though you may have many years of experience in prayer—or, better, I should say reflection because perfect prayer in the end removes these bad habits.[13]

Sensual Pleasure

God created us to both feel and desire pleasure. Pleasure in itself is by no means sinful but is a wonderful capacity God has given us to delight in what is truly delightful. Francis de Sales regularly points out how God draws us to Himself by the pleasure He gives us from being in relationship with Him, and how He, in fact, takes pleasure in His relationship with us.[14] Yet all created pleasures are but a very limited participation in and shadows of the eternal pleasure of knowing God and dwelling forever in His kingdom. When we direct ourselves to the pursuit of sensual pleasure in a disordered manner or degree it becomes an obstacle to the greatest pleasure, union with God. God has created earthly pleasures as signs, foretastes, and invitations to the pleasure of eternity. When they are sought apart from God as ends in themselves or not in accord with their purpose, they become obstacles. We are at the same time sensual and spiritual in our natures. If we pursue the sensual in a disproportionate or disordered way, we can end up becoming less than human, truly beasts, whose "god is the belly" and whose "end is destruction" (Phil. 3:19). What helps us to avoid this idolatry and its disastrous consequences is to remember that our true home is in heaven and that we are awaiting the return of Jesus, "who will change our lowly body to be like his glorious body." (Phil. 3:20–21). (Of course, the opposite can also be true. An imbalanced, delusional "spirituality" that ignores the authentically human can also make us less than human and more demonic than angelic.) In fact, as in the case with greed, the excessive seeking of sensual pleasure can truly become idolatrous (cf. Eph. 5:5). When we give the greater part of our time, attention, thoughts, affections to something that is not God, we run the risk of idolatry—of worshipping (adoring, contemplating, praising, seeking, thanking) something that is not truly God.

Sexual Pleasure

There are many God-given pleasures, but let's take for an example one that's so fundamental to our natures and so prominently focused on in our culture, that of sexual pleasure.

God created human beings with sexual desires and drives. Because of the deep wound in our natures caused by the Fall there is a disorder in our desires and drives that must be brought under the reign of Christ and the rule of the Holy Spirit for sexual desire to find its proper expression.

Bernard points out that the body in itself is not the problem, but the disorder that sin has brought to the body.

> For "so long as we are in this body we are exiles from the Lord" (2 Cor. 5:6). Not because we are embodied, but because we are in this body which has a sinful lineage, and is never without sin. So you may know that it is not our bodies but our sins that stand in the way.[15]

The path to true freedom in this area begins by coming to know God's purpose for our sexuality as revealed to us in His Word and as understood by the Church. Jesus spoke of this essential link between acting on the truth, as it is known, coming to understand it more deeply through our obedience to it, and experiencing true freedom.

If you continue in my word, you are truly my disciples, and you will know the truth, and the truth will make you free. (Jn. 8:31)

Without going into a treatise on the Church's teaching on sexuality, let's review some of the basic truths and then consider the wisdom of the saints as to how to conduct ourselves in various situations so that we don't become "slaves" or "idolaters" in this area. The purpose of sexuality is for a man and a woman to enter into a lifetime commitment to love and care for each other and be open to bringing forth new life. In the framework of marriage the expression of sexuality is intended to express and develop communion between the husband and wife and, God willing, to bring forth children. Any exercise of sexuality outside of marriage or contrary to these purposes is a violation of God's will, and besides being sinful in a lesser or greater degree, puts us at great risk of becoming slaves to disordered sexual desire.

Practical Advice on Chastity

The advice of the saints in this area is to be very clear about what the truth is, ask God's help to live in accordance with it, and exercise practical wisdom in dealing with sexual temptation.

Francis de Sales points out that chastity is necessary for everyone, single or married, understanding by chastity the proper exercise or restraint of the sexual capacity. He makes clear that any involvement in sexual pleasure outside of marriage is not permitted and that we need to guard our minds, hearts, memories, and senses so as to obtain and preserve appropriate purity in this regard. The best defense is an early one.

Be very quick to turn away from whatever leads or allures to lewd conduct. . . . Such things are always easier to avoid than to cure. . . . It is an act of impurity to look at, hear, speak, smell, or touch anything immodest if our heart is entertained thereby and takes pleasure in it. . . . Certainly chastity may be lost in as many ways as there are immodest and wanton acts . . . some weaken it, others wound it, and still others cause it to die completely.[16]

The words of Saint Paul come to mind:

But immorality and all impurity or covetousness must not even be named among you, as is fitting among saints. Let there be no filthiness, nor silly talk, nor levity, which are not fitting; but instead let there be thanksgiving. Be sure of this, that no immoral or impure man, or one who is covetous (that is, an idolater), has any inheritance in the kingdom of Christ and of God. (Eph. 5:3–5)

Francis speaks of three degrees in exercising the virtue of chastity. The first degree of this virtue is expressed by not voluntarily giving in to sexual pleasure apart from marriage or sexual pleasure within marriage that may violate the laws of loving communion and openness to new life. The second degree is, as much as possible, not pursuing pleasures, even when permitted, apart from what truly serves the purposes of the relationship. The third degree is not setting one's heart and mind on the sexual pleasure that is necessary and appropriate for the marriage relationship, that is, not becoming preoccupied or obsessed with an important but subordinate part of life and marriage.[17]

He particularly cautions us to avoid starting down the path of sexual curiosity, whether married or single, as it can easily lead to sexual obsession and enslavement. In a pornographic, immodest culture such as the one in which we live, this advice is extremely important. Citing Saint Jerome, Francis cautions single people not to be deceived by the devil, who magnifies the delight and pleasure of imagined sex so as to tempt them violently to abandon chastity. The devil tries to present these pleasures "as infinitely more pleasurable and delightful than they actually are."[18] His advice is to turn away from such thoughts immediately and not be drawn into sexual curiosity.

Bernard identifies curiosity as a means that the devil uses to lead many to sin, not just sexual sins. He places curiosity as the first step in a twelve-step descent from humility to pride, from grace into damnation. His advice: we should only concern ourselves with what we need to know, moment by moment.

> And so the first step of pride is curiosity. You can recognize it by these indications. You see a monk of whom you had thought well up to now. Wherever he stands, walks, sits, his eyes begin to wander. His head is lifted. His ears are alert. You can tell from his outward movements that the inner man has changed . . . his soul has fallen sick. He has grown careless about his own behavior. He wastes his curiosity on other people . . . for just as death entered the world through sin (Rom. 5:12), so it enters the mind through these windows (Jer. 9:21).[19]

Bernard reminds us that it was curiosity that led to the Fall originally, and speaks of Eve.

> Why are you always glancing at it [the forbidden fruit]? What is the good of looking at what you are forbidden to eat? . . . For when you are looking intently at something, the serpent slips into your heart and coaxes you. He leads on your reason with flattery; he awakes your fear with lies. . . . He increases your interest while he stirs up your greed. He sharpens your curiosity while he prompts your desire. He offers what is forbidden and takes away what is given. He holds out an apple and snatches away paradise.[20]

Francis acknowledges that the concept of chastity within marriage is a startling concept for many people. Chastity within marriage obviously doesn't mean abstaining from sexual relations but rather exercising appropriate restraint by using the sexual faculty as much as possible in the service of love and life. Francis acknowledges that this is challenging and that complete abstinence may in fact be easier to accomplish than an appropriate exercise of sexuality within marriage.

He makes a comparison with the scriptural admonition to "Be angry but sin not" (Ps. 4:4), commenting that it is actually harder to exercise appropriate anger than to not get angry at all. He acknowledges the legitimate "holy freedom" appropriate to married sexuality but points out how easy it is for this to drift into "license and from use to abuse."[21]

Sometimes circumstances within marriages require total abstinence from sexual expression for a period of time, such as is required in long illnesses or unavoidable separations. He speaks of two kinds of chastity then for married people: absolute abstinence for such separations, and a chastity of "moderation" for ordinary circumstances.[22] We will have occasion to return in more detail to the reality of married love and friendship in the spiritual life in the next chapter.[23]

Money and possessions are a powerful force in our life that must be dealt with. So also, as we have just considered, is sexuality. We now come to pride, which many spiritual writers, based on their analysis of the primordial sin recounted in Genesis, identify as the root of all sin.

Pride

It was an act of pride that led to the Fall—"You shall be like gods!" (Gen. 3:5)— and it was an act of loving, obedient, humility that brought the possibility of redemption. Scripture repeatedly speaks strongly about the profound evil of pride.[24]

> Have this mind among yourselves, which was in Christ Jesus, who, though he was in the form of God, did not count equality with God a thing to be grasped, but emp-

tied himself, taking the form of a servant, being born in
the likeness of men. And being found in human form he
humbled himself and became obedient unto death, even
death on a cross. (Phil. 2:6–9)

Being detached from self-centered, possessive seeking—the
breaking of pride—is essential for progress in the spiritual life.
Bernard identifies pride as the beginning of all sin.

Just as the fear of the Lord is the beginning of wisdom
(Ps. 110: 10; Sir. 1:16), so pride is the beginning of all
sin (Sir. 10:15). . . . For this is pride, this is how all sin
originates—that you are greater in your own eyes than
you are before God, than you are in truth.[25]

The profound wound in our being caused by pride needs to be
healed before union with God can be restored as it was "in the beginning." And God has so ordered His plan for saving the human race
that salvation cannot happen without pride being broken. Faith is the
simple but powerful key that breaks pride and releases salvation.[26]

All have sinned and fallen short of the glory of God, they
are justified by his grace as a gift, through the redemption
which is in Christ Jesus, whom God put forward as an
expiation by his blood, to be received by faith. Then what
becomes of our boasting? It is excluded. (Rom. 3:23–27)

Much is said in these few verses, and the themes treated here are
developed throughout the Bible. In short: as result of the Fall, everybody is cut off from God; through the sacrifice of Christ, everybody is
undeservedly offered a gift of redemption by God. If we truly understand our situation and how undeserving we are of salvation, how
much it is a pure gift of God, we have nothing to boast of—except the
Cross of Christ, and our weakness and need, two things the Scripture
tells us that are appropriate to boast of! It is our deep recognition of

this truth, lived out in our daily lives, that allows pride to be broken. We have to receive, not achieve, in order to be saved. There's nothing we can do to merit or earn or deserve salvation. Properly understood, this is profoundly humbling. It's supposed to be.

> For Christ did not send me to baptize, but to preach the gospel—not with worldly "wisdom," however, lest the cross of Christ be rendered void of its meaning! . . . Since in God's wisdom the world did not come to know him through "wisdom," it pleased God to save those who believe through the absurdity of the preaching of the gospel. Yes, Jews demand "signs" and Greeks look for "wisdom," but we preach Christ crucified—a stumbling block to the Jews, and an absurdity to Gentiles; but to those who are called, Jews and Greeks alike, Christ the power of God and the wisdom of God. For God's folly is wiser than men, and his weakness more powerful than men. . . . God chose those whom the world considers absurd to shame the wise; he singled out the weak of this world to shame the strong. He chose the world's lowborn and despised, those who count for nothing, to reduce to nothing those who were something; so that mankind can do no boasting before God. . . . "Let him who would boast, boast in the Lord." (1 Cor. 1:17–31)

Bernard makes very clear time and time again that our hope for salvation rests not in our own merits or efforts but in the blood of Christ.

> Your Passion is the ultimate refuge, a remedy that is unique. When our wisdom lets us down, when our righteousness falls short, when the merit of our holiness founder, your Passion becomes our support. . . . Unless your blood cries out on my behalf, I am not saved.[27]

The blood of Christ wins for us the gift of the Spirit which makes of us a new creation, or, as Bernard puts it, truly human.

As I have pointed out, nature can never shake off this evil by its own strength, nor regain the oil of innate kindness once it has been destroyed. But what nature cannot do, grace can. And therefore the man on whom the merciful unction of the Holy Spirit deigns to pour out again the grace of its gentleness, will be immediately restored to a truly human condition, and will obtain from grace gifts far greater than nature could bestow.[28]

Even the holiest among us, Bernard declares, needs to depend on the mercy of Christ and not our own righteousness.

For if he marks what is done amiss, even by the elect, who can abide it (Ps. 129:3)? In his sight the stars are not clean (Job 15:15), and even in the angels he finds corruption (Job 4:18). . . . Therefore even the saints have need to ask pardon for their sins, that they may be saved by mercy, not trusting in their own righteousness. For all have sinned, and all need mercy.[29]

These fundamental insights into the reality of our condition and the basic truths about salvation remain obscure to many contemporary Catholics. More and more, however, contemporary voices are being raised to witness to these important truths, echoing those of the saints. Father Raniero Cantalamessa, official preacher to the papal household for many years, is one of these voices.

However, Saint Paul strongly insists on one thing: all this comes about "gratuitously" (*dorean*), through grace, as a gift; he comes back to this point numerous times using different terms. And we wonder why God is so determined on this point! It's because he wants to exclude from the new creation the canker that ruined the first creation: man's boasting. . . . Man hides in his heart the innate tendency to "pay God his price." But "no man can ransom himself or give to God the price of his life" (Ps. 49:8). To want to pay God his price through our own merits is another form of the never ending effort to be autonomous and independent of God, and not just autonomous and independent but actually God's creditors because "to one who works, his wages are not reckoned as a gift but as his due" (Rom. 4:4).[30]

It is all too easy on the spiritual journey to begin to think that the salvation of the world and our own salvation depend only on us, on the structures we erect—on our customs, our patterns, our leadership, our group, our longevity, our virtue, our faithfulness, our character, our history, our discipline, our devotions, our buildings, our traditions, our intellect, our will. There's a tremendous danger that in our response to Christ we may allow these things to overshadow the supreme place of the Cross of Christ in our lives, the life of the Church, and the life of the world. If we allow ourselves to gradually transfer our trust to things other than the unmerited grace won for us on Calvary, we end up placing our confidence in the works of our own hands or the deeds of our own flesh. It is *essential* for those who think we are "something" to be reduced to "nothing," so that we have no grounds of boasting before God. That's humbling, and it's supposed to be.

> To you all flesh must come
>   with its burden of wicked deeds.
> We are overcome by our sins,
>   only you can pardon them. (Ps. 65:3–4, NAB)

A proud person always thinks he's right. Humility is being able to say, "I'm wrong; you're right," both to God and others.

One of the great battles which the Lord called the apostle Paul to fight was to keep clear what was new about the New Covenant. Paul continually faced the tendency both within and without the Church to drift back into depending on religious externals or self-effort rather than on the saving Person and deeds of Jesus.

For by grace you have been saved through faith; and this is not your own doing, it is the gift of God—not because of works, lest any man should boast. For we are his workmanship, created in Christ Jesus for good works, which God prepared beforehand, that we should walk in them. (Eph. 2:8–10)

For who sees anything different in you? What have you that you did not receive? If then you received it, why do you boast as if it were not a gift? (1 Cor. 4:7)

That is why it depends on faith, in order that the promise may rest on grace. (Rom. 4:16)

The tendency to want to save ourselves, not to have to depend utterly on God, is very strong in all of us, especially in today's modern world. Yves Congar, the great French theologian, warns of this also:

With the constant progress of science, man has gradually lost the awareness that he depends on another. Yet salvation essentially consists in this awareness of dependence. Man cannot save himself by his own efforts. Another saves us. Catholics also are running this risk.[31]

For the sake of the world, for our own sakes, and for the sake of God we desperately need, as individuals and as a Church, not to behave as if what we have in the way of spiritual or material goods is due to our own merit or a result of our own will or strength. Rather, it is the pure grace of God.

Of course, our faith can't be genuine if it doesn't express itself progressively in a life of morality, prayer, and love for others (through which we truly merit). But even here, of course, it's God's grace that enables us to live in such a way as to please God. We owe Him thanks even for the good deeds—the "merits"—which He has prepared for us in advance to carry out.

We are truly his handiwork, created in Christ Jesus to lead the life of good deeds which God prepared for us in advance. (Eph. 2:10)

It is God who in his good will towards you begets in you any measure of desire or achievement. (Phil. 2:13)

Bernard wants to make very sure that we know that even our "merits" are a result of grace, a gift.

There is no way for grace to enter, if [a sense of] merit has taken residence in the soul. A full acknowledgement of grace then is a sign of the fullness of grace. Indeed if the soul possesses anything of its own, to that extent grace must give place to it: whatever you impute to merit you steal from grace. I want nothing to do with the sort of merit which excludes grace.[32]

Bernard is aware how easy a disguised, prideful, self-satisfaction can hide itself among those who are "religious." His commentary on the parable about the Pharisee and the Publican brings this out clearly.

"Because the pieties that our mouths proclaim will not justify the pride of our hearts in the sight of him who is repelled by the arrogant (Ps. 137:6). 'God is not mocked (Gal. 6:7), O Pharisee. What do you have that was not given to you (1 Cor. 4:7)?'"

The truly wise, Bernard admonishes, will humbly recognize and openly admit that their merits are gifts from God and give *all* the glory to Him.[33]

For if a man who is very good takes the credit for his goodness he becomes correspondingly evil. For this is a very evil thing. If anyone says "Far be it from me! I know that it is by the grace of God I am what I am (1 Cor. 15:10)," and then is careful to take a little of the glory for the favor he has received, is he not a thief and a robber (Jn. 10:1)? Such a man will hear these words: "Out of your own mouth I judge you, wicked servant (Lk. 19:22)." What is more wicked than for a servant to usurp the glory due his master?[34]

Bernard wants us to know that the glory of God is simply passing through us, not originating with us.[35]

Faith and Works

Bernard, who could hardly emphasize our total dependence on grace more, is also clear that appropriate obedience (merit) must be our response to such grace. A test of the genuineness of our faith is how we live our lives. This is a strong message of the Scriptures and also, of course, of the teaching of the saints.

> It is enough for merit to know that merit is not enough. But as merit must not presume on merit, so lack of merit must bring judgment. Furthermore, children re-born in baptism are not without merit, but possess the merits of Christ; but they make themselves unworthy of these if they do not add their own—not because of inability, but because of neglect; this is the danger of maturity. Henceforward, take care that you possess merit; when you possess it, you will know it as a gift. Hope for its fruit, the mercy of God, and you will escape all danger of poverty, ingratitude, and presumption.[36]

Saving faith is a faith that issues in works. Saving faith is not just an inner act or disposition but the expression of that inner act or disposition in deeds (cf. Gal. 5:6, 6:15; 1 Cor. 7:19; 1 Jn. 2:3; Jn. 14:15). The final judgment is based not just on our interior faith alone but on actions we take in our lives by the grace of God, actions that flow from that faith (cf. Rev. 22:12; Mt. 16:26–27, 25:31–46; Rom. 2:5–11; 1 Cor. 3:10–15; 2 Cor. 5:10).

The apostle James puts it very directly.

> What does it profit, my brethren, if a man says he has
> faith but has not works? Can his faith save him? . . . You
> believe that God is one; you do well. Even the demons
> believe—and shudder. . . . You see that man is justified by
> works and not by faith alone. (Jas. 2:14, 19, 24)

It is the grace that comes through faith that empowers us to do
the works. In that sense we are dependent on the grace of God not
only to strengthen us in faith, but in works also.

> For this I labor and struggle, in accord with the exercise
> of his power working within me. (Col. 1:29, NAB)

Properly understood, there is no conflict between grace and law,
or faith and works, as Father Cantalamessa expresses so well:

> In the new economy there is no contrast or incompatibil-
> ity between the interior law of the Spirit and the written
> external law; on the contrary there is full collaboration;
> the one is given to guard the other: "Law was given so
> that we might seek grace and grace was given so that we
> might observe the law" (Saint Augustine, *De Spir. Litt.*
> 19, 34). The observance of the commandments and, in
> fact, obedience, is the proof of love; it is the sign that
> shows whether we are living "according to the Spirit" or
> "according to the flesh." The law doesn't therefore sud-
> denly become a giver of life; it remains exactly what it
> was, that through which the will of God is shown and
> nothing more. The difference is, though, that now, after
> the coming of the Spirit, its limited function is openly
> recognized and therefore it is positive, whereas before,
> when it was expected to give life, it was misleading and
> only encouraged the pride of man and sin. The very "let-
> ter" is, in other words, only safe in the Spirit.[37]

Bernard expresses this same truth.

The Lawgiver was not unaware that the burden of the law exceeded the powers of men, but he judged it useful for this reason to advise men of their own insufficiency, that they might know the proper end toward which they ought to strive according to their powers. Therefore in commanding impossible things he made men humble, not prevaricators, so that every mouth may be stopped and the whole world be made subject to God, because nobody will be justified in his sight by the works of the law (Rom. 3:19–20). Accepting that command then, and conscious of our deficiency, we shall cry to heaven and God will have mercy on us (1 Mac. 4:10). And on that day we shall know that God has saved us, not by the righteous works that we ourselves have done, but according to his mercy (Tit. 3:5).[38]

God arranged the plan of salvation with a fundamental purpose: that no one would have any grounds for boasting in a self-glorifying way. Self-delusion and self-righteousness are characteristic of us fallen creatures; the very root of sin is pride. The only way to break pride and allow God's grace to triumph is to admit the awesome truth: we're all in desperate need of God, of His forgiveness, of His love, of His Holy Spirit, and all of us need to abandon our pride, admit our need, and come to the foot of the Cross to receive mercy and forgiveness. And we need to stay there.

As Father Benedict Groeschel, CFR, Director of Spiritual Development for the Archdiocese of New York, and founder of a reformed order of Capuchins, has pointed out, the admission of need and helplessness expressed in the twelve steps of Alcoholics Anonymous, now utilized by various other groups, gets to the heart of the Gospel.

If you have not given sufficient thought in your own life to the complete destitution and helplessness of the person symbolized by the prodigal son, you should review the twelve steps of Alcoholics Anonymous. . . . Many spiritual writers rightly assume that the utter destitution that these steps reflect is actually the spiritual state of all men. . . . Jesus requires that his followers repent in such a way that they admit their powerlessness over sin and their inability to save themselves.[39]

Isn't this also an important message that the Spirit is speaking to our Church, today?

> For you say, I am rich, I have prospered, and I need nothing; not knowing that you are wretched, pitiable, poor, blind, and naked. (Rev. 3:17)

In order to keep clear about my fundamental need for God I find it helpful to periodically say straight out, as members of the twelve-step groups do: "My name is Ralph, and I'm a sinner." This helps me to remember who God is and who I am, which is so important as a foundation for all growth.

Father Cantalamessa points out another reason why God has chosen faith as the gateway to the kingdom.

> If you had been told: the door to the Kingdom is innocence, the door is the strict observance of the commandments, the door is this or that virtue, you could have found excuses and said: It's not for me! I'm not innocent, I haven't got that virtue. But you are being told: the door is faith. Believe! This is not something above or beyond you, it is not so far removed from you.[40]

Father Cantalamessa, from his extensive experience with religious life and his study of the history of the Church, points out how important the emphasis on grace is:

> The newness of the Christian message becomes clouded when preaching, catechesis, spiritual guidance and all other formative activities of faith unilaterally insist on

duties, virtues, vices, punishment and, in general, on what man "should do," presenting grace as an aid that comes to man in the course of his commitment to make up for what he is not able to do alone and not, on the contrary, as something that comes before these efforts and which makes them possible; when "duty" is created by the law and not by grace and when duty is consequently not conceived as our debt of gratitude to God but rather as something that creates, if we accomplish it, a debt of gratitude on God's part towards us; when, in other words, morals become separated from the *kerygma*. In a stricter sphere, the religious life is similarly clouded when in the formation given to young people and novices, in retreats and on other occasions, more time is spent on talking about the charism, traditions, rules and constitutions and the particular spirituality of the order (often very poor and inconsistent) than talking of Christ the Lord and his Holy Spirit. The center of attention imperceptibly moves from God to man and from grace to the law.[41]

There is a deep tendency in all of us to gradually drift into understanding grace as an afterthought rather than as the very foundation of our lives. Father Cantalamessa's vivid words help us to guard against this pernicious drift into self-reliance and false autonomy.

Growing in Virtue

Detachment from disordered love of the things of this world—from money, from inordinate sensual pleasure, from pride, from our very selves—is not an end in itself. The emptying that detachment brings about prepares us for an infilling of something greater. The something greater is not only a greater delight in God but a greater and truer delight in all He has created. The proper ordering of lesser loves places us in a position to receive and embody a greater love for both God and our neighbor. Turning away from vice allows the growth of virtue. Virtue is not only the fruit of our discipline and effort but the fruit of our relationship with Christ Himself. Bernard tells us:

Only those can be called prudent who are imbued with his teaching; only those are just who have had their sins pardoned through his mercy; only those are temperate who take pains to follow his way of life; only those are courageous who hold fast to the example of his patience when buffeted by sufferings. Vainly therefore will anyone strive to acquire the virtues, if he thinks they may be obtained from any source other than the Lord of the virtues.[42]

Bernard frequently returns to this theme in his teaching.

Christ the Lord is the ultimate source of all virtue and knowledge. . . . Hence from him as from a wellhead comes the power to be pure in body, diligent in affection and upright in will. Nor is this all. From him too come subtlety of intellect, splendor of eloquence, urbanity of bearing; from him, knowledge and words of wisdom. Indeed in him are hidden all the treasures of wisdom and knowledge (Col. 2:3). Shall I add still more? Chaste thoughts, just judgments, holy desires—are they not all streams from that one spring?[43]

Ultimately, it is the love of Christ poured into us through the Spirit that enables us to experience transformation and be more like Him.

The fraternal love that I exercise, my zeal for righteousness, is the fruit of my beloved's love in me.[44]

As we experience the Bridegroom's love, more and more "pride melts away" and humility grows. Knowing that the deepest key to its transformation, the power needed to free it from vice and open it to virtue, is simply the love of Christ, the soul cries out:

Lord Jesus, if only you would once say to my soul: "How beautiful you are." . . . It would be enough for me to hear it even once.[45]

With great eloquence, Bernard reminds us of a sure path to grace—turning to our Mother Mary, and asking for her help.

> I know what I will do; servant though I am I shall have recourse to her who is the friend. In my dwarfish ugliness I shall be filled with wonder by her multiform loveliness; I shall rejoice at the voice of the Bridegroom (Jn. 3:29) as he too marvels at a beauty so great. . . . Mary never lost her holiness, yet she did not lack humility; and so the king desired her loveliness (Ps. 44:12).[46]

Humility

Although simply knowing the Lord and His love is the key to growth and transformation, we, as always, have a part to play by actively cooperating with His grace.

One help in overcoming pride is to reflect on the reality of our situation in relationship to God, which we have just done in our treatment of pride, sin and the gospel of grace and faith. Another help is to consciously choose to humble ourselves rather than exalt ourselves as we encounter the manifold circumstances of life in which such decisions must be made. We can eventually, with patient effort and God's help, change patterns of proud response to patterns of humble response, change vice into virtue.

Francis counsels us to love our own weakness, abjection, and spiritual and human poverty. He advises us not to try to hide it, cover it over, or pretend it isn't there, but to love it. This, at first hearing, is startling advice, but it is based on the basic facts of our situation before God. The virtues that are born here are humility in relationship with God, and meekness in relationship to our neighbor and our self.

Bernard counsels us to accept the necessity of humiliations as a means to growing in the virtue of humility.

> It is only when humility warrants it that great graces can be obtained, hence the one to be enriched by them is first

humbled by correction that by his humility he may merit
them. And so when you perceive that you are being humiliated, look on it as the sign of a sure guarantee that grace is
on the way (Ps. 85:17). Just as the heart is puffed up with
pride before its destruction, so it is humiliated before being
honored (Prov. 16:18) . . . "the Lord resists the proud and
gives his grace to the humble" (Jas. 4:6).[47]

Sometimes the humbling circumstance comes from the hand
of God, or sometimes from our fellow human beings, but, in both
cases, humiliation doesn't automatically become humility—that
depends on our response.

Do you see that humility makes us righteous? I say
humility and not humiliation. How many are humiliated
who are not humble! There are some who meet humiliation with rancor, some with patience, some again with
cheerfulness. The first kind are culpable, the second are
innocent, the last just. . . . He who can say: "It was good
for me that you humiliated me" (Ps. 118:71), is truly
humble. The man who endures it unwillingly cannot say
this; still less the man who murmurs. To neither of these
do I promise grace on the grounds of being humiliated . . .
because it is not to the humiliated but to the humble that
God gives grace. But he is humble who turns humiliation
into humility.[48]

Ironically, our humiliation, when taken in all humility, opens
up the joyful dimension of wholeheartedly following the Lord and
making progress on the spiritual journey. Bernard sees it as playing
a particular role here.

We know that "God loves a cheerful giver (2 Cor.
9:7).". . . For it is the possession of a joyful and genuine humility that alone enables us to receive grace. . . .
It is not sufficient that one keep his self-possession by
patience when he is humbled; to receive grace one must

embrace humiliation willingly. You may take as a general rule that everyone who humbles himself will be exalted (Lk. 14:11). It is significant that not every kind of humility is to be exalted, but that which the will embraces; it must be free of compulsion or sadness.[49]

Bernard cites Paul as an example of a man who joyfully accepted his humiliation and therefore received an infusion of God's grace (see 2 Cor. 12:9).

And do we not hear the startling music of the revelation of God here?

> Count it all joy, my brethren, when you meet various trials. . . . (Jas. 1:2)

Let's now look at some particular circumstances that we commonly encounter where there are opportunities to renounce pride and embrace humility, and to grow in true freedom and appropriate detachment.

Our Reputation

Francis acknowledges that having and preserving a good reputation is not necessarily an expression of sinful pride but is useful for social relationships and for avoiding scandal. There is then, oftentimes, an obligation to have and preserve a good reputation. On the other hand, self-will, vanity, a lack of trust in God, anger and hatred, can all hide themselves in efforts to "defend our reputation." Francis therefore advises us not to be "too ardent, precise, and demanding in regard to preserving our good name," if for no other reason than for pragmatic ones. "Those who try too carefully to maintain their reputation lose it entirely. By such sensitivity they become captious, quarrelsome, and unbearable and thus provoke the malice of detractors." Francis points out that, generally speaking, it is far better to ignore injuries or calumnies than to respond with "resentment, fighting, and revenge. Contempt for injuries causes them to vanish, whereas if we become angry, we seem to admit them . . . detraction hurts only those who are vexed by it. Excessive fear of losing our good name reveals great distrust in its foundation, which is really a good life."[50]

Francis says we should make reasonable efforts to refute lies that are being told about us, but if our efforts are not effective, we should simply go on with our lives trusting in God to care for us, continuing to humble ourselves. If He permits our reputation to be taken away from us it will either be "to give us a better one or to make us profit by holy humility, of which a single ounce is preferable to a thousand pounds of honor."[51]

He agrees with Saint Gregory the Great that if we are accused of a fault of which we are indeed guilty, we should admit it and humbly ask forgiveness. Gregory tells those who are falsely accused to "excuse yourself meekly and deny your guilt, for you owe respect to truth and to the edification of your neighbor. If they continue to accuse you after you have made your true and legitimate explanation, don't be disturbed and don't try to make them accept your explanation."[52]

> Let us always keep our eyes fixed on Jesus Christ crucified and go forward in his service with confidence and sincerity but with prudence and discretion. . . . By surrendering our reputation together with our soul into God's hands, we safeguard it in the best way possible.[53]

Not defending herself was a struggle for Thérèse of Lisieux and a significant step forward for her on her spiritual journey. On one occasion she tells us that someone was needed to help supervise a workman and the opportunity was offered to another sister and Thérèse. Thérèse, who would have loved to go, decided to move slowly to give the other sister a chance to respond first, out of charity. The superior saw Thérèse's slowness and interpreted it as a reluctance to do a chore and publicly criticized her. The whole community then, Thérèse supposed, interpreted her slowness as a manifestation of selfishness. She knew she shouldn't defend herself and this incident also helped her see more the "vanity" of human praise and blame.

> This incident prevents me from being vain when I am judged favorably because I say to myself: Since one can take my little acts of virtue for imperfections, one can also be mistaken in taking for virtue what is nothing but imperfection.[54]

She knew that only God can justly judge the human heart, as Paul explained concerning the imperfection of human judgment (cf. 1 Cor. 4: 3–4).

Our Health

We normally like to be and to appear healthy, strong, handsome or beautiful, young looking, and so on. And yet illness, old age, bodily defects of various kinds, genetic and acquired, sweep over the whole race. This is one of the reasons why the Resurrection of Jesus and our own promised resurrection are so important and give us so much hope and joy. We can respond to the distress of these bodily afflictions with pride, anger, rebellion, vanity, and deception, or we can respond with humility, meekness, and deeper trust in God—the choice is ours.

Francis advises that when evil befalls us we should try to remedy it in reasonable ways but "wait with resignation for the results it may please God to send." If God relieves us of the evil we should humbly give Him thanks; if He wills that we continue to endure the evils we should humbly give thanks and trust in the goodness of His purpose and the power of His providence. As regards illness, we should follow the advice of competent physicians, and desire to get well so we can serve God, but not refuse to remain ill if that would serve Him better. In the meantime, while we are sick and the outcome is not

known, we can very meaningfully offer our suffering in union with
the suffering of Jesus for the salvation of the world.

We recall Francis's advice in this regard.

> When you are sick offer up all your grief, pain, and weak-
> ness as a service to our Lord and beseech him to join
> them to the torments he suffered for you. Obey your
> physician; take your medicine, food, and other remedies
> out of love of God, remembering the gall he drank out of
> love of you. Desire to get well so that you may serve him,
> but do not refuse to lie ill so that thus too you may obey
> him and prepare for death, if that is his will, so that you
> may praise him and be happy with him forever.[55]

Appropriate detachment regarding our health also has to extend
to the very type of illness that God may permit us to experience.

> One man has a cancer in his arm and another on his
> face; the first has only the disease, while the other suf-
> fers contempt, disgrace, and abjection along with the
> disease. Hence I hold that we must not only love the
> disease, which is the duty of patience, but we must also
> embrace the abjection, and this is done by the virtue
> of humility.[56]

Francis though, as always, is remarkably balanced and attuned
to the nuance.

> If I should have some disagreeable infection in my face, I
> will try to have it cured, although not with an intention
> to forget the abjection I received from it.[57]

Teresa of Avila is amazingly insightful—and very witty—in her
comments about our tendencies to exaggerate little illnesses and use
them as excuses to pull back from prayer and service. She points out
that the more we pamper and comfort our bodies, the more pam-

pering and comfort we will think we need. In talking to her nuns she tries to get them to stop complaining about little indispositions which can be borne "on their feet." She tells, with some sarcasm, the story of how some nuns in her convent stop showing up for community prayer when they have a headache and stay away after it goes away so they don't get one again.

> Hardly does our head begin to ache than we stop going to choir, which won't kill us either. We stay away one day because our head ached, another because it was just now aching, and three more so that it won't ache again. . . . Oh, God help me, this complaining among nuns!. . . For if the devil begins to frighten us about losing our health, we shall never do anything.[58]

Teresa reassures her nuns that a really serious condition will make its presence clear enough. She points out how many married women are bearing "serious illnesses and heavy trials," but in order not to trouble their husbands dare not complain. She points out the incongruousness of nuns complaining more and looking for more comfort than married women living in the world. She urges them to "learn how to suffer a little for love of God without having everyone know about it!"[59] She challenges them even further by urging them to change their mindset and determine to "come to die for Christ, not to live comfortably for Christ."[60]

Hundreds of years earlier, Bernard observed that some of his fellow monks were more preoccupied with what they were going to eat than how to live. He points out that it is the wisdom of the world that teaches us to save our lives in this world; Christ teaches us to lose them in order to truly find them. We need to be clear what master and what wisdom we're following.

> But the man who complains: "This is bad for my eyes, that gives me headache, this affects my heart, that upsets

my stomach—he shows clearly who his master is . . . the wisdom of the flesh (Rom. 8:7), whereby a man either abandons himself to sensual indulgence or pays excessive attention to the body's health.[61]

Bernard quotes a telling passage from Scripture: "I loved wisdom more than health or beauty" (Wis. 7:10). Relevant words for our culture as well, which is almost exclusively focused on health and beauty—goods for this life only—and virtually ignores the health and beauty of the soul, which lasts forever!

Jesus brought this home to His disciples again and again in many different contexts.

> Do not labor for the food which perishes, but for the food which endures to eternal life, which the Son of man will give to you; for on him has God the Father set his seal. (Jn. 6:27)

Some of Bernard's observations, as Teresa's, are downright humorous. He describes a monk who was very focused on his food.

> "Beans," he says, "produce flatulency, cheese causes dyspepsia, milk gives me headache, water is bad for my heart, cabbages bring on melancholy, I feel choleric after onions, fish from the pond or from muddy water does not agree with my constitution." Are you not actually saying that food to your taste is not available in all the rivers, the fields, the gardens and the cellars?
>
> I earnestly request that you remember you are a monk, not a physician, and that you will be judged not on the quality of your constitution but on your profession.[62]

Teresa of Avila scarcely had a day in her adult life without some annoying illness. She regularly suffered from ringing in the ears, dizziness, nausea, and sometimes had flare-ups of other illnesses, so she very much had to practice what she preached. She makes the ironic, self-deprecating remark that the Lord permitted her to be sickly to give her a reason for looking after her comfort, which she would have done anyway!

Through the humor and sarcasm both Teresa and Bernard are making a very serious point: being overly concerned for our comfort and health is a serious obstacle to making progress on the spiritual journey. Teresa makes the observation that if she had waited to feel better she never would have prayed or served.

> If we do not determine once and for all to swallow death and the lack of health, we will never do anything. Strive not to fear them; abandon yourselves totally to God, come what may. So what if we die? If our body has mocked us so often, shouldn't we mock it at least once?[63]

She even found that oftentimes only when she would stop pampering herself or allowing herself to be pampered by others would her health improve.[64]

Bernard points out that overcoming these excessive fears and disordered desires leads to and preserves a genuine realm of freedom, true beauty, and strength for the soul.[65]

I must admit when I read these comments of Teresa and understood how she pressed on in prayer and service even though she hardly ever felt well, it opened my eyes to a whole new way of relating to the little indispositions that I occasionally have. Amen, Sister Teresa, so what if we die!

On the other hand, Teresa acknowledges that there are times when the sickness is a big enough factor that some adjustments in our way of life need to be made for a time: "The changes in the weather and the rotating of the bodily humors often have the result that without their fault souls cannot do what they desire but suffer in every way." In these circumstances we shouldn't force the soul to keep to the same routine, or things will get worse and the soul will get "smothered." If our discernment shows that this isn't a temptation from the devil, "the hour of prayer ought to be changed, and often this change will have to continue for some days." Also, doing exterior things like "works of charity and spiritual reading," may be helpful, "although at times it will not even be fit for these." Another method she suggests is to engage in some "holy conversations, provided they are truly so, or going to the country, as the confessor might counsel." She has confidence that we will learn from experience how to handle these situations and reminds us that "His yoke is easy and it is very helpful not to drag the soul along, as they say, but to lead it gently for the sake of its greater advantage."[66]

Detachment and humility, Teresa points out, always go together as "inseparable sisters."[67] As many of the saints point out, the virtues are inextricably linked, and working on one of them often brings about growth in others. As we grow in detachment and humility, we will soon find ourselves needing to grow also in patience and obedience.

Patience

Pride and lack of detachment can often manifest itself in impatience. Impatience is often rooted in pride, as it is an expectation that things should go the way I want them to go, that people should behave in a way that I consider responsible, that misfortunes and unforeseen circumstances shouldn't happen to me, and so on. Detaching ourselves from our own self-centered demands, opinions, judgments, and expectations is an important dimension of growth in humility.

Bernard speaks of the importance of patience:

> So I must put innocence first, and if I can join self-control to it I shall consider myself rich. . . . But if I can add a third to these—patience—I shall be a king.[68]

Francis de Sales points out that it is not uncommon for us to be selectively patient—patient with things we think it is reasonable to be patient with, or that we have a sympathy for, but impatient with the rest. He points out that our patience has to become a universal submission to the will of God, in humility.

> Do not limit your patience to this or that kind of injury and affliction. Extend it universally to all those God will send you or let happen to you.[69]

Francis points out that selective patience is often rooted in a disguised self-seeking.

> Some men wish to suffer no tribulations except those connected with honor, for example, or to be wounded or made a prisoner in war, persecuted for religion, or impoverished by some lawsuit they win. Such people do not love tribulation but the honor that goes with it. The truly patient man and true servant of God bears up equally under tribulations accompanied by ignominy and those that bring honor.[70]

It is easier to be criticized by a person of no repute; it is harder to be criticized by someone well regarded. It is easier to have a "noble" illness, harder to have an embarrassing one. It is easier to handle difficulty that is anticipated, harder to handle difficulty that is unforeseen. It is easier to handle interruptions when we're working on something less important, harder when it's something more important and difficult.

Francis also counsels us to be patient not only with the afflictions themselves but also with the annoying secondary aspects of them. True humility must involve detachment from our own impatient reactions, expectations, and judgments that are rooted in pride.

There is perhaps no saint that had a deeper grasp of the importance of patience than Catherine of Siena. While Teresa and Francis stress the link between humility and patience, Catherine stresses the link between charity and patience.

> The soul, therefore, who chooses to love me must also choose to suffer for me anything at all that I give her. Patience is not proved except in suffering, and patience is one with charity.[71]

Catherine, as we will recall, simply transmits what she hears the Father tell her. She points out that patience, and all the virtues, are tested and grow in our interactions with one another. Other people are the pathway to growth of virtue.

> You test the virtue of patience in yourself when your neighbors insult you. Your humility is tested by the proud, your faith by the unfaithful, your hope by the person who has no hope. Your justice is tried by the unjust, your compassion by the cruel, and your gentleness and kindness by the wrathful. Your neighbors are the channel through which all your virtues are tested and come to birth, just as the evil give birth to all their vices through their neighbors.[72]

When we respond in patient love, we release a power into the lives of those who are testing our virtue. Catherine speaks of the "power of charity and perfect patience in one who takes up the burden of the sins of the wicked and bears with their anger."[73]

Humility is rooted in self-knowledge and knowledge of God. Knowledge of our own sinfulness, the shortness and fragility of human life, the great mercy and goodness of God, and the length of eternity all deepen humility and enable us to practice patience. Patience is impossible without the humility that brings with it a deep knowledge of and confidence in the goodness and providence of God.

Catherine explains that even though nobody can avoid physical pain in this life because of the fragility of our bodies, the deeper pain is rooted in the opposition of our will to God's will. As our will comes into greater and greater conformity with God's will—one of the definitions of holiness used by many of the saints—the spiritual and psychological anguish of being in opposition to God subsides and the physical pain can be more easily endured, as all the virtues grow.

> This is why I told you that they suffer physically but not spiritually, because their sensual will—which afflicts and pains the spirit—is dead. Since they no longer have a selfish will, they no longer have this pain. So they bear everything with reverence, considering it a grace to suffer for me. And they want nothing but what I will . . . They pass through life joyfully, knowing themselves and untroubled by suffering.[74]

Catherine strikingly describes the freedom and joy that can come to those who are made perfect in detachment and humility, willing what God wills in complete trust.

> They may suffer at the hands of others, or from illness or poverty or the instability of the world. They may lose their children or other loved ones. All such things are thorns the earth produced because of sin. They endure them all, considering by the light of reason and holy faith that I am goodness itself and cannot will anything but good. And I send these things out of love, not hatred. . . . They learn that all suffering in this life is small with the smallness of time. Time is no more than the point of a needle, and when time is over, so is suffering—so you see how small it is. Therefore they endure it patiently.[75]

I waited patiently for the Lord; he inclined to me
    and heard my cry. (Ps. 40:1)

Obedience

Many of the saints talk about the link between obedience, patience, humility, and love. Catherine states this quite bluntly.

> The sign that you have this virtue [obedience] is patience, and impatience is the sign that you do not have it.[76]

Even though we distinguish the various virtues, Catherine points out that they really exist together and are linked to each other.

> Love never stands alone, but has as her companions all the true solid virtues, because all the virtues have life from charity's love. . . . And among love's companions is patience, the very marrow of love and the clear sign of whether the soul is in grace and is loving in truth or not. This is why charity, the mother, has given obedience patience as a sister and has so joined the two together that the one can never be lost without the other. Either you have both or you have neither.
>
> Obedience has a wet nurse, true humility, and the soul is as obedient as she is humble, and as humble as she is obedient.[77]

Just as with poverty and chastity, obedience in the life of a layperson is different than for those who take the vow of obedience in a religious order or as a priest, yet it is nonetheless essential for making progress on the spiritual journey. Francis de Sales makes clear that the essence of holiness is to be completely ordered towards love—love of God and neighbor, thereby being fully conformed to God's will. He also makes clear that detachment, particularly in the areas of poverty, chastity, and obedience, are essential means for attaining to such love and union.

Francis also distinguishes between necessary obedience and voluntary obedience. Necessary obedience is what we owe to those who are in legitimate authority over us in both state and church as well as in the family. Francis makes clear that in God's plan, for the good of the family, of society, and of the Church, legitimate authority must be respected and appropriately obeyed. It's not an absolute obedience, however—we can never obey an order to do something sinful, for example. Besides this necessary obedience, Francis also advises us, as a way of growing in perfect obedience, to follow the advice of our authorities—even in their desires and inclinations, and even when they have not given us an order—"as far as charity and prudence will permit."[78]

In our current culture, where sensitivity to the abuse of authority has necessarily had to increase, Francis's qualifications on the limits of obedience are important to note. We should never obey a request to do something that is sinful and should be alert to possible violations of charity and prudence.[79]

The spirit in which we obey is also important:

> In short, obey meekly and without arguing, quickly and without delay, cheerfully and without complaining. Above all obey lovingly out of love of him who for love of us "made himself obedient unto death, even death on a cross" (Phil. 2:8).[80]

Francis also has some surprising advice about how to train ourselves for such obedience to our superiors, namely, in our relations with one another. He advises us that in order to learn how to obey our superiors with ease, one must "adapt . . . easily to the will of your equals by giving in to their opinions in what is not sinful and by not being contentious or obstinate." And for those whom we may have authority over he advises us to "accommodate yourself cheerfully to your inferiors' wishes as far as reason permits and do not exercise imperious authority over them so long as they are good."[81]

Bernard agrees.

> It counts for little, however, that you are submissive to God, unless you be submissive to every human creature

for God's sake (1 Pet. 2:3), whether it be the abbot as first superior or to the other officers appointed by him. I go still further and say: be subject to your equals and inferiors. "It is fitting," said Christ, "that we should in this way do all that righteousness demands" (Mt. 3:15. If you seek an unblemished righteousness, take an interest in the man of little account, defer to those of lesser rank, be of service to the young.[82]

With an eagle eye for self-delusion in the spiritual life, Francis reminds us that "it is an illusion for us to think that if only we were members of some religious community we would obey readily although we are slow and stubborn in obeying those God has placed over us."[83]

Francis also talks about the possibility of voluntarily entering into a relationship of obedience that is not required of us as a way of growing in the virtue. He suggests this possibility in relationship to our confessor or spiritual director. The possibility of asking our confessor or spiritual director to order us to do those things helpful for our growth in Christ, both as a help in doing them and also as a way of increasing their value, will give us new opportunities to exercise obedience as well. He gives as an example that of Teresa of Avila who, in addition to the obedience she owed necessarily to her religious order superiors, also made a vow of obedience to one of her confessors.

I know that in my own life at a certain point I felt that I should be spending more time in prayer each day. I had been feeling this for quite a while—several years—but would make only sporadic efforts to do something about it. One day I was telling my spiritual director about this, and he totally surprised me by ordering me to increase my prayer time to the amount that I had felt called to do, but wasn't doing. It wasn't his normal style, but the Spirit must have inspired him to know that this was the right thing to do in the situation. It was just what I needed. While I had not made a formal vow of obedience in relationship to this priest, I assumed that I would obey whatever he asked me to do. When he actually asked me to obey his directive to pray more—which I truly believed the Lord was asking me to do—I was both shocked and pleased. It was what I knew I should be doing. It gave me the extra motivation and impetus to actually increase my prayer time, and I'm very grateful.

Francis summarizes the areas to which our obedience to God's will extends.[84] In first place, is obedience to God's will as expressed in the commandments, docility to basic morality, to basic Christian life. In second place, is obedience to the will of God as expressed in the "evangelical counsels," which we have just been considering: poverty, chastity, and obedience, as means to the freedom necessary to love God and neighbor more completely. In third place, Francis mentions obedience to the will of God as manifested in inspirations of God, which we will consider in a later chapter. In fourth place, Francis mentions obedience to the will of God expressed in the circumstances, afflictions, and trials that God allows to be in our lives.

Growing in freedom from our disordered attachments brings about a growth in virtue that is nothing else, at root, than a growth in love. It is time now to consider explicitly how the whole spiritual journey is essentially a growth in love.

Chapter Eleven

GROWING IN LOVE

W<small>HAT THE SPIRITUAL JOURNEY IS ALL ABOUT</small> is growing in love, fulfilling the great commandment to love God and our neighbor completely. The New Testament, speaking to already committed Christians, frequently encourages continued growth in that holiness that is love.

> Beloved, if God so loved us, we also ought to love one another. No man has ever seen God; if we love one another, God abides in us and his love is perfected in us. (1 Jn. 4:11–12)

The Lord puts this love into our hearts as we grow in relationship with Him.

> He has put into my heart a marvelous love
> for the faithful ones who dwell in his land. (Ps. 16:3)[1]

Bernard describes the dynamic growth in love which is the purpose of the spiritual journey:

> The capacity of any man's soul is judged by the amount of love he possesses; hence he who loves much is great, he

who loves little is small, he who has no love is nothing, as Paul said: "If I have not love, I am nothing" (1 Cor. 13:2). But if he begins to acquire some love however, if he tries at least to love those who love him (Lk. 6:32), and salutes the brethren and others who salute him (Mt. 5:4&), I may no longer describe him as nothing because some love must be present in the give and take of social life (Phil. 4:15). In the words of the Lord however, what more is he doing than others (Mt. 5:47)? When I discover a love as mediocre as this, I cannot call such a man noble or great: he is obviously narrow minded and mean.[2]

Bernard brings us right into the heart of Jesus' challenge to us in the Sermon on the Mount: to extend the boundaries of our love and our hearts beyond the natural affections of family and friends. He gives us a picture of what this expanded heart will look like and encourages us as to its possibility.

But if his love expands and continues to advance till it outgrows these narrow, servile confines, and finds itself in the open ranges where love is freely given in full liberty of spirit; when from the generous bounty of his goodwill he strives to reach out to all his neighbors, loving each of them as himself (Mt. 19:19), surely one may no longer query, "What more are you doing than others?"[3]

Bernard continues to fill in the picture as he describes the remarkable identification of the soul with God that is characteristic of the spiritual marriage.

Indeed he has made himself vast. His heart is filled with a love that embraces everybody, even those to whom it is not tied by the inseparable bonds of family relationship; a love that is not allured by any hope of personal gain, that possesses nothing it is obliged to restore, that bears no burden of debt whatever, apart from that one of which it is said: "Owe no one anything, except to love

one another" (Rom. 13:8). Progressing further still . . .
instead of shutting off your affections from your enemies
(1 Jn. 3:17), you will do good to those who hate you,
you will pray for those who persecute and slander you
(Mt. 5:44), you will strive to be peaceful even with those
who hate peace (Ps. 119:7). Then the width, height and
beauty of your soul will be the width, height and beauty
of heaven itself.[4]

The Three Stages of Growth in Love

Catherine of Siena similarly describes the stages of the spiritual
journey in terms of a progressive purification and deepening of
love. She uses the image of Christ's body hanging on the Cross as an
image of the spiritual journey.[5]

At the first stage, where our affections begin to undergo conversion and turn away from sin, we embrace His feet. This is the
purgative stage, where purification is the primary note and where
our love still may be quite self-centered and perhaps fear-based.
Catherine speaks of the "slavish fear" present in this stage, in contrast with the filial fear of the Lord which is the gift of the Holy
Spirit and the "beginning of wisdom."[6] A major motivation for our
conversion at this stage is to save ourselves, to avoid the pain in
this life of living in sin, and to avoid eternal damnation. This is a
great place to start, and a place we should always keep in mind as
we progress.

Bernard also uses the image of Christ's feet in connection with
repentance and conversion. Repentance for sin at the feet of Christ
is where the journey must begin. Bernard suggests that the bride in
the Song of Songs is only able to aspire to the lover's kiss because
she "wept bitterly [Lk. 22:62], she sighed deeply from her heart, she
sobbed with a repentance that shook her very being, till the evil that
inflamed her passions was cleansed away" (cf. Song 1:2, 5) The "kiss
of the mouth" spoken of in the Song of Songs is not to be lightly
sought or prematurely expected.

> They may not rashly aspire to the lips of a most benign
> Bridegroom, but let them prostrate with me in fear at the
> feet of a most severe Lord. . . .
>
> It is up to you, wretched sinner, to humble your-
> self as this happy penitent did so that you may be rid of
> your wretchedness. Prostrate yourself on the ground, take
> hold of his feet, soothe them with kisses, sprinkle them
> with your tears and so wash not them but yourself.[7]

The second stage of the spiritual journey—where we grasp
something more of Christ's love and begin to understand important
truths about God and ourselves—is symbolized by the wounded
side of Christ. This is the illuminative stage, where growth in virtue
and understanding is the dominant note, although purification still
continues. Our love at this stage is that of a servant or a mercenary.
We love the Lord and are willing to serve Him, but very much
expect a reward both now and in eternity; there is a continuing self-
centeredness to our love.

Bernard makes a point similar to Catherine's but uses a slightly
different image, that of kissing the hands of Christ, as an essential
part of ascension to the mouth. Solid virtue must be established on
the way to the fullness of union, symbolized by moving on to the
kiss of the mouth.

> Though you have made a beginning by kissing the feet,
> you may not presume to rise at once by impulse to the kiss
> of the mouth; there is a step to be surmounted in between,
> an intervening kiss on the hand. . . . I must confess that I
> am not entirely satisfied with the first grace by which I am
> enabled to repent of my sins: I must have the second as
> well, and so bear fruits that befit repentance (Lk. 3:8), that
> I may not return like the dog to its vomit (Prov. 26:11).[8]

Bernard traces the same path that Catherine does from "slavish
fear," which may be characteristic of the first stage, to a growth in

virtue and love characteristic of the second stage, which is, neverthe-less, imperfect and "mercenary."

> Fear is the lot of a slave, unless he is freed by love. . . .
> Love is a great reality: but there are degrees to it. . . . I
> suspect the love which seems to be founded on some
> hope of gain. It is weak, for if the hope is removed it may
> be extinguished, or at least diminished. It is not pure, as
> it desires some return.[9]

Many people, Bernard points out, are "with" the Lord, but few have the Lord's interests primarily at heart.

> Not all those whom you see today waiting on the Bride
> and hanging around her, as the expression is, are friends
> of the bridegroom (Jn. 3:29). There are very few of them
> among all her lovers (Lam. 1:2) who are not concerned
> with their own interests (1 Cor. 13:5). It is gifts that they
> love . . .[10]

Francis de Sales tells us that normally a slow cure is the best cure, and in this Bernard agrees. To try to rush forward to full union without reconstructing the depths of the soul is to court disaster. The "illuminative stage" of the journey is necessary.

> I do not wish to be suddenly on the heights, my desire
> is to advance by degrees. The impudence of the sinner
> displeases God as much as the modesty of the penitent
> gives him pleasure. You will please him more readily if
> you live within the limits proper to you, and do not set
> your sights at things beyond you (Sir. 3:22). It is a long
> and formidable leap from the foot to the mouth, a man-
> ner of approach that is not commendable. Consider for
> a moment: still tarnished as you are with the dust of sin,
> would you dare touch those sacred lips? Yesterday you
> were lifted from the mud, today you wish to encounter
> the glory of his face? No, his hand must be our guide to

that end. First it must cleanse your stains, then it must raise you up. How raise you? By giving you the grace to dare to aspire. . . . First of all you must glorify him because he has forgiven your sins, secondly because he has adorned you with virtues.[11]

Thus Bernard makes clear that the "kiss of the mouth" is "reserved for the pure of heart."[12]

The third stage is symbolized by the mouth of Christ. This is the unitive stage, where profound, abiding union with Christ is established. Our love has grown and become purified to that of a truly loving, faithful son or daughter, or friend, or spouse. Catherine tends to favor the description of this highest stage of union and love as being "filial," meaning that of a son or daughter. Bernard favors the image of the bride or bridegroom to describe this stage,[13] or sometimes, "close, dear friend."[14]

In either case their description of the purity of this love, and its contrast with the "mercenary" love of the second stage, is similar. We love the Lord—and, as we will see, others as well—with a purified, unselfish love that truly cares for the well-being and interests of the other, irrespective of our own selves. The focus now is not on what we are getting from the relationship but on what we can give, by way of profound filial love, faithful friendship, and spousal union. Our focus is on the Other and how to please Him.[15]

Bernard speaks of the unitive or third stage, this way:

> Once you have had this twofold experience of God's benevolence in these two kisses, you need no longer feel abashed in aspiring to a holier intimacy. Growth in grace brings expansion of confidence. You will love with greater ardor, and knock on the door with greater assurance, in order to gain what you perceive to be still wanting to you. "The one who knocks will always have the door opened to him" (Lk. 11:10). It is my belief that to a person so disposed, God will not refuse that most intimate kiss of all, a mystery of supreme generosity and ineffable sweetness.[16]

Bernard further describes the love present in the third stage, or unitive way:

> Pure love has no self-interest. Pure love does not gain strength through expectation, nor is it weakened by distrust. This is the love of the bride, for this is the bride—with all that means. Love is the being and the hope of a bride. She is full of it, and the bridegroom is contented with it. He asks nothing else, and she has nothing else to give. This is why he is the bridegroom and she the bride; this love is the property only of the couple. No one else can share it, not even a son.[17]

Since his major work is a commentary on the Song of Songs, Bernard offers many descriptions of the nature of this union.

> Although the creature loves less, being a lesser being, yet if it loves with its whole heart nothing is lacking, for it has given all. Such love, as I have said, is marriage, for a soul cannot love like this and not be beloved; complete and perfect marriage consists in the exchange of love. . . . Happy the soul who has been permitted to experience the embrace of such bliss! For it is nothing other than love, holy and chaste, full of sweetness and delight, love utterly serene and true, mutual and deep, which joins two beings, not in one flesh, but in one spirit, making them no longer two but one. As Paul says: "He who is united to God is one spirit with him" (1 Cor. 6:17).[18]

Sometimes Bernard describes the person at this stage as "wise."

> Give me a man who loves God before all things and with his whole being, self and neighbor in proportion to their love of God, the enemy as one who perhaps some day will love, his physical parents very deeply because of the natural bond, but his spiritual guides more generously because of grace. In like manner let him deal with the other things of God too with an ordered love, disregard-

ing the earth, esteeming heaven, using this world as if
not using it (Cor. 7:31), and discriminating between the
things used and those enjoyed with an intimate savoring
in his mind. Let him pay but passing attention to things
that pass, as existing need demands. Let him embrace
eternal things with an eternal desire. Give me such a man,
I repeat, and I shall boldly proclaim him wise, because he
appreciates things for what they truly are, because he can
truthfully and confidently boast and say: "he set love in
order in me" (Song 2:4). "But where is he, and when shall
these be? In tears I ask" (Phil. 3:18).[19]

Neither Bernard nor Catherine intends that these divisions
be understood as totally exclusive of one another. We recall what
Catherine says: "These are three stages for which many have the
capacity, and all three can be present in one and the same person."[20]
Teresa of Avila also didn't intend her seven-stage division of the
spiritual journey to be airtight; she acknowledges that aspects of
several different mansions or stages can be present in one person
at the same time. Each of the saints offers these "road maps" of the
soul's journey to God as broad but very helpful indicators that help
us to know the direction and the specific ways in which the Spirit is
moving us, so that we can better understand and cooperate with the
process of transformation.

Love of Neighbor

We will have occasion in a later chapter to consider in more detail
additional means that God uses to purify our love for Him, but now
we need to look at the essential link between love of God and love
of neighbor, so strongly emphasized by all the saints. Basing their
advice on Scripture as they do, it is easy to understand the central
role they give to love of neighbor.

We know that we have passed out of death into life,
because we love the brethren. He who does not love

remains in death. Any one who hates his brother is a murderer, and you know that no murderer has eternal life abiding in him. (1 Jn. 3:14–15)

If any one says, "I love God," and hates his brother, he is a liar, for he who does not love his brother whom he has seen, cannot love God whom he has not seen. And this commandment we have from him, that he who loves God should love his brother also. (1 Jn. 4:20–21)

A result of the "merciful unction of the Holy Spirit" is the restoration of a "truly human condition," characterized by gentleness, compassion, and brotherly love—marks of true holiness.[21]

The purification of our lives that comes through growing in holiness makes us more capable of sincerely loving others. The Scriptures make this clear time and time again.

Having purified your souls by your obedience to the truth for a sincere love of the brethren, love one another earnestly from the heart. (1 Pet. 1:22–23)

Teresa of Avila, ever the spiritual mother, reminds us:

"Let us understand my daughters, that true perfection consists in love of God and neighbor; the more perfectly we keep these two commandments the more perfect we will be. . . . This mutual love is so important that I would never want it to be forgotten."[22]

And she adds:

"For perfection as well as its reward does not consist in spiritual delights but in greater love and in deeds done with greater justice and truth."[23]

The Father tells Catherine that the more the soul grows in love for God, the more the soul will also grow in love for its neighbor.

Some of the specific ways of loving our neighbor that Catherine lists are intercessory prayer, good example, counsel, advice, and spiritual and material help.[24]

Bernard teaches that love is not just a feeling, although feelings of love are good, but it must be demonstrated by action. He points out that when Jesus tells us to love—whether it's to love our enemies, or to love Him—He tells us specific actions that constitute love.

> When the Lord said: "Love your enemies," he referred right afterwards to actions; "Do good to those who hate you" (Lk. 6:27). Scripture also says: "If your enemy is hungry feed him; if he is thirsty, give him drink (Rom. 12:20)." Here you have a question of actions, not of feeling . . . .. "If you love me keep my words" (Jn. 14:15) . . ..
> It would have been superfluous for him to warn us to act if love were but a matter of feeling.[25]

The Father also communicates to Catherine that He purposefully created the human race so that no one would be self-sufficient. We were made to need one another, not just for material things but for spiritual things as well.

> For I could well have supplied each of you with all your needs, both spiritual and material. But I wanted to make you dependent on one another so that each of you would be my minister, dispensing the graces and gifts you have received from me. . . . I have made you my ministers, setting you in different positions and in different ranks to exercise the virtue of charity. . . . All I want is love. . . . If you are bound by this love you will do everything you can to be of service wherever you are.[26]

This passage could have been taken right out of the documents of Vatican II, which so inspiringly give a vision of the life of the Church involving the activity of all the baptized, using the gifts and graces God has given to each to build up the Body of the Church and to reveal Christ to the world.[27]

Bernard, as we know, was very aware of the link between love and action. He often speaks of the necessity of periodically leaving his preferred "contemplation" to meet the needs of others.

> In spite of her longing for the repose of contemplation she is burdened with the task of preaching; and despite her desire to bask in the Bridegroom's presence she is entrusted with the cares of begetting and rearing children. . . . We learn from this that only too often we must interrupt the sweet kisses to feed the needy with the milk of doctrine. No one must live for himself but all must live for him who died for all (2 Cor. 5:15).[28]

Gratuitous Love

Since all our love for God is ultimately a response to His love for us, we can never love Him in the same way He loves us, namely, gratuitously. Since we are fundamentally dependent on God and in His debt for our creation and redemption, our love is always owed to Him, a duty, a response to His love. But we can love our *neighbor* in the same way that He loves us, gratuitously—not because of anything the neighbor has done for us or because of anything that we owe him, but simply because love has been freely given to us. We thereby greatly please the Father. God the Father tells Catherine:

> This is why I have put you among your neighbors: so that you can do for them what you cannot do for me—that is, love them without any concern for thanks and without looking for any profit for yourself. And whatever you do for them I will consider done for me.[29]

Virtue for Catherine, as for all the saints, is something that is intrinsically bound up with our relationships with our neighbors. And just as our love of God starts out in a mixture of motivations and needs to be purified, so also does our love for neighbor. The "selfish-sensuality" that Catherine identifies as a primary manifestation of sin in our lives affects our relationship with God, and this in turn also affects our relationship with our neighbor. And of course, by neighbor, Catherine means everyone who intersects with our lives. Love for neighbor must then be purified, grow, and deepen.

How to Tell If Our Love Is Selfish

Catherine indicates that our tendency to use people for our own selfish purposes and be possessive in our relationships needs to be brought out into the light. Sometimes, God permits selfish relationships to be established in order to manifest to us their imperfection and draw us on to deeper and purer love. Catherine identifies certain indicators in our responses to others that can tell us when our relationships need to be purified.

> Do you know how you can tell when your spiritual love is not perfect? If you are distressed when it seems that those you love are not returning your love or not loving you as much as you think you love them. Or if you are distressed when it seems to you that you are being deprived of their company or comfort, or that they love someone else more than you. . . . All this comes of the failure to dig out every bit of the root of spiritual selfishness. This is why I often permit you to form such a love, so that you may come through it to know yourself and your imperfection in the way I have described.[30]

As the Lord permits us to see our selfishness in relationships, we have the opportunity to resolve to renounce such selfishness, asking God's help to do so. Seeing our sin becomes an opportunity to renounce it and embrace more fully the will and love of God for our life and relationships.

Thérèse tells us about how she was once attracted to a relationship that was "too ardent." God protected her by making her love go unreciprocated.

My heart, sensitive and affectionate as it was, would have easily surrendered had it found a heart capable of understanding it. I tried to make friends with little girls my own age, and especially with two of them. I loved them and they, in their turn, loved me insofar as they were *capable*. But alas! How *narrow* and *flighty* is the heart of creatures! Soon I saw my love was misunderstood. . . . I felt this and I did not *beg* for an affection that was refused. . . . How can I thank Jesus for making me find *"only bitterness in earth's* friendships" With a heart such as mine, I would have allowed myself to be taken and my wings to be clipped, and then how would I have been able to "*fly and be at rest?*" (Ps. 54:7). How can a heart given over to the affection of creatures be intimately united with God? I feel this is not possible. Without having drunk the poisoned cup of a too ardent love of creatures, I *feel* I cannot be mistaken. I have seen so many souls, seduced by this *false light*, fly like poor moths and burn their wings, and then return to the real and gentle light of *Love*, that gives them new wings which are more brilliant and delicate, so that they can fly toward Jesus, that Divine Fire "which burns without consuming" [John of the Cross, *The Living Flame of Love*, 2:2–3]. Ah! I feel it! Jesus knew I was too feeble to be exposed to temptation. . . . I encountered only bitterness where stronger souls met with joy, and they detached themselves from it through fidelity. I have no merit at all, then, in not having given myself up to the love of creatures. I was preserved from it only through God's mercy![31]

Francis de Sales goes into helpful—and sometimes amusing—detail in helping us to identify this possessive, selfish love. Francis talks about the superficiality of relationships based primarily on sensual attraction.

Listen to how most girls, women, and young men talk. They do not hesitate to say that so and so is a very accomplished gentleman and has many fine qualities. He is a

good dancer, plays all sorts of games well, dresses fashion-
ably, sings delightfully, chats pleasantly, and makes a fine
appearance. . . . All such things concern the senses and
therefore friendships proceeding from them are termed
sensual, vain, and frivolous and deserve to be called folly
rather than friendship. Ordinarily such are the friendships
of young people when based on a fine moustache or head
of hair, smiling glances, fine clothes, superior attitudes,
and idle talk. . . . Such friendships are only passing things
and melt away like snow in the sun.[32]

Francis points out that such flirtatious relationships—he calls
them "fond loves"—even when they start off with no intention
of ending in sexual immorality, often lead there. He states that
even though these relationships may go on for years, satisfied with
"indulging in the pleasure of wishes, desires, sighs, love taps, and
similar folly and vanity,"[33] they often in the end degenerate into
outright immorality. Even though the intention may be to keep the
relationship on the level of "flirting," Francis points out that this is
nonetheless a dangerous path.

> You think that you will take in only a spark but you will
> be amazed to see that in a moment it has seized your
> whole heart and reduced your resolutions to ashes and
> your reputation to smoke.[34]

One thinks of the good advice that Paul gives in this regard.

> But immorality and all impurity or covetousness must
> not even be named among you, as is fitting among saints.
> Let there be no filthiness, nor silly talk, nor levity, which
> are not fitting; but instead let there be thanksgiving.
> (Eph. 5:3–4)

Bernard has his own incisive remarks on the dangers of too-inti-
mate a companionship between members of the opposite sex who
aren't married to each other.

To be always in a woman's company without having carnal knowledge of her—is this not a greater miracle than
raising the dead? You cannot perform the lesser feat; so
do you expect me to believe that you can do the greater?
Every day your side touches the girl's side at table, your
bed touches hers in your room, your eyes meet hers in
conversation, your hands meet hers at work—do you
expect to be thought chaste? It may be that you are, but
I have my suspicions.[35]

The Value of Godly Friendships

Even though there are dangers in relationships Francis and
Bernard are strongly of the opinion that godly friendships are
important for the spiritual journey. One of the very first counsels
Francis gives to those setting out on the journey is to find a spiritual
friend as a help and a guide.

Do you seriously wish to travel the road to devotion? If
so, look for a good man to guide and lead you. This is the
most important of all words of advice.[36]

While Francis strongly recommends the value of having the
friendship of a spiritual director, he knows this isn't always possible
and acknowledges how hard it is to find one. Besides the great value
of having a spiritual director Francis also acknowledges the great
value of spiritual friendship in the Christian life.

He quotes the beautiful lines from the Book of Sirach to this
effect.

A faithful friend is a sturdy shelter;
    he that has found one has found a treasure.
There is nothing so precious as a faithful friend,
    and no scales can measure his excellence.
A faithful friend is an elixir of life;
    and those who fear the Lord will find him.
Whoever fears the Lord directs his friendship aright,
    for as he is, so is his neighbor also. (Sir. 6:14–17)

Bernard also strongly emphasizes the need to seek out help from reliable spiritual guides. Speaking sadly of those who "begin in the Spirit but end in the flesh (Gal. 3:3)," disastrously stepping off the sound path, he says:

> Let this be a warning to those who are not afraid to enter the paths of life without anyone to guide and teach them, but act as their own pupils as well as their own teachers in the spiritual life. Nor are they satisfied with this; they even collect disciples, the blind leading the blind. How many have we seen wander from the right path, to their great peril, as a result of this? For their ignorance of the wiles and tricks of Satan bring it about that those who began in the spirit finish in the flesh. They are led seriously astray and fall damnably.[37]

Because friendship so affects the depths of our being, Francis advises us to be careful in our choices. Since "friendship is mutual love," it should be formed only with those who can share love for Christ and the life of virtue. Such friendship then "will be excellent because it comes from God, excellent because it leads to God, excellent because its bond will endure eternally in God."[38]

Francis teaches that such friendship doesn't take away from the universal charity that we should have for everyone, nor does it mean that we should neglect our relationships with parents, relatives, neighbors, coworkers, or pre-existing ties.

Francis also directly addresses the warnings against "particular friendships" that were so commonly given in spiritual writing at that time, primarily addressed to those in religious life. Francis allows that in dedicated religious communities there may not be a need for such particular friendships as the bond among all the members of the community is the way friendship should be expressed. "Particular friendships" in these situations can be incompatible with the form of community life one is committed to and can lead to "partiality" and possessiveness. Yet Francis insists that this is clearly not the case for people living their life in the world.

> For those who live in the world and desire to embrace true virtue it is necessary to unite together in holy, sacred friendship. By this means they encourage, assist, and lead one another to perform good deeds. Men walking on level ground do not have to lend one another a hand, while those who are on a rugged, slippery road hold on to one another in order to walk more safely. So also members of religious orders have no need for particular friendships, whereas people in the world need them to keep safe and assist one another in the many dangerous places they must pass through.[39]

Francis points out how Jesus Himself had particularly close friendships with John, Martha, Mary, and Lazarus. The apostle Paul shared a deep bond with Timothy and others of his close associates. Francis also cites the close friendship shared between Saint Gregory Nazianzen and Saint Basil. He quotes the words of Gregory:

> It seemed that in us there was only a single soul dwelling in two bodies. Although we do not believe those who say that all things are in all things, yet of us you can believe that we, were both together in each of us and that each was in the other. We had each of us only one purpose, to cultivate virtue and to adapt all the purposes of our life to our future hopes, in this way leaving mortal earth before we died in it.[40]

Francis goes on to cite the many holy friendships the saints have had throughout history which were not an obstacle to their growth in union with God, but a help. He also points out that Saint Thomas Aquinas considered true friendship a virtue. Francis concludes:

Hence perfection consists not in having no friendships, but in having only those which are good, holy, and sacred.[41]

Bernard of Clairvaux has provided us with one of the most remarkable testimonies to the power of Christian friendship in the eulogy he gave for his brother Gerard. Gerard was Bernard's blood brother as well as a monk in the same monastery. He took care of many of the administrative responsibilities of the monastery in order to free Bernard for prayer and preaching. Bernard felt Gerard's loss profoundly.

> Both of us were so happy in each other's company, sharing the same experiences, talking together about them; now my share of these delights has ceased and you have passed on, you have traded them for an immense reward. . . he who shouldered every burden that I might be free. . . . It was only right that I should depend entirely on him, he was all in all to me. . . . I could not but feel secure with a man who enabled me to enjoy the delights of divine love, to preach with greater facility, to pray without anxiety . . . through you, my dear brother, I enjoyed a peaceful mind and a welcome peace; my preaching was more effective, my prayer more fruitful, my study more regular, my love more fervent. . . . O, if I could only die at once and follow you!. . . Flow on, flow on, my tears, so long on the point of brimming over; flow on, for he who dammed up your exit is here no longer.[42]

Bernard was well aware of the spiritual teaching that warned against "particular friendships" as well as the teaching that frowned on the show of emotion or passion, and specifically addressed it.

> My soul cleaved to his. We were of one mind, and it was this, not blood relationship, that joined us as one. . . . I have made public the depth of my affliction, I make no attempt

to deny it. Will you say then that this is carnal? That it is human, yes, since I am a man. . . . I am certainly not insensible to pain. . . . I feel it, the wound is deep. . . . It is but human and necessary that we respond to our friends with feeling: that we be happy in their company, disappointed in their absence. . . . My deepest wound is in the ardor of my love for you. And let no one embarrass me by telling me I am wrong in yielding to this feeling, when the kind-hearted Samuel poured out the love of his heart for a reprobate king, and David for his parricidal son, without injury to their faith, without offending the judgment of God. . . . At the tomb of Lazarus Christ neither rebuked those who wept nor forbade them to weep, rather he wept with those who wept. The Scripture says: "And Jesus wept" (Jn. 11:35). These tears were witnesses to his human kindness, not signs that he lacked trust. . . . In the same way, our weeping is not a sign of a lack of faith, it indicates the human condition. . . . You gave me Gerard, you took him away; and if his removal makes me sad, I do not forget that he was given to me, and offer thanks for my good fortune in having had him. . . . You entrusted Gerard to us, you have claimed him back; you have but taken what was yours. These tears prevent me speaking further; impose a limit on them O Lord, bring them to an end.[43]

Saint Augustine, struggling with the Greek philosophical ideal of not feeling or showing emotion (*apatheia*), which had an influence on Christian spirituality, had to break through this to defend the proper role of affection, emotion, and passion in Christian life. He found his answer in the presence of deep emotions in the lives of Jesus and the apostles.

If these emotions and affections, which come from love of the good and from holy charity, are to be called vices, then let us allow that real vices should be called virtues. But since, when they are exhibited in the proper circumstances, these affections are the consequences of right reason, who would then dare to say that they are unwholesome or vicious passions. Hence, when the Lord Himself deigned to live a human life in the form of a servant, though having no sin, He displayed these emotions. . . . For human emotion was not feigned in Him Who truly had the body of a man and the mind of a man. . . . Moreover if *apatheia* is to be defined as a condition such that the mind cannot be touched by any emotion whatsoever, who would not judge such insensitivity to be the worst of all vices? It can, therefore, be said without absurdity that our perfect blessedness which is to come will be free from the pangs of fear and from any kind of grief; but who save one wholly estranged from the truth would say that there will be no love and no gladness there? Moreover, if *apatheia* is a condition such that there is no fear to terrify and no pain to torment, then it is a condition to be avoided in this life if we wish to live rightly, that is, according to God.[44]

The Father communicates to Catherine some deep insight into the enduring love in true Christian friendship, showing how love that begins in this life, in Christ, doesn't lessen but grows more intense in the life of heaven. Love, in Christ, then, can truly be eternal. We have considered these texts (in chapter 4) previously in the context of heaven; now let us consider them in the context of love. In speaking of the life of the blessed in heaven the Father tells Catherine,

And though they are all joined in the bond of charity, they know a special kind of sharing with those whom they loved most closely with a special love in the world, a love through which they grew in grace and virtue. They helped each other proclaim the glory and praise of my name in themselves and in their neighbors. So now in everlasting life they have not lost that love; no, they still love and share with each other even more closely and fully, adding their love to the good of all.[45]

Not only does the love of the blessed in heaven that began on earth increase, but their love for those they loved on earth increases also.

> Their desires are a continual cry to me for the salvation of others, for they finished their lives loving their neighbors, and they did not leave that love behind but brought it with them when they passed through that gate which is my only-begotten Son. So you see that in whatever bond of love they finish their lives, that bond is theirs forever and lasts eternally. . . . What these blessed ones want is to see me honored in you who are still on the way, pilgrims running ever nearer your end in death. Because they seek my honor they desire your salvation, and so they are constantly praying to me for you. I do my part to fulfill their desire provided only that you do not foolishly resist my mercy.[46]

Not only is there a continuing mutual love between the blessed in heaven and Christians on earth, but Bernard tells us that there is also love between angels and men, since men are destined to fill in the ranks of the fallen angels!

> When he uses the ministry of angels for the salvation of the human race, is it not so that the angels may be loved by men? For it is clear that men are loved by the angels because they are not unaware that the losses in their ranks will be made up by men. Indeed, it would not be right that the kingdom of charity, which men and angels are to rule together, should be governed by other laws than those of mutual love and pure affection for each other and for God.[47]

Bernard speaks of the angels and blessed in heaven continuing to take a very strong concern for what happens to those of us who are still on our earthly pilgrimage.

> Would they leave us in the midst of the flames and great waters which they have passed through, without taking the trouble to stretch out a hand to us, their children? Surely not. . . . Your guardians are the holy angels, your watchmen are the spirits and souls of the righteous (Dan. 3:86). . . . And they each have their special care for you: the saints because they will not themselves be made perfect without you; the angels because without you their full number cannot be restored. . . . Thus all things await their consummation from you, some the completion of their numbers, others the fulfillment of their desires.[48]

Bernard tells us that the love of the saints and angels in heaven for those on earth "overflow with kindness. . . . Far from begrudging us the glory they enjoy, they want us to share it . . . sedulously watching over us and our concerns."[49]

The deepest desire of the human heart is to find love and relationships that last forever. Popular love songs throughout the centuries speak of the dream of "forever" and "always," of a love that's true, deep, faithful, and lasting. Love and relationships that are in Jesus are the only love and relationships that can fulfill the dream of the human heart.

Francis, as we have seen, also speaks of the bond of friendship in Christ that will "endure eternally."

> How good it is to love here on earth as they love in heaven and to learn to cherish one another in this world as we shall do eternally in the next!
> Here I do not refer to the simple love of charity we must have for all men but of that spiritual friendship by which two, three, or more souls share with one another their devotion and spiritual affections and establish a single spirit among themselves.[50]

Thérèse, as we have seen, is a strong witness to the beauty and value of deep Christian friendships. The bond in Christ, and in common love and suffering, between Celine and Thérèse was "stronger than blood."[51] It was, so to speak, "the same soul giving us life."[52] Their common experience of Christ's presence reminded her of the special contemplative union that Monica and Augustine experienced for a few moments at the seaport of Ostia shortly before Monica's death.[53]

As she grew in the spiritual life Thérèse's friendships with her own blood sisters, and others as well, deepened.

> When the human heart gives itself to God, it loses nothing of its innate tenderness; in fact, this tenderness grows when it becomes more pure and more divine.[54]

So far we have talked about the value and enduring worth of Christian friendship. How does what the saints speak about in this connection apply to the reality of that form of friendship which is Christian marriage? This is an important question for Christian spirituality.

Married Love

As in so many other areas, Francis de Sales is able to grasp the positive message of Scripture about marriage, as well as its message about the holiness and mission of lay people—insights that weren't brought to the center of the Church's consciousness until Vatican II. Francis, as does Scripture, speaks of marriage as a "great sacrament" or "mystery" (Eph. 5:32).

> It is "honorable to all" (Heb. 13:4) persons, in all persons, and in all things, that is, in all its parts. It is honorable to all persons because even virgins must honor it with humility, in all persons because it is equally holy in the rich and in the poor, in all things because its origin, purpose, advantages, forms, and matter are holy. It is the nursery of Christianity, which supplies the earth with faithful souls to fill up the number of the elect in heaven. Hence the

preservation of holy marriage is of the highest importance for the state since it is the origin and source of all that flows from the state.[55]

Bernard—in resisting demonically-inspired Manichean religious aberrations of his day (as Augustine did in his day) that would "forbid marriage and abstain from foods which God has created" (1 Tim. 4:1–3)—points out that those who are pushed into trying to live like angels (not really having the gift of celibacy) can actually end up living like beasts.

> Take from the Church the honorable estate of marriage and the purity of the marriage bed (Heb. 13:14), and you will surely fill it with concubinage, incest, masturbation, effeminacy, homosexuality—in short, with every kind of filthiness (1 Cor. 6: 10).[56]

Bernard responds to over-strict, non-biblical views about who is able to marry (only virgins, no remarriage after the death of one's spouse, etc.) with these words:

> Why do you shorten God's arm (Is. 59:1)? Why do you limit the abundant blessings of marriage?[57]

It wasn't that Bernard and Francis were blind to the low way in which many marriages are entered into and lived. In their days, marriage was as often dishonored by those who engaged in it as it was honored, as it is in our own day. Nevertheless, both Bernard and Francis knew its intrinsic importance and great potential as a way to holiness.

Francis touchingly reflects on what a difference it would make if Jesus were invited to the celebration of each marriage.

> Would to God that his well-beloved Son was invited to every marriage, as he was to the marriage at Cana, for then

the wine of his consolation and blessing would never be lacking to it. The supreme reason why there is little of that wine at the beginning of married life is because Adonis is invited instead of our Lord and Venus instead of our Lady. . . . The man who wishes to have a happy married life must reflect on his wedding day on the sanctity and dignity of this sacrament. Instead of this there are countless unseemly things done in play, feasting, and speech. It is not surprising that its effects are so disordered.[58]

Sounds distressingly familiar, doesn't it?

If the love of marriage primarily remains on the biological level, Francis tells us, it's hardly different than animal love. If it primarily remains on the merely human level of affection and mutual convenience, it is hardly different than the love of the pagans. If it participates though in the love of Christ, it is truly a Christian marriage. Pope Benedict XVI describes this as the "maturing" or "healing" of "eros," which restores "its true grandeur."[59] As Francis put it:

> With the great apostle I say to you, "Husbands, love your wives as Christ also loved the Church," (Eph. 5:25) and you wives, love your husbands as the Church loves her Savior. God brought Eve to Adam, our first father, and gave her to him in marriage. It was God too, my friends, who with an unseen hand tied your holy marriage bond and gave you to one another. Why then do you not cherish each other with a completely holy, completely sacred, and completely divine love?[60]

Francis must have given good homilies at marriages!

He makes clear that much of what has been said of Christian friendship also applies to Christian marriage, as the mutual love of true Christian friendship is an essential component of marriage.

> Exchange of carnal pleasures involves mutual inclination and animal allurement. . . . If there were no other

exchange in marriage, there would be no true friendship there at all. However, in marriage there is communication of life, work, goods, affection, and indissoluble fidelity and therefore married friendship is true, holy friendship.[61]

Francis identifies three effects of true married love and friendship: the indissoluble union of hearts, the inviolable fidelity of each party to the other, and the birth and raising of children. Francis notes what a great honor it is for God to allow us to participate in bringing forth new life with eternal destinies. He urges husbands to "preserve a tender, constant, heartfelt love for your wives," and wives to "love the husbands God has given you with a love that is tender and heartfelt and yet filled with respect and reverence."[62] While urging respect for the scriptural order of the husband/wife relationship, Francis makes clear that there is to be no "lording over" one another as the pagans might do, but a love appropriate to those who are companions on the journey together, imitating the mutual love of Christ and the Church.

Francis makes clear that the holiness of married love must be tender and affectionate.

> Love and fidelity joined together always produce familiarity and mutual trust, and hence in their married life the saints, both men and women, have used many reciprocal caresses, truly affectionate but chaste, tender, sincere caresses.[63]

And what about the sexual relationship in marriage? Does Francis have insight here? He does. He attempts to illuminate the complexity of the sexual dimension of the relationship by using the analogy of food and eating. He starts by acknowledging the goodness of eating to preserve our bodily life and the parallel goodness of the sexual relationship in producing new life. He then makes clear, though, that eating food to survive isn't all that eating food is about. He acknowledges that sharing meals with others plays an important role in building and sustaining relationships. So also, Francis acknowledges, the sexual relationship is an important way of expressing and building the relationship of mutual love, the need to be close, and the consolation of the communion of persons. He emphasizes in this regard that this dimension is such a basic part of married love that Scripture talks of it as a "debt" or "obligation" that the spouses owe to one another.

> Just as eating not merely for the preservation of life but to maintain the mutual association and consideration we owe one another is an extremely just and virtuous act, so also mutual, lawful satisfaction of both parties in holy matrimony is called a debt by Saint Paul (1 Cor. 7:2). It is a debt so great that he grants neither party exemption from its payment without the free, voluntary consent of the other. This holds even in reference to exercises of devotion. . . . How much less can there be self-exemption on the score of some fanciful pretext of virtue or out of anger or disdain?[64]

The vulnerability of the spouses to one another as they give themselves over in marriage causes Francis to urge great care and sensitivity in the sexual dimension. Francis urges the spouses to give themselves freely in the sexual expression of love and union, and not as if fulfilling an obligation—just as "those who eat in order to maintain friendly association with others must eat freely and not as if compelled to do so and must show an appetite for their food."[65]

Francis is aware that sometimes the sexual relationship in the intention of the spouses is not primarily about having children or even about deepening the relationship by expressing affection but is sometimes just about fulfilling a need or desire. While there is nothing particularly praiseworthy about this exercise of sexuality, Francis allows that it is a permissible exercise of sexuality. He uses the eating analogy again as a way of illustrating this point.

> To eat for neither of the reasons given but merely to sat-
> isfy our appetite may be tolerated but not commended.
> Mere pleasure in satisfying a sensual appetite cannot be a
> sufficient reason to make an action praiseworthy but it is
> sufficient if the action is permissible.[66]

There has always been a recognition that a legitimate dimension of the marriage relationship was the legitimate satisfaction of sexual desire, a "remedy for concupiscence."

Just as with eating, there can be excess and disorder in the exercise of the sexual dimension. Francis explains that "to eat not merely to gratify our appetite but in an excessive and inordinate way is something more or less worthy of censure according as the excess is great or small. . . . Marital intercourse, which is so holy, virtuous, and praiseworthy in itself and so profitable to society, is nevertheless in certain cases a source of danger to those who exercise it."[67]

Francis indicates that simple excess can be a venial sin but more serious perversions of the sexual function can in fact be mortal sins, particularly when the procreative dimension is violated and perverted in a way that is contrary to the Church's understanding of Christ's will in this matter.

The sexual dimension is an important dimension of the marriage relationship, but it has to be subordinate to and in the service of love and the journey to union with God. To dwell inordinately on the sensual pleasures of married life is problematic. As Francis puts it, "They should not keep their affections fixed on the sensual pleasures they have indulged in as part of their vocation in life."[68] Just as people who approach eating in an excessive or inordinate way can end up making "a god of their bellies" (Phil. 3:19), so too excess in the area of sexuality can have analogous results.

What a blessing it is when believing husband and believing wife sanctify each other in true fear of the Lord![69]

In one of his meditations Francis shares a "vision" of the married living a devout life where, in the words of Pope Benedict XVI, the "inseparable connection" between agape and eros becomes manifest.[70]

> See the crowded ranks of the married who live so calmly together in mutual respect, which cannot be had without great charity. See how these devout souls wed care of the exterior house to that of the interior, that is, the love of their earthly spouse with that of the heavenly Spouse. . . . Look upon the eyes of the Savior who comforts them, and see how all of them together aspire to him. . . . The crucified King calls you by name, "Come, my well-beloved, come, that I may crown you."[71]

Chapter Twelve

GROWING IN PRAYER

GROWING IN PRAYER IS SIMPLY ANOTHER DIMENSION of growing in love. Nevertheless, it's useful to consider our progress in love from the perspective of prayer, which is our direct, focused, conscious communing with God. We've already considered some of the basics about prayer in an earlier chapter (chapter 7), such as its importance, its basic method, and the difficulties we may encounter. Now we want to consider the perspective that the saints give us on progressing in prayer along with the challenges we encounter along the way.

We have already seen how Teresa of Avila insists that the essence of prayer, whether it is vocal or "mental," is paying attention to God, speaking and listening to Him. She also talks about some of the things that often happen as we grow in prayer.

Teresa points out that at the beginning of the Christian journey it seems as if we ourselves are doing most of the work (in the first through the third mansions) but as we progress, we become more aware of the initiative and action of God working in us, leading, guiding, and transforming (in the fourth through the seventh mansions). She talks of beginning to include moments of "recollection" or a quieting of the soul in our meditation and recitation of established prayers, where we find ourselves better able to be aware of God and simply be in His presence. This "recollection" can then deepen into the "prayer of quiet." (Teresa talks about the prayer of recollection and the prayer of quiet when she is describing the fourth mansion or stage of the spiritual journey.) Teresa describes the prayer of quiet as an absorption in the Lord in which, at varying degrees of depth, the will is fixed on the Lord, even though our intellect, memory, and imagination may still wander and be distracted.

She then explains that this prayer of quiet can reach deeper levels of absorption in the Lord and be described as the "prayer of union" (the fifth mansion). In this prayer not only is the will fixed on the Lord but the other faculties are absorbed in Him as well. Teresa makes clear that the prayer of union is not normally experienced for lengthy periods of time while we're still on this earth. She mentions how the first time she experienced this depth of absorption in the Lord it lasted only as long as the length of a "Hail Mary." The longest she experienced this "prayer of union" was for about a half hour.[1]

Let us consider now in more detail the various stages of growth in prayer.

The Challenge of Meditation and Prayer

Meditation—reflecting on the Scriptures or spiritual reading—is an important and necessary component of prayer. More strictly defined, meditation is thinking about God. Prayer is actually speaking to God, either in words or in silent contemplation. For almost everyone meditation and prayer are difficult at various times and in various degrees, as they were for Teresa herself.

> The greatest labor is in the beginning because it is the beginner who works while the Lord gives the increase. In the other degrees of prayer the greatest thing is enjoying; although whether in the beginning, the middle, or the end, all bear their crosses even though these crosses be different.[2]

And isn't it encouraging that the greatest saints have had periods of time—sometimes long periods—in their journey to God when they were watching the clock during their prayer times?

> And very often, for some years, I was more anxious that the hour I had determined to spend in prayer be over than I was to remain there and more anxious to listen for the striking of the clock than to attend to other good things.[3]

Thérèse shares about her own long struggle not to fall asleep during prayer times, and offers some interesting advice in the process.

> Really, I am far from being a saint, and what I have just said is proof of this; instead of rejoicing, for example, at my aridity, I should attribute it to my little fervor and lack of fidelity; I should be desolate for having slept (for seven years) during my hours of prayer and my *thanksgivings* after Holy Communion; well I am not desolate. I remember that *little children* are as pleasing to their parents when they are asleep as well as when they are wide awake; I remember, too, that when they perform operations, doctors put their patients to sleep. Finally, I remember that: *"The Lord knows our weakness, that he is mindful that we are but dust and ashes."*[4]

Those of us who are parents know that we sometimes love our children even more when they finally go to sleep! Thérèse's message is one of great confidence in God's love for us. He knows our weaknesses and loves us anyway. If we just do the little bit we can, He'll be able to continue the process of transformation, even if prayer is sleepy and dry.

Of course, sleepiness during prayer times has been a human reality throughout the centuries. Bernard comments on it periodically in his sermons.

Should we come to an end for the sake of those who are asleep down there? I thought that with one sermon I should fulfill my promise about the two kinds of ignorance, and I would have, but it is already too long for those who are tired of it. Some, I can see, are yawning, and some are asleep. And no wonder, for last night's vigils were prolonged; that excuses them. But what shall I say to those who were asleep then, and now sleep again?[5]

And it's encouraging that even this very imperfect, distracted, dutiful prayer is valuable to the Lord and allows Him to work in our lives. As Teresa of Avila puts it:

After I had made this effort, I found myself left with greater quiet and delight than sometimes when I had the desire to pray.[6]

Teresa witnesses to the fact that even if we are not fully attentive in our prayer, little by little, even imperfect prayer will change us. Simply "showing up" for prayer time evidences our desire to be with the Lord. Even though sometimes it seems that we are more there physically than spiritually, our desire allows Him to draw us closer.[7]

Even if our prayer doesn't seem to be bearing fruit on the level of our conscious intellect, it may very well bear fruit on the level of strengthening our will. By persevering we embrace the Cross.

For there are many who begin, yet they never reach the end. I believe this is due mainly to a failure to embrace the cross from the beginning; thinking they are doing nothing, they become afflicted. When the intellect ceases to work, they cannot bear it. But it is then perhaps that their will is being strengthened and fortified, although they may not be aware of this.[8]

Teresa likens this first stage of prayer, or discursive meditation, to the work of drawing water from a deep well by hand, with a rope and bucket, in order to cultivate the garden of our soul.[9] The temptation here is to think that such apparently insignificant results aren't worth the laborious effort necessary to persevere in this kind of prayer. Yet Teresa counsels that even if our prayer seems barren and unproductive, our perseverance "serves and gives pleasure to the Lord of the garden."[10]

> These labors take their toll. Being myself one who endured them for many years . . . , I know that they are extraordinary. It seems to me more courage is necessary for them than for many other labors of this world. But I have seen clearly that God does not leave one, even in this life, without a large reward; because it is certainly true that one of those hours in which the Lord afterward bestowed on me a taste of Himself repaid, it seems to me, all the anguish I suffered in persevering for a long time in prayer.[11]

Recollection

As we immerse ourselves in Christian teaching and the practice of the Christian life through participation in the liturgical life of the Church and prayer, spiritual reading, and contact with our fellow Christians, we are more able to think of and pay attention to the Lord. We will eventually begin to experience a certain calming or recollection of our soul where we are more able just to be in the Lord's presence and be aware of Him.

A distinction is made by theologians between *acquired* recollection, and infused or *contemplative* recollection. Acquired recollection is a certain stilling of the soul that comes about through our work and effort of meditation, spiritual reading, making acts of faith, hope, and love, and so on. We may use music, or purposely close our eyes, or light a candle, or any of a number of things to help us focus. At one point Teresa tells her sisters that if they faithfully practice meditation and prayer, in a year or even half a year this acquired recollection will be achieved.[12]

Infused Prayer (Contemplation)

Infused or contemplative recollection is a recollection that comes or is enhanced by a "touch of God" in the soul. It's a becoming aware of God's presence and closeness. It is something to which our own efforts can dispose us but never bring to pass simply by our effort or will. It is another example of the primacy of grace in the spiritual life. Teresa describes the way in which these first touches of "infused contemplation" may be experienced.

> It is a recollection that also seems to me to be supernatu-
> ral because it doesn't involve being in the dark or closing
> the eyes, nor does it consist in any exterior thing, since
> without first wanting to do so, one does close one's eyes
> and desire solitude.[13]

Teresa describes the beginning of this infused contemplation or recollection as a "hearing" or "being drawn" by God to open to His presence and pay attention. She makes clear, again, that it is not a matter of imagining being with Him, or thinking about the truth of the interior indwelling—although these are good elements of meditation as they are founded on the important truth of God being within us—but of an almost imperceptible interior hearing of the gentle whisper of the "shepherd's whistle."[14]

> It wasn't through the ears, because nothing is heard. But
> one noticeably senses a gentle drawing inward, as anyone
> who goes through this will observe. . . . It seems to me I
> have read where it was compared to a hedgehog curling
> up or a turtle drawing into its shell. . . . In the case of this
> recollection, it doesn't come when we want it but when
> God wants to grant us the favor.[15]

Bernard also clarifies that when people speak of "hearing" the Lord it is normally not an audible voice that they hear but a more subtle, spiritual communication.

> So whenever you hear or read that the Word and the soul converse together, and contemplate each other, do not imagine them speaking with human voices nor appearing in bodily form. Listen, this is rather what you must think about it: The Word is a spirit (Jn. 4:24), the soul is a spirit; and they possess their own mode of speech and mode of presence in accord with their nature. The speech of the Word is loving kindness, that of the soul, the fervor of devotion. . . . When the Word therefore tells the soul, "You are beautiful," and calls it friend (Song 1:14), he infuses into it the power to love, and to know it is loved in return. . . . The speech of the Word is an infusion of grace, the soul's response is wonder and thanksgiving.[16]

Teresa reiterates that the granting of this "touch" from God has some relationship to our turning away from the things of the world—detachment—and a growing desire to make room in our lives for God.

> I for myself hold that when His Majesty grants it, He does so to persons who are already beginning to despise the things of the world. I don't say that those in the married state do so in deed, for they cannot, but in desire; for He calls such persons especially so that they might be attentive to interior matters. So I believe that if we desire to make room for His Majesty, He will give not only this but more, and give it to those whom He begins to call to advance further.[17]

Bernard also teaches that contemplative prayer is usually given after a period of time in which the virtues are growing. He particularly mentions keeping the commandments and practicing acts of love and obedience.[18]

Teresa compares this prayer of infused recollection (as well as the prayer of quiet which we are about to consider) to the method of getting water for the garden by turning a waterwheel and bringing the water through aqueducts. It is not as hard as drawing water from the well by buckets by hand, and one can rest more without working.[19]

The first traces of contemplative prayer—this insight into God or flaring up of love given by God—grows, deepens, and becomes more constant and stable until it reaches the depth and stability of the state of spiritual marriage or transforming union of the seventh mansion.

The word "contemplation" does not appeal to many people today. Few are willing to claim to be "contemplatives," being uncertain about what this really means. The term brings to mind images of cloistered nuns or monks, or canonized saints who experienced remarkable things from God. The related terms appear nebulous and rather lofty. I myself prefer not to often use them precisely because of these problems. Nonetheless, "contemplation" is a key term used in the mystical tradition, and so we must use it occasionally and provide some definition, as the saints themselves do in their writings.

The Catechism of the Catholic Church, attempting to summarize the tradition, describes contemplation in a variety of ways. In its glossary of terms it gives this definition: "A form of wordless prayer in which mind and heart focus on God's greatness and goodness in affective, loving adoration; to look on Jesus and the mysteries of his life with faith and love" (cf. 2628, 2715).

But in the text of the Catechism itself there are other definitions of contemplation that broaden its meaning. For example, the Catechism cites Teresa of Avila's definition of "mental prayer" as a good description of contemplative prayer.

> What is contemplative prayer? St. Teresa answers: "Contemplative prayer [*oración mental*] in my opinion

is nothing else than a close sharing between friends; it means taking time frequently to be alone with him who we know loves us [St. Teresa of Jesus, *The Book of Her Life*, 8, 5]." (CCC 2709)

The Catechism variously goes on to describe contemplation as a prayer in which, "under the prompting of the Holy Spirit," we "enter into the presence of him who awaits us. We let our masks fall and turn our hearts back to the Lord who loves us, so as to hand ourselves over to him as an offering to be purified and transformed." It is a matter of the "forgiven sinner" welcoming love and wanting to love in return, but knowing that "the love he is returning is poured out by the Spirit in his heart, for everything is grace from God." Contemplation is "a *gaze* of faith, fixed on Jesus" (CCC 2711–2712, 2715).

There is a tendency to equate contemplative prayer with silent prayer. This is a mistake. We can contemplatively recite memorized prayers, the prayers of the liturgy, the prayers of the Bible, or our own spontaneous prayers. We can sing contemplatively. Contemplative prayer can also be jubilant and expressive, as we will see later on when we consider the fruits of the "spiritual marriage." The Spirit—the Giver of contemplation—can inform our prayer in silence, in whispers, in words, in groans, in longing, or in various forms of jubilation such as shouting, dancing, or leaping, to name a few. The Psalms, as does the Book of Revelation, gives us an example of the whole range of contemplative prayer: deeply personal and yet profoundly communal and liturgical, from reflecting on our beds in silence to solemn, sung worship in the temple, from "being still" to "reflecting or meditating" to "gazing on the Lord" to "yearning" to "shouting with joy." Jesus Himself tells us to "rejoice and leap for joy" when we find ourselves being joined to the sufferings of Christ as we encounter persecution for being His disciples (Lk. 6:23).

In essence, contemplative prayer is a communication with God that isn't simply our own mental or affective effort, but has at least some dimension of "givenness" by God, some infusion of light or love or presence that transcends our own efforts.

Let's continue now as Teresa teaches us about growth in prayer.

The Prayer of Quiet

Teresa speaks of different dimensions of the prayer of quiet but explains that in its essence it is a captivating of our will by the Lord, even though our other faculties may wander to one degree or another.

> I have already mentioned that in this first recollection and quiet the soul's faculties do not cease functioning. But the soul is so satisfied with God that as long as the recollection lasts, the quiet and calm are not lost since the will is united with God even though the two faculties are distracted; in fact, little by little the will brings the intellect and the memory back to recollection. Because even though the will may not be totally absorbed, it is so well occupied, without knowing how, that no matter what efforts the other two faculties make, they cannot take away its contentment and joy.[20]

At another point Teresa describes the beginning of this prayer like this:

> It used to happen, when I represented Christ within me in order to place myself in His presence, or even while reading, that a feeling of the presence of God would come upon me unexpectedly so that I could in no way doubt He was within me or I totally immersed in Him.[21]

She also mentions that there can be a form of contemplative intercession in this prayer.

> It [the soul] should be aware that we are very near His Majesty and ask for His gifts and pray for the Church

and for those who have asked for our prayers and for the souls in purgatory, not with the noise of words but with longing that He hear us.[22]

Even while reciting prayers in common or alone, such as the Divine Office of the Hours, contemplative prayer can express itself, even when one doesn't completely understand the language one is praying in!

> And in fact, it has happened to me that while in this quietude, and understanding hardly anything of the Latin prayers, especially of the psalter, I have not only understood how to render the Latin verse in the vernacular but have gone beyond to rejoicing in the meaning of the verse.[23]

Teresa notes that the Lord often gives small "pledges" or "little sips" of what will be given in abundance in the kingdom.

> But there are times when, tired from our travels, we experience that the Lord calms our faculties and quiets the soul. As though by signs, He gives us a clear foretaste of what will be given to those He brings to His Kingdom. . . . Those who experience this prayer call it the prayer of quiet.[24]

At certain points Teresa describes a more intense form of the prayer of quiet which she calls the "sleep of the faculties." In this "sleep of the faculties" the other faculties as well as the will are under the rule of the Lord in a time of prayer, but not in an as deep or all-absorbing way as they are in the prayer of union.[25] Teresa now uses the illustration of bringing water to the garden not by a bucket raised by hand, or even by a waterwheel and aqueducts, but by way of rivers and streams that flow right into the garden.

Teresa goes on to mention the situation of an elderly nun who experienced great distraction during mental prayer. For years, this nun's prayer had consisted only of the simple but heartfelt recitation of the "Our Father," yet she was often raised to the heights of prayer. She came to Teresa, disturbed that she wasn't able to practice mental prayer or contemplation, but Teresa quickly saw that God was indeed bringing this nun into deep contemplation through these numberless devout repetitions of the Lord's Prayer.[26]

> It may seem to anyone who doesn't know about the matter that vocal prayer doesn't go with contemplation; but I know that it does. Pardon me, but I want to say this: I know there are many persons who while praying vocally, as has already been mentioned, are raised by God to sublime contemplation [without striving for anything or understanding how.][27]

Bernard tells us that a simple repetition of words and affections infused by the Spirit can be signs of a profound communication between the Lord and the soul.

> The speech of the Word is an infusion of grace, the soul's response is wonder and thanksgiving. The more she feels surpassed in her loving the more she gives in love and her wonder grows when he still exceeds her. Hence, not satisfied to tell him once that he is beautiful, she repeats the word, to signify by that repetition the pre-eminence of his beauty.[28]

Consolations in Prayer: Invitations to Go Deeper

It may happen, Teresa notes, that many who experience this prayer of quiet don't continue to grow and advance on the spiritual journey. The experience of this prayer must be interpreted as a call from the Lord to continue on the journey, not as a stopping point. She urges us to realize that to be united with the Lord in such a manner is a great gift and privilege. Her advice: be careful, be appreciative, be faithful, be a friend.

This prayer, then, is a little spark of the Lord's true love which He begins to enkindle in the soul. . . . And if we don't extinguish it through our own fault, it is what will begin to enkindle the large fire that . . . throws forth flames of the greatest love of God. . . . This little spark is the sign or the pledge God gives to this soul that He now chooses it for great things if it will prepare itself to receive them. This spark is a great gift, much more so than I can express. . . . God desires to choose them to bring profit to many others, especially in these times when staunch friends of God are necessary to sustain the weak. And those who are aware of this favor within themselves may consider that they are such friends if they know how to respond according to the laws that even a good friendship in the world demands.[29]

The Lord's Visits

Bernard asks: "And who is qualified to investigate and comprehend those countless affective movements of the soul caused by the presence of the Bridegroom dispensing his multiform graces?"[30]

Bernard, depending on the light of the Holy Spirit, volunteers to share some of his own experiences—by an interweaving of biblical allusions—of these "visits" from the Lord to help us understand their significance. Whether they be of the type that Teresa describes as the "prayer of quiet" or the deeper absorption of the "prayer of union," which we are about to consider, Bernard's commentary is useful.

Now bear with my foolishness for a little. I want to tell you of my own experience, as I promised. Not that it is of any importance. But I make this disclosure only to help you, and if you derive any profit from it I shall be consoled for my foolishness; if not, my foolishness will be revealed. I admit that the Word has also come to me—I speak as a fool—and has come many times. But although he has come to me, I have never been conscious of the moment of his coming. I perceived his presence, I remembered afterwards that he had been with me; sometimes I had a presentiment that he would come, but I was never conscious of his coming or his going. And where he comes from when he visits my soul, and where he goes, and by what means he enters and goes out, I admit that I do not know even now.

Bernard describes how these "visits" of the Lord's presence awakened his lethargic soul, revealed and healed his faults, gave him insight and aroused praise, brought his human longings into subjection, and instilled awe at God's mercy and goodness.

> But when the Word has left me, all these spiritual powers become weak and faint and begin to grow cold, as though you had removed the fire from under a boiling pot, and this is the sign of his going. Then my soul must needs be sorrowful until he returns and my heart again kindles within me—the sign of his returning.[31]

Bernard ends another description of these visits with a characteristic expression of his sensitivity to the joy of union with God.

> The fire of holy desire ought to precede his advent to every soul whom he will visit, to burn up the rust of bad habits and so prepare a place for the Lord. The soul will know that the Lord is near when it perceives itself to be aflame with fire . . . and that soul's angel . . . must be dancing with joy![32]

Thérèse is another witness to this direct action of God in the soul, which sometimes brought her to tears of joy.

> The way I was walking was so straight, so clear, I needed no other guide but Jesus. I compared directors to faithful mirrors, reflecting Jesus in souls, and I said that for me God was using no intermediary, He was acting directly![33]

Thérèse remarks that the secrets Jesus was showing her were so extraordinary that learned theologians would be astounded at the understanding that He had given to a fourteen year old girl. In fact, one of her directors, seeing how Jesus was acting directly in her soul, told her: "My child, may Our Lord always be your Superior and your Novice Master."[34] She explicitly states that such knowledge comes primarily not through study but through poverty of spirit, and quotes beautiful stanzas from John of the Cross's poem *The Dark Night* to explain what she was experiencing.

> On that glad night,
> In secret, for no one saw me,
> Nor did I look at anything,
> With no other light or guide
> Than the one that burned in my heart.
>
> This guided me
> More surely than the light of noon
> To where he was awaiting me
> —Him I knew so well—
> —There in a place where no one appeared.[35]

Thérèse speaks about how many lights she received from reading John of the Cross, particularly between the ages of seventeen and eighteen (she also had his writings on her bedside table when she died). She also admits that sometimes no book of spiritual reading was able to help her break through periods of aridity in prayer, and then only Holy Scripture, especially the Gospels, and Thomas à Kempis's *The Imitation of Christ* provided any help. But she realizes that in the midst of the aridity Jesus was accomplishing and teaching deep things.

> I understand and know from experience that *"The kingdom of God is within you"* (Lk. 17:21). Jesus has no need of books or teachers to instruct souls; He teaches

without the noise of words [*Imitation*, III, 43:3]. Never have I heard Him speak, but I feel that he is within me at each moment; He is guiding and inspiring me with what I must say and do. I find just when I need them certain lights that I had not seen until then, and it isn't most frequently during my hours of prayer that these are most abundant but rather in the midst of my daily occupations.[36]

How familiar we are with this work of Jesus in souls; from the Old Testament through the New, the Lord Himself shepherds and teaches His flock directly.[37] These saints are living the reality of the New Covenant—the direct presence of God in the soul—a reality we are all called to experience.

The Prayer of Union

As Teresa discusses the stages of prayer she makes clear that she's talking primarily about a difference of degree in the intensity with which we're absorbed in the Lord in prayer. In the fifth mansion she talks about the prayer of union, in which not only the will but also the memory, imagination, and intellect are "captured" by the Lord in yet a deeper absorption. This absorption can be so deep that the person experiencing it is not aware of anything around them. The faculties now are not just lightly "sleeping" but are suspended.

> There is no need to use any technique to suspend the mind since all the faculties are asleep in this state—and truly asleep—to the things of the world and to ourselves. As a mater of fact, during the time that the union lasts the soul is left as though without its senses, for it has no power to think even if it wants to. In loving, if it does love, it doesn't understand how or what it is it loves or what it would want. In sum, it is like one who in every respect has died to the world so as to live more completely in God. . . . It is so stunned that, even if consciousness is not completely lost, neither a hand nor a foot stirs.[38]

In another place she describes the prayer of union like this:

> When there is *union* of all the faculties, things are very
> different because none of them is able to function. The
> intellect is as though in awe; the will loves more than it
> understands, but it doesn't understand in a describable
> way whether it loves or what it does; there is no memory
> at all, in my opinion, nor thought; nor even during that
> time are the senses awake, but they are as though lost,
> that the soul might be more occupied in what it enjoys.
> This union passes quickly.[39]

Bernard too speaks of the relatively short time it is possible to
experience deep contemplation while on this earth, in the body.

> For who can enjoy the light of contemplation—I do not
> say continually but even for long—while she remains in
> the body?[40]

And, in another place:

> But there is a place where God is seen in tranquil rest,
> where he is neither Judge nor Teacher but Bridegroom. To
> me—for I do not speak for others—this is truly the bed-
> room to which I have sometimes gained happy entrance.
> Alas! How rare the time, and how short the stay![41]

Teresa says that one of the main signs that the prayer of union
has really happened is the unforgettable nature of the experience.
Even as its exterior awareness is suspended, the soul remembers with
acute conviction that God has visited it.

> For during the time of this union it neither sees, nor
> hears, nor understands, because the union is always short
> and seems to the soul even much shorter than it probably
> is. God so places Himself in the interior of that soul that

when it returns to itself it can in no way doubt that it was in God and God was in it. This truth remains with it so firmly that even though years go by without God's granting that favor again, the soul can neither forget nor doubt that it was in God and God was in it.[42]

Teresa acknowledges that there are varying degrees of intensity in union. In "lighter" experiences of the prayer of union, one could hear someone talking and decide whether to answer or not; in "deeper" experiences of the union, one might not even be able to respond to outside stimuli.[43] She uses another water analogy to describe this deeper prayer of union as water falling on the soul as if directly from above, in a soaking downpour.

Teresa also acknowledges that one can go in and out of the prayer of union over longer prayer times, spending intervals of time in less absorbing levels of prayer such as meditation, recollection, and quiet. She notes how the will can be held steadily for longer periods of time but the intellect, imagination, and memory seem to take up their wandering ways much sooner.[44]

The purpose of the Lord granting these various forms of infused contemplation or various degrees of absorption is to help us to more fully be united to Him and to His will. It is important to remember that for Teresa and all the saints, prayer is not something that is primarily about technique, or having certain experiences, but it's about growing in a relationship.

Teresa encourages us to do all we can to dispose ourselves for the action of God so our lives can be transformed, like an ugly silkworm into a beautiful butterfly.

> Courage, my daughters! Let's be quick to do this work and weave this little cocoon by getting rid of our self-love and self-will, our attachment to any earthly thing, and by performing deeds of penance, prayer, mortification, obedience, and of all the other things you know. Would

to heaven that we would do what we know we must. . . .
Let it die; let this silkworm die, as it does in completing
what it was created to do![45]

As we dispose ourselves for union by turning from sin and from
all inordinate attachments as best we can, and as we focus our lives
on God, the Lord by degrees gives us graces in prayer such as Teresa
has been describing, which help to bring about the transformation.

> When the soul is, in this prayer, truly dead to the world,
> a little white butterfly comes forth. Oh, greatness of
> God! How transformed the soul is when it comes out
> of this prayer after having been placed within the great-
> ness of God and so closely joined with Him for a little
> while—in my opinion the union never lasts for as much
> as a half hour.[46]

The Union of Wills

The experience of union in prayer, Teresa makes very clear, is
intended to help make more possible the union of our wills with
God's will, in a more profound obedience and love. Teresa also
makes clear that God is able to bring people to this essential union
of wills without necessarily bringing them through the experience of
the prayer of union, with its full suspension of all the faculties.

> Since so much gain comes from entering this place [the
> fifth mansion, the prayer of union] it will be good to
> avoid giving the impression that those to whom the
> Lord doesn't give things that are so supernatural are left
> without hope. True union can very well be reached with
> God's help, if we make the effort to obtain it by keeping
> our wills fixed only on that which is God's will. . . . The
> Lord has the power to enrich souls through many paths
> and bring them to these dwelling places without using
> the short cut that was mentioned.[47]

The "shortcut" that Teresa is talking about is the deep experience of the prayer of union. This prayer helps one to die to oneself but there are other ways by which the Lord can bring this about. The death to self is essential; the prayer of union isn't.

> It is necessary for the silkworm to die, and moreover, at a cost to yourselves. In the delightful union [the prayer of union], the experience of seeing oneself in so new a life greatly helps one to die; in the other union [the union of wills], it's necessary that, while living in this life, we ourselves put the silkworm to death.[48]

Teresa acknowledges that this takes real effort but that it is possible and has its own reward.

> I confess this latter death will require a great deal of effort or more than that; but it has its value. Thus if you come out victorious the reward will be much greater. But there is no reason to doubt the possibility of this death any more than that of true union with the will of God. This union with God's will is the union I have desired all my life; it is the union I ask the Lord for always and the one that is clearest and safest.[49]

While Teresa is a master at describing the various kinds of experiences we may have in our journey to full union with God, she is also relentless in insisting that the goal is not the experience, but the union, manifested in a greater conformity of our will to God's will, in love of God and neighbor. "Self-love, self-esteem, judging one's neighbors (even though in little things), a lack of charity for them, and not loving them as ourselves" are like little worms gnawing away at our life with God.[50]

God's will for us is our perfection, our total conformity to love of God and neighbor. Although we can't always be sure if we're loving God more perfectly—although there are reliable indicators—we can be sure whether we're loving our neighbor. And the surest way to love our neighbor, Teresa advises, is not to dream of doing big deeds for our neighbor "one day," but to take advantage of the little, everyday opportunities that present themselves in ordinary life. This is what pleases the Lord.

> He desires that if you see a Sister who is sick to whom you can bring some relief, you have compassion on her and not worry about losing this devotion; and that if she is suffering pain, you also feel it; and that, if necessary, you fast so that she might eat—not so much for her sake as because you know it is your Lord's desire. This is true union with His will, and if you see a person praised, the Lord wants you to be much happier than if you yourself were being praised. This, indeed, is easy, for if you have humility you will feel sorry to see yourself praised. But this happiness that comes when the virtues of the Sisters are known is a very good thing; and when we see some fault in them it is also a very good thing to be sorry and hide the fault as though it were our own. . . . And force your will to do the will of your Sisters in everything even though you may lose your rights; forget your own good for their sakes no matter how much resistance your nature puts up; and, when the occasion arises, strive to accept work yourself so as to relieve your neighbor of it. Don't think it won't cost you anything or that you will find everything done for you. Look at what our Spouse's love for us cost Him; in order to free us from death, He died that most painful death of the cross.[51]

Bernard teaches that "everyone who lives among us in harmony with the community, who not only mingles with his brothers without complaining, but with a very friendly attitude even makes himself available to all for any occasion of loving service" is bearing the fruit of genuine spiritual experience.[52]

While stressing the importance of love of neighbor and warning against self-delusion, Teresa is also immensely encouraging.

If we fail in love of neighbor we are lost. . . . When you
see yourselves lacking in this love even though you have
devotion and gratifying experiences that make you think
you have reached this stage, and you experience some little suspension in the prayer of quiet (for to some it then
appears that everything has been accomplished), believe
me you have not reached union. And beg our Lord to
give you this perfect love of neighbor. Let His Majesty
have a free hand, for He will give you more than you
know how to desire because you are striving and making
every effort to do what you can about this love.[53]

Teresa makes some very strong statements about what is necessary
to make progress but then, almost immediately, knowing that we
might feel overwhelmed and think progress is impossible, gives us
some strong encouragement about what reliance on God can accomplish. For Teresa, obstacles on the journey to God are opportunities
to admit our helplessness and ask God for help. When we honestly
confess our spiritual poverty, we qualify for "divine welfare."

When Thérèse of Lisieux was pondering the big steps in the spiritual life that she felt called to take, yet incapable of, she wondered if
there was some kind of spiritual "shortcut" or spiritual "elevator" that
could lift her up these too difficult steps. She felt that God the Father
showed her that there was such an "elevator": the arms of Jesus.

Let's listen to what Thérèse says about this discovery.

You know, Mother, I have always wanted to be a saint.
Alas! I have always noticed that when I compared myself
to the saints, there is between them and me the same difference that exists between a mountain whose summit is
lost in the clouds and the obscure grain of sand trampled
underfoot by passers-by. Instead of being discouraged, I
said to myself: God cannot inspire unrealizable desires. I
can, then, in spite of my littleness, aspire to holiness. It
is impossible for me to grow up, and so I must bear with
myself such as I am with all my imperfections. But I want

to seek out a means of going to heaven by a little way, a way that is very straight, very short, and totally new.

We are living now in an age of inventions, and we no longer have to take the trouble of climbing stairs, for, in the homes of the rich, an elevator has replaced these very successfully. I wanted to find an elevator which would raise me to Jesus, for I am too small to climb the rough stairway of perfection. I searched, then, in the Scriptures for some sign of this elevator, the object of my desires, and I read these words coming from the mouth of Eternal Wisdom: "*Whoever is a* LITTLE ONE, *let him come to me*" (Prov. 9:4). And so I succeeded. I felt I had found what I was looking for. But wanting to know, O my God, what You would do to *the very little one* who answered Your call, I continued my search and this is what I discovered: "*As one whom a mother caresses, so will I comfort you; you shall be carried at the breasts, and upon the knees they shall caress you* (Is. 66: 12-13). Ah! Never did words more tender and more melodious come to give joy to my soul. The elevator which must raise me to heaven is Your arms, O Jesus! And for this I had no need to grow up, but rather I had to remain *little* and become this more and more.[54]

The Father showed Thérèse how much she could depend on and rely on the love and mercy of Christ to make up for what was lacking in her own strength or virtue. She felt that becoming a saint was beyond her, and it was. Only by radically entrusting herself to the love of Jesus, weaknesses and all, was there any hope of Thérèse, or any of us, becoming a saint.

Bernard was taught the same wisdom, as were all the saints.

I cannot restrain my joy that this majesty did not disdain to bend down to our weakness in a companionship so familiar and sweet, that the supreme Godhead did not scorn to enter into wedlock with the soul in exile and to reveal to her with the most ardent love how affectionate was this bridegroom whom she had won. . . . What do you think she will receive there [heaven], when now she is favored with an intimacy so great as to feel herself embraced by the arms of God, cherished on the breast of God, guarded by the care and zeal of God lest she be roused from her sleep by anyone till she wakes of her own accord.[55]

It is so clear that a fundamental message of the saints is the importance of placing our confidence in the infinite mercy of Christ, who is the One who both calls us to holiness and works it in us. Prayer is simply a way of opening ourselves up to this mercy. As Bernard puts it:

But as for me, whatever is lacking in my own resources I appropriate for myself from the heart of the Lord, which overflows with mercy.[56]

Chapter Thirteen

HELP FROM HEAVEN

AFTER MANY YEARS OF STRUGGLE and considerable progress in the life of virtue, the soul cries out for more. Having experienced the grace of conversion and repentance at the feet of Christ, the soul asked for greater intimacy; the Lord's hand molded the soul in virtue and stability and drew it closer; but now the soul desires more. Bernard expresses it strikingly:

> I ask, I crave, I implore; let him kiss me with the kiss of his mouth. Don't you see that by his grace I have been for many years now careful to lead a chaste and sober life (Tit. 2:12), I concentrate on spiritual studies, resist vices, pray often; I am watchful against temptations, I recount all my years in the bitterness of my soul (Is. 38:15). As far as I can judge I have lived among the brethren without quarrel (Phil. 3:6). I have been submissive to authority (Tit. 3:1). . . . I do not covet goods not mine; rather do I put both myself and my goods at the service of others. With sweat on my brow I eat my bread. Yet in all these practices there is evidence only of my fidelity, nothing of enjoyment. What can I be but . . . a well trained heifer that loves to tread the threshing floor (Hos. 10:11)? . . . I obey the commandments, to the best of my ability I

hope, but in doing so "my soul thirsts like a parched land" (Ps. 142:6). If therefore he is to find my holocaust acceptable (Ps. 19:4), let him kiss me I entreat, with the kiss of his mouth.[1]

As the work of transformation continues there may be, at certain points, an acceleration of the process. Direct actions of God in the soul, graces of various kinds, may increase, and there also may be an intensification of trials and difficulties—graces of another sort. In this chapter we will consider the various "touches" that God may give to the soul as a way of preparing it for deeper union, and the appropriate way of responding. (In the next chapter we will consider the intensification of trials.) Teresa speaks of these touches of God in her sixth mansion, where they are presented as preparations for the upcoming "spiritual betrothal" and, later on, the "spiritual marriage." John also speaks of these touches of God in great detail, but refers his readers to Teresa's even more exhaustive and detailed treatment. They both make clear that not every soul will experience all these phenomena—and some may experience very little or even none, since they are not essential for the process of transformation—but they want to be exhaustive about the type of experiences that are possible so as to provide a resource to everyone, whatever their situation or experience.

Solitude

Teresa has already told us how important desire for God is to make progress on the spiritual journey and now she tells us how God Himself increases that desire in us by means of various graces. She begins by speaking of how God acts in the soul by means of various "woundings." One of the results of these "wounds" is that the person now "strives for more opportunities to be alone and, in conformity with its state, to rid itself of everything that can be an obstacle to this solitude."[2] As the Lord calls us to a deeper union with

Him, we seek for ways that we can respond by spending more time in prayer and eliminating unnecessary things that distract from this union. For lay people this "greater solitude" can involve reducing or eliminating certain entertainments or activities that aren't necessary or are excessive, such as time spent in passive media exposure like watching TV, listening to the radio, reading the newspaper, playing computer games, reading novels, listening to music, card-playing, watching sports, and so on. It can also involve decisions to increase times of prayer, spiritual reading, participation in the liturgy, taking periodic "retreat days," and the like.

Let's take another look at Bernard's excellent insights into solitude. He points out that while physical solitude may be helpful from time to time, there is a recollection of our spirit—a mental and spiritual solitude—that can be practiced in the midst of ordinary life.

> Therefore you must withdraw mentally rather than physically, in your intention, in your devotion, in your spirit . . . although physical withdrawal can be of benefit when the opportunity offers, especially in time of prayer. . . .
>
> Apart from that the only solitude prescribed for you is that of the mind and spirit. You enjoy this solitude if you refuse to share in the common gossip, if you shun involvement in the problems of the hour and set no store by the fancies that attract the masses; if you reject what everybody covets, avoid disputes make light of losses, and pay no heed to injuries (2 Sam. 19:19). Otherwise you are not alone even when alone. Do you not see that you can be alone when in company and in company when alone? However great the crowds that surround you, you can enjoy the benefits of solitude if you refrain from curiosity about other people's conduct and shun rash judgment. Even if you should see your neighbor doing what is wrong, refuse to pass judgment on him, excuse him instead. Excuse his intention even if you cannot excuse the act, which may be the fruit of ignorance or surprise or chance.[3]

Wounds of Love

Teresa describes some of the effects of these "visits" from the Lord that produce what she calls "wounds of love."

> That meeting left such an impression that the soul's whole desire is to enjoy it again. . . . Now the soul is fully determined to take no other spouse. But the Spouse does not look at the soul's great desires that the betrothal take place, for He still wants it to desire this more, and He wants the betrothal to take place at a cost; it is the greatest of blessings . . . for the soul to endure such delay it needs to have that token or pledge of betrothal that it now has.[4]

The "meeting" and "token of betrothal" that Teresa is speaking about is that experience of the prayer of union. These times of deeper prayer are intended to serve as invitations, "tokens" of the more substantial "betrothal" or "engagement" that precedes the spiritual marriage. While desire is enkindled and increased by these experiences of deeper prayer, the Lord wants our desire and longing for Him to increase still more. To this end He periodically gives the grace of "wounds of love."

Teresa says it is quite a challenge to describe these wounds of love and doubts she will be successful, but she tries to explain:

> He makes it [the soul] desire Him vehemently by certain delicate means the soul itself does not understand. . . . They proceed from very deep within the interior part of the soul. . . . For often when a person is distracted and forgetful of God, His Majesty will waken it. His action is as quick as a falling comet. And as clearly as it hears a thunderclap, even though no sound is heard, the soul understands that it was called by God. . . . It feels that it is wounded in the most exquisite way. . . . It knows clearly that the wound is something precious, and it would never want to be cured. . . . The wound satisfies it much more than the delightful and painless absorption

of the prayer of quiet . . . a whisper so penetrating that
the soul cannot help but hear it.[5]

Bernard describes the "wound of love" that Mary, the mother of
Jesus, experienced in the "transpiercing" of her whole being with the
sword of God's Word and love.

> In the process she experienced through her whole being
> a wound of love that was mighty and sweet; and I would
> reckon myself happy if at rare moments I felt at least the
> prick of the point of that sword. Even if only bearing
> love's slightest wound, I could still say: "I am wounded
> with love." (Song 2:5, Septuagint). How I long not only
> to be wounded in this manner but to be assailed again
> and again till the color and heat of that flesh that wars
> against the spirit is overcome (1 Pet. 2:11).[6]

As often as she speaks of dryness and trials, Thérèse speaks also
of remarkable "lights" that were given to her. Occasionally, these
lights were heightened and became "transports of love" that "rav-
ished" her soul.[7]

These communications from God increase our desire for God
in such a way that they are both agonizingly painful and exquisitely
delightful at the same time.

> This action of love is so powerful that the soul dissolves
> with desire. . . . This pain reaches to the soul's very depths
> and that when He who wounds it draws out the arrow, it
> indeed seems, in accord with the deep love the soul feels,
> that God is drawing these very depths after Him. . . .
> This delightful pain—and it is not pain—is not continu-
> ous, although sometimes it lasts a long while; at other
> times it goes away quickly.[8]

True "wounds of love" produce solid spiritual fruit, including a
"desire to have many trials, and the determination to withdraw from

earthly satisfactions and conversations and other similar things." Teresa notes that the devil never gives delightful pain like this, and would never increase our desire for God and our desire to bring our life into greater conformity with His will. When the devil tries to simulate these experiences they come from more external regions of our personality and produce disturbances and contentions, not true spiritual delight with its subsequent fruit.[9]

Francis de Sales, in speaking of the various delights and consolations that the Lord gives, also gives us some indicators to tell if they are from the Lord or not.

> With regard to the affections and passions of the soul . . . the general teaching is that we must know them by their fruits (Mt. 7:16). . . . If these delights, tender feelings, and consolations make us more humble, patient, adaptable, charitable, and sympathetic towards our neighbor, more fervent in mortifying our desires and evil inclinations, more faithful to our exercises, more cooperative and submissive to those we are bound to obey, more sincere in our lives, then . . . they certainly come from God. If they are sweet only to ourselves and make us selfish, harsh, quarrelsome, impatient, obstinate, haughty, presumptuous, and severe to our neighbors while we think that we are little saints and resent being subject to direction or correction, then beyond doubt such consolations are false and pernicious.[10]

Francis also gives advice about how to respond to these kinds of graces, with an interesting interpretation of what it means in practice to "kiss" the Lord.

> When we have thus humbly received them, let us use them carefully according to the intention of the giver. What is God's purpose in giving us these sweet consolations? It is to make us sweet toward everyone and loving toward him. The mother gives a piece of candy to her

child to induce him to kiss her. Let us then kiss the Savior who grants us these delights. To kiss him is to obey him, keep his commandments, do his will, and follow his desires, in brief, to embrace him with tender obedience and fidelity. Therefore whenever we receive any spiritual consolation on that very day we must be more diligent in doing good and humbling ourselves.[11]

Bernard and Catherine concur with Francis as he advises us to turn our eyes from the gifts to the Giver, periodically making sure that we're not seeking the consolations and gifts of the Lord for themselves rather than for God.

> Besides all this we must from time to time renounce such delights, tender feelings, and consolations by withdrawing our heart from them and protesting that although we humbly accept them and love them because God sends them and they arouse us to his love, yet it is not such things that we seek but God and his holy love. It is not the consolations we seek but the Consoler, not their sweetness but the sweet Savior, not their tenderness but him who is the delight of heaven and earth. In this spirit we must resolve to stand fast in a holy love of God even though we may never find any consolation throughout our whole life. We must be ready, as ready on Mt. Calvary as on Mount Tabor, to say, "Lord, it is good for me to be with you, whether you are on the Cross or in your glory."[12]

Teresa gives similar advice on what our response should be to these graces.

> Let his great fear be that he might prove ungrateful for so generous a favor, and let him strive to better his entire life, and to serve, and he will see the results and how he receives more and more.[13]

Again, the test of the authenticity of spiritual experience is the fruit it produces in how our lives are actually lived, the test of love and virtue. And again, the "kingdom principle" is applicable: he who is faithful in responding to small graces will be given greater.

Words from God

Another means that God uses to prepare people for union is by communicating various "words." Teresa and John identify four different kinds of "words" that may be experienced.

Exterior words

Sometimes the Lord actually communicates in an audible voice that we actually perceive through the sense of hearing. Most commonly though His communications are interior, words given to our understanding in various kinds of ways.

Successive locutions

Locutions are words communicated to the interior of the soul and perceived with the understanding. Successive locutions are communications that aren't instantaneously infused but are "built up" over a period of some time—it may be rather short—with a noticeable activity of our own mind and spirit. Perhaps an idea or a particular word or phrase seems to be "given," and then, as the mind and spirit pays attention, more of the communication is filled in with the obvious involvement of our own mind, drawing on memory, imagination, and study, as well as present inspiration. These are the weakest and least "powerful" of the interior locutions, and the most subject to distortion by our own involvement.

John acknowledges that the Lord gives locutions like these and that they impart some real grace, but is rather skeptical about the rather large number of claimed locutions that he encountered in sixteenth century Spain.

I greatly fear what is happening in these times of ours: If any soul whatever after a few pennies worth of reflection experiences one of these locutions in some recollection, it will immediately baptize all as coming from God and, supposing this, say, "God told me," "God answered me." Yet this will not be true but, as we pointed out, these persons will themselves more often be the ones who speak the words.

Furthermore, the desire for such locutions and attachment to them will cause these persons to answer themselves and think that God is responding and speaking to them. They will commit serious blunders if they do not practice great restraint and if their directors do not oblige them to renounce such discursive methods. For through these methods they usually derive more vanity of speech and impurity of soul than humility and mortification of spirit. They think something extraordinary has occurred and that God has spoken, whereas in reality little more than nothing will have happened, or nothing at all, or even less than nothing. For whatever does not engender humility, charity, mortification, holy simplicity, silence, and so on, of what value is it?[14]

John teaches that the benefit to be gained from successive locutions "will not come from focusing one's attention on it [writing it down or having others write it down] but by refusing to focus the intellect on what is communicated supernaturally and simply centering the will on God with love."[15]

The successful restoration of the New Testament gift of prophecy in the Church today depends on wise pastoral guidance which is aware of the variation in quality among the diverse phenomena that can be described as "words from the Lord."

Formal Locutions

The third kind of locution that John describes is one in which the whole "form" (wording) is given all at once. Rather than being built up in bits and pieces through the use of our memory, imagination, study, and direct inspiration, it is given all at once and thereby is less subject to distortion through our "work" with it. It has a more powerful effect on our spirit.

> It comes independently of whether the spirit is recollected or not. I give it the name "formal locution" because another person formally utters it to the spirit without intervention of the soul . . . ordinarily given merely for the purpose of teaching or shedding light upon some truth. . . . Successive locutions do not move the spirit as much as formal ones do.[16]

Even though formal locutions are less subject to human imagination than are successive locutions, and although they have a more powerful effect on the soul, John's advice remains the same. Don't focus on the locution, but let the power of the locution increase your desire to love God and neighbor and to give yourself more fully to Him. John puts it bluntly: "My main teaching is to pay no heed whatever to them."[17]

After we have considered some of the other special communications that God makes to the soul we will consider in more detail the reasons why John's main advice, which appears startling and even paradoxical, is not to pay attention to these communications. We will also see that John acknowledges some exceptions to this general advice.

Substantial Locutions

Substantial locutions are formal locutions that impress themselves on the soul with such power that they actually bring about the effect of which they speak. For example, if the Lord were to speak interiorly to the soul words such as "Be not afraid," the soul would be delivered from fear and experience peace and confidence. Or if the Lord were to communicate interiorly, "Be good," the soul would immediately be substantially good.[18]

Bernard gives a similar example of such a locution.

> When the Word therefore tells the soul, "You are beauti-
> ful," and calls it friend (Song 1:14), he infuses into it the
> power to love, and to know it is loved in return.[19]

These communications are so pure and so powerful that "the soul
has nothing to do, desire, refrain from desiring, reject, or fear."[20]

These substantial locutions are "in a class of their own," and
John's normal advice to basically ignore the lesser locutions doesn't
apply here.

> These locutions are as important and valuable as are the
> life, virtue, and incomparable blessings they impart to
> the soul. A locution of this sort does more good for a
> person than a whole lifetime of deeds. . . . There is noth-
> ing to be done, because God never grants them for that
> purpose, but he bestows them in order to bring about
> what they express. . . . It need not fear any deception
> because neither the intellect nor the devil can intervene
> in this communication.[21]

Visions

Another whole class of communications from God include various
types of visions. John and Teresa provide an exhaustive analysis of the
kinds of visions, only the main lines of which we will present here.

Bernard, like John, believes that the angels play a significant role
in many of these communications and provides some interesting
insight into why they are given in the form that they are.

The angels, Bernard indicates, contribute to "the construction
of certain spiritual images in order to bring the purest intuitions
of divine wisdom before the eyes of the soul that contemplates, to
enable it to perceive, as though puzzling reflections in a mirror, what
it cannot possibly gaze on as yet face to face (1 Cor. 13:12)."[22]

Bernard, guided by Scripture (cf. 1 Cor. 13:12, 19), recognizes
that while our knowledge and our prophecy is imperfect while we

are still in the body, there are occasional moments where unusually clear light is given.

> But when the spirit is ravished out of itself (2 Cor. 5:13) and granted a vision of God that suddenly shines into the mind with the swiftness of a lightning-flash, immediately, but whence I know not, images of earthly things fill the imagination, either as an aid to understanding or to temper the intensity of the divine light. So well-adapted are they to the divinely illumined senses, that in their shadow the utterly pure and brilliant radiance of the truth is rendered more bearable to the mind and more capable of being communicated to others. My opinion is that they are formed in our imaginations by the inspirations of the holy angels, just as on the other hand there is no doubt that evil suggestions of an opposite nature are forced upon us by the bad angels (Ps. 77:49).[23]

Let's consider now the different types of visions that John identifies.

Corporeal visions

Sometimes we may actually see, with our biological eyes, figures of Jesus, Mary, or various saints or angels. These types of visions are most subject to tampering by the devil or a spiritually immature response on our part. When they come from God, they are intended to lead us on to deeper and purer love and union; but sometimes we focus on their corporeal nature in a way which blocks the spiritual good from having its effect. John explains what bad effects can follow from being overly impressed by these kinds of corporeal visions. He applies these same comments to other sensory perceptions such as smells, sounds, lights, and the like.

> They are a ready occasion for the breeding of error, presumption and vanity in the soul. Palpable, tangible,

and material as they are, they strongly affect the senses so that in one's judgment they seem more worthwhile on account of their being more sensible. A person, then, forsaking faith, will follow after these communications, believing that their light is the guide and means to the goal, which is union with God. But the more importance one gives to these communications the further one strays from faith, the way and means.[24]

John always brings us back to the absolutely essential nature of faith as the primary means of growing in union with God. He is a master at detailing how our fallen, possessive, short-sighted, and easily impressed nature can foolishly grasp at these corporeal communications and miss their intended purpose—to lead us to fuller trust in and surrender to the Communicator.

Catherine also speaks of the inappropriateness of focusing on the gift rather than on the One who is giving the gift to us, who is inestimably more valuable than the gift itself.

> When a soul has reached the third stage, the love of friendship and filial love, her love is no longer mercenary. Rather she does as very close friends do when one receives a gift from the other. The receiver does not look just at the gift, but at the heart and the love of the giver, and accepts and treasures the gift only because of the friend's affectionate love.[25]

John emphasizes how vulnerable we are in spiritual things to falling into pride and vanity.

> Furthermore, persons receiving these apprehensions often develop secretly a special opinion of themselves—that now they are important in God's eyes. Such a view is contrary to humility.
>
> The devil too is adept at suggesting to individuals a secret self-satisfaction that becomes truly obvious at times.[26]

John advises us—using strong language—to "reject" such communications. He knows that he is using what may appear to many as blunt, extreme language but wants to make sure we don't miss his point. He wants to be sure that we don't get slowed down, detoured, or damaged in our spiritual journey by a misdirected fascination with the communications rather than the Communicator. Again, he is interested in pointing out to us the most direct and straightforward way of reaching the summit of "Mount Carmel." As Teresa of Avila once told her sisters, if you can reach your journey's end in eight days, why take a year? (At the same time she acknowledges that the journey is taking her longer than she hoped!). John writes:

> Such representations and feelings, consequently, must always be rejected. Even though some may be from God, this rejection is no affront to him. Nor will one, by rejecting and not wanting them, fail to receive the effect and fruit God wishes to produce through them.[27]

The reason John gives for his advice is that if the corporeal vision or feeling in the senses has a divine origin it produces its effect in the spirit at the very moment of its perception, irrespective of any deliberation about wanting or not wanting it.

> Those from the devil, even though the soul does not desire them, cause in the spirit agitation, or dryness, or vanity, or presumption. . . . The communications from God, however, penetrate the soul, move the will to love, and leave their effect within. The soul, even if it wants to, can no more resist their effect than can a window withstand the sunlight shining on it.[28]

Imaginative visions

Imaginative visions are those that appear interiorly, to the imagination. The "seeing" is not with the biological eyes but with the "eyes of the mind." Interiorly, we may "see" images of Jesus or the various saints, or scenes of heaven or hell, angels or devils, or even scenes on this earth, with strangers or people we know. The interior vision may sometimes have a "prophetic" character. John acknowledges that the Lord works in these ways with the goal of increasing "knowledge, love or sweetness."[29]

His advice, though, remains the same. Yes, God works by means of imaginative visions at times, but we don't need to waste time discerning them, since, if they are from God, the effect is produced automatically in the soul. If they're from the devil or our own imagination, that is all the more reason not to pay attention to them. He again warns us of the danger of getting preoccupied or attached to these communications in a way that blocks our progress in genuine love and union. He urges us to let these graces do their work by increasing understanding and love and our desire for God and moving on, guided by faith, strengthened by hope, acting in love.

John, very aware at the consternation that his teaching can provoke in his listeners, explains that God works by means of these corporeal or imaginative visions because in some cases it is the best way to lead us on to higher union, taking into account our bodily natures.

> God perfects people gradually, according to their human nature, and proceeds from the lowest and most exterior to the highest and most interior. . . .
>
> He first perfects the corporeal senses, moving one to make use of natural exterior objects that are good, such as hearing sermons and Masses, seeing holy objects, mortifying the palate at meals, and disciplining the sense of touch through penance and holy rigor.
>
> When these senses are somewhat disposed, he is wont to perfect them more by granting some supernatural favors and gifts to confirm them further in good (e.g. corporeal visions of saints or holy things, very sweet odors, locutions, and extreme delight in the sense of touch). These senses are greatly confirmed in virtue through these communications and the appetites withdrawn from evil objects.[30]

John is aware that despite the great insight he has been given into the process of spiritual growth, and despite his wide experience in giving spiritual direction, God can never be put "in a box." John acknowledges that this is generally how God works, but of course God is free to work however He wants, through whatever means, and in whatever order.

> This is God's method to bring a soul step by step to the innermost good, although it may not always be necessary for him to keep so mathematically to this order, for sometimes God bestows one kind of communication without the other, or a less interior one by means of a more interior one, or both together. The process depends on what God judges expedient for the soul, or on how he wants to grant it favors. But his ordinary procedure conforms with our explanation.[31]

While there is a remarkable unity of witness in the descriptions given by these Doctors of the Church, the elements of the spiritual journey can never rightfully be presented with the "control" characteristic of a mechanical or mathematical system. Freedom always remains, both for God and for the believer, and no method can hope to eliminate the risk that is inherent in this freedom without distorting the journey.

John is very concerned to make his points strongly because he knows how subject to delusion we are in these areas. He even may tend sometimes to attempt to make his advice "foolproof" in a way that goes a bit too far. For example, when talking about his basic advice—not attaching ourselves to any kind of supernatural communications or experience, "renouncing" everything that is less than God himself, proceeding only by faith, hope, and love—he makes the statement: "This method provides complete security against the cunning of the devil and the power of self-love in all its ramifications."[32] Of course, "complete security," may really be more than can or should be attempted. Attempts to provide a "foolproof" method usually result in creating a system that truncates the range of God's action and the freedom of the believer.

Exceptions to the General Rule

John reluctantly realizes that he needs to leave room for "exceptions."

As regards visions and other forms of supernatural communications, John acknowledges that while there is an objective progression of worth in moving from the corporeal to the imaginative and then to the intellectual that doesn't mean that a "lower" form of communication, may not, in a particular case, bring about a greater good.

> Yet this does not mean that some of the exterior corporeal visions may not be more effective [than the more interior imaginative visions], since after all God gives his communications as he pleases. But we are dealing with these visions insofar as they are in themselves more spiritual.[33]

John recognizes how difficult it is when making a strong point to do so with sufficient nuance and balance.

> And I think I was too brief in only explaining that a person should be careful never to accept them [corporeal visions]—unless in some rare case and with extremely competent advice, and then without any desire for them.[34]

Even though these communications should be "forgotten" and "renounced" and "not paid any attention to," those who may be experiencing certain spiritual phenomena should disclose them to their confessor or spiritual director, not just as a protection but also as a way of further releasing the power of their effect.

God is so pleased that the rule and direction of humans be through other humans and that a person be governed by natural reason that he definitely does not want us to bestow entire credence on his supernatural communications, or be confirmed in their strength and security, until they pass through this human channel of the mouth of another human person. . . .

Thus God announces that he does not want the soul to believe only by itself the communications it thinks are of divine origin or for anyone to be assured or confirmed in them without the Church or her ministers. God will not bring clarification and confirmation of the truth to the heart of one who is alone. Such a person would remain weak and cold in regard to the truth.[35]

His advice to confessors and spiritual directors about how to respond to these kinds of spiritual experiences also adds some important nuance to his advice.

It ought to be noted in this regard that, even though we have greatly stressed rejection of these communications and the duty of confessors to forbid souls from making them a topic of conversation, spiritual fathers should not show severity, displeasure, or scorn in dealing with these souls. With such an attitude they would make them cower and shrink from a manifestation of these experiences, would close the door to these souls and cause them many difficulties. Since God is leading them by this means, there is no reason to oppose it or become frightened or scandalized over it. The spiritual father should instead proceed with much kindness and calm . . . [and] should guide them in the way of faith by giving them good instruction on how to turn their eyes from all these things and on their obligation to denude their appetite and spirit of these communications in order to advance. They should explain how one act done in charity is more precious in God's sight than all the visions and communications possible—since these imply neither merit nor demerit—and how it is that many individuals who have not received these experiences are incomparably more advanced than others who have received many.[36]

It is useful to recall here Teresa of Avila's reflections that the reason why God may be giving some souls these supernatural communications such as visions or locutions is because they are weaker and are in greater need of this help than those who are more able, by God's grace, to travel more directly by faith, hope, and love.

Intellectual visions

The third type of vision that John discusses is the intellectual vision—a more purely spiritual "seeing" that doesn't involve the bodily senses or the work of the imagination as do the corporeal and imaginative visions. The "seeing" here may involve corporeal beings (John cites John the Evangelist's vision of the heavenly Jerusalem as of this type), but it is of a different quality than the previous visions. It's like a "door opening" in heaven and the capacity to see clearly and distinctly is given for a short period of time.

> These visions are similar to the imaginative corporeal visions but are far clearer and more delicate. . . . Through the supernatural light a soul may behold with greater facility and clarity the earthly and heavenly objects he desires it to see. . . .
> The vision takes place at times as though a door were opened and the soul could see as it would if a flash of lightning were to illumine the dark night and momentarily make objects clearly and distinctly visible. . . . These objects of the soul's vision are impressed so strongly [in the memory] that they are never entirely removed, although in the course of time they do become somewhat more remote.[37]

The "seeing" here may also be a more purely "intellectual" grasp or insight of a mystery of the faith or an aspect of God's being that's not attained by our own reasoning or study but is given spiritually. There may also be, for example, as Teresa of Avila describes it, an "intellectual" vision of the Trinity that's more than just an additional insight but is in some sense a non-visual, non-conceptual "seeing" of the Trinity itself, which in Teresa's case went on for long periods of times. She viewed these visions as connected with the spiritual marriage described in her seventh mansion.

John acknowledges that these visions are higher forms of knowledge and less subject to self-deception or demonic interference but nevertheless are not without dangers. In fact, he understands the vision that Satan gave to Jesus of all the kingdoms of this world as this kind of vision. Overall, his advice remains substantially the same: don't cling to these communications, but keep focused on God Himself through faith, hope, and love.

Although John doesn't encourage us to spend time in "discerning" any of these communications, he nevertheless describes the effects of both genuine and spurious communications of this sort.

When the visions or insights are genuinely from God they produce in the soul "quietude, illumination, happiness resembling that of glory, delight, purity, love, humility and an elevation and inclination toward God. Sometimes . . . [they are] more intense, sometimes less; sometimes one effect predominates, at other times another. The diversity is due to the spirit that receives them and to God's wishes."[38]

The devil can produce these visions and when he does they produce "spiritual dryness in one's communion with God and an inclination to self-esteem, to admitting them and considering them important. In no way do they cause the mildness of humility and the love of God."[39]

In so far as these visions are "intellectual" visions of creatures—saints, angels, scenes of heaven—they cannot serve as *proximate* means for union with God. But when these more purely spiritual visions communicate a dimension of knowledge of God Himself—

one of His attributes, for example, being "sublimely experienced"—John terms this an experience of "pure contemplation" and an actual participation in this life in the union which is our goal, the spiritual marriage.

John describes what these communications are like.

> This sublime knowledge can be received only by a person who has arrived at union with God, for it is itself that very union. It consists in a certain touch of the divinity produced in the soul and thus it is God himself who is experienced and tasted there. Although the touch of knowledge and delight that penetrates the substance of the soul is not manifest and clear, as in glory, it is so sublime and lofty that the devil is unable to meddle or produce anything similar. . . . This knowledge tastes of the divine essence and of eternal life. . . . Some of these divine touches produced in the substance of the soul are so enriching that one of them would be sufficient not only to remove definitively all the imperfections that the soul would have been unable to eradicate throughout its entire life but also to fill it with virtues and blessings from God.
>
> These touches engender such sweetness and intimate delight in the soul that one of them would more than compensate for all the trials suffered in life, even though innumerable. Through these touches individuals become so courageous and so resolved to suffer many things for Christ that they find it a special suffering to observe that they do not suffer.[40]

God may grant these graces at totally unexpected times. Their sovereign, gratuitous nature is stressed by John.

> God usually grants these divine touches, which cause certain remembrances of him, at times when the soul is least expecting or thinking of them. Sometimes they are produced suddenly through some remembrance that may concern only some slight detail. They are so sensible that

they sometimes cause not only the soul but also the body to tremble. Yet at other times with a sudden feeling of spiritual delight and refreshment, and without any trembling, they occur very tranquilly in the spirit. Or again they may occur on the uttering or hearing of a word from Sacred Scripture or from some other source. . . . They are not always felt so forcibly because they are often very weak. Yet no matter how weak they may be one of these divine awakenings and touches is worth more to the soul than numberless other thoughts and ideas about God's creatures and works.[41]

John here makes an important exception to his strongly stated general rule that we should ignore these communications, put them behind us, and move on, as they automatically produce their good effects, and to linger with them risks slowing us down or diverting us from the single-minded pursuit of God himself. Because these kinds of communications are a purer form of contemplative communication, they actually are a participation in the union for which we are striving.

I do not say that people should behave negatively regarding this knowledge, as they should with the other apprehensions, because this knowledge is an aspect of the union toward which we are directing the soul and which is the reason for our doctrine about denudation and detachment from all other apprehensions. God's means for granting such a grace are humility, suffering for love of him, and resignation as to all recompense. God does not bestow these favors on a possessive soul since he gives them out of a very special love for the recipient. The individual receiving them is one who loves with great detachment . . . [the fulfillment of Jn. 14:21]. . . . This manifestation includes the knowledge and touches that God imparts to a person who has reached him and truly loves him.[42]

In other words, our renouncing of the lesser visions and communications and experiences have now reached their intended purpose: to bring us to this direct, contemplative participation in the very union with God that is our goal in this life and is an anticipation of the beatific vision itself. This kind of contemplative participation in knowing and loving does not need to be renounced as it is the goal towards which we have been striving.

John goes on to say that this knowing and loving is still not the knowing and loving of heaven and the beatific vision but it is as far as is generally possible in this life, with perhaps some exceptions!

Just as "substantial" locutions accomplish what they communicate and are correspondingly rare, so too do "substantial" visions impart the essence of spiritual substances and are even rarer, if even possible, in this life. They require a higher light, the light of glory which is usually not accessible in this life.

> These visions of incorporeal substances (angels, and souls) do not occur in this life, nor can we while in this mortal body view such substances. If God should desire to let the soul see these substances essentially (as they are in themselves), it would immediately depart from the body and be loosed from this mortal life.[43]

However, it's just possible that Moses, Elijah, and Paul had a transitory experience of such substantial visions, "for God imparts this kind of vision only to those who are very strong in the spirit of the church and God's law, as were these three."[44]

Bernard, without systematically analyzing the various kinds of communications as much as John does, has a very similar view of the ascending order of purity and power of the various communications. Bernard too is aware that virtually all of the communications we receive from the Lord are not unmediated revelations of how He is in Himself—the beatific vision—but rather adapted to our current capabilities in surviving such encounters with the Lord.

But this vision is not for the present life; it is reserved for the next, at least for those who can say: "We know that when he appears we shall be like him, for we shall see him as he is. (1 Jn. 3:2)" Even now he appears to whom he pleases, but as he pleases, not as he is. Neither sage nor saint nor prophet can or could ever see him as he is, while still in this mortal body; but whoever is found worthy will be able to do so when the body becomes immortal. Hence, though he is seen here below, it is in the form that seems good to him, not as he is.[45]

Nevertheless, Bernard, as does John, indicates that the communications can become closer and closer to an actual participation in the beatific vision, even in this life.

One who is so disposed and so beloved will by no means be content either with that manifestation of the Bridegroom given to the many in the world of creatures (Rom. 1:20), or to the few in visions and dreams. By a special privilege she wants to welcome him down from heaven into her inmost heart, into her deepest love; she wants to have the one she desires present to her not in bodily form but by inward infusion, not by appearing externally but by laying hold of her within. . . .

Not yet have I come round to saying that he has appeared as he is, although in this inward vision he does not reveal himself as altogether different from what he is. Neither does he make his presence continuously felt, not even to his most ardent lovers, nor in the same way to all.[46]

Before we move on to considering another mode of God's work to draw us into union—the mode of trials—we need to take a look at two more ways in which God communicates with us and John's advice about how to respond: that of the "prophetic" and that of the "natural."

The Prophetic Dimension of God's Communications

Many of the saints both recognized and personally experienced the reality of the prophetic workings of the Spirit in the Christian life. As Bernard put it on one occasion:

> To have believed is to have seen. Not only is it possible for him who sees by a spirit of prophecy (Rev. 19:10), but also for him who sees by faith. And if a man claims to see in the spirit, I think he may well be right.[47]

There are two perspectives from which John evaluates various prophetic workings of the Spirit: the perspective of us being recipients of such graces, and the perspective of us being ministers of such graces for the building up of the Body. It is only the first of these aspects that we will consider here.[48]

John clearly acknowledges that God communicates prophecy in many different ways, including prophetic visions, dreams, locutions, signs, revelations and specific prophesies. He again advises not to make too much out of these communications and to keep moving forward in faith. If the prophetic communications are truly from the Lord, they will produce their fruit in due time. In many cases it is only after a considerable period of time passes that their true import can be properly understood.

When the apostle Paul describes prophecy (cf. 1 Cor. 12–14), he acknowledges its importance as a way of building up the Church but also warns of our very limited and imperfect perception of supernatural things, which he describes as seeing "in a mirror dimly"(1 Cor. 13:12).

John goes through example after example of how prophecy functioned in the history of God's people, showing in brilliant detail how its interpretation and application were often very problematic.[49] He shows how, although God's promise to Abraham that he would possess the land of the Canaanites was true, it didn't come to pass as perhaps Abraham and his contemporaries would have expected; it came to pass only hundreds of years after Abraham's death, through his descendents. He also mentions that although God's promise to Jacob that he would return from Egypt was true, it wasn't to be when he was alive—only his bones would return from Egypt!

John points out that oftentimes prophecy is implicitly conditional and should not be considered an absolute statement of what will happen, no matter what. He also demonstrates through various examples that oftentimes prophecy is given not so that it can be immediately understood but so that in the future, when certain events take place, one may then receive light about them. He points out that when Jesus prophesied about the future to His disciples He specifically cited this as its purpose (see Jn. 12:16, Jn. 14:26).

> The event may not turn out as expected, and frequently no one but God knows why.
> God usually affirms, teaches, and promises many things, not so there will be an immediate understanding of them, but so that afterward at the proper time, or when the effect is produced, one may receive light about them. . . . Christ acted this way with his disciples. . . . As a result many particular works of God can come to pass in a soul that neither the soul nor its director can understand until the opportune time.[50]

John gives yet another example that illustrates his point in a very clear way.

> An example: A soul has intense desires to be a martyr. God answers, "You shall be a martyr" and bestows deep interior consolation and confidence in the truth of this promise. Regardless of the promise, this person in the end does not die a martyr; yet the promise will have been true. Why, then, was there no fulfillment of the promise? Because it will be fulfilled in its chief, essential meaning: the bestowal of the essential love and reward of a martyr.

God truly grants the soul what it formally desired and what he promised it because the formal desire of the soul was not a manner of death but the service of God through martyrdom and the exercise of a martyr's love for him. Death through martyrdom in itself is of no value without this love, and God bestows martyrdom's love and reward perfectly by other means. Even though the soul does not die a martyr, it is profoundly satisfied since God has fulfilled its desire.[51]

While John acknowledges the role that God gives to prophetic communications he is concerned to point out the dangers of deception and the way that vanity and curiosity in "seeking a word from God" can give a big opening to the devil to get us off the track of humility and obedience. He reminds us of how much God desires to communicate to us through the gift of reason that he has given, and the great and inexhaustible revelation that has been given to us in the gospel, centering on His Son.

If I have already told you all things in my Word, my Son, and if I have no other word, what answer or revelation can I now make that would surpass this? Fasten your eyes on him alone because in him I have spoken and revealed all and in him you will discover even more than you ask for and desire. You are making an appeal for locutions and revelations that are incomplete, but if you turn your eyes to him you will find them complete. For he is my entire locution and response, vision and revelation, which I have already spoken, answered, manifested, and revealed to you by giving him to you as a brother, companion, master, ransom, and reward. . . . In Him are hidden all the treasures of the wisdom and knowledge of God. (Col. 2:3)[52]

Don't Despise the Natural

While John acknowledges the important role of the supernatural in God preparing our soul for union, he also warns that we can become "over spiritual" and mistakenly devalue the many normal and ordinary ways in which God seeks to communicate with us and lead us to union. A great deal of God's will and wisdom can come to us through "ordinary" means: thinking, common sense, seeking advice, and our interaction with others.

> [God] usually does not effect or reveal to people what can be arrived at through human effort or counsel, even though he may frequently and affably commune with them. . . .
>
> Usually God does not manifest such matters through visions, revelations, and locutions, because he is ever desirous that insofar as possible people take advantage of their own reasoning powers. . . .
>
> People should not imagine that just because God and the saints converse amiably with them on many subjects, they will be told their particular faults, for they can come to the knowledge of these through other means. Hence there is no motive for assurance, for we read in the Acts of the Apostles what happened to Saint Peter. Though he was a prince of the Church and received immediate instruction from God, he was mistaken about a certain ceremony practiced among the Gentiles. And God was so silent that Saint Paul reproved Peter. . . .
>
> On judgment day God will punish the faults and sins of many with whom he communed familiarly here below and to whom he imparted much light and power, for they neglected their obligations and trusted in their converse with him and the power he bestowed on them.[53]

How important that we are open to humbly listening to those with whom we interact, who may see things about us that we are blind to! Teresa of Avila, aware of the possibility of great spiritual depth and blindness to certain faults existing side by side, sought out an environment where fraternal correction would be possible. She got together a small group of committed people—widows, a married man, priests—whom she believed could help one another make progress on the journey.

> I should like the five of us who at present love each other
> in Christ . . . to gather together some time to free each
> other from illusion and to speak about how we might
> mend our ways and please God more since we do not
> know ourselves as well as others who observe us if they
> do so with love and concern for our progress.[54]

Many of the contemporary renewal movements in the Church place a strong emphasis on the importance of mutual support for perseverance on the journey to God. Right after I made a Cursillo when I was a senior at the University of Notre Dame, I began meeting in a small group with other men to help each other review how we were doing on our journey. I've been in such a group now for more than forty years, and it's been an important help for me and for millions of others as well—just as it was for Teresa.

Bernard praises the merits of fraternal correction when lovingly administered.

> We must not therefore despise the good man's rebuke
> which destroys sin, gives healing to the heart and makes
> a path for God to the soul.[55]

And the saints even remark that we can benefit a great deal not just from a "good man's rebuke" but also from ill-motivated, unkind rebukes from "bad men"!

The Active Night of the Spirit: Our Faith Response

All of this advice about how to respond to these kinds of graces John refers to as the "active night of the spirit." What he means by this is that we need to play our role in moving into deeper union with God by not clinging to whatever kinds of communications may be granted to us (with some notable exceptions as described above). God is preparing our soul for union by giving us these graces but our job is not to possessively grasp them, but simply let them do their work and move on towards the goal of union with God Himself.

Bernard emphasizes strongly the central role of faith in the journey toward full union with God.

> Believe, and you have found him. Believing is having found. The faithful know that Christ dwells in their hearts by faith (Eph. 3:17). What could be nearer? . . . How can faith fail to find him? It reaches what is unreachable, makes known what is unknown, grasps what cannot be measured, plumbs the uttermost depths, and in a way encompasses even eternity itself in its wide embrace. . . . I hold fast by faith what I cannot grasp with my mind.[56]

He also frequently refers to those strong passages from Scripture that talk of the foundational role faith plays in the whole Christian journey.[57]

> Without faith it is impossible to please him [God]. (Heb. 11:6)

> Whatever does not proceed from faith is sin. (Rom. 14:23b)

> He who through faith is righteous shall live. (Rom. 1:17b)

He emphasizes that here on earth our primary means of making progress is "walking in faith, not by sight" (2 Cor. 5:7). The role of faith is to deepen our desire and cleanse our heart (cf. Acts 15:9), preparing it for the beatific vision.[58] Bernard also points out that "not everyone who has the faith lives by faith" but that living by faith is a way of life that is cultivated by daily decisions to believe and act in the light of faith.[59]

Bernard is aware, of course, as is John, that even though we walk by faith and faith comes by hearing the Word of God and believing it (Rom. 10:17), "faith is strengthened by seeing."[60] Bernard is talking of the role of miracles and charismatic workings of the Spirit in this context, but it also applies to the whole realm of consolations that we have been considering. But while "seeing" and "experiencing" strengthen faith, faith has to be able to function *without* seeing and experiencing, in order to grow stronger and purer. So, there is interplay between experience and faith that is recognized by all the saints we are learning from, with the primacy being given to faith during our journey on earth, but the end being the experience of the beatific vision. And in the beatific vision, the need for faith (and hope) will be removed for all eternity, for then we will be "seeing," "knowing," and "experiencing" in an infinite ecstasy of eternal love. In the meantime though, this alternation of believing and experiencing is characteristic of the journey on earth. Bernard tells us,

> What they do not know from experience, let them believe, so that one day, by virtue of their faith, they may reap the harvest of experience.[61]

To sum up then, echoing John's cry: enough of the messengers![62] Bernard also eloquently cries out for union with Jesus Himself.

> No longer am I satisfied to listen to Moses, for he is a slow speaker and not able to speak well (Ex. 4:10). Isaiah is "a man of unclean lips" (Is. 6:5), Jeremiah does not know how to speak, he is a child (Jer. 1:6); not one of the prophets makes an impact on me with his words. But he, the one whom they proclaim, let him speak to me, "let him kiss me with the kiss of his mouth." I have no desire that he should approach me in their person, or address me with their words, for they are "a watery darkness, a dense cloud" (Ps. 17:12), rather in his own person "let him kiss me with the kiss of his mouth"; let him whose presence is full of love, from whom exquisite doctrines flow in streams, let him become "a spring inside me, welling up to eternal life" (Jn. 4:14). For his living, active word (Heb. 4:12) is to me a kiss, not indeed an adhering of the lips that can sometimes belie a union of hearts, but an unreserved infusion of joys, a revealing of mysteries, a

marvelous and indistinguishable mingling of the divine light with the enlightened mind, which, joined in truth to God, is one spirit with him (1 Cor. 6:17). With good reason then I avoid trucking with visions and dreams; I want no part with parables and figures of speech; even the very beauty of the angels can only leave me wearied. For my Jesus utterly surpasses these in his majesty and splendor. There I ask of him what I ask of neither man nor angel; that he kiss me with the kiss of his mouth.[63]

We have been considering in this chapter "helps from heaven"—the various communications that the Lord gives to expand our souls and increase our desire and capacity for union. But there is another way in which God also works to prepare our souls for union, and that is by the wise and powerful use of trials, temptations and suffering to make our souls more capable of a deeper and purer faith, hope, and love. This way of God's working to prepare us for union John refers to as the "passive night of the spirit." And it is to this important reality that we now turn.

Chapter Fourteen

A DEEPER PURIFICATION

WE HAVE SEEN HOW IMPORTANT detachment from a disordered love of the things and people of this world is if we want to make progress in the spiritual life. Selfishly grasping creatures and the creation significantly blocks progress in union with God. We have spent a great deal of time presenting the specific ways in which we need to do our part in preparing ourselves for such union. We have also recognized that despite all our efforts—which are only possible because of God's grace—we will fall short unless the Lord Himself acts deeply within us to bring about this purification and union. As John has said, the desires of our fallen natures are so strong that a stronger love is needed to overcome them—the love of the Bridegroom.

We have seen how the Lord gives grace in prayer to enkindle this greater love. But the purification that's needed goes deeper than that of the sensory attractions and attachments that we have. It goes to the depth of the soul, the spirit, where the wounds of sin have affected the highest and most spiritual part of our being. There needs to be a profound purification of our spirit, as well as a deeper purification of our senses. As the psalm says:

> Search me, O God, and know my heart!
> Try me and know my thoughts!

And see if there be any wicked way in me,
And lead me in the way everlasting! (Ps. 139:23–24)

Even when John of the Cross is discussing the passive night (purification) of the senses through temptations, trials, and aridities, he shows how selfish sensuality and the spiritual can be profoundly intertwined. Using his keen insight into subtle and hidden attachments he shows how the "capital" sins (pride, covetousness or avarice, lust, anger, gluttony, envy, sloth) not only have a sensual component but also a deeply rooted existence in the depths of the human spirit, and can even hide themselves in spiritual trappings. Even though certain levels of these ingrained patterns of sin have been dealt with in earlier stages of the spiritual journey, the deepest roots may remain.

It's important that we take another look at the depth of transformation that is needed.

Pride

When we think of pride we think of an exaltation of the self in our own eyes or in the eyes of others. John points out that even our desire for perfection can cloak a deep pride. Speaking of those who are trying to make progress on the spiritual journey, he says:

> Sometimes they minimize their faults, and at other times they become discouraged by them, since they felt they were already saints and they become impatient and angry with themselves, which is yet another fault.
> They are often extremely anxious that God remove their faults and imperfections, but their motive is personal peace rather than God. They fail to realize that were God to remove their faults they might very well become more proud and presumptuous."[1]

John also points out that this hidden pride can also manifest itself by trying to impress our confessor (even going to a different confessor to confess our serious sins), vying to outdo our spiritual "rivals," speaking of spiritual things so as to be praised, or by condemning others in our heart who don't appear to have the same devotion as us.

Bernard points out how prideful self-will can be deeply intertwined with all kinds of spiritual practices, recalling the words of Jesus to that effect on the Sermon on the Mount.

> If my fasting reflects my own self-will (Is. 58: 3–5), it will not be acceptable to him, and he will find no fragrance in my fasting, since its odor is not that of the lily of obedience, but the weed of self-will. And the same thing, I feel, must be true not only of fasting but of silence, vigils, prayer, spiritual reading, manual labor, and indeed of every detail of the monk's life when self-will is found in it instead of obedience. . . . Self-will is a great evil and through it your good deeds become not good for you.[2]

Spiritual Avarice (Greed, Covetousness)

When we think of avarice or greed we think of desiring to have things that don't belong to us or having more of what we already have to a disordered degree. Sad to say, it is entirely possible for us human beings to focus our greed and covetousness on spiritual things as well!

John piercingly points out that many never have enough of pursuing "spiritual input" through hearing talks, seeking advice, or reading books, and become "peevish" and discontent if they don't find the consolation in these things that they are seeking. Attempting to "possess" or amass spiritual things, John points out, is ironically just the opposite of that poverty of spirit that is necessary to enter the kingdom. True worship, in spirit and truth, is sometimes short circuited by a "religiosity" that is truly blind to the meaning of the spiritual journey, that self-emptying obedience in love to God and neighbor.

Furthermore they weigh themselves down with over decorated images and rosaries. . . and they prefer one cross to another because of its elaborateness. . . decked out in relics and lists of saints' names. . . . This attachment—possessiveness of heart—is contrary to poverty of spirit, which is intent only on the substance of the devotion, benefits by no more than what procures this sufficiently, and tires of all other multiplicity and elaborate ornamentation. Since true devotion comes from the heart and looks only to the truth and substance represented by spiritual objects, and since everything else is imperfect attachment and possessiveness, any appetite for these things must be uprooted if some degree of perfection is to be reached.[3]

Bernard also notes that "possessiveness" actually causes the loss of the gifts of God. In speaking of Satan's loss of his wisdom, beauty, and place in heaven, Bernard remarks:

But Satan lost this when he appropriated it as his own, so that to lose wisdom through his own elegance to lose it through his own wisdom. Possessiveness brings about the loss. It was because he was wise in his own eyes (Prov. 26:5), not giving God the glory (Jn. 9:24), nor returning grace for grace (Jn. 1:16), and not walking in grace following truth (2 Jn. 4) but distorting it for his own purposes, that he lost it. Indeed, to possess it is to lose it. . . . "Anything I do not possess before God I have lost" (Rom. 4:2). Nothing can be lost as that which is outside the presence of God.[4]

Spiritual Lust

When we think of lust we think of the desire to satisfy sexual appetites in ways that violate God's purposes. John points out the surprising but common appearance of lustful desires even in the midst of spiritual exercises. Because of the close link between the spiritual and the sensory, joy and delight in the spiritual can trigger sensory activity.

> It happens frequently that in a person's spiritual exercises themselves, without the person being able to avoid it, impure movements will be experienced in the sensory part of the soul, and even sometimes when the spirit is deep in prayer or when receiving the sacraments of Penance or the Eucharist. . . . It may happen that while a soul is with God in deep spiritual prayer, it will conversely passively experience sensual rebellions, movements, and acts in the senses, not without its own great displeasure. This frequently happens at the time of Communion. Since the soul receives joy and gladness in this act of love—for the Lord grants the grace and gives himself for this reason— the sensory part also takes its share. . . . Once the sensory part is reformed through the purgation of the dark night, it no longer has these infirmities.[5]

Even though it may generally be the case that this unsettling appearance of sexual temptation in connection with spiritual activity diminishes as the spiritual rules over the sensory we know from the testimony of other saints that strong sexual temptation can unexpectedly reappear even in higher stages of union with God.[6]

Sometimes, also, John points out, the devil takes advantages of our fear and confusion in experiencing lustful temptations at holy moments to tempt us to give up prayer.

> To make them cowardly and afraid, he brings vividly to their minds foul and impure thoughts. And sometimes the thoughts will concern spiritually helpful things and persons. . . . The devil excites these feelings while souls are at prayer, instead of when they are engaged in other works, so that they might abandon prayer.[7]

Not only can lust express itself in the midst of spiritual activities, it also can become a factor in how we relate to others spiritually.

> Sometimes, too, in their spiritual conversations or works, they manifest a certain sprightliness and gallantry on

considering who is present, and they carry on with a kind of vain satisfaction . . . a byproduct of spiritual lust.[8]

John points out, as does Catherine, that our "attraction" to someone may be led more by lust—even if it's not explicitly sexual, but simply "possessive"—than by the spirit.

> Some spiritually acquire a liking for other individuals that often arises from lust rather than from the spirit. This lustful origin will be recognized if, on recalling that affection, there is remorse of conscience, not an increase in the remembrance and love of God. The affection is purely spiritual if the love of God grows when it grows, or if the love of God is remembered as often as the affection is remembered, or if the affection gives the soul a desire for God. . . . As the love of God increases, the soul grows cold in the inordinate affection and comes to forget it.[9]

The contrary is also true. If the lustful affection grows, the love of God will grow colder and will tend to disappear, not without remorse.

Strong—and merciful—medicine is needed, to bring order to our loves and enable us truly to be "led by the Spirit." This is precisely the medicine the Lord provides in the various purifying and healing measures He undertakes on our behalf.

Anger

When we think of anger we think of losing our temper when someone cuts us off in traffic or does something that offends us very much. Anger, too, can express itself in spiritual things; John says imperfections involving anger are common. For example, it is not uncommon for people making progress on the spiritual journey to become angry at the sins and failings of others, "setting themselves up as lords of virtue," as John says,[10] but this is contrary to spiritual meekness and must be purified in the aridities and trials of the passive dark night of the senses.

An impatient anger toward ourselves is also an imperfection that the Lord desires to deal with by leading us to a greater meekness.

> Others in becoming aware of their own imperfections grow angry with themselves in an unhumble impatience. . . . They want to become saints in a day. . . . [They] make numerous plans and great resolutions, but since they are not humble and have no distrust of themselves, the more resolves they make the more they break, and the greater becomes their anger. They do not have the patience to wait until God gives them what they need, when he so desires.[11]

Keeping everything in proper proportion and balance is challenging. John is quick to point out that "some are so patient about their desire for advancement, that God would prefer to see them a little less so."[12]

Besides an unhumble and impatient anger at others and ourselves there can be a generalized anger or "peevishness" that affects one's overall disposition. This commonly expresses itself when consolation and delight in prayer passes and the soul is left "vapid and zestless."

> And because of this distastefulness, they become peevish in the works they do and easily angered by the least thing, and occasionally they are so unbearable that nobody can put up with them.[13]

This too, John tells us, will be taken care of in the purification that God will work in the soul in large part by means of the very dryness which initially causes the unbearable irritability or peevishness.

Spiritual Gluttony

When we think of gluttony we think of overeating or overdrinking, an inordinate satisfying of what is in itself a legitimate appetite. John shows us how this gluttonous spirit can express itself in spiritual things as well. This "selfish sensuality" (as Catherine of Siena frequently calls it) can express itself in the spiritual life in surprising ways. Spiritual gluttony can express itself by desiring to do the pious practices that we prefer rather than what is most helpful and most in harmony with our state in life or in obedience to a spiritual director. Whether it be fasting, prayer, or spiritual reading, devotions or particular ministries, a desire for spiritual gratification can be an underlying motivation rather than a desire to conform ourselves to God's will. As John puts it: "Their only yearning and satisfaction is to do what they feel inclined to do. . . . They think that gratifying and satisfying themselves is serving and satisfying God."[14]

Francis de Sales makes a similar point when he teaches that we should strive to develop those virtues most necessary to fulfill the duties of our state in life rather than those virtues that we find most attractive or most to our taste.[15]

Learning to be led by the Spirit of God rather than by our own appetites is a major theme of the spiritual journey. John paints a vivid picture of this often hidden and subtle struggle.

> With their hearts set on frequent Communion, they make their confessions carelessly, more eager just to receive Communion than to receive it with a pure and perfect heart. . . .
>
> In receiving Communion they spend all their time trying to get some feeling and satisfaction rather than humbly praising and reverencing God dwelling within them. . . . They fail to understand that the sensory benefits are the least among those that this most blessed Sacrament bestows, for the invisible grace it gives is a greater blessing. God often withdraws sensory delight and pleasure so that souls might set the eyes of faith on this invisible grace. . . . They do this in other exercises as well.[16]

When we start looking for or seeking a certain feeling or sensation in our spiritual activities rather than God Himself we have departed from the straight path of faith and have begun to seek ourselves rather than God. John and many of the saints point out that God may then withdraw the feelings and sensations that initially encouraged us, in order to give us the opportunity to more maturely, deeply, and purely seek and follow Him in faith, for His own sake rather than our own gratification. God does this, of course, with great wisdom and love.

> God very rightly and discreetly and lovingly denies this satisfaction to these beginners. If he did not, they would fall into innumerable evils because of their spiritual gluttony and craving for sweetness. This is why it is important for these beginners to enter the dark night and be purged of this childishness.
>
> Those who are inclined towards these delights have also another serious imperfection, which is that they are weak and remiss in treading the rough way of the cross. A soul given up to pleasure naturally feels aversion toward the bitterness of self-denial. These people incur many other imperfections because of this spiritual gluttony, of which the Lord in time will cure them through temptations, aridities, and other trials, which are all a part of the dark night.[17]

Teresa of Avila, as we have already seen, has identical advice about seeking the Cross rather than our own pleasure in the spiritual journey.

> It's an amusing thing that even though we still have a thousand impediments and imperfections and our virtues have hardly begun to grow—and please God they may have begun—we are yet not ashamed to seek spiritual delights in prayer or to complain about dryness. May this never happen to you. . . . Embrace the cross your Spouse has carried and understand that this must be your task.[18]

Spiritual Envy

When we think of envy we may think of envying someone's car or house or good looks or job or position in life. John shows how envy can also express itself in spiritual things as well. He identifies spiritual envy as being in particular opposition to the characteristics of love as identified in 1 Corinthians 13.

> In regard to envy, many of them feel sad about the spiritual good of others and experience sensible grief in noting that their neighbor is ahead of them on the road to perfection, and they do not want to hear others praised. Learning of the virtues of others makes them sad. They cannot bear to hear others being praised without contradicting and undoing these compliments as much as possible. Their annoyance grows because they themselves do not receive these plaudits and because they long for preference in everything. All of this is contrary to charity (1 Cor. 13:6).[19]

By this point John is aware that his analysis of imperfections could be getting a little overwhelming so he states he's going to hurry over the last few capital sins as they express themselves in spiritual things.

Spiritual Sloth

When one thinks of sloth, one thinks of laziness. Just as laziness is a problem in terms of getting chores done, accomplishing work-related, or family-related projects, so too, laziness is a big impediment to making progress on the spiritual journey.

> Regarding spiritual sloth, these beginners usually become weary in exercises that are more spiritual and flee from them since these exercises are contrary to sensory satisfaction. Since they are so used to finding delight in spiritual practices, they become bored when they do not find

it. . . . They either give up prayer or go to it begrudgingly. Because of their sloth, they subordinate the way of perfection (which requires denying one's own will and satisfaction for God) to the pleasure and delight of their own will. As a result they strive to satisfy their own will rather than God's.

Many of these beginners want God to desire what they want, and they become sad if they have to desire God's will. They feel an aversion toward adapting their will to God's. Hence they frequently believe that what is not their will, or brings them no satisfaction, is not God's will, and on the other hand, that if they are satisfied, God is too. They measure God by themselves and not themselves by God, which is in opposition to his teaching in the Gospel that those who lose their life for his sake will gain it and those who desire to gain it will lose it (Mt. 16:25).

Beginners also become bored when told to do somethings unpleasant. Because they look for spiritual gratifications and delights, they are extremely lax in the fortitude and labor perfection demands. Like those who are reared in luxury, they run sadly from everything rough, and they are scandalized by the cross, in which spiritual delights are found. . . . Since they expect to go about in spiritual matters according to the whims and satisfactions of their own will, entering by the narrow way of life, about which Christ speaks, is saddening and repugnant to them (Mt. 7:14).[20]

Not everyone has these problems in the same degree of difficulty but all of us have some of these imperfections to deal with.

The number of these imperfections is serious in some people and causes them a good deal of harm. Some have fewer, some have more, and yet others have little more than the first movements toward them. But there are scarcely any beginners who at the time of their initial fervor do not fall victim to some of these imperfections.[21]

In all of this analysis the bad news is that sin has really messed us up; very deep selfishness and imperfections permeate our lives. Bernard indicates that the great capacity of the soul for eternity is oftentimes not realized because the soul has become "bent" or crippled, and "limps."[22] The good news is that God has a provision for bringing about healing and transformation, bringing us into conformity with our destiny to be with Him forever in glory. The provision is primarily, of course, the liberating truth of the Gospel and the teaching of Christ and His Church, the sacraments, the power and presence of His Person, the power of the Holy Spirit, and the love of the Father which enlightens and draws us. In the previous chapter we examined a whole range of various ways in which the Lord communicates His love to us, thereby changing us through contact with Him. It's a power and presence that sometimes, however, because of the nature of the wounding, has to work through trials of various kinds to effect the necessary changes.

John makes very clear that, while we have to do everything we can to deny ourselves in all these various manifestations of selfishness and sin, our efforts will be doomed to failure unless the Lord Himself acts through the "darkness" of a faith that remains true and continues to deepen in a dry contemplation in the midst of such trials.

There's an initial purification in the earlier stages of the spiritual journey (John's active and passive nights of the senses, Teresa's first, second, and third mansions, Catherine's "purgative" stage) that brings these appetites under a reasonable control and places these various loves "in reasonable order."[23]

John insists that on a deeper level the roots of this profound selfishness, this "bentness," still exist; as the spiritual journey continues, a deeper purification is necessary. In previous chapters we examined what we can do by our own efforts (the active nights of the senses and spirit) to purify our senses, mind, memory, and will of any attachments to even spiritual things that are less than God Himself. As always, our own efforts are necessary, but not sufficient. Our own efforts dispose ourselves towards God but are unable to reach union with Him by themselves. God Himself must act, and He does—by the infusion of love and light that we examined in the previous chapter, but also by an infusion that happens in apparent dryness and aridity but bears great fruit. John calls this deeper purification the passive purification of the dark night of the spirit.

The Dark Night of the Spirit: God's Action

Even though the initial purification (night of the senses) described by John, Catherine, Francis, and Teresa sounds comprehensive, in an important sense, it isn't. While bringing about a reasonable ordering of our appetites, the night of the senses cannot unearth the deepest roots of our sinful habits.

> The real purgation of the senses begins with the spirit. Hence the night of the senses, as previously explained, should be called a certain reformation and bridling of the appetite rather than a purgation. The reason is that all the imperfections and disorders of the sensory part are rooted in the spirit and from it receive their strength. All good and evil habits reside in the spirit and until these habits are purged, the senses cannot be completely purified of their rebellions and vices.[24]

Nevertheless, the soul may go on for years in this relatively stable, peaceful state, enjoying a measure of contemplative prayer, a measure of stable virtue and engagement in service, experiencing intervals of purification but nothing sustained and enduring. Those who are in this "illuminative way"—or intermediate stage—are called by John "proficients." The soul knows, though perhaps in an intuitive way, that deeper levels of purification are needed and that not everything that needs to be dealt with has been.

> If His Majesty intends to lead the soul on, he does not put it in this dark night of spirit immediately after its

going out from the aridities and trials of the first purgation and night of sense. Instead, after having emerged
from the state of beginners, the soul usually spends many
years exercising itself in the state of proficients.

In this new state, as one liberated from a cramped prison cell, it goes about the things of God with much more
freedom and satisfaction of spirit and with more abundant
interior delight than it did in the beginning before entering the night of sense. Its imagination and faculties are
no longer bound to discursive meditation and spiritual
solicitude as was their custom. The soul readily finds in
its spirit, without the work of meditation, a very serene,
loving contemplation and spiritual delight. Nevertheless
the purgation of the soul is not complete. The purgation
of the principal part, that of the spirit, is lacking. . . . As a
result, certain needs, aridities, darknesses, and conflicts are
felt. These are sometimes far more intense than those of
the past and are like omens or messengers of the coming
night of the spirit. But they are not lasting, as they will be
in the night that is to come. For after enduring the short
period or periods of time, or even days, in this night and
tempest, the soul immediately returns to its customary
serenity.[25]

The initial purification, as John says, is like cutting off the tops
of a weed but leaving the root, or it is like rubbing out a new stain
but leaving the older, more deeply embedded ones. A deeper purification is needed—one that is able to eradicate the roots of sin and
erase the old, deeply embedded stains as well. On an even deeper
level, any natural dullness of spirit or distractedness that is in us
must be transformed into an attentiveness of spirit.

The habitual [imperfections] are the imperfect affections
and habits still remaining like roots in the spirit, for the
sensory purgation could not reach the spirit. The difference between the two purgations is like the difference
between pulling up roots or cutting off a branch, rubbing
out a fresh stain or an old, deeply embedded one. . . .

> These proficients also have the natural dullness
> everyone contracts through sin, and a distracted and inat-
> tentive spirit. The spirit must be illumined, clarified, and
> recollected by means of the hardships and conflicts of this
> night . . . [in order to experience] the perfect state of the
> union of love.[26]

John also indicates that even though we try not to become
attached to the spiritual blessings, which we may be receiving, there
is a great temptation that many fall into when enticed by the devil,
a temptation to "become audacious with God and lose holy fear . . .
falling into vanity, presumption and pride."[27]

How does this deeper purification come about? Very much like
the initial purification but in a deeper and more intense form. The
very fallenness of the world, the flesh, and the devil are turned into
means to draw us into deeper union with God. And God Himself
acts in the soul directly.

As we have previously noted: "Through many tribulations we
must enter the kingdom of God" (Acts 14:22b). This is a foundational biblical principle. The grain of wheat must fall into the
ground and die if it is to bear fruit (cf. Jn. 12:24).

> The trials that those who are to reach this state [trans-
> forming union] suffer are threefold: trials, discomforts,
> fears, and temptations from the world; and these in many
> ways: temptations, aridities, and afflictions in the senses;
> and tribulations, darknesses, distress, abandonment,
> temptations, and other trials in the spirit.[28]

It's useful to remember when we hear descriptions of the types of
trials and depths of purification that we must undergo to be able to be
fully united to God that this purification isn't optional. It's necessary.
It's not a question of "if" but of "when." If the purification doesn't
take place in this life it will have to happen in purgatory if we are to be
able to see God. We also should recall that the sooner this purification

takes place the better, for us and for everyone else in our life. The root of all our unhappiness is the result of sin and its effects. The sooner we are free from the distortions and crippling of sin the sooner we will experience a fuller joy and freedom as sons and daughters of God, and be able more and more to be a blessing to others.

> Since unpurified souls must undergo the sufferings of fire in the next life to attain union with God in glory, so in this life they must undergo the fire of these sufferings to reach the union of perfection. This fire acts on some more vigorously than on others, and on some for a longer time than on others, according to the degree of union to which God wishes to raise them, and according to what they must be purged of. [29]

Fire is an important image of the purifying action of God's Spirit, both in Scripture and in the writing of the mystics. One of John's most illuminating descriptions of how this purifying action of God's Spirit works and what it accomplishes is based on his analogy of a burning log. He considers this a particularly useful analogy that "illustrates many of the things we are saying and will say."

> For the sake of further clarity in this matter, we ought to note that this purgative and loving knowledge, or divine light we are speaking of has the same effect on a soul that fire has on a log of wood. The soul is purged and prepared for union with the divine light just as the wood is prepared for transformation into the fire. Fire, when applied to wood, first dehumidifies it, dispelling all moisture and making it give off any water it contains. Then it gradually turns the wood black, makes it dark and ugly, and even causes it to emit a bad odor. By drying out the wood, the fire brings to light and expels all those ugly and dark accidents that are contrary to fire. Finally, by heating and enkindling it from without, the fire transforms the wood into itself and makes it as beautiful as it is itself.

John explains how this analogy pertains to the purification of the soul.

> Similarly, we should philosophize about this divine, loving fire of contemplation. Before transforming the soul, it purges it of all contrary qualities. It produces blackness and darkness and brings to the fore the soul's ugliness; thus one seems worse than before and unsightly and abominable. This divine purge stirs up all the foul and vicious humors of which the soul was never before aware; never did it realize there was so much evil in itself, since these humors were so deeply rooted. And now that they may be expelled and annihilated they are brought to light and seen clearly through the illumination of this dark light of divine contemplation. Although the soul is no worse than before, either in itself or in its relationship with God, it feels clearly that it is so bad as to be not only unworthy that God sees it but deserving of his abhorrence. In fact, it feels that God now does abhor it.[30]

Bernard too, as steeped in Scripture as he is, often uses the image of fire to describe the purifying and divinizing action of God. He makes a distinction between the "fire that goes before God" that reveals sin and lays bare what must be purified, and the "fire that is God."

> The fire that is God does indeed devour but it does not debase; it burns pleasantly, devastates felicitously. It is a coal of desolating fire (Ps. 119:4), but a fire that rages against vices only to produce a healing unction in the soul. Recognize therefore that the Lord is present both in the power that transforms you and in the love that sets you aglow.

Bernard then talks about what this purifying fire of God's Spirit produces in the soul.

Furthermore, when this fire has consumed every stain of sin and the rust of evil habits, when the conscience has been cleansed and tranquilized and there follows an immediate and unaccustomed expansion of the mind, an infusion of light that illuminates the intellect to understand Scripture and comprehend the mysteries—the first given for our own satisfaction, the second for the instruction of our neighbors—all this undoubtedly means that his eye beholds you, nurturing your uprightness as a light and your integrity as the noonday.[31]

Let's examine now the nature of the purifying sufferings of this "dark night," and the great fruit that they bring.

Purifying Sufferings

First of all, we need to say that the reality of the "dark night" of a deeper purification isn't an invention of John of the Cross. It's an observation, a discovery, of how God works with souls that many of the saints speak about using a variety of different terminologies. It's a reality that's spoken about directly in Scripture—as we have seen and will continue to see—that the saints have been able to describe in some detail because of their experience and the gift of teaching that God has given some of them, most particularly the Doctors of the Church on whom we are focusing.

Many of the saints, especially John, make a point of explicitly relating their teaching to Scripture.

In speaking of this deeper purification that he calls the "dark night," John states: "So many are the scriptural passages we could cite that we would have neither the time nor the energy to put it all in writing."[32] John has analyzed this process of purification and developed a technical and poetic language to describe it perhaps better than anyone else, but there is a wide testimony to the reality and necessity of this purification that we will consider as we proceed.

Teresa categorizes the sufferings of this deeper purification—the dark night of the spirit—into exterior and interior trials. She teaches that as we are drawing closer to union with God, He prepares the soul for deeper union by accelerating the process of preparation through both gifts and graces, wounds of love—which we examined in the previous chapter—and also by trials of all kinds.

Exterior Trials

Teresa specifically names several exterior trials that she underwent: the harsh, judgmental criticism of others, the praise of others, the bad advice and lack of understanding by indecisive and inexperienced confessors, rejection by friends, and the suffering of physical illness.[33] The apostle Paul likewise cites a long list of sufferings that tested and purified him: afflictions, hardships, constraints, beatings, imprisonments, riots, labors, vigils, fasts, dishonor, and insults (cf. 2 Cor. 6:4–10).

"Dark nights" can be experienced intermittently or for more extended periods of time, and at varying levels of intensity. Thérèse talks of the anguish of waiting three days for her uncle to give approval for her to enter the convent as a "dark night."[34] The profound trial of her father's mental deterioration, which lasted three years, was a deeper and longer lasting "dark night." She speaks of the unbearable anguish, as the profound sorrow of her heart was soon joined by a deep aridity of her soul. Yet, as painful as it was, she wouldn't have traded it for the world. She knew the value of suffering. In the mysterious embrace of the Cross of suffering Thérèse knew that she and her sisters were "flying" towards God.[35] The deepest night of all was not to come until the last year and a half of her life when, while suffering from tuberculosis, she experienced acute and continuing temptations to abandon faith itself. We will learn more about this shortly.

Teresa of Avila mentions that physical illnesses, when the pains are acute, are the greatest of the exterior trials because the pain of the body affects the soul "in such a way that it doesn't know what to do with itself . . . although they do not last long in this extreme form."[36]

The purpose of what might seem like overwhelmingly impossible trials is to purify and to lead us to a deeper trust in God and abandonment to His will, "supernaturalizing" our hopes and dreams.

Paul remarks of his own afflictions experienced in Asia:

> We were so utterly, unbearably crushed that we despaired of life itself. Why, we felt that we had received the sentence of death; but that was to make us rely not on ourselves but on God who raises the dead. (2 Cor. 1:8–9)

Teresa encourages us, as usual, and reminds us that "God gives no more than what can be endured and His Majesty gives patience first" (cf. 1 Cor. 10:13).[37] She herself testifies that since she first began to experience the initial touches of the prayer of union when she was just twenty-two years old and only a few years in the convent—she was about sixty-two years old when she wrote this—she hadn't a day without some kind of physical illness and other trials of various kinds. She claims that this is because of her wretchedness and the fact that she deserved hell and that others, who haven't offended the Lord as much, might be led by a different path.[38]

While the external trials can be severe, particularly in the case of serious illness, both Teresa and John explain that the interior trials of this deeper purification are even more difficult.

Interior Trials

The most serious of the interior trials involves the suffering that comes from feeling that one has perhaps been abandoned by God or has seriously gotten off track. Sometimes the absence of feeling in prayer and in the overall relationship with God—aridity—combined with the tempting of the devil, can produce a hellish, agonizing experience of abandonment and almost hopeless condemnation.

Teresa of Avila explains that, as in the case of Job, the Lord sometimes gives permission for the devil to test the soul even to the point of thinking it is rejected and abandoned by God.[39] During these times of profound interior trial, she explains, the presence of grace is so hidden that not even a tiny spark of it is visible.

> The soul doesn't think that it has any love of God or that it ever had any, for if it has done some good, or His Majesty has granted it some favor, all of this seems to have been dreamed up or fancied. As for sins, it sees certainly that it has committed them.[40]

Nothing satisfies during these times. Solitude is unbearable but so is being with other people. All kinds of prayer, vocal and mental, feel empty and useless. And even though the soul tries to maintain a positive disposition during this time, it finds it impossible to do so, and "goes about with a gloomy and ill-tempered mien that is externally very noticeable." It also suffers the added humiliation of everyone seeing how "down" it is.[41]

In this state, nothing seems to be able to relieve the soul's misery. Even if a spiritual director were to explain what one was experiencing and why, explaining about the "dark night" and how it would eventually lift, it probably would not help. The reason is that this trial "comes from above and earthly things are of no avail in the matter. Our great God wants us to know our own misery and that He is king; and this is very important for what lies ahead."[42]

Teresa explains that, since this is a divine work, nothing we do can get rid of the trial, but a good way of enduring it "is to engage in external works of charity and to hope in the mercy of God who never fails those who hope in Him." In fact she makes clear that "there is no remedy in this tempest but to wait for the mercy of God."[43]

The reason for the depth of this trial is so that we can know on a much deeper level our incapacity for union with God and our absolute need of His grace and mercy if we are to be able to love Him and follow Him. And then, when this phase of the preparation has been accomplished, "at an unexpected time, with one word alone or a chance happening," this very great trial will be over. The soul will emerge, deeply humbled, and with great joy, delight, praise, and gratitude, having been made ready to enter the seventh mansion.[44]

John of the Cross makes clear that what we are undergoing is not just a trial, a suffering, or a temptation, but an actual work of God deep in the soul. He explains that in this passive night of the spirit God infuses pure light and love into the soul ("dark contemplation"). It is only because of our limitations and sinfulness that what is in itself purely delightful is experienced by us, in our fallen condition, as painful and distressing.

> These proficients are still very lowly and natural in their communion with God and in their activity directed toward him. . . . Wishing to strip them in fact of this old self and clothe them with the new, which is created according to God in the newness of sense, as the Apostle says [Col. 3:9–10, Eph. 4:22–24, Rom. 12:2], God divests the faculties, affections, and senses, both spiritual and sensory, interior and exterior. He leaves the intellect in darkness, the will in aridity, the memory in emptiness, and the affections in supreme affliction, bitterness, and anguish by depriving the soul of the feeling and satisfaction it previously obtained from spiritual blessings. . . . The Lord works all of this in the soul by means of a pure and dark contemplation.[45]

John is eager, as always, to show the scriptural foundation for what he is teaching. He is attempting to "unpack" the dense layers of meaning contained in what Scripture describes in more succinct terms. Besides the New Testament passages speaking of complete transformation that John often cites, he also discerns the same "passive night of the spirit" in the profound testing and trials that great figures of the Old Testament underwent. In this regard he often cites the experiences of Job, Jonah, David, Joseph, Abraham, and Jeremiah as illuminative of what he is calling, in his poetic language, a "dark night."[46]

Job, of course, is almost a prototype of the dark night of purification. Besides the experience of abandonment by God, John points out that Job felt a lack of understanding and rejection from those close to him, for "such persons also feel forsaken and despised by creatures, particularly by their friends."[47]

As with the story of Job, so also Psalm 88 provides a striking description of many of the elements of the dark night.[48] It speaks of apparent abandonment by God, rejection by friends, anguish of soul and body, darkness of understanding, temptations against faith and trust. It can be rightly called a "psalm for the dark night."

And how descriptive of this purification are the words of the prophet Malachi:

> "For he is like a refiner's fire and like fullers' soap; he will sit as a refiner and purifier of silver, and he will purify the sons of Levi and refine them like gold and silver, till they present right offerings to the LORD." (Mal. 3:2b–3)

These themes of profound affliction and the experiential absence of God surface in much of the Scripture, most notably in Jesus' recitation of Psalm 22 in His own agony on the Cross. No matter how deep the darkness and agony may seem, despair never wins; faith and trust in the midst of darkness remain the only light, and ultimately lead to the glory of the Resurrection and the beatific vision. Jesus is our leader, and we have only to follow Him through the darkness.

> In the days of his flesh, Jesus offered up prayers and supplications, with loud cries and tears, to him who was

able to save him from death, and he was heard for his godly fear. Although he was a Son, he learned obedience through what he suffered; and being made perfect he became the source of eternal salvation to all who obey him. (Heb. 5:7–9)

The dark night calls from us in the deepest part of our being a deeper and purer faith, hope, and love. In the dark night, God is giving us the grace to believe (cf. Ps. 116:10) even when afflicted. He is lovingly guiding us on our way even when there is no perception of His presence. Even though we are in darkness, we are not to focus on the darkness, as perhaps some non-Christian forms of meditation might suggest, but we need to focus on Jesus who remains the "pioneer and perfecter" (Heb. 12:2) of our faith. If we do this, the darkness will eventually turn into an immense light.

> And I will lead the blind
>   in a way that they know not,
> in paths that they have not known
>   I will guide them.
> I will turn the darkness before them into light,
>   the rough places into level ground.
> These are the things I will do,
>   and I will not forsake them. (Is. 42:16)

Although we "go forth weeping," we shall "come back rejoicing" at the fruitfulness that has been revealed, as we persevere in faith, hope, and love (Ps. 126:6).

John also explains clearly that everything that comes from God is good; this "dark contemplation" that comes into the soul is experienced as painful only because of our unclean, untransformed condition.

> When this pure light strikes in order to expel all impurity, persons feel so unclean and wretched that it seems God is against them and they are against God. . . .

The soul understands distinctly that it is worthy neither of God nor of any creature. And what most grieves it is that it thinks it will never be worthy, and there are no more blessings for it. This divine and dark light causes deep immersion of the mind in the knowledge and feeling of one's own miseries and evils; it brings all these miseries into relief so the soul sees clearly that of itself it will never possess anything else. . . .

Persons suffer affliction . . . because of their natural, moral and spiritual weakness. Since this divine contemplation assails them somewhat forcibly in order to subdue and strengthen their soul, they suffer so much in their weakness that they almost die, particularly at times when the light is more powerful. Both the sense and the spirit, as though under an immense and dark load, undergo such agony and pain that the soul would consider death a relief.[49]

Teresa mentions that this desire to die and have it all done with, which is characteristic of this phase of purification, gives way in the seventh mansion to a peaceful love of God's will—so much so that even if He wanted us to spend another thousand years on earth undergoing extraordinary sufferings we would be delighted to do so out of love for Him and His will.

In the meantime, however, the soul undergoes a deep purification, and John vividly describes the feelings that accompany it.

And the soul not only suffers the void and suspension of these natural supports and apprehensions, which is a terrible anguish (like hanging in midair unable to breathe), but it is also purged by this contemplation. As fire consumes the tarnish and rust of metal, this contemplation annihilates, empties, and consumes all the affections and imperfect habits the soul contracted throughout its life. Since these imperfections are deeply rooted in the substance of the soul, in addition to this poverty, this natural and spiritual emptiness, it usually suffers an oppressive undoing and an inner torment. . . . For the prophet [Ezekiel 24:10–11] asserts that in order to burn away the rust of the affections the soul must, as it were, be annihilated and undone in the measure that these passions and imperfections are connatural to it.[50]

And remember, Bernard also talks of the purifying fire.

The fire that is God does indeed devour but it does not debase; it burns pleasantly, devastates felicitously. It is a coal of desolating fire (Ps. 119:4), but a fire that rages against vices only to produce a healing unction in the soul.

This fire consumes "every stain of sin and the rust of evil habits."[51]

This language and the concept of "annihilation" are strong. Is it biblical? Indeed, the biblical equivalent, I believe, would be that of "crucifixion." Indeed, to be "crucified with Christ" is to be "crucified to the world and the world to me," and is a death that is radical, total, and irrevocable.

And those who belong to Christ Jesus have crucified the flesh with its passions and desires. (Gal. 5:24)

We know that our old self was crucified with him so that the sinful body might be destroyed, and we might no longer be enslaved to sin. (Rom. 6: 6)

Is this not the violence that Jesus speaks of as being required for "taking" the Kingdom (cf. Mt. 11:12)?

Saint Vincent de Paul speaks of the violence of the sculptor who chips off marble that doesn't belong so that the beautiful figure that he is carving may be revealed.

The very essence of being a Christian, expressed in the baptismal and Easter liturgy, speaks of death and crucifixion.

> We were buried therefore with him by baptism into death. . . . We know that our old self was crucified with him so that the sinful body might be destroyed, and we might no longer be enslaved to sin. For he who has died is freed from sin. But if we have died with Christ, we believe that we shall also live with him. (Rom. 6:4, 6–8)

The image that Jesus uses of the seed falling into the ground and dying (Jn. 12:24) is similar, very much like Teresa's silkworm. Everything unclean must go. Everything twisted and bent as a result of sin must be straightened. Everything crippled and sick in the depths of our soul must be healed, and everything out of its proper order must be put into order. Every attachment that is not to the Lord and in the Lord must be broken. The illness we suffer from is grave and life threatening; the medicine to cure this "sickness unto death" must itself be very strong to be effective.

What must "die," "be crucified," or, in the language of John of the Cross, "be annihilated" is not the human personality or even the body, but the distortions that sin has worked in the depth of the human person. This must happen in order for each of us, body and soul, to truly live as we were created to live, beginning on this earth and continuing in fullness when we live with risen bodies. Oh, blessed death! Oh, blessed crucifixion! Oh, blessed annihilation!

Catherine of Siena also speaks of the intensity of this purification, without using the terminology of "dark night." In speaking about the intensity of trials, temptations and dryness in prayer that a soul trying to make progress encounters, the Father gives Catherine the answer to a question that all of us have surely asked: Why must we undergo this trial? The answer is in harmony with what Teresa, Bernard, and John have explained.

> And why do I keep this soul, surrounded by so many enemies, in such pain and distress? Not for her to be captured and lose the wealth of grace, but to show her my

providence, so that she will trust not in herself but in me. Then she will rise up from her carelessness and her concern will make her run for protection to me her defender, her kind Father, the provider of her salvation. I want her to be humble, to see that of herself she is nothing and to recognize that her existence and every gift beyond that comes from me, that I am her life. She will recognize this life and my providence when she is liberated through these struggles, for I do not let these things last forever. They come and go as I see necessary for her. Sometimes she will think she is in hell, and then, through no effort of her own, she will be relieved and will have a taste of eternal life. The soul is left serene. What she sees seems to cry out that God is all-aflame with loving fire, as she now contemplates my providence. For she sees that she has come safely out of this great flood not by any effort of her own. The light came unforeseen. It was not her effort but my immeasurable charity, which wanted to provide for her in time of need when she could scarcely take anymore.[52]

We hear the same message: this purification is necessary for humility to deepen and to know our total dependence on God. It is not an end in itself but raises us to a higher level of union with God. God will not let us be tested beyond our strength, even though sometimes it will seem like we are. The revelation of our weaknesses, mistakes, sins, or failures in our relationships or work may all be means that God makes use of to draw us more radically to Himself.

John of the Cross also notes that purification varies in intensity and does not last forever. Depending on how God deems best to work with each individual soul, it may come in intervals, alternating with consolations.

God humbles the soul greatly in order to exalt it greatly afterward. And if he did not ordain that these feelings, when quickened in the soul, be soon put to sleep again, a person would die in a few days. Only at intervals is one aware of these feelings in all their intensity. Sometimes that experience is so vivid that it seems to the soul that it sees hell and perdition open before it. These are the ones who go down into hell alive (Ps. 55:15), since their purgation on earth is similar to what takes place there.[53]

Here John is talking about the purifying process of "purgatory," not the eternal damnation of hell. He then makes the remarkable statement, which is echoed by many saints, that the more purification that can be undergone here on earth, the better.

For this purgation is what would have to be undergone there. The soul that endures it here on earth either does not enter that place, or is detained there for only a short while. It gains more in one hour here on earth by this purgation than it would in many there.[54]

The sooner the purification can happen and the more advanced it can become, the better for us and everyone else. As we have previously noted—and will keep on noting!—the more we are purified and conformed to God's will and image, the happier we will be and the better able to truly love God and everyone else in our life, and to live our life in a way that's a blessing for others.

As John explains, what an individual will actually experience in this purification will vary greatly, depending on how much needs to be purified and to what degree of union God is leading the person. Both Teresa and John try to include everything in their descriptions that they believe people could possibly experience, while knowing that what an individual will actually experience will vary considerably and that very few, if any, will experience everything of which they speak.[55]

Francis de Sales also talks of this deep purification. He describes how Saint Francis of Assisi went through such a time of intense purification.

> The glorious father of whom we speak was himself once assailed and disturbed by such deep spiritual melancholy that he could not help showing it in his conduct. If he wanted to talk with his religious he could not do so; if he withdrew from their company it was worse. Abstinence and bodily mortification weighed him down and prayer gave him no relief. He went on in this way for two years so that he seemed completely abandoned by God. Finally, after he had humbly endured this violent storm, the Savior in a single instant restored him to a happy calm.[56]

The conclusion which Francis de Sales draws for us is that, if even the greatest of saints had to undergo such purification, we should not be astonished that we lesser servants have to undergo purification in some measure also.

In commenting on the purification of Job and of the apostles, Francis links such purifications to the unique and mysterious sufferings of Jesus.

> In like manner our divine Savior was incomparably afflicted in his civil life, being condemned as guilty of treason against God and man; beaten, scourged, reviled, and tormented with extraordinary ignominy; in his natural life, dying in the most cruel and sensible torments that heart could conceive; in his spiritual life enduring sorrows, fears, terrors, anguish, abandonment, interior oppressions, such as never had, nor shall have their like. . . . So in the sea of passions by which Our Lord was overwhelmed, all the faculties of his soul were, so to say, swallowed up and buried in the whirlpool of so many pains, excepting only the point of his spirit, which, exempt from all trouble, remained bright and resplendent with glory and felicity.[57]

Just as Jesus at the "point of his spirit" maintained the experience of the beatific vision, although all else was darkness, Francis indicates that when we are going through the most intense of purifications, so too will the "heights of the spirit" of our souls maintain some perception, however obscure, of the link with God.

John makes the same point when speaking about the experience of abandonment of Jesus on the Cross. Even though His whole being experienced the desolation of crucifixion in all its sensory and spiritual dimensions, the "higher" part of His soul remained in the peace of the beatific vision.

Thérèse witnesses to the same truth:

> In a word, everything was sadness and bitterness. And still *peace,* always *peace,* reigned at the bottom of the chalice.[58]

Emptied in Order to Be Filled

Trials, temptations, sufferings, and purifications are not ends in themselves. They are means to a positive end. They are preparing us for union. They are enlarging the capacity of our soul so we can "grasp fully, with all the holy ones, the breadth and length and height and depth of Christ's love, and experience this love which surpasses all knowledge, so that you may attain to the fullness of God himself" (Eph. 3:18–19).

In retrospect it is possible to see the great grace of this deeper purification. In John's words:

> I departed from my low manner of understanding, and my feeble way of loving, and my poor and limited method of finding satisfaction in God. . . . This was great happiness and a sheer grace for me, because through the annihilation and calming of my faculties, passions, appetites, and affections, by which my experience and satisfaction in God were base, I went out from my human operation and way of acting to God's operation and way of acting. . . .
>
> My intellect departed from itself, changing from human and natural to divine. For united with God through this purgation, it no longer understands by

means of its natural vigor and light, but by means of the divine wisdom to which it was united. And my will departed from itself and became divine. United with the divine love, it no longer loves in a lowly manner, with its natural strength, but with the strength and purity of the Holy Spirit. . . .

The memory, too, was changed into eternal apprehensions of glory. And finally, all the strength and affections of the soul, by means of this night and purgation of the old self, are renewed with divine qualities and delights.[59]

As Thérèse looked back on her life, she saw the same thing: "My soul has matured in the crucible of exterior and interior trials." Like a flower after the storm, she could finally raise her head and see the promises of Scripture realized in her. Knowing on a deep level that the Lord was her shepherd, she lost her fear.[60]

Reflecting on the call of Carmel to save souls and to pray for priests, Thérèse remarks that one must use the proper means; the means by which Jesus saved the world was an obedient love that bore suffering for the sake of souls. As Thérèse put it:

Yes, suffering opened wide its arms to me and I threw myself into them with love. . . . This was my way for five years; exteriorly nothing revealed my suffering, which was all the more painful since I alone was aware of it. Ah! what a surprise we shall have at the end of the world when we shall read the story of souls.[61]

This suffering continued to purify Thérèse of the "stubbornness," the "self-love mingled with spiritual conversations," and the "excessive self-love" that at times led people to call her a "rascal" or a "brat."[62] Thérèse marveled at the changes that God was able to make in her through the embrace of suffering.

I really made a big fuss over *everything*! I was just the opposite of what I am now, for God has given me the grace not to be down cast at any passing thing. When I think of the past, my soul overflows with gratitude when I see the favors I received from heaven. They have made such a change in me that I don't recognize myself.[63]

But the change produced in Thérèse not just a stability and maturity of virtue and character—holiness—but also an identification with Christ that enabled her to participate in His redemptive suffering and in His love for the salvation of souls.

She was able, as Saint Paul puts it, to "complete what is lacking in Christ's afflictions for the sake of his body, that is, the church" (Col. 1:24).

Every aspect of the purification is an expression of the great mercy of God. Every painful aspect of the transformation is rooted in the immense desire God has to make us capable of sharing in the fullness of His joy. Every suffering is temporary, making us capable of an eternal weight of glory.

> Even though this happy night darkens the spirit, it does so only to impart light concerning all things; and even though it humbles individuals and reveals their miseries, it does so only to exalt them; and even though it impoverishes and empties them of all possessions and natural affection, it does so only that they may reach out divinely to the enjoyment of all earthly and heavenly things with a general freedom of spirit in them all.[64]

The process of letting go of inordinate attachments (this clinging to the things and people of this world out of fear or greed) once the purification has been completed, paradoxically leads to the ability to love and enjoy the things and people of this world in a much greater measure of love and in great freedom of spirit.

In summary, John prays,

> For you, O divine life, never kill unless to give life, never wound unless to heal. When you chastise your touch is

gentle, but it is enough to destroy the world. . . . You have wounded me in order to cure me, O divine hand, and you have put to death in me what made me lifeless, what deprived me of God's life in which I now see myself live. . . . And your only begotten Son, O merciful hand of the Father, is the delicate touch by which you touched me with the force of your cautery and wounded me.[65]

PART III

TRANSFORMING UNION

(The Unitive Way)

—∿—

Chapter Fifteen

DEEP UNION

THIS IS HOW POPE JOHN PAUL II sums up the principles of the
spiritual journey:

> It is a journey totally sustained by grace, which nonethe-
> less demands an intense spiritual commitment and is
> no stranger to painful purifications (the "dark night").
> But it leads, in various possible ways, to the ineffable joy
> experienced by the mystics as "nuptial union." How can
> we forget here, among the many shining examples, the
> teachings of Saint John of the Cross and Saint Teresa of
> Avila? (NMI 33)

The painful aspects of the journey, as John Paul II and the saints
tell us, are "worth it" because of what they make possible, what the
saints call the "spiritual marriage" or "nuptial union." What is this
union that the whole spiritual journey is preparing us for? What are
its signs? What are its fruits or effects?

The third stage of the spiritual journey is called the *unitive* way.
This stage usually comes only after the soul has been prepared by
many years spent in the struggle against selfish appetites, in the
development of virtue, in faithful prayer and good works, in the

patient endurance of trials and suffering, and in docility to the graces that God gives in many different forms. Teresa and John speak of the reality of a "betrothal" which ushers in the unitive way and leads to the even deeper "spiritual marriage." Bernard also puts it in these terms: "When she will have attained to it and become perfect she will celebrate a spiritual marriage. . ."[1]

While the saints don't usually map out their personal experience of the journey and relate it to their teachings, it is sometimes possible to infer from their writings when and how they progressed through the stages of the spiritual life. Teresa of Avila, for one, relates enough of her own experience that we are reasonably able to map the stages of her journey. She tells us that during her first years in the convent, in her early twenties, she occasionally experienced aspects of the prayer of union that she speaks about in her fifth mansion. She also speaks of a period of laxness that came to an end when she was thirty-nine years old, after which she experienced a new spiritual awakening or reconversion to a fervent quest for holiness. At the age of forty-seven, eight years later, she experienced the "betrothal" that she speaks about in the sixth mansion. Ten years later, at the age of fifty-seven, she experienced the spiritual marriage that she describes in her seventh mansion. At the age of sixty-seven, she died, exhausted from her labors.

We know from the testimony of Catherine and Thérèse that their own journeys were accelerated because of the early ages at which they would die. We can also surmise that John of the Cross's prison experience was a significant step in his journey: while in captivity he composed *The Spiritual Canticle*, a work in which he outlines the intense purification of the dark night of the spirit and how the dark night leads to spiritual marriage. In any case, while there is great variation in the timing and circumstances of each person's spiritual journey, the underlying "laws of the spiritual life" can be detected in each.

The Betrothal: Peace, Promise, and Imperfections

The "betrothal" is like a "spiritual engagement"—using the analogy of marriage—which bespeaks of a reasonable assurance that the long sought-for marriage will indeed come to pass. There is a mutuality of commitment and expectation that, if the journey continues as it has been, the end of "marriage" will be reached. The moment of betrothal may be experienced by way of some kind of spiritual communication, such as vision, locution, or some other spiritual touch. Or the moment may not in itself be clearly recognized by such a clear communication but rather in retrospect, by its subsequent fruits. Or there may simply be a quiet realization that a level of stable holiness and a depth of transformation have been reached where thoughts of marriage may now be considered. As Bernard explains,

> The soul which has attained this degree now ventures to think of marriage. Why should she not, when she sees that she is like him and therefore ready for marriage? His loftiness has no terrors for her, because her likeness to him associates her with him, and her declaration of love is a betrothal.[2]

John identifies the spiritual betrothal as a state of relationship where "the loyal and mutual love of betrothed persons" is expressed.[3] The seriousness and stability of a deep, mutually loyal and attentive relationship brings to the soul a basic tranquility and is usually characterized by abundant communications of various kinds. However, this tranquility is most fully experienced in what John calls the "superior" part of the soul. The sensory part of the soul "never completely loses the dross left from bad habits or brings all its energies into subjection" until the spiritual marriage.[4]

This is an important distinction. It takes a long time for all of our energies to come into submission to the Lord. Even when freely chosen sin is eliminated, there still remain to one degree or another various attachments, preferences, and "appetites" after which we follow. John in his poem speaks of this as following after the "herd" of such attachments. He clearly indicates that we are not freed from these attachments until the spiritual marriage takes place. His descriptions of what remains to be purified, even after having reached a rather advanced stage of the spiritual journey—that of the spiritual betrothal of the unitive way—is illuminating.

> It should be known that however spiritual a soul may be there always remains, until she reaches this state of perfection [spiritual marriage], some little herd of appetites, satisfactions, and other imperfections, natural or spiritual, after which she follows in an effort to pasture and satisfy it.
>
> In the intellect there usually reside some imperfect appetites for knowing things.
>
> The will is usually allowed to be captivated by some small appetites and gratifications of its own. These may involve temporal things, such as some little possession, or the attachment to one object more than to another, or some presumptions, judgments, punctilios, and other small things having a worldly savor or tinge. These latter may concern natural things, such as eating, drinking, finding more gratification in this than in that, choosing and desiring the best. Or they may concern spiritual things, such as the desire for spiritual satisfactions or other trifles we would never finish listing that are characteristic of spiritual persons who are not yet perfect.[5]

Thérèse speaks of overcoming her preference for beautiful objects, her desire for spending time with people for whom she had a natural attraction, her pride and defensiveness regarding what people thought of her—examples of what John is speaking about here.[6]

> In the memory there are usually many wanderings, cares, and useless imaginings after which she [the soul] follows.
>
> Regarding, too, the four passions of the soul, there are many useless hopes, joys, sorrows, and fears that she follows.

Some have more and others less of this herd, and they follow until having entered the interior wine cellar to drink, all transformed in love, they lose it entirely. In this wine cellar these herds of imperfections are more easily consumed than are the rust and tarnish of metal consumed by fire. Thus the soul now feels free of all the childish likes and trifles she pursued; and she can say: "And lost the herd which I was following."[7]

A little later on in his commentary on his own poem, John further elaborates on the composition of this "herd" that the soul follows.

Before reaching this gift and surrender of herself and her energy to the Beloved, the soul usually has many unprofitable occupations by which she endeavors to serve her own appetite and that of others. . . . These habitual imperfections can be, for example, the trait or "work" of speaking about useless things, thinking about them, and also carrying them out, not making use of such actions in accord with the demands of perfection. She usually has desires to serve the appetites of others, which she does through ostentation, compliments, flattery, human respect, the effort to impress and please people by her actions, and many other useless things. In this fashion she strives to please people, employing for them all her care, desires, work, and finally energy.[8]

Thérèse may be indirectly letting us know the point of surrender to God's will that she had reached—the spiritual marriage—when she quotes the very stanzas of *The Spiritual Canticle* (nos. 26, 28) in which John speaks of "losing the herd." She tells us further that at one point, after she had asked Jesus as a sign that her father had gone right to heaven to inspire the nuns in her convent to admit her sister Celine—a request that was granted—she no longer had any desires except "to love Jesus unto folly."

And now I have no other desire except *to love* Jesus unto folly. My childish desires have all flown away. . . . Neither do I desire any longer suffering or death, and still I love them both; it is *love* alone that attracts me, however. I desired them for a long time; I possessed suffering and believed I had touched the shores of heaven, that the little flower would be gathered in the springtime of her life. Now, abandonment alone guides me. I have no other compass. I can no longer ask for anything with fervor except the accomplishment of God's will in my soul without any creature being able to set obstacles in the way. I can speak these words of the Spiritual Canticle of Saint John of the Cross:

> In the inner wine cellar
> I drank of my Beloved, and, when I went abroad
> Through all this valley
> I no longer knew anything,
> And lost the herd that I was following.
>
> Now I occupy my soul
> And all my energy in his service;
> I no longer tend the herd,
> Nor have I any other work
> *Now that my every act is* **LOVE**.[9]

Bernard encourages us by noting that even if these imperfections or lesser attachments are not quite taken care of during the course of our life, the purification surrounding the process of death can remove the remaining imperfections.

> I do not say that this soul is deformed, but it has not attained to perfect beauty, for it worries and frets about so many things (Lk. 10:38–42), and is bound to be stained to some degree with the grime of worldly affairs. This however is quickly and easily cleansed at the hour of a death made holy by the grace of a pure intention and a good conscience.[10]

The Spiritual Marriage: Deep Union of Personal Love

John further explains the difference between the spiritual betrothal and the spiritual marriage.

> In spiritual marriage there are striking advantages over this state of betrothal, for although the bride, the soul enjoys so much good in these visits of the state of betrothal, she still suffers from her Beloved's withdrawal and from disturbances and afflictions in her sensory part and from the devil; all of these cease in the state of marriage.[11]

Bernard describes the state of spiritual marriage like this:

> When you see a soul leaving everything (Lk. 5:11), and clinging to the Word with all her will and desire, living for the Word, ruling her life by the Word, conceiving by the Word what it will bring forth by him, so that she can say, "For me to live is Christ, and to die is gain" (Ph. 1:21), you know that the soul is the spouse and bride of the Word.[12]

And isn't Mary the model of such complete union? And so Pope Benedict XVI describes her:

> The *Magnificat*—a portrait, so to speak, of her soul—is entirely woven from threads of Holy Scripture, threads drawn from the Word of God. Here we see how completely at home Mary is with the Word of God, with ease she moves in and out of it. She speaks and thinks with the Word of God; the Word of God becomes her word, and her word issues from the Word of God. Here we see how her thoughts are attuned to the thoughts of God, how her will is one with the will of God. Since Mary is completely imbued with the Word of God, she is able to become the Mother of the Word Incarnate.[13]

John reminds us that while the foundation of this marriage was established on the Cross, it unfolds in our personalities over the course of a lifetime, after a long journey. In one sense, the marriage is effected all at once, on the Cross, and communicated to us in Baptism; in another sense, it unfolds only gradually, little by little, at a pace that the wounded soul can endure.[14]

Again, John reminds us that what unfolds in our lives is an eminently personal union of love.

> When there is union of love, the image of the Beloved is so sketched in the will, and drawn so intimately and vividly, that it is true to say that the Beloved lives in the lover and the lover in the Beloved. Love produces such likeness in this transformation of lovers that one can say each is the other and both are one. The reason is that in the union and transformation of love each gives possession of self to the other and each leaves and exchanges self for the other. Thus each one lives in the other and is the other, and both are one in the transformation of love.
>
> This is the meaning of Saint Paul's affirmation: I live, now not I, but Christ lives in me (Gal 2:20).[15]

Bernard describes the intimate union of the spiritual marriage in a similar way.

> When she loves perfectly, the soul is wedded to the Word. . . . You approach the Word with confidence, cling to him with constancy, speak to him as to a familiar friend, and refer to him in every matter with an intellectual grasp proportionate to the boldness of your desire. Truly this is a spiritual contract, a holy marriage. It is more than a contract, it is an embrace: an embrace where identity of will makes of two one spirit. . . . This bond is stronger even than nature's firm bond between parents and children. . . . You see how strong this feeling is between bride and bridegroom—it is stronger not only than other affections, but even than itself. . . . Although the creature loves less, being a lesser being, yet if it loves with its whole heart (Mt. 22:37) nothing is lacking, for it has given all. Such love, as I have said, is marriage, for

a soul cannot love like this and not be beloved; complete and perfect marriage consists in the exchange of love.[16]

Sometimes he speaks of this union as similar to being invited into the private quarters of the king after a long day of work, to "chill out" or "debrief" "with a few companions whom he welcomes to the intimacy of his private suite. . . . His placid gaze sees about him none but well-loved friends."[17]

At another time Bernard uses the strong imagery of "eating" the Lord and "being eaten" by Him to convey a mutuality of complete indwelling that, while redolent with Eucharistic imagery, extends to an abiding state of relationship.

> I myself am his food. . . . I am chewed as I am reproved by him; I am swallowed as I am taught; I am digested as I am changed; I am assimilated as I am transformed; I am made one as I am conformed. Do not wonder at this (Jn. 5:28), for he feeds upon us and is fed by us that we may be the more closely bound to him. Otherwise we are not perfectly united with him. For if I eat and am not eaten, then he is in me but I am not yet in him (Jn. 6:57). . . . But he eats me that he may have me in himself, and he in turn is eaten by me that he may be in me, and the bond between us will be strong and the union complete, for I shall be in him and he will likewise be in me . . . feeding somehow upon God, and being fed by God.[18]

John reminds us that even in the spiritual marriage our journey is not yet over: the beatific vision, the "transformation in glory," yet awaits us when the veil of death is penetrated and we are transformed fully in a "face-to-face" encounter with the Lord.

Bernard also keeps before us the "not yet" present even in the highest union possible in this life.

> What do you think she will receive there, when now she is favored with an intimacy so great . . .[19]

And John concurs.

> Although transformation in this life can be what it was
> in Saint Paul, it still cannot be perfect and complete even
> though the soul reaches such transformation of love as is
> found in the spiritual marriage, the highest state attain-
> able in this life. Everything can be called a sketch of love
> in comparison with that perfect image, the transforma-
> tion in glory.[20]

Bernard also makes clear that the union awaiting us in the beatific vision is beyond anything possible in this life.

> And if both the ability and will to contemplate are
> prolonged eternally, what is lacking to total happiness?
> Those who contemplate him without ceasing are short of
> nothing; those whose wills are fixed on him have nothing
> more to desire.
>   But this vision is not for the present life; it is reserved
> for the next, at least for those who can say: "We know
> that when he appears we shall be like him, for we shall see
> him as he is" (1 Jn. 3:2). Even now he appears to whom
> he pleases, but as he pleases, not as he is. Neither sage nor
> saint nor prophet can or could ever see him as he is, while
> still in this mortal body; but whoever is found worthy will
> be able to do so when the body becomes immortal.[21]

John speaks about our fallen nature as an "old man," with its disordered passions as having "withered" or "fallen asleep"—a terminology
that other saints also use.[22] John seems to give the impression that
once in the spiritual marriage, there is virtually no possibility of ever
turning away so as to lose one's salvation. This is one of the very few
areas where there is a divergence of views between John and Teresa
of Avila as well as most of the other Doctors we are studying. The
preponderance of opinion is that even at the highest states of union
possible in this life, turning away remains a possibility, and careful

vigilance remains necessary. It is this preponderance of opinion that we would be wise to follow. Bernard expresses this view as well.

> For who has so completely cut away from himself all superfluous things that he thinks he has nothing worth pruning? Take my word for it, what is pruned will sprout again, what is banished will return, what is quenched will blaze again, things lulled to sleep will reawaken. To prune once therefore is of little worth. One must prune often, even, if possible, always, for you will always find something to prune if you aren't dishonest with yourself. No matter what progress you make in this life, you are wrong if you think vices are dead when they are only suppressed. Whether you like it or not, the Jebusite dwells within your borders (Judges 1:21). He can be subdued but not exterminated.[23]

Teresa of Avila, when considering how it is possible that someone even in the spiritual marriage could yet turn away, tells us such tragedies occur through small, almost imperceptible infidelities that gradually lead to bigger infidelities.

Even though it still may be possible to turn away from God until the very end, the nature of the spiritual marriage is truly extraordinary.

> In this interior union God communicates himself to the soul with such genuine love that neither the affection of a mother, with which she so tenderly caresses her child, nor a brother's love, nor any friendship is comparable to it. The tenderness and truth of love by which the immense Father favors and exalts this humble and loving soul reaches such a degree—O wonderful thing, worthy of all our awe and admiration!—that the Father himself becomes subject to her for her exaltation, as though he were her servant and she his lord. And he is as solicitous in favoring her as he would be if he were her slave and she his god. So profound is the humility and sweetness of God.[24]

Catherine of Siena describes the intimate union of the unitive way as that of a close friendship or a deeply filial relationship, or even "another me."

> And if anyone should ask me what this soul is, I would say: She is another me, made so by the union of love.
>
> What tongue could describe the marvel of this final unitive stage and the many different fruits the soul receives when its powers are so filled? . . . Not even the soul's own will stands between us, because she has become one thing with me.[25]

Bernard speaks of a mutual "holding" of each other.

> "I have hold of him, and will not let him go" (Song 3:4). But perhaps he wishes to be held, for he says, "My delight is to be with the sons of men" (Prov. 8:31). . . . What bond can be stronger than this, which is secured by the single strong will of the two who make it. . . . She holds him by her strong faith and devoted affection. Yet she could not hold for long unless she herself was held. She is held by the power and mercy of God.[26]

The mutuality of friendship or spousal union is characteristic of the spiritual marriage. John describes it like this:

> In this high state of spiritual marriage the Bridegroom reveals his wonderful secrets to the soul as to his faithful consort, with remarkable ease and frequency, for true and perfect love knows not how to keep anything hidden from the beloved.[27]

Among these communications are deep insights into the Incarnation and Redemption and many other mysteries as well.

Let us now consider what the fruits of this blessed union are.

Chapter Sixteen

THE FRUITS OF UNION

IT'S NOT THAT THE REMARKABLE FRUITS present in the spiritual marriage appear all of a sudden or for the first time. These fruits have been growing all along, but in the spiritual marriage they deepen, blossom, and stabilize in a way that is remarkable indeed. Not only is John of the Cross a master at precisely identifying what holds us back or delays us on the journey to God, but he is also a master at describing the wonderful fruits that appear as we progress on the journey.

Fruitfulness in Work

One of the fruits that John identifies as flowing from the spiritual marriage is a remarkable purity and power in the works we undertake.

> God causes in this union the purity and perfection necessary for such a surrender. And since he transforms her in himself, he makes her entirely his own and empties her of all she possesses other than him.
>
> Hence, not only in her will but also in her works she is really and totally given to God without keeping anything back, just as God has freely given himself entirely to her. This union is so effected that the two wills are mutually paid, surrendered, and satisfied (so that neither fails the other in anything) with the fidelity and stability of an espousal.[1]

This brings about a freedom from self-concern and fear of what others will think that enables one to act with a daring and determination in obedience to God's will and His interests.[2]

Bernard also speaks of the daring actions characteristic of this union.

> There is nothing that a pure heart, a good conscience, and an unfeigned faith will not venture.[3]

Teresa of Avila speaks of the same transition into apostolic desire and fruitful actions in connection with the spiritual marriage. And Catherine of Siena exemplified the union of the contemplative and active dimensions of the Christian life: after an intense three-year process of purification and transformation, she emerged from her room to engage in a very active life of service. Bernard puts it like this:

> Men and women of this kind undertake great deeds . . . and what they undertake they achieve, in accord with the promise which runs: "Everyplace on which the sole of your foot treads shall be yours" (Deut. 11: 24). Great faith deserves great rewards; and if you step out with the trust where the good things of the Lord are to be found, you will possess them.[4]

An Immense Fortitude

An immense fortitude is characteristic of the soul in the spiritual marriage, rooted as it is in God. It's a fortitude and strength that enables the soul to act always in the service of love. John again reminds us that what holiness is all about is growing in love.

> Since in this state she has reached perfection, the form and nature of which, as Saint Paul says, is love (Col. 3:14), and since the more a soul loves the more completely it loves, this soul that is now perfect is all love, if one may express it so, and all her actions love. She employs all her faculties and possessions in loving . . . the love of God in and

through all things. . . . The soul easily extracts the sweetness of love from all the things that happen to her; that is,
she loves God in them. Thus everything leads her to love.
And being informed and fortified as she is with love, she
neither feels nor tastes nor knows the things that happen
to her, whether delightful or bitter, since as we said the soul
knows nothing else but love. . . .

God makes use of nothing other than love.[5]

Continual Prayer

This love expresses itself in continual prayer, not only in adoration and thanksgiving to God but in intercession for the salvation
of others.

Catherine puts it like this:

> She gives forth a fragrance to the whole wide world, the
> fruit of constant humble prayers. The fragrance of her
> longing cries out for the salvation of souls; with a voice
> without human voice she cries out in the presence of my
> divine majesty.[6]

Sensitivity to Others

Souls at this level of union with God also develop a great sensitivity to others and a keen ability to reach out to them in their need.
Bernard describes it like this:

> She [the soul] becomes all things to all, mirrors in herself
> the emotions of all and so shows herself to be a mother to
> those who fail no less than to those who succeed.[7]

Love, we are reminded, at the beginning, at the middle, and at
the end of the journey, is the substance of true holiness and the fruit
of genuine union with God.

> The soul must grow and expand, that it may be roomy
> enough for God. Its width is its love. . . . His heart is
> filled with a love that embraces everybody, even those to

whom it is not tied by the inseparable bonds of family relationship; a love that is not allured by any hope of personal gain, that possesses nothing it is obliged to restore, that bears no burden of debt whatever, apart from that one of which it is said: "Owe no one anything, except to love one another" (Rom. 13:8).[8]

On a personal note, Bernard tells his monks that while they shouldn't unnecessarily interrupt someone engaged in contemplation, when necessary, by all means, interrupt! He tells them that while he appreciates people being sensitive to the busyness of his life, what with the constant visitors and his need for prayer, he doesn't want them to become so sensitive that they don't interrupt when there is genuine need. He'd rather err on the side of love. "I shall accommodate myself to them as far as I can, and as long as I live I shall serve God in them in unfeigned love."[9]

In harmony with the counsel of other saints, Bernard even advises that prayers, spiritual reading, and even Mass should sometimes be skipped in favor of helping someone.

> Who will doubt that in prayer a man is speaking with God? But how often, at the call of charity, we are drawn away, torn away, for the sake of those who need to speak to us or be helped! How often does dutiful repose yield dutifully to the uproar of business! How often is a book laid aside in good conscience that we may sweat at manual work! How often for the sake of administering worldly affairs we very rightly omit even the solemn celebration of Masses! A preposterous order; but necessity knows no law. Love in action devises its own order.[10]

Contemplation and Action

And Bernard, again in harmony with many of the saints, speaks of the link between contemplation and action. He speaks of these as the two offspring from the spiritual marriage.

But notice that in spiritual marriage there are two kinds of birth, and thus two kinds of offspring, though not opposite. For spiritual persons, like holy mothers, may bring souls to birth by preaching, or may give birth to spiritual insights by meditation. . . . The children are dear, they are pledge of his love, but his kisses give her greater pleasure. It is good to save many souls, but there is far more pleasure in going aside to be with the Word.[11]

Sometimes the fire of contemplation burns so strong that there is no desire to ever leave the time of prayer. Sometimes the fire of contemplation burns in such a way that a great desire to bring others to know the love of Christ arises.

It is characteristic of true and pure contemplation that when the mind is ardently aglow with God's love, it is sometimes so filled with zeal and the desire to gather to God those who will love him with equal abandon that it gladly foregoes contemplative leisure for the endeavor of preaching.[12]

Yet Bernard, as we have seen, is realistic in noting that even though the link between contemplation and action is important, it may often be perplexing to figure out the proper balance and realize what is truly pleasing to God at a particular moment. Indeed, finding the balance may be a lifelong process.

Quite often though the mind is tossed to and fro amid these changes, fearful and violently agitated lest it cling more than is justified to one or the other of these rival attractions and so deviate from God's will even momentarily. . . . That is, when at prayer I accuse myself of indifference at work; when at work of upsetting my prayer. . . . For this man the only remedy, the last resort, is prayer and frequent appeals to God that He would deign to show us unceasingly what he wishes us to do, at what time, and in what measure.[13]

A Stable Instinct for Good

This process of transformation or "deification" reaches such a point that the soul "does not even suffer the first movements contrary to God's will" but inclines towards God even in the first movements (inclinations or reactions towards things, people, situations) of the soul.

> As an imperfect soul is ordinarily inclined toward evil, at least in the first movements of its will, intellect, memory, and appetites, and as it has imperfections, so conversely the soul in this state ordinarily inclines and moves toward God in the first movements of its intellect, memory, will, and appetites, because of the great help and stability it has in God and its perfect conversion toward him. . . .

John cites Psalm 62:2 as a scriptural witness to what he is saying: "He only is my rock and my salvation, my fortress; I shall not be greatly moved."[14]

Finally, all the energies and capacities of the soul, interior and exterior, spiritual and bodily, are conformed to God's will and habitually act in harmony with Him. Its "instinctive" reactions to things are now in harmony with God's will, in harmony with truth and love. Its instincts have finally become in a real sense the "instincts" of God Himself.

> By directing the activity of the interior and exterior senses toward God, [the soul's] use of the body is now conformed to his will. She also binds the four passions of the soul to him, for she does not rejoice except in God or hope in anything other than God; she fears only God and has no sorrow unless in relation to him. And likewise all her appetites and cares go out only to God.[15]

This union is so habitual that the soul may not even be aware in particular situations how it is acting in conformity with God's will. It may even no longer find it necessary to explicitly "pray" before starting an activity, so habitual is the soul's union with God, so instinctual is its response to situations from within its relationship with Him.

> All this energy is occupied in God and so directed to him that even without advertence all its parts which we have mentioned, are inclined from their first movements to work in and for God . . . although, as I say, the soul may not advert to the fact that she is working for him. As a result she frequently works for God, and is occupied in him and in his affairs, without thinking or being aware that she is doing so. For her custom and habit of acting in this way cause her to lack advertence and care and even the fervent acts she used to make in beginning some work.[16]

Apostolic Fruitfulness

John remarks that "a little of this pure love is more precious to God and the soul and more beneficial to the Church, even though it seems one is doing nothing, than all these other works put together. . . . After all, this love is the end for which we were created."[17]

He then gives a very practical exhortation to those who think that apostolic work can be fruitful without giving the primacy to grace, to prayer, and to the journey towards union.

> Let those, then, who are singularly active, who think they can win the world with their preaching and exterior works, observe here that they would profit the Church and please God much more, not to mention the good example they would give, were they to spend at least half of this time with God in prayer, even though they might not have reached a prayer as sublime as this. They would then certainly accomplish more, and with less labor, by one work than they otherwise would by a thousand. For through their prayer they would merit this result, and themselves be spiritually strengthened. Without prayer they would do

a great deal of hammering but accomplish little, and some-times nothing, and even at times cause harm. . . .

However much they may appear to achieve exter-nally, they will in substance be accomplishing nothing; it is beyond doubt that good works can be performed only by the power of God.[18]

Bernard makes a similar point, claiming that someone who is not living under the lordship of Christ, in true communion with Him, should not exercise authority in the Church.

One who has not been admitted to this room should never take charge of others. This wine should be the inspiring influence in the lives of those who bear author-ity. . . . Your desire is venal if you hanker to rule over others without the will to serve them; your ambition is unprincipled if you would hold men in subjection with-out concern for their salvation. I have also named this the room of grace . . . because grace is especially found here in its fullness.[19]

John and Bernard's reflections are very similar to John Paul II's call to the whole Church:

I have no hesitation in saying that all pastoral initiatives must be set in relation to *holiness*. . . . Stressing holiness remains more than ever an urgent pastoral task. . . .

Our Christian communities must become *genuine "schools" of prayer*, where the meeting with Christ is expressed not just in imploring help, but also in thanks-giving, praise, adoration, contemplation, listening, and ardent devotion until the heart truly "falls in love." Intense prayer, yes, but it does not distract us from our commitment to history: by opening our heart to the love of God it also opens it to the love of our brothers and sisters, and makes us capable of shaping history according to God's plan. (NMI 30, 33)

A Purified, Joy-filled Love

In the spiritual marriage, as Catherine of Siena has expressed it, our love for God is no longer rooted in fear of punishment or motivated by hope of reward, but stems primarily from a pure and unselfish love of the Other—God—for His own sake.

> When a soul has reached the third stage, the love of friendship and filial love, her love is no longer mercenary.[20]

John echoes Catherine's teaching and shows once again how this teaching permeates the New Testament.

> Anyone truly in love will let all other things go in order to come closer to the loved one . . . with no desire to gain anything for herself. . . .
> The one who walks in the love of God seeks neither gain nor reward, but seeks only to lose with the will all things and self for God; and this loss the lover judges to be a gain [cf. Mt. 6:24, 16:25; Phil. 1:21].[21]

John, like Catherine, emphasizes again the great diversity of ways in which each human personality will reflect the perfection of love. Although all the saints share in common a profound love of God and neighbor, they express this love in an amazing variety of ways.

> Each runs along according to the way and kind of spirit and state God gives, with many differences of spiritual practices and works.[22]

Or as Catherine puts it:

> They find joy in everything. They do not sit in judgment on my servants or anyone else, but rejoice in every situation and every way of living they see, saying, "Thanks to you, eternal Father, that in your house there are so many dwelling places!" And they are happier to see many dif-

ferent ways than if they were to see everyone walking the
same way, because this way they see the greatness of my
goodness more fully revealed.[23]

Catherine lived this truth in her guidance of her disciples. She
didn't channel them all into one way of living for God, but encouraged them to pursue a whole variety of vocations, including married life, priesthood, religious life or consecrated life in the world,
depending on how each one was called.

From within the Father's Heart: Rediscovering Creation

The path of renunciation of disordered desires, the path of emptying, of death to sinful inclinations, leads to a realm of freedom and
joy where it is possible, for the first time, to truly enjoy the wonders
of creatures and the creation. People and things, the material universe
itself, are rediscovered in all their glory now that we are habitually
"resting filially within the Father's heart" (NMI 33). In *The Spiritual
Canticle,* John puts his poetic gifts to the task to express the wonder
and glory of God, reflected in His creation. We find striking phrases
from the poem itself such as "silent music" and "sounding solitude."

> So creatures will be for the soul a harmonious symphony
> of sublime music surpassing all concerts and melodies of
> the world. . . .
> When these spiritual faculties are alone and empty of
> all natural forms and apprehensions, they can receive in a
> most sonorous way the spiritual sound of the excellence
> of God, in himself and in his creatures. . . .
> In this same way the soul perceives in that tranquil
> wisdom that all creatures, higher and lower ones alike,
> according to what each in itself has received from God,
> raise their voice in testimony to what God is.[24]

This rediscovery of the creation in God—seeing it as it truly is, as
an expression of His glory—is, of course, what the Psalms continu-

ally tell us. The heavens and earth truly do declare the glory of God, for those who have ears to hear and eyes to see.

Bernard reminds us of the basis in truth for the earth now being the true homeland of men and of the Son of Man.

> He who is from heaven (Jn. 3:3–12) speaks of the earth so agreeably and intimately, as if he were someone from the earth . . . when he says "our land" (Song 2:12). . . . Notice then the utter happiness of hearing the God of heaven say: "in our land." . . . This is clearly not the language of domination but of fellowship and intimate friendship. He speaks as Bridegroom, not as lord. . . . It is not enough for him to be on a par with men, he is a man. Hence he lays claim to our land for himself, not as a possession but as his homeland. And why not claim it? From there is his bride, from there his bodily substance, from there the Bridegroom himself, from there the two become one flesh (Eph. 5:31). If one flesh, why not also one homeland? "The heavens are the Lord's heavens, but the earth he has given to the sons of men" (Ps. 113:24). Therefore as man he inherits the earth, as Lord he rules over it, as Creator he controls it, as Bridegroom he shares it.[25]

As we have already seen, Thérèse of Lisieux witnesses often to how much the creation spoke to her of God and His greatness.

> Never will I forget the impression the sea made upon me; I couldn't take my eyes off it since its majesty, the roaring of its waves, everything spoke to my soul of God's grandeur and power.[26]

And her trip by train through the Swiss Alps on the way to Rome remained a reference point that continually called her back to realize the grandeur and power of God.

> First, there was Switzerland with its mountains whose summits were lost in the clouds, its graceful waterfalls gushing forth in a thousand different ways, its deep

valleys literally covered with gigantic ferns and scarlet heather. Ah! Mother, how much good these beauties of nature, poured out *in such profusion,* did my soul. They raised it to heaven which was pleased to scatter such masterpieces on a place of exile destined to last only a day. I hadn't eyes enough to take in everything. Standing by the window I almost lost my breath; I would have liked to be on both sides of the car. . . .

At times, we were climbing a mountain peak, and at our feet were ravines the depths of which our glance could not possibly fathom. They seemed about to engulf us. A little later, we were passing through a ravishing little village with its graceful cottages and its belfry over which floated immaculately white clouds. . . .

When I saw all these beauties very profound thoughts came to life in my soul. I seemed to understand already the grandeur of God and the marvels of heaven. . . . I said to myself: When I am a prisoner in Carmel and trials come my way and I have only a tiny bit of the starry heavens to contemplate, I shall remember what my eyes have seen today.[27]

Remarkable as she was for her single-minded desire for heaven, Thérèse was equally remarkable for her sensitivity to all that is human, all that is created as a witness to the reality of God. Whether it be through her response to nature, or her love for her pet birds or the family dog, or her great sensitivity and appreciation for the depth of affection in her family relationships, Thérèse was continually called on toward God by all these things, which she experienced, more and more, in God. Her strong desire to be and to have all—to touch, to feel, to experience—led her inexorably on to the Source of all that is. Whether pushing past the barriers that kept her from entering the actual House of Loretto, or sneaking past the guards to go into the Coliseum to pick up stones, Thérèse craved contact with the original. God had put within her an overwhelming desire to touch the source of the innermost depth of things, which is God Himself.

I always had to find a way of *touching* everything. . . .
Really, I was far too brazen! Happily, God who knows
the depths of our hearts was aware that my intention was
pure and for nothing in the world would I have desired
to displease Him. I was acting toward Him like a *child*
who believes everything is permitted and looks upon the
treasures of its Father as its own.[28]

But Thérèse knew she needed to push on in order to really possess
creation as she desired to possess it, in order to plumb the depths of its
beauty and majesty from within the very heart of the Creator.

Ah! What poetry flooded my soul at the sight of all these
things I was seeing for the first and last time in my life!
It was without regret I saw them disappear, for my heart
longed for other marvels. It had contemplated *earthly
beauties* long enough; *those of heaven* were the object of its
desires and to win them for *souls* I was willing to become
a *prisoner.*[29]

For Thérèse, entering the enclosure of the Carmelite monastery
in Lisieux, becoming a "prisoner," was the most direct path into the
very heart of Beauty, into the vast expanses of the Creator's heart and
mind. It was her way of renunciation, total surrender, and single-
hearted pursuit of God. And she entered, she knew, not just for herself
but for others as well. She wanted her life to open a path to this heart
of Love for others. And she wanted to "return" to earth after her
death to carry out this mission.

In the state of union that characterizes the spiritual marriage, we
no longer primarily know God through creation, but we know creation through God. Our vantage point has changed. We no longer
are looking at God through creation, but we are looking at creation
from within the Father's heart. As Thérèse put it:

Since the time I took my place in the arms of Jesus, I am
like the watchman observing the enemy from the highest

turret of a strong castle. Nothing escapes my eyes; I am frequently astonished at seeing so clearly.[30]

This heightened sense of seeing, this perspective from within "the arms of Jesus," is a remarkable characteristic of the spiritual marriage, whether it should reveal the work of evil in a human soul or in the world at large, or the work of God in ordering all things to the good.

Bernard, commenting on the Song of Songs, expresses a similar insight.

> As she lies back he cushions her head on one of his arms, embracing her with the other, to cherish her at his bosom. Happy the soul who reclines on the breast of Christ (Jn. 13:25), and rests between the arms of the Word! "His left arm under my head, his right arm will embrace me" (Song 2:6).[31]

The purified soul not only is able to perceive creation as it truly is, but it does so by being able to participate in the very knowing and loving and "breathing" of God.

> There are many kinds of awakening that God effects in the soul, so many that we would never finish explaining them all . . . but it also seems that all the virtues and substances and perfections and graces of every created thing glow and make the same movement all at once . . . [as God moves in the soul] . . . in this awakening they not only seem to move, but they all likewise disclose the beauties of their being, power, loveliness, and graces, and the root of their duration and life. For the soul is conscious of how all creatures, earthly and heavenly have their life, duration, and strength in him. . . . It knows these things better in God's being than in themselves.
>
> And here lies the remarkable delight of this awakening: The soul knows creatures through God and not God through creatures. . . . God always acts in this way—as the

soul is able to see—moving, governing, bestowing being, power, graces, and gifts on all creatures, bearing them all in himself by his power, presence, and substance.[32]

A Habitual Embrace

John speaks of the union of the spiritual marriage as being a "habitual embrace." Now that the passions have been calmed and a deeper peace and a greater joy have been brought about, light from God may flow into the soul unimpeded.

> She finds in this state a much greater abundance and fullness of God, a more secure and stable peace, and an incomparably more perfect delight than in the spiritual betrothal; here it is as though she were placed in the arms of her Bridegroom. As a result she usually experiences an intimate spiritual embrace, which is a veritable embrace, by means of which she lives the life of God. . . . She would be unable to endure so intimate an embrace if she were not now very strong. . . . This union is found only in the spiritual marriage, in which the soul kisses God without contempt or disturbance from anyone. For in this state neither the devil, the flesh, the world, nor the appetites molest her.[33]

The "storms of life" continue to come and go; trials and suffering continue to be part of life; but the depth of union is such that these storms are now like storms on the surface of the ocean—deep underneath there is a solid calm. The Father speaks to Catherine of this:

> Those who reach the third stage . . . are perfect in every situation once they have come into this glorious light. No matter what I send them, they hold it in due reverence. . . . They consider themselves deserving of sufferings and outrages from the world, worthy to be deprived of any consolation at all that may be theirs. And just as they consider themselves deserving of suffering, so they also count themselves unworthy of any fruit that may come to them

from their suffering. These have known and tasted in the light my eternal will, which wants only your good and permits you these things so that you may be made holy in me. . . . They find joy in everything.[34]

John describes the "glorious illumination" the Lord sometimes bestows on the soul.

This habitual embrace, which is a certain spiritual turning toward her in which he bestows the vision and enjoyment of this whole abyss of riches and delight he has placed within her, our words would fail to explain anything about it. . . .

She is now so clearly illumined and strong and rests so firmly in her God that the devils can neither cause her obscurity through their darknesses, nor frighten her with their terrors, nor awaken her by their attacks. Nothing can reach or molest her now. . . .

This sweetness takes such an inward hold on her that nothing painful can reach her.[35]

Bernard speaks of the great confidence that comes from this union.

Consider how great is the grace of intimacy which results from this encounter of the soul and the Word, and how great the confidence which follows this intimacy![36]

The deep trust in the providence of God, which the Father speaks to Catherine about, is the foundation of the constant peace and joy in the union of the spiritual marriage. At its core, as Teresa and all the saints remind us, this union is that of our will with God's will.

In whatever way they use their lifetime for my honor, they are happy and find spiritual peace and quiet.

Why? Because they choose to serve me not in their own way but in mine. So the time of consolation is worth as much to them as the time of trial, prosperity as much as adversity. The one is worth as much as the other because they find my will in everything and they think of nothing but conforming themselves to that will wherever they find it.

They have seen that nothing is done apart from me or without mystery and divine providence—except sin, which *is* nothing. Therefore, they hate sin and hold all else in reverence. This is why they are so firm and constant in their will to walk along the path of truth, and do not slow down. Faithfully they serve their neighbors, paying no attention to their lack of recognition or gratitude or to the fact that sometimes vicious people insult and reprove them for their good works.[37]

Catherine also speaks of the "glorious" illumination of the faculties of the soul that is characteristic of this stage of union. This light helped her to express her love, as the Father told her, by "loving what I love and hating what I hate."[38]

This stage of union even has an impact on the devil. John explains that at a certain point in our transformation in Christ our union with Him becomes so deep that the devils are now afraid of us, rather than us being afraid of the devils!

In this state the soul is so protected and strong in each of the virtues and in all of them together . . . that the devils not only fear to attack her but do not even venture to appear before her. For they become greatly frightened on seeing her so exalted, courageous, and bold, with the perfect virtues in the bed of her Beloved. When she is united with God in transformation they fear her as much as they do him, and they dare not even look at her. The devil has an extraordinary fear of the perfect soul.[39]

The Father communicated a similar insight to Catherine:

So the devil is afraid of the club of their charity, and that is why he shoots his arrows from far off and does not dare come near. The world strikes at the husk of their bodies, but though it thinks it is hurting, it is itself hurt, for the arrow that finds nowhere to enter returns to the one who shot it. So it is with the world and its arrows of insult and persecution and grumbling: When it shoots them at my most perfect servants, they find no place at all where they can enter because the soul's orchard is closed to them. So the arrow poisoned with the venom of sin returns to the one who shot it.[40]

Teresa of Avila comments on this reality also.

And I would dare say that if the prayer is truly that of union with God [the fifth mansion] the devil cannot even enter or do any damage. His majesty is so joined and united with the essence of the soul that the devil will not dare approach nor will he even know about this secret.[41]

And Bernard agrees:

If the demons encounter a soul of this quality I can hear then now crying out: "Let us flee from before Israel, for the Lord is fighting for him" (Ex. 14:25).[42]

While the union of the spiritual marriage is habitual, it is not always "actualized" in a way that totally absorbs and engages the faculties, as Teresa of Avila describes when speaking of the prayer of union.

Perhaps this is how to best understand Bernard's meaning when he comments:

Neither does he make his presence continuously felt, not even to his most ardent lovers, nor in the same way to all.[43]

The same is true in terms of the "activation" of virtues that the Lord has given but aren't always in operation.

Even though [the soul] is filled with perfect virtues she is not always enjoying them actually; although, as I said, she ordinarily does enjoy the peace and tranquility they cause. We can say that in this life they are present in the soul as flower buds in a garden. It is sometimes a wonderful thing to see them all open through the Holy Spirit and diffuse a marvelous variety of fragrance. . . . Even though the soul is always in this sublime state of spiritual marriage once God has placed her in it, the faculties are not always in actual union although the substance is. Yet in this substantial union of the soul the faculties are frequently united too . . . [but the union] is not, nor can be, continuous in this life.[44]

While neither this state of absorption nor the actualization of the virtues can be constant, the experience of the almost continual presence of God is characteristic of the spiritual marriage.

Continual Presence

Normally (we will consider later on some special exceptions) once the spiritual marriage is attained there is a constant, virtually uninterrupted experience of the Lord's presence. Teresa tells us that every now and then the Lord may remove His presence for a few hours or a few days at most, to remind us that this union is a gift and not an achievement of ours; it depends on God's continual grace and our continual humility for it to continue.

The Father tells Catherine, we may recall, that the "lover's game" he plays with the soul as a means of growth, by removing the experience of His presence periodically, now ceases in the stage of union.

To such as these it is granted never to feel my absence. I told you how I go away from others (in feeling only, not in grace) and then return. I do not act thus with these most perfect ones who have attained great perfection and are completely dead to every selfish impulse. No, I am always at rest in their souls both by grace and by feeling. In other words, they can join their spirits with me in loving affection whenever they will. For through loving affection their desire has reached such union that nothing can separate it from me. Every time and place is for them a time and place of prayer. . . . I am their bed and table. . . . You see, then, how they feel me constantly present to their spirits. And the more they have scorned pleasure and been willing to suffer, the more they have lost suffering and gained pleasure. . . . They are like the burning coal that no one can put out once it is completely consumed in the furnace, because it has itself been turned into fire. So it is with these souls cast into the furnace of my charity, who keep nothing at all, not a bit of their own will, outside of me, but are completely set afire in me. There is no one who can seize them or drag them out of my grace. They have been made one with me and I with them. I will never withdraw from their feelings. No, their spirits always feel my presence within them, whereas of the others I have told you that I come and go, leaving in terms of feeling, not in terms of grace, and I do this to bring them to perfection. When they reach perfection I relieve them of this lover's game of going and coming back. I call it a "lover's game" because I go away for love and I come back for love—no, not really I, for I am your unchanging and unchangeable God; what goes and comes back is the feeling my charity creates in the soul."[45]

John testifies also to this fruit of the union.

She enjoys now in this state habitual sweetness and tranquility that is never lost or lacking to her.[46]

This strong awareness of the Lord's presence can flower into actual "jubilation."

Great Jubilation
This union produces a state of joy that wells up into jubilation and song, both interiorly and exteriorly.

In this state of life so perfect, the soul always walks in festivity, inwardly and outwardly, and it frequently bears on its spiritual tongue a new song of great jubilation in God, a song always new, enfolded in a gladness and love arising from the knowledge the soul has of its happy state.[47]

The inspired jubilation of the Psalms is realized in a habitual manner.

> Rejoice in the LORD, O you righteous
> > Praise befits the upright
> Praise the LORD with the lyre,
> > make melody to him with the harp of ten strings!
> Sing to him a new song,
> > play skillfully on the strings, with loud shouts.
> (Ps. 33:1–3)

This song of joy, John explains, is a participation in the jubilant song of the Lord Himself, welling up from within the union of hearts.

> The bride feels that this voice of the Bridegroom speaking within her is the end of evil and the beginning of good. . . . [She] sings a new and jubilant song together with God, who moves her to do this. He gives his voice to her that so united with him she may give it together with him to God.[48]

We think of what the prophet Zephaniah tells us of the Lord's song of joy, in which we participate.

> Sing aloud, O daughter of Zion;
> > shout, O Israel!
> Rejoice and exult with all your heart,
> > O daughter of Jerusalem! . . .
> The LORD your God is in your midst,
> > a warrior who gives victory;
> he will rejoice over you with gladness,
> > he will renew you in his love;

he will exult over you with loud singing
    as on a day of festival. (Zeph. 3:14, 17–18)

Bernard also witnesses to the presence of joyful praise as a characteristic of this union with the Lord. He teaches that the "holy anointing" of the Holy Spirit is characterized by "gladness and thanksgiving" and declares that "nothing more appropriately represents on earth the state of life in the heavenly fatherland than spontaneity in this outpouring of praise. Scripture implies as much when it says: 'Happy those who live in your house and can praise you all day long'" (Ps. 83:5).[49]

Bernard further explains that the one whom the Scripture calls "blessed" or "happy" is the one whose "joyfulness of spirit begets a radiance in his face and his deeds" (2 Cor. 9:7).[50] Bernard connects this "joyful spirit" with certain biblical declarations: "God loves a cheerful giver" (2 Cor. 9: 7), and "The joy of the Lord is your strength" (Neh. 8:10).

From time to time, Bernard tells us, there may be special outbreaks of jubilant praise.

> We may even find ourselves at times living beyond our normal powers through the great intensity of our affections and our spiritual joy, in jubilant encounters, in the light of God, in sweetness in the Holy Spirit (2 Cor. 6:6), all showing that we are among those envisioned by the Prophet when he said: "Lord, they will walk in the light of your favor; they will rejoice in your name all day and exult in your righteousness." (Ps. 88:16–17)[51]

Bernard further counsels us that when the anointing of joy falls upon us, we should yield to it.

> But if at times, when the heart expands in love at the thought of God's graciousness and mercy, it is all right to surrender our mind, to let it go in songs of praise and gratitude. . . . Unless I am mistaken, he will look in with

greater pleasure the more he is honored by the sacrifice of praise. (Ps. 49:23)[52]

And:

> As men feel the infusion of spiritual health they refuse to conceal their good fortune. The inward experience finds outward expression. Stricken with remorse I speak out his praise, and praise is a sign of life. . . . But see! I am conscious, I am alive![53]

Teresa also speaks of this ecstatic prayer of jubilation.

> Our Lord sometimes gives the soul feelings of jubilation and a strange prayer it doesn't understand.[54]

She explains that sometimes this interior joy of union with God is so great, and the impulse to express it externally is so strong, that it leads to dramatic expression. She gives examples of how people sometimes thought the saints were crazy, such as when Saint Francis of Assisi went running through the fields crying out he was the herald of the great King.

> To be silent and conceal this great impulse of happiness when experiencing it is no small pain. . . . Oh what blessed madness, Sisters! If only God would give it to us all![55]

Teresa gives us a glimpse of how this jubilation can occasionally "break out" into the life and relationships of the Christian community. She speaks of how this happens occasionally in her convents.

> I would want you to praise Him often, Sisters; for the one who begins, awakens the others. . . .
> May it please His Majesty to give us this prayer often since it is so safe and beneficial; to acquire it is impossible because it is something very supernatural. And it may last a whole day. The soul goes about like a person who has

drunk a great deal but not so much as to be drawn out of his senses. . . .

The joy makes a person so forgetful of self and of all things that he doesn't advert to, nor can he speak of anything other than the praises of God which proceed from his joy.

Let us all help this soul, my daughters. Why do we want to have more discretion? What can give us greater happiness? And may all creatures help us forever and ever, amen, amen, amen![56]

One thinks of Jesus' endorsement of jubilant praise.

As he was now drawing near, at the descent of the Mount of Olives, the whole multitude of the disciples began to rejoice and praise God with a loud voice for all the mighty works that they had seen, saying, "Blessed is the King who comes in the name of the Lord! Peace in heaven and glory in the highest!" And some of the Pharisees in the multitude said to him, "Teacher, rebuke your disciples." He answered, "I tell you, if these were silent, the very stones would cry out." (Lk. 19:37–40)

John Paul II called us to make this life of jubilation part of the authentic renewal the Holy Spirit is leading the Church into today, and has pointed out the need to let joy be manifested outwardly as well as inwardly as an invitation to others to join in the joy of salvation.

The term "Jubilee" speaks of joy, not just an inner joy but a jubilation which is manifested outwardly, for the coming of God is also an outward, visible, audible and tangible event, as Saint John makes clear (cf. 1 Jn. 1:1). It is thus appropriate that every sign of joy at this coming should have its own outward expression. This will demonstrate that *the Church rejoices in salvation.* She invites everyone to rejoice, and she tries to create conditions to ensure that the power of salvation may be shared by all.[57]

Inebriation in the Holy Spirit

This tradition of jubilant praise flows from the encounter with God and is a sign of the presence of the Spirit. We find it already in the wholehearted response of David dancing before the ark and praising God, embodied and carried forward in the Psalms, and deeply rooted in the New Testament vision of the Church.

When the Spirit rushed on the disciples in the upper room at Pentecost they began to speak "as the Spirit gave them utterance" in such a way that the crowd thought they must be inebriated. This interpretation of the assembled crowd—that they were drunk— had to be explicitly disavowed by Peter.

> For these men are not drunk, as you suppose, since it is only the third hour of the day; but this is what was spoken by the prophet. (Acts 2:15–16)

The continued presence of the Spirit in the life of the Church makes possible a continuing, fervent jubilation, which Saint Paul explicitly encourages:

> And do not get drunk with wine, for that is debauchery; but be filled with the Spirit, addressing one another in psalms and hymns and spiritual songs, singing and making melody to the Lord with all your heart, always and for everything giving thanks in the name of our Lord Jesus Christ to God the Father. (Eph. 5:18–20)

The mystical tradition of the Church that we are exploring, as we have already seen, regularly witnesses to this "inebriation" or jubilation as a sign of the encounter with God and His Spirit.

Bernard, writing in the twelfth century, comments on this fruit of union with God. On one occasion he interprets the "wine cellar" spoken of in the Song of Songs as the upper room where the early Church experienced the Pentecostal outpouring of the Spirit.

"The King led me into the wine-cellar, he set love in order in me.". . . It is not surprising if one who entered the wine-cellar should be tipsy with wine. . . . But she also does not deny that she is drunk in the spirit, but with love, not wine—except that love is wine. . . . Peter, the friend of the bridegroom, standing in their midst said on behalf of the bride: "These men are not drunk as you suppose." Take note that he denies not that they are drunk, but drunk in the manner supposed by the people. For they were drunk, but with the Holy Spirit, not with wine . . . intoxicated by the abundance of that house and drunk from a torrent of a pleasure so great.[58]

Bernard indicates that such contemplative "intoxication" continues to happen.

But if anyone obtains, while praying, the grace of going forth in spirit into the mystery of God, and then returns in a glowing ardor of divine love, overflowing with zeal for righteousness, fervent beyond measure in all spiritual studies and duties, so that he can say: "My heart became hot within me; as I mused the fire burned" (Ps. 38:4), since the abundance of love shows he has clearly begun to live in that state of good and salutary intoxication, he is not unjustly said to have entered the wine-cellar. . . . A tender affection, a heart glowing with love, the infusion of holy ardor, and the vigor of a spirit filled with zeal are obviously not acquired from any place other than the wine-cellar.[59]

Bernard is speaking with such joyful confidence here that one can't help but suspect that he is experiencing the very spiritual intoxication of which he is writing.

Can she [the bride] be possibly drunk? Absolutely drunk! And the reason? It seems most probably that when she uttered those passionate words she had just come out from the cellar of wine (Song 1:3; 2:4). . . . David in his turn cried out to God concerning people such as the bride: "They shall be inebriated with the plenty of your house; and you will make them drink of the torrent of your pleasure" (Ps. 35:9). How great this power of love: what great confidence and freedom of spirit! What is more manifest than that fear is driven out by perfect love! (1 Jn. 4:18).[60]

John of the Cross, writing in the sixteenth century, tells us that being filled with the Spirit in this way can be so bountiful that it indeed produces a state that appears to be a form of spiritual inebriation.

This spiced wine is another much greater favor that God sometimes grants to advanced souls, in which he inebriates them in the Holy Spirit with a wine of sweet, delightful, and fortified love. . . . They cause her to direct toward him, efficaciously and forcefully, flowings or outpourings of praise, love, and reverence, and so on. . . . And she does this with admirable desires to work and suffer for him.

This favor of sweet inebriation, because it has more permanence, does not pass away as quickly as the spark . . . [it] usually lasts, together with its effect, a long while, and sometimes a day or two, or many days, though not always in the same degree of intensity, because its lessening and increasing are beyond the soul's power. . . . *My heart grew hot within me, and in my meditation a fire shall be enkindled* [Ps. 39:3].[61]

Teresa's description of the spontaneous praise and jubilation that would break out in her convent and its effects which would last for days seems to be exactly what John and Bernard are talking about.

John and Bernard attribute this inebriation, as does the apostle Paul, to the working of the Holy Spirit in the life of the Christian and the Christian community, and draw our attention to the testimony to such spiritual inebriation found in the Scripture.

Citing the same psalm as Bernard, John tells us:

> *They shall be inebriated with the plenty of your house; and*
> *you will give them to drink of the torrent of your delight,*
> *because with you is the fountain of life* [Ps. 36:8–9]. What
> fulfillment the soul will have in her being, since the drink
> given her is no less than a torrent of delight! This torrent
> is the Holy Spirit.[62]

The Enhancement of Natural Knowledge

John strongly holds that the supernatural knowledge given to
us by God about Himself and His plan are far superior in importance to any natural knowledge we can obtain through observation
or study.

> She is being informed with supernatural knowledge, in
> the presence of which all natural and political knowledge
> of the world is ignorance rather than knowledge. . . . The
> natural sciences themselves and the very works of God,
> when set beside what it is to know God, are like igno-
> rance. For where God is unknown, nothing is known.[63]

Even though "natural" knowledge is vastly less important than
supernatural knowledge it nevertheless has its place in God's plan.
The infusion of supernatural knowledge doesn't destroy natural
knowledge, but actually enhances it and perfects it.

Thérèse testifies to the enhancement of her ability to master
natural knowledge (especially history and science) after God healed
her wounded soul and set her free to more maturely follow Him; she
calls this the grace of her "complete conversion."

> God was able in a very short time to extricate me from
> the very narrow circle in which I was turning without
> knowing how to come out. . . . Freed from its scruples
> and its excessive sensitiveness, my mind developed. . . . I
> had always loved the great and the beautiful, but at this

epoch in my life I was taken up with an extreme desire for learning . . . in a few months I acquired more knowledge than during my years of study.[64]

With the knowledge that comes with the spiritual marriage, we don't forget our knowledge of a foreign language or math—in fact, we may actually speak French or do math better than before. Yet in heaven, as John speculates, such natural knowledge, while not being forgotten, may be of even less use and importance.

> It should not be thought that because she remains in this unknowing she loses there her acquired knowledge of the sciences; rather, these habits are perfected by the more perfect habit of supernatural knowledge infused in her. Yet they do not reign in such a way that she must use them in order to know, although at times she may still use them. . . . When a faint light is mingled with a bright one, the bright light prevails and is what illumines. Yet the faint light is not lost; rather it is perfected even though it is not the light that illumines principally. Such, I believe, will be the case in heaven. The habits of acquired knowledge of the just will not be supplanted, but they will not be of great benefit either, since the just will have more knowledge through divine wisdom than through these habits.[65]

It is to heaven that Bernard, John, Teresa, Catherine, Thérèse, Francis, and Augustine finally direct our thoughts. Our journey from baptism to the beatific vision has almost reached its destination. We are almost at journey's end. We have almost reached the fulfillment of all desire.

Chapter Seventeen

THERE'S ALWAYS MORE

THE SAINTS MAKE CLEAR that although the spiritual marriage, or the "third stage" or unitive way, is the highest mode of union possible in this life, it is nevertheless not a static union. It continues to be a place of growth. The growth is characterized by a yet greater conformity to Christ and a yet deeper participation in His crucified, redemptive love for the human race. Therefore, paradoxically, while this stage of union is characterized by a virtually unshakable peace and joy, growth within it happens through a deeper participation in both the suffering and the Resurrection of Jesus.

The Father speaks to Catherine of it in this way:

> For the soul is never so perfect in this life that she cannot become yet more perfect in love. My beloved Son, your head, was the only one who could not grow in any sort of perfection, because he was one with me and I with him. His soul was beatified in his union with my divine nature. But you, his pilgrim members, can always grow to greater perfection. Not that you would advance to another stage once you had reached that final state of union with me. But you can make that very union grow in whatever kind of perfection you choose with the help of my grace.[1]

The Father tells Catherine that the human soul of Jesus actually participated in the fullness of the beatific vision while He was on earth, but the rest of us always have room to grow in deeper union in this life. This growth in deeper union happens the same way that growth in earlier stages happened: through both suffering and blessing.

> For there is no one in this life, no matter how perfect, who cannot grow to greater perfection . . . (Jn. 15:1–5). And so that your fruit may grow and be perfect, I prune you by means of trials: disgrace, insults, mockery, abuse, and reproach, with hunger and thirst, by words and actions, as it pleases my goodness to grant to each of you as you are able to endure. For trial is a sign that shows whether the soul's charity is perfect or imperfect.
>
> Patience is proved in the assaults and weariness I allow my servants, and the fire of charity grows in the soul who has compassion for the soul of her abuser. For she grieves more over the offense done to me and the harm done to the other than over her own hurt. This is how those behave who are very perfect, and so they grow. And this is why I permit all these things. I grant them a stinging hunger for the salvation of souls so that they knock day and night at the door of my mercy, so much so that they forget themselves. . . . And the more they abandon themselves the more they find me. . . . If they only saw it, there would be no one who would not seek suffering with great solicitude and joy.[2]

While at earlier stages suffering that came through trials and difficulties was perhaps primarily purgative—purifying the disorder in our souls—at this highest stage, our sufferings, while not without its purgative purpose, now also have a strongly redemptive purpose. The sufferings at this stage are now more directly a participation in the suffering love of Jesus for the salvation of the human race.

The Father also indicates to Catherine that sometimes the sufferings of this stage are characterized by an accompanying "condition" that makes clear the weakness of the vessel carrying the great treasure of Christ. The Father gives as an example Paul's "thorn in the flesh" described in Scripture. Speculation abounds about what this troubling condition might have been. Some speculate that it was an annoying physical condition or illness, or some kind of humiliating natural defect or embarrassing ongoing temptation. While the exact nature of the condition has not been revealed, its important spiritual function, for Paul and for others, is evident: humility and compassion are among the chief fruits of bearing such an ongoing condition of weakness in patience and in faith.

> Sometimes my providence leaves my great servants a pricking, as I did to my gentle apostle Paul, my chosen vessel. After he had received my Truth's teaching in the depths of me the eternal Father, I still left him the pricking and resistance of his flesh (2 Cor. 12:7).
>
> Could I and can I not make it otherwise for Paul and the others in whom I leave this or that sort of pricking? Yes. Then why does my providence do this? To give them opportunity for merit, to keep them in the self-knowledge whence they draw true humility, to make them compassionate instead of cruel toward their neighbors so that they will sympathize with them in their labors. For those who suffer themselves are far more compassionate to the suffering than are those who have not suffered. They grow to greater love and run to me all anointed with humility and ablaze in the furnace of my charity. And through these means and endless others they attain perfect union—such union and knowledge of my goodness that while they are still in their mortal bodies they taste the reward of the immortal. . . . And whoever loves much will have great sorrow; therefore those whose love grows will know more sorrow.[3]

Catherine summarizes what the Father says to her about this, recapitulating some of the themes with which we have become familiar.

You see then in how many different ways I provide for these perfect ones, for as long as you are alive you can still grow in perfection and merit. This is why I purge them of every selfish and disordered love, whether temporal or spiritual, and prune them by means of many trials so that they may produce more and better fruit. And because of the great suffering they endure when they see me offended and souls deprived of grace, every lesser emotion of theirs is quelled, until they consider any burden they could bear in this life to be less than nothing. This is why they care equally about trial and consolation, because they are not seeking their own consolation. They do not love me with a mercenary love for their own selfish pleasure; rather, it is the honor and glory and praise of my name they seek.[4]

Personal Calls: The Story of Thérèse's Soul

While the Father has revealed to the saints an amazing amount of detail about the general progression of the spiritual journey, He—and they—make clear that there is nevertheless an irreducibly unique personal dimension to each person's journey. We see such a personal call within the vocation of Thérèse of Lisieux.[5]

While steeped in the biblical worldview and the deep tradition of her own fellow Carmelites, Teresa and John, Thérèse didn't attempt to write a systematic treatise on the spiritual life as they did. She simply told her story, but communicated in the course of telling it a great deal of spiritual truth; in her own inimitable way, she witnessed to what it was like for one person to embody the teachings of Teresa and John. The story of her soul's journey, while uniquely hers, sheds light for us all.

As we have seen in earlier chapters, Thérèse's vocation was special from the beginning. God worked in her quickly, for His plan for her anticipated an early death. This plan included significant purification and healing of a soul that was deeply wounded and turned in on itself by the early death of her mother and the traumatic departure for the convent of her "second mother," Pauline. While Thérèse didn't exactly pinpoint when the spiritual betrothal or spiritual marriage happened for her (although, as we have seen, we have some indication), it is clear that she had reached a very high degree of union certainly within a few years of her death.

Yet the last year and a half of her life took a surprising turn. Shortly after the first signs of tuberculosis appeared, a very deep spiritual darkness set in, which involved deeply disturbing temptations against faith. The whole longing of her life had focused on heaven, and now her faith in the reality of heaven was being assailed in the most unremitting manner!

In order to understand this unexpected turn of events we must look carefully at what she says she began to pray in the months after her first Communion. In the days when receiving Communion at every Mass was not considered appropriate for most people, Thérèse had received permission to receive communion on all the principal Feasts. We must consider carefully what she tells us happened the day after one of these Communions, when a special vocation was offered to her and she accepted.

> The day after my Communion . . . I felt born within my heart a *great desire* to suffer, and at the same time the interior assurance that Jesus reserved a great number of crosses for me. I felt myself flooded with consolations so *great* that I look upon them as one of the *greatest* graces of my life. Suffering became my attraction; it had charms about it which ravished me without my understanding them very well. Up until this time, I had suffered without *loving* suffering but since this day I felt a real love for it. I also felt the desire of loving only God, of finding my joy only in Him. Often during my Communions, I repeated these words of the Imitation [*The Imitation of Christ* III, 26, 3]: "O Jesus, unspeakable *sweetness*, change all the consolations of this earth into *bitterness* for me." This prayer fell from my lips without effort, without

constraint; it seemed I repeated it not with my will but like a child who repeats the words a person he loves has inspired in him.[6]

The whole notion of "loving suffering," which appears occasionally in the writings of the saints, can be startling. But this too has a sound biblical basis. When we are able to grasp the dimensions of what we have called the "biblical worldview," things can appear very different than they do to the "natural" man. Very different indeed!

Peter tells us to "rejoice in so far as you share Christ's sufferings, that you may also rejoice and be glad when his glory is revealed. If you are reproached for the name of Christ, you are blessed, because the spirit of glory and of God rests upon you" (1 Pet. 4:13–14).

Paul tells us that when we understand the good that suffering is producing in our lives, we will rejoice in it!

> We rejoice in our sufferings, knowing that suffering produces endurance, and endurance produces character, and character produces hope, and hope does not disappoint us, because God's love has been poured into our hearts through the Holy Spirit who has been given to us. (Rom. 5:3–5)

James has similar advice.

> Count it all joy, my brethren, when you meet various trials, for you know that the testing of your faith produces steadfastness. And let steadfastness have its full effect, that you may be perfect and complete, lacking in nothing. (Jas. 1:2–4)

There's a certain progression in the journey to God regarding our attitude towards suffering. In the beginning, we flee from suffering. As we mature, we reluctantly accept it as necessary. As the Spirit works more deeply in our hearts, we little by little lose our fear of suffering and become able to rejoice in it, even to love it.

While there was much suffering in Thérèse's life, much of which she doesn't reveal to us, the suffering of the last year and a half of her life was not anticipated.

> At this time I was enjoying such a living faith, such a clear *faith*, that the thought of heaven made up all my happiness, and I was unable to believe there were really impious people who had no faith. . . . He permitted my soul to be invaded by the thickest darkness, and that the thought of heaven, up until then so sweet to me, be no longer anything but the cause of struggle and torment. This trial was to last not a few days or a few weeks, it was not to be extinguished until the hour set by God Himself and this hour has not yet come.[7]

Thérèse describes her experience as being caught in the suffocating confines of a "dark tunnel," sharing with us some of the terrifying evil temptations that the voices of the demons insinuated into her mind.

> The darkness, borrowing the voice of sinners, says mockingly to me: "You are dreaming about the light, about a fatherland embalmed in the sweetest perfumes; you are dreaming about the *eternal* possession of the Creator of all these marvels; you believe that one day you will walk out of this fog that surrounds you! Advance, advance; rejoice in death which will give you not what you hope for but a night still more profound, the night of nothingness."[8]

Thérèse gives us a wonderful glimpse of the means she used to combat these horrible voices communicating evil doubt. She kept on living her life, doing the right things (including writing some of her most inspiring poems although she herself was not experiencing any sensible "inspiration"). She countered the temptations by making acts of the opposite virtue, faith; she didn't get into conversations with the devil but ran toward Jesus. She offered the suffering of the lack of consolation and the experience of darkness and temptations as an act of love to the Lord and in reparation for (or to prevent) sins against faith.

> Ah! May Jesus pardon me if I have caused Him any pain, but He knows very well that while I do not have *the joy of faith*, I am trying to carry out its works at least. I believe I have made more acts of faith in this past year than all through my whole life. At each new occasion of combat, when my enemies provoke me, I conduct myself bravely. Knowing it is cowardly to enter into a duel, I turn my back on my adversaries without deigning to look them in the face; but I run toward my Jesus. I tell Him I am ready to shed my blood to the last drop to profess my faith in the existence of *heaven*. I tell Him, too, I am happy not to enjoy this beautiful heaven on this earth so that He will open it for all eternity to poor unbelievers. Also, in spite of this trial which has taken away *all my joy*, I can nevertheless cry out: "*You have given me DELIGHT, O Lord, in ALL your doings.*" For is there a *joy* greater than that of suffering out of love for You? . . . But if my suffering was really unknown to You, which is impossible, I would still be happy to have it, if through it I could prevent or make reparation for one single sin against *faith*.[9]

Packed into this paragraph is an immense amount of spiritual teaching and insight. While Thérèse's description of the violence of the temptations and the profundity of the darkness reminds us of John's classic descriptions of the "dark night" that may precede the spiritual marriage, there are also clear indications that what is happening is not just the "dark night" that comes before the spiritual marriage, but perhaps a special vocation to bear the sins of nineteenth-century atheism, as Jesus bore all our sins on the Cross. Thérèse voluntarily accepted the terrible trial as an offering for sin, in the pattern of Jesus' own acceptance of the agony of the Crucifixion and the experience of abandonment for the sins of the world.

It is also important to note that even though profound darkness may exist—the total absence of sensible joy, as well as violent and deeply disturbing temptations—there can be underneath it all a deep joy, rooted in suffering that is willingly offered out of love for Jesus. It's the very joy and peace that John of the Cross indicates is always there, even in the deepest of dark nights, the joy and peace of being in union with God's will no matter what the circumstances might be. It's the very joy and peace that John indicates that Jesus had in the "higher" part of His soul, even in the agony of pain, rejection, and abandonment on the Cross.

Not that an element of ongoing purification doesn't remain with us. As we have already seen earlier in this chapter in the teaching of Catherine and John, even within the spiritual marriage there is an ongoing growth and deeper purification through suffering which the Lord offers to us. Thérèse makes this element explicit:

> Never have I felt before this, dear Mother, how sweet and merciful the Lord really is, for He did not send me this trial until the moment I was capable of bearing it. A little earlier I believe it would have plunged me into a state of discouragement. Now it is taking away everything that could be a natural satisfaction in my desire for heaven. . . . Dear Mother, it seems to me now that nothing could prevent me from flying away, for I no longer have any great desires except that of loving to the point of dying of love.[10]

These words, written on the second anniversary of her Oblation of June 9, 1895, speak of the yet deeper purification the Lord was working in her through these trials. Whatever was natural or selfish in her desire for heaven was being taken away. Any willful preferences were being dissolved, and she was coming to the point, more completely than ever before, of truly preferring God's will above all other things, including her own spiritual desires. This of course is what holiness is: truly preferring God's will to all other things. As the purity of her love increased still more, even in the midst of darkness and desolation and struggle, what remained for her was to "fly away"—to die of such purity and strength of love, the body no longer able to keep the soul from flying to God.

In the last months of her life, as she was confined to the infirmary of the convent in Lisieux, her bedside reading consisted of the Bible and John of the Cross. She read John's words on the "death of love" and desired it for herself. But she knew that in her case there might be a difference.

And what did John teach about "dying of love"?

John taught that as the soul in the unitive stage reached spiritual marriage and continued to grow in that union, it would reach a point where it would leave the body, so great was the fervor of its love, and death would occur. Even though it might appear that such a person had died of old age or physical illness, it would really be a "death of love."

> It should be known that the natural death of persons who have reached this state is far different in its cause and mode from the death of others, even though it is similar in natural circumstances. If the death of other people is caused by sickness or old age, the death of these persons is not so induced, in spite of their being sick or old; their soul is not wrested from them unless by some impetus and encounter of love far more sublime than previous ones; of greater power, and more valiant since it tears through this veil and carries off the jewel, which is the soul.
>
> The death of such persons is very gentle and very sweet, sweeter and more gentle than was their whole spiritual life on earth. . . . The soul's riches gather together here, and its rivers of love move on to enter the sea, for these rivers, because they are blocked, become so vast that they themselves resemble seas. . . .
>
> A person having reached this stage knows full well that it is characteristic of God to take to himself, before their time, souls that love him ardently perfecting them in a short while by means of that love, which in any event they would have gained at their own pace. . . .

It is vital for individuals to make acts of love in this life so that in being perfected in a short time they may not be detained long either here on earth or in the next life, before seeing God.[11]

John teaches further that any desire at a previous stage of union to be loosed from the body in death and be with the Lord was still imperfect and rooted in an impatience that wanted to cut short the process of purification that life on this earth provides. Teresa speaks of this desire to have done with the weariness of this life and be with the Lord as a desire that commonly is experienced in the sixth mansion, where the soul is being prepared for spiritual betrothal. But now, John indicates, the soul is truly ready; it has come to truly prefer and love God and His will above all things.

> Previously my requests did not reach your ears, when, in the anxieties and weariness of love in which my sense and my spirit suffered because of considerable weakness, impurity, and lack of strong love, I was praying that you loose me and bring me to yourself because my soul longed for you, and impatient love did not allow me to be so conformed to the conditions of this life in which you desired me still to live. The previous impulses of love were not enough, because they did not have sufficient quality for the attainment of my desire; now I am so fortified in love that not only do my sense and spirit no longer faint in you, but my heart and my flesh, reinforced in you, rejoice in the living God (Ps. 84:2), with great conformity between the sensory and spiritual parts. What you desire me to ask for, I ask for; and what you do not desire, I do not desire, nor can I, nor does it even enter my mind to desire it. My petitions are now more valuable and estimable in your sight, since they come from you, and you move me to make them and I make them in the delight and joy of the Holy Spirit, *my judgment now issuing from your countenance* (Ps. 17:2), that is, when you esteem and hear my prayer. Tear, then, the

thin veil of this life and do not let old age cut it naturally, that from now on I may love you with the plenitude and fullness my soul desires forever and ever.[12]

Thérèse had come to this point of true detachment and "perfect" love. She was ready to have the veil torn and enter into the beatific union. The words of Job came to her mind:

> "Even though he should kill me, yet will I trust him," always fascinated me in my childhood days. It took me a long time, however, to reach that degree of surrender. Now I have reached it; God has placed me in this degree, for He has taken me up into His arms and placed me there.[13]

Yet she knew that her death might not look quite so "very gentle and very sweet" as such deaths of love often were. She also knew that her sisters were conceiving in their minds a picture of her death based on John's teachings and on their own sentimentality, a picture that perhaps would be so different in reality that it might disturb them. And so Thérèse taught them by her progressive relinquishments to trust God no matter what the external circumstances. When she was no longer able to receive Communion because of her illness, she told them:

> No doubt, it is a great grace to receive the sacraments. When God does not permit it, it is good too! Everything is a grace![14]

She wanted to prepare them for what might happen by directing their gaze to the most perfect death of love, the death of Jesus on the Cross.

In June, a few months before her death, she once again reassured them:

> Do not be troubled, little sisters, if I suffer very much and if you see in me, as I have already said to you, no sign

of joy at the moment of death. Our Lord really died as a Victim of Love, and see what His agony was!

And in July:

> Our Lord died on the Cross in anguish, and yet His was the most beautiful death of love. To die of love does not mean to die in transports. I tell you frankly, it appears to me that this is what I am experiencing.[15]

And that, indeed, is what she experienced. Her physical and spiritual agony was great. Suffocating from the tuberculosis in her lungs—during her last month only half of one lung was functioning—and besieged by the most awful of temptations, Thérèse's last months were difficult.

She was moved to the infirmary, in a bed around which brown curtains could be drawn. Thérèse pinned to these curtains her favorite holy pictures—the Holy Face of Christ, the Blessed Virgin, and Blessed Théophane Vénard, the young French priest martyred in Vietnam. They also brought in the Martin family statue of the "Virgin of the Smile." Often, spitting up blood, her head and side aching, she vomited up the milk prescribed for her.

She had reached the point where she could truly say:

> I do not desire to die more than to live; it is what He does that I love.[16]

Even in the midst of her suffering she did not lose her sense of humor. When they told her that there was a danger of gangrene setting in to her intestines, she replied:

> Well, all the better! While I am at it I may as well suffer very much and all over—and even have several sicknesses at the same time![17]

Nor did her human affection desert her. Deeply purified, she now could freely ask for one of her favorite things, a chocolate éclair, and for a big kiss from one of her sisters, "a kiss that makes lots of noise."[18]

While there was an intermittent lessening of her suffering in the final months, it always returned strongly. Her humanity was evident.

> What would become of me if God did not give me courage? A person does not know what this is unless he experiences it. No, it has to be experienced![19]

> Pray for those who are sick and dying, little sisters. If you only knew what goes on! How little it takes to lose control of oneself! I would not have believed this before. . . . My "little life" is to suffer; that's it![20]

When someone suggested that she pray to Mary for help, her reply was devastating:

> Oh! I prayed fervently to her! But it is pure agony; there is no consolation![21]

As her physical and spiritual suffering became desperate, she had to cling to God all the more and fight off fear.

> Mama! Earth's air is leaving me. . . . When will God give me the air of heaven? Ah! My breathing has never been so short! . . . I am afraid I have feared death. I am not afraid of what happens after death; that is certain! I don't regret giving up my life; but I ask myself: What is this mysterious separation of the soul from the body? It is the first time that I have experienced this, but I abandoned myself immediately to God.[22]

She turned her agony into a prayer, offering it for the good of the Church and for souls.

Everything I have, everything I merit, is for the good of
the Church and for souls.[23]

In the months before her death she began to have stronger
glimpses of the mission the Lord might have in mind for her when
she finally joined him on the "other side."

> How unhappy I shall be in heaven if I cannot do little
> favors for those whom I love. . . . I will return! I will come
> down! . . . I feel that my mission is about to begin, my
> mission of making others love God as I love Him, my
> mission of teaching my little way to souls. If God answers
> my requests, my heaven will be spent on earth up until
> the end of the world. Yes, I want to spend my heaven in
> doing good on earth.[24]

And even from her deathbed, she sought to encourage priests, by
way of prayer and letters. She wrote to one in particular:

> When I shall have arrived at port, I will teach you how to
> travel dear little brother of my soul, on the stormy sea of
> the world: with the surrender and the love of a child who
> knows his Father loves him and cannot leave him alone
> in the hour of danger. . . . The way of simple love and
> confidence is really made for you.[25]

A few weeks before her death, the convent celebrated the seventh
anniversary of her profession and brought flowers into her room.

> Exteriorly I am surrounded by flowers; but interiorly I
> am always in my trial; however, I am at peace! . . . Ah!
> What darkness! However, I am still at peace![26]

Even when, on her deathbed, she was corrected for impatience,
her faith and confidence in the greatness of God's mercy and love
triumphed through the insensitivity of those closest to her.

Oh! how happy I am to see myself imperfect and to be in need of God's mercy so much even at the moment of my death![27]

At various times the sisters thought that her last agony was starting; on September 21, nine days before her death, they once again thought Thérèse was nearing the end.

Ah! What is the agony? It seems I am always in it.[28]

And then the day before she died:

When am I going to suffocate entirely? . . . I can't stand any more! Ah! Pray for me! Jesus! Mary! I will it![29]

Thérèse died the next day: September 30, 1897. The darkness and trial of faith lifted a few moments before she died.

Thérèse sighed: *"Mother! Isn't this the agony? Am I not going to die?"*

"Yes, my poor child, but God perhaps wills to prolong it for several hours."

"Well, all right! Ah! I would not want to suffer a shorter length of time."

Her head fell back on the pillow and was turned toward the right. The Prioress had the infirmary bell rung, and the sisters quickly returned. . . . Hardly had the community knelt at her bedside when Thérèse pronounced very distinctly, while gazing at her crucifix: *"Oh! I love Him!"* And a moment later: *"My God, I love you!"*

Suddenly her eyes came to life and were fixed on a spot just a little above the statue of the Blessed Virgin. Her face took on the appearance it had when Thérèse enjoyed good health. She seemed to be in ecstasy. This look lasted for the space of a "Credo." Then she closed her eyes and expired. It was 7:20 in the evening. . . .

A mysterious smile was on her lips. She appeared very beautiful.[30]

Her mission had begun.

While most "deaths of love" may look as John of the Cross describes, Thérèse's didn't, at least until its very last moments. God works with each of us in a unique way, as individuals; and yet the principals of the spiritual journey described by the saints and Doctors we are considering remain immensely helpful for understanding what is happening and how we can cooperate.

Personal Calls: Mother Teresa of Calcutta

When Mother Teresa of Calcutta's writings were initially released, many were shocked by her open admission of her own very long, unremitting experience of desolation in the midst of a joy-filled apostolate.

Surrounded by the tangible experience of grace, including significant locutions and visions of the Lord as she founded her new order, she went through most of the rest of her life not only without the continuation of such special graces but in a state of great dryness and desolation. It is unusual for this dark night of the spirit to last such a great length of time, but with Mother Teresa we are again in the presence of a unique vocation, in which these lengthy years of desolation were "fitting."

Father Raniero Cantalamessa, who has been for many years the official preacher to the papal household, offered some reflections in his Advent meditations, given during 2003, on why this might have been part of Mother Teresa's unique vocation.

Father Raniero suggested that the Lord perhaps offered her this lengthy spiritual aridity because of the media adulation that was to surround Mother Teresa, as a protection against temptation and a help in continuing to live that poverty of spirit and humility which is essential to holiness. He also suggested that this extreme spiritual poverty was also a means by which the Lord helped her identify with the extremely poor and abandoned people for whom she cared. Perhaps, as was the case with Thérèse, this darkness was also a means by which the Lord gave the grace of an especially intimate participation in the abandonment and darkness that Jesus experienced on the Cross, sharing in His redemptive suffering for the human race.

At the same time we must note that the simultaneous presence of both great suffering and great joy—as we have seen in the life of Thérèse and in the teaching of John, and most especially in the life and death of Jesus—is again evident in the case of Mother Teresa.

The Father tells Catherine that we should not be shocked at the particular shape the vocation to holiness may assume. We must expand our conception of the profundity of God's providence.

> Sometimes I let the whole world be against the just, and in the end they die a death that leaves worldly people stunned in wonder. It seems to them unjust to see the just perishing now at sea, now in fire, now mangled by beasts, now physically killed when their houses collapse on top of them. How unreasonable these things seem to the eye unenlightened by most holy faith! But not so to the faithful, for through love they have found and experienced my providence in all those great things. Thus they see and grasp that I do what I do providentially, only to bring about your salvation. Therefore they hold everything in reverence. They are not scandalized in themselves nor in my works nor in their neighbors, but pass through everything with true patience. My providence is never denied to anyone; it seasons everything.

And the Father makes clear that His surprising providence extends to the unjust as well, for their salvation.

> Sometimes people think that the hail and storms and lightning I rain upon their bodies are cruel. In their judgment I have no care for their wellbeing. I have done

these things to rescue them from eternal death, but they believe the opposite.

Thus do worldly people try to distort my every work and interpret it after their own base understanding.[31]

Whether the profound purification of the dark night or the special participation in the suffering of Christ works itself out in the external circumstances of our lives through illness or persecution or pain-filled relationships, or whether it manifests itself more interiorly, in a way that no one would suspect, the truth is that there is always more, for all of us. Whatever the unique dimensions of our own journey may be—whether it be an intermittent experience of the purifying dark night over a long period of time, or an intense, shorter experience of the dark night, or a special vocation of a more lengthy abandonment and trial that is no longer primarily purifying but primarily redemptive—what's true for all of us is that there's always more.

Even in the highest states of union, obedience, humility, and love, there *is* always more. John, as with many of the saints, is eager to have us keep our eyes on the goal: the beatific union. He points out time and again that even the greatest experience or knowledge of God's love or goodness or holiness or power in this life is as nothing in comparison to what the face-to-face encounter of heaven will be like. He encourages us not to cling to anything less than this, and to keep ourselves moving towards this ultimate goal of our journey.

Journey's End: The Fulfillment of All Desire
When John tries to describe (and no one does it better!) some of the things the soul experiences in the higher stages of union even in this life, it seems as if his mind, his heart, even the very words he uses are about to burst.

Once the soul is placed at the peak of perfection and freedom of spirit in God, and all the repugnancies and contradictions of sensuality have ceased, she no longer has any other activity to engage her than surrender to the delights and joys of intimate love of her Bridegroom. . . . One thing only is left for her to desire: perfect enjoyment of God in eternal life.[32]

As John contemplates the nature of the relationship with God in heaven—the beatific vision—language reaches its limits and moves into praise that is beyond intelligible words:

> Let us so act that by means of this loving activity we may attain to the vision of ourselves in your beauty in eternal life. That is: That I be so transformed in your beauty that we may be alike in beauty, and both behold ourselves in your beauty, possessing then your very beauty; this, in such a way that each looking at the other may see in the other their own beauty, since both are your beauty alone, I being absorbed in your beauty; hence, I shall see you in your beauty, and you will see me in your beauty, and I shall see myself in you in your beauty, and you will see yourself in me in your beauty; that I may resemble you in your beauty, and you resemble me in your beauty, and my beauty be your beauty and your beauty my beauty; wherefore, I shall be you in your beauty, and you will be me in your beauty, because your very beauty will be my beauty; and thus we shall behold each other in your beauty.[33]

The beauty of God enraptures the soul and makes it yearn for the beatific vision with great longing. Bernard too describes this well.

> What can the bride do but yearn for that place of rest, of security, of exultation, of wonder, of overwhelming joy. . . . Who would not be filled with vehement longing to be fed in that place, on account of its peace, on account of its richness, on account of its super-abundance? There one experiences neither fear nor distaste, nor any want. Paradise is a safe dwelling-place, the Word is sweet nourishment, eternity, is wealthy beyond calculation.[34]

Bernard then makes the even more radical statement that no matter how much the Holy Spirit enlivens the sacraments and faith itself, it's not enough. The soul longs for what the sacraments and faith point towards—God Himself in the beatific vision. The sacraments and faith will pass away—they are simply means for the journey—but at journey's end they will no longer be needed but give way to what they prepared for, God Himself.

> I too have the Word, but the Word made flesh: and the Truth is set before me, but in the sacrament. An angel is nourished with the richness of the wheat (Ps. 80:17) is satiated with the pure grain; but in this life I have to be content with the husk, as it were, of the sacrament, with the bran of the flesh, with the chaff of the letter, with the veil of the faith. And these are the kind of things whose taste brings death (Job 6:6) unless they are seasoned in some degree with the first fruits of the Spirit (Rom. 8:23). . . . For without the Spirit the sacrament is received as a judgment (1 Cor. 11:29), the flesh is of no avail (Jn. 6:64), the letter kills (2 Cor. 3:6), and faith is dead (Jas. 2:20). It is the Spirit who must give these things life if I am to find life in them (Jn. 6:64). But no matter how great the effusion of the Spirit that enriches these (Ps. 147:14), the husk of the sacrament is not received with the same pleasure as the fat of the wheat, nor is faith the equivalent of vision (2 Cor. 5:7), nor memory of presence, nor time of eternity, nor a face of its reflection, nor the image of God (Col. 1:15) of a slave's condition (Phil. 2:7). . . . Let us make haste then my sons, let us make haste to a place that is safer, to a pasture that is sweeter, to a land that is richer and more fertile. Let us make haste to a place where we may dwell without fear, where we may abound and never want, where we may feast and never weary.[35]

John also tells us that the soul longs for deeper insight into the knowledge, the wisdom, and the "judgments" of God.

She is dying with the desire to penetrate them deeply. Knowledge of them is an inestimable delight surpassing all understanding. . . . Hence the soul ardently wishes to be engulfed in these judgments and know them from further within. And in exchange, it will be a singular comfort and happiness for her to enter all the afflictions and trials of the world and everything, however difficult and painful, that might be a means to this knowledge, even the anguish and agony of death, all in order to see herself further within her God. . . .

Suffering is the means of penetrating further, deep into the thicket of the delectable wisdom of God. The purest suffering brings with it the purest and most intimate knowing, and consequently the purest and highest joy, because it is a knowing from further within . . . even to the agony of death in order to see God. . . .

The gate entering into these riches of his wisdom is the cross, which is narrow, and few desire to enter by it, but many desire the delights obtained from entering there.[36]

Ultimately the soul's desire is to see Christ and to be engulfed in all the mysteries contained in Him. To see Christ and comprehend the depths of His wisdom and love in the great mystery of the Incarnation, as John puts it, "is by no means the lesser part of beatitude." Here John turns to Scripture and illuminates in it the depths of the mystery it points to.

One of the main reasons for the desire to be dissolved and to be with Christ (Phil. 1:23) is to see him face to face and thoroughly understand the profound and eternal mysteries of his Incarnation, which is by no means the lesser part of beatitude. As Christ himself says to the Father in St. John's Gospel: *This is eternal life, that they know you, the one true God, and your Son Jesus Christ whom you have sent* (Jn. 17:3). The first thing a person desires to do after having come a long distance is to see and converse with a deeply loved one; similarly, the first thing the soul desires on coming to the vision of God is to know and enjoy the deep secrets and mysteries of the Incarnation and the ancient ways of God dependent on it.[37]

To comprehend in much greater measure than ever before the interplay of God's mercy and justice throughout human history, to ponder the judgments of God as they bring about the salvation of the human race, to marvel at the wisdom of God's predestination of the just and His foreknowledge of the damned, leads to depths of adoration, now offered more perfectly and fully than ever before, through our unimpeded union with Jesus.

John points out that in heaven we will never exhaust the treasures and depths of God's wisdom contained in Jesus. He cites Colossians 2:3: "*In Christ dwell hidden all treasures and wisdom.*" And in the happiness of seeing Christ, in some real measure, we will be able to know as we are presently known. "For now we see in a mirror dimly, but then face to face. Now I know in part; then I shall understand fully, even as I have been fully understood" (1 Cor. 13:12).[38]

In the union that is effected in the state of glory the soul will also be able to love God as she is loved by Him.

> As her intellect will be the intellect of God, her will then will be God's will, and thus her love will be God's love. The soul's will is not destroyed there, but is so firmly united with the strength of God's will, with which he loves her, that her love for him is as strong and perfect as his love for her; for the two wills are so united that there is only one will and love, which is God's. Thus the soul loves God with the will and strength of God himself, united with the very strength of love with which God loves her. This strength lies in the Holy Spirit in whom the soul is there transformed, for by this transformation of glory he supplies what is lacking in her, since he is given to the soul for the sake of the strength of this love.[39]

This knowing and loving grow during life on earth, of course, reaching great heights in the spiritual marriage by the power of the Holy Spirit, but they attain an entirely different level in the life of glory. John draws our attention to the mysterious promises of the life of glory contained in chapters 2 and 3 of the Book of Revelation as a way of getting an additional glimpse of what this life is like. In the inspired, poetic images of the apostle John, John of the Cross finds a deep resonance with his own contemplation.

Bernard also sheds light on the already and the not yet of the vision of God, as God speaks to the soul.

> But to be drawn up through the clouds, to penetrate to where light is total, to plunge through seas of splendor and make your home where light is unapproachable (1 Tim. 6:16), that is beyond the scope of an earthly life or an earthly body. That is reserved for you at the end of all things, when I shall take you, all glorious, to myself, without spot or wrinkle or any such thing (Eph. 5:27). . . . The time will come when I shall reveal myself, and your beauty will be complete, just as my beauty is complete; you will be so like me that you will see me as I am (1 Jn. 3:2). Then you will be told: "You are all fair my love, there is no flaw in you" (Song 4:7). But for now, though there is some resemblance, there is also some want of resemblance, and you must be content with an imperfect knowledge (1 Cor. 13:9).[40]

John of the Cross also draws our attention to the great depth of revelation contained in Jesus' profound prayer to the Father on behalf of His disciples of all times, praying for the profound union of the Persons of the Trinity with us, contained in chapter 17 of John's Gospel. One of John's traveling companions tells us that John of the Cross used to recite the seventeenth chapter of John with great devotion as they traveled.

It's perhaps his meditation on these passages and others like it that led to his descriptions of the "breathing" of the Holy Spirit within us.

By his divine breath-like spiration, the Holy Spirit elevates the soul sublimely and informs her and makes her capable of breathing in God the same spiration of love that the Father breathes in the Son and the Son in the Father. This spiration of love is the Holy Spirit himself, who in the Father and the Son breathes out to her in this transformation in order to unite her to himself. . . .

In the transformation that the soul possesses in this life, the same spiration passes from God to the soul and from the soul to God with notable frequency and blissful love, although not in the open and manifest degree proper to the next life. Such I believe was St. Paul's meaning when he said: *Since you are children of God, God sent the Spirit of his Son into your hearts, calling to the Father* (Gal. 4:6).[41]

Bernard tells us that the beatific vision is nothing else than love itself.

It is assuredly a thing most marvelous and astonishing, that likeness which accompanies the vision of God, and is itself the vision. I can only describe it as subsisting in charity. This vision is charity, and the likeness is charity. . . . Then the soul will know as it is known (1 Cor. 13:12) and love as it is loved, and the Bridegroom will rejoice over the Bride, knowing and known, loving and loved (Is. 62:5), Jesus Christ Our Lord, who is God above all, blessed forever. Amen.[42]

What John of the Cross does in his teaching, he tells us, is to unpack the meaning of Scripture as it pertains to the transformation of the human person, from conversion to the beatific vision. And now, as he attempts to explain the dynamics of the beatific vision, he returns more and more explicitly to the Scriptures that refer to these mysteries. As breathtaking as John's descriptions of the glory that waits us are, he reminds us that he is simply drawing out the implications of what Scripture tells us when the apostle Peter states that our destiny is to be "*made partakers of the divine nature.*" (2 Pt. 1:2–5)[43]

In case any of his readers by this point have still not determined to "sell all" to obtain this priceless pearl of heaven, John makes an impassioned last-minute appeal to conversion:

> O souls, created for these grandeurs and called to them! What are you doing? How are you spending your time? Your aims are base and your possessions miseries! O wretched blindness of your eyes! You are blind to so brilliant a light and deaf to such loud voices because you fail to discern that insofar as you seek eminence and glory you remain miserable, base, ignorant, and unworthy of so many blessings![44]

John ends his comments here with a tender prayer, intended to give hope and encouragement to everyone on the journey to the fulfillment of all desire. He knows clearly that it's the mercy of God that brings anyone to the fullness of union.

> May the most sweet Jesus, Bridegroom of faithful souls, be pleased to bring all who invoke his name to this marriage.[45]

May it always and everywhere be so!

—⁓—

FINAL ENCOURAGEMENT

SOMETIMES WE CAN BE OVERWHELMED with the challenge of making progress on the spiritual journey. Sometimes we can become discouraged and be tempted to think that we can never hope to reach our destination. Every saint and Doctor we have learnt from in the pages of this book wants us to know beyond a shadow of a doubt that this journey *is* for everyone, and that if we persevere, by His grace, we will surely reach journey's end. Let's meditate on these words of encouragement addressed to us by those who truly are our friends and companions on the journey.

> In the first place it should be known that if anyone is seeking God, the Beloved is seeking that person much more.[1] (John of the Cross)

> The soul seeks the Word, but has been first sought by the Word. . . . Let her seek him as she can, provided she remembers that she was first sought, as she was first loved; and it is because of this that she herself both seeks and loves.[2]
> It is my belief that to a person so disposed, God will not refuse that most intimate kiss of all, a mystery of supreme generosity and ineffable sweetness.[3] (Bernard of Clairvaux)

We have seen how every soul—even if burdened with sin, enmeshed in vice, ensnared by the allurements of pleasure, a captive in exile, imprisoned in the body, caught in mud, fixed in mire, bound to its members, a slave to care, distracted by business, afflicted with sorrow, wandering and straying, filled with anxious forebodings and uneasy suspicions, a stranger in a hostile land, and, according to the Prophet, sharing the defilement of the dead and counted with those who go down into hell—every soul, I say, standing thus under condemnation and without hope, has the power to turn and find it can not only breathe the fresh air of the hope of pardon and mercy, but also dare to aspire to the nuptials of the Word, not fearing to enter into alliance with God or to bear the sweet yoke of love with the King of angels.[4] (Bernard of Clairvaux)

Concerning souls that have entered the third dwelling places, for the Lord has done them no small favor, but a very great one, in letting them get through the first difficulties. I believe that through the goodness of God there are many of these souls in the world. They long not to offend His Majesty, even guarding themselves against venial sins; they are fond of doing penance and setting aside periods for recollection; they spend their time well, practicing works of charity toward their neighbors; and are very balanced in their use of speech and dress and in the governing of their households—those who have them. Certainly this is a state to be desired. And, in my opinion, there is no reason why entrance even into the final dwelling place should be denied these souls, nor will the Lord deny them this entrance if they desire it; for such a desire is an excellent way to prepare oneself so that every favor may be granted.[5] (Teresa of Avila)

May the most sweet Jesus, Bridegroom of faithful souls, be pleased to bring all who invoke his name to this marriage.[6] (John of the Cross)

Oh Jesus! Why can't I tell all *little souls* how unspeakable is Your condescension? I feel that if You found a soul weaker and littler than mine, which is impossible, You would be pleased to grant it still greater favors, provided it abandoned itself with total confidence to Your Infinite Mercy. But why do I desire to communicate Your secrets of Love, O Jesus, for was it not You alone who taught them to me, and can You not reveal them to others? Yes, I know it, and I beg You to do it. I beg You to cast Your Divine Glance upon a great number of *little* souls. I beg You to choose a legion of *little* Victims worthy of your *love!*[7] (Thérèse of Lisieux)

And how shall this come to pass for each one of us?

"The Holy Spirit will come upon you, and the power of the Most High will overshadow you." (Lk. 1:35)

May all of us wholeheartedly say with Mary, in all simplicity, humility and trust:

May it be done to me according to your word. (Lk.1: 38)

Blessed saints—Augustine, Bernard, Catherine, Teresa, John, Francis, Thérèse—pray for us!

ENDNOTES

Introduction

[1] Individual audio albums devoted to the teachings of each of these saints are available both in cassette and CD versions through Renewal Ministries. Visit www.renewalministries.net or call (734) 662-1730 ext. 27.

[2] Bernard of Clairvaux, *On the Song of Songs*, in four volumes, trans. Kilian Walsh, Irene Edmonds, (Kalamazoo, MI: ICS Publications, 1971–1980), vol. IV sermon 76, no. 7, p. 115.

Chapter One

[1] John Paul II, Apostolic Letter at the Close of the Jubilee Year *Novo Millennio Ineunte* (January 6, 2001). Available from www.vatican.va/holy_father/john_paul_ii/apost_letters/index.htm. (hereafter cited in text as NMI)

[2] The other two rediscoveries that John Paul II identifies are "the Church as communion" and "the charismatic dimension" of the Church.

[3] Thérèse of Lisieux, *Story of a Soul*, trans. John Clarke, OCD (Washington, DC: ICS Publications, 1996), chap. I, p. 14.

[4] Thérèse of Lisieux, *Story of a Soul*, epilogue, p. 264.

[5] Teresa uses the image of the soul as a grand castle with many concentric layers of mansions or grouping of rooms. She explains the spiritual journey in terms of moving from the outer rooms into the very center of the soul, where the Lord Himself is. The first mansion is the outermost mansion and the seventh mansion the innermost.

[6] Bernard of Clairvaux, *On the Song of Songs*, vol. IV, sermon 76, no. 6, p. 114.

[7] Ibid., p. 115.

Chapter Two

[1] Catherine of Siena, *The Dialogue*, trans. Suzanne Noffke, OP, *The Classics of Western Spirituality* (Mahwah, NJ: Paulist Press, 1980), chap. 56, p. 111.

Chapter Three

[1] Father Thomas Dubay, S.M. has written an excellent introduction to the teachings of Teresa of Avila and John of the Cross, *Fire Within: St. Teresa of Avila, St. John of the Cross and the Gospel—on Prayer*, (San Francisco, CA: Ignatius Press, 1989).

[2] Teresa of Avila, *Her Life, The Collected Works of St. Teresa of Avila*, trans. Kieran Kavanaugh and Otilio Rodriguez, OCD, 2nd ed., vol. 1(Washington, D.C.: ICS Publications, 1987), chap. 2, no. 3, p. 58.

[3] Teresa of Avila, *Her Life*, chap. 4, no. 7, p. 67.

[4] Ibid., chap. 5, no. 3, p. 71.

[5] Teresa of Avila, *The Way of Perfection, The Collected Works of St. Teresa of Avila*, trans. Kieran Kavanaugh and Otilio Rodriguez, 2nd ed., vol. 2 (Washington, D.C.: ICS Publications, 1987), chap. 41, no. 3, p. 197.

[6] Teresa of Avila, *Her Life*, chap. 6, no. 4, pp. 78–79.

[7] Teresa of Avila, *The Interior Castle, The Collected Works of St. Teresa of Avila*, trans. Kieran

Kavanaugh and Otilio Rodriguez, 2nd ed., vol. 2 (Washington, D.C.: ICS Publications, 1987), sect. II, chap. 1, no. 2, p. 297.

[8] Teresa of Avila, *Her Life*, chap. 19, no. 15, p. 171.

[9] Teresa of Avila, *The Way of Perfection*, chap. 32, no. 14, p. 165, emphasis in original.

[10] Ibid., chap. 41, no. 4, p. 198.

[11] Teresa of Avila, *The Interior Castle*, sect. II, chap.1, no. 9, p. 302.

[12] Teresa of Avila, *Her Life*, chap. 13, no. 2, pp. 123–24.

[13] Teresa of Avila, *The Way of Perfection*, chap. 31, no. 11, pp. 158–59.

[14] Bernard of Clairvaux, *On the Song of Songs*, vol. III, sermon 57, no. 3, p. 97.

[15] Ibid., vol. III, sermon 57, no. 4, p. 99.

[16] Ibid., vol. IV, sermon 78, no. 7, p. 153.

[17] Ibid., vol. III, sermon 66, no. 7, p. 198.

[18] Ibid., vol. II, sermon 38, no. 2, p. 188.

[19] Ibid., vol. II, sermon 38, no. 2, p. 188.

[20] In the early Church sometimes popular candidates for priestly or episcopal office were acclaimed by the people, and ordained quickly. This happened in the case of Ambrose, the Bishop of Milan who baptized Augustine, as well as with Augustine himself.

[21] Saint Augustine, *Confessions,* trans. Henry Chadwick (Oxford: Oxford University Press, 1992), bk. VIII, no. 1, 2, pp. 133–34.

[22] Ibid. bk. VIII, no. 4, p. 136.

[23] Ibid., bk. VIII, no. 6, p. 137.

[24] Ibid., bk. VIII, no. 10, p. 139.

[25] Ibid., bk. VIII, nos. 10–11, p. 140.

[26] Bernard of Clairvaux, *On the Song of Songs*, vol. IV, sermon 81, no. 7, pp. 163–64.

[27] Ibid., vol. III, sermon 56, no. 6, pp. 92–93.

[28] Augustine, *Confessions*, bk. VIII, nos. 11, 12, pp. 140–41.

[29] Ibid., bk. VIII, no. 13, p.141.

[30] Ibid., bk. VIII, no. 15, p.143.

[31] Ibid., bk. VIII, no. 15, pp.143–44.

[32] Ibid., bk. VIII, nos. 16, 17, pp. 144–45.

[33] Ibid., bk. VIII, nos. 18, 19, pp.145–46.

[34] Ibid., bk. VIII, nos. 25–26, pp. 150–51.

[35] Ibid., bk. VIII, no. 27, pp. 151.

[36] Ibid., bk. VIII, no. 28, pp. 152.

[37] Ibid., bk. VIII, no. 29, pp. 152–53.

[38] Thérèse of Lisieux, *Story of a Soul,* chap. IV, p. 83, emphasis in original.

[39] Francis de Sales, *Treatise on the Love of God*, trans. Dom Henry Benedict Mackey, OSB, (Rockford, IL: TAN Publishers, 1997) chap. XI, no. 6, pp. 478–81.

[40] Thérèse of Lisieux, *Story of a Soul*, chap. I, pp. 13, 15.

[41] Ibid., chap. III, pp. 65–66.

[42] Ibid., chap. IV, p. 72.

[43] Bernard of Clairvaux, *On the Song of Songs*, vol. IV, sermon 82, no. 7, p. 178.

[44] Ibid., vol. IV, sermon 84, no. 2, p. 189.

Chapter Four

[1] Sister Mary Ann Fatula, O.P. has written a fine introduction to the teaching of Catherine of Siena, *Catherine of Siena's Way*, which is volume four in "The Way of the Christian Mystics" series (Wilmington, Delaware: Michael Glazier, 1987).

[2] Blessed Raymond of Capua, *The Life of St. Catherine of Siena*, trans. George Lamb (Rockford, IL: TAN Publishers, 2003).

3 Bernard of Clairvaux, *Song of Songs*, vol. IV, sermon 72, no. 8, p. 70.

4 Ibid., vol. IV, sermon 69, no. 3, pp. 29–30.

5 Catherine of Siena, *The Dialogue*, chap. 27, p. 67; chap. 42, p. 87.

6 Bernard of Clairvaux, *On the Song of Songs*, vol. IV, sermon 75, no. 5, p. 101.

7 Ibid., vol. II, sermon 26, no. 11, p. 71.

8 Ibid., vol. IV, sermon 72, no. 5, p. 67.

9 Catherine of Siena, *The Dialogue*, chap. 38, pp. 80–81.

10 Ibid. chap. 42, pp. 86–87.

11 Bernard of Clairvaux, *On the Song of Songs*, vol. II, sermon 23, no. 12, p. 36.

12 See also Ps. 4:5, Ps. 33:11, Ps. 25:12.

13 Bernard of Clairvaux, *On the Song of Songs*, vol. II, sermon 23, no. 14, pp. 37–38.

14 Catherine of Siena, *The Dialogue*, chap. 41, pp. 84–85.

15 Bernard of Clairvaux, *On the Song of Songs*, vol. IV, sermon 72, nos. 9–10, pp. 72–73.

16 Catherine of Siena, *The Dialogue*, chap. 41, p. 83.

17 Ibid., chap. 41, pp. 83–84.

18 Pope John Paul II is a notable exception to this silence on the life of heaven. Over the course of several years he delivered many talks devoted to a consideration of the "theology of the body" which included several addresses devoted to a consideration of how our identities as male and female persons may find expression in the risen life of heaven. The General Audiences of December 9, 1981; January 13, 1983, and February 10, 1982 are of particular interest in this regard. The whole series of talks on the "theology of the body," including these particular audiences, have been published in book-length editions by several publishers. One such edition is *The Theology of the Body: Human Love in the Divine Plan* by John Paul II, published by Pauline Books and Media.

19 Catherine of Siena, *The Dialogue*, chap. 43, pp. 88–89.

20 Bernard of Clairvaux, *On the Song of Songs*, vol. III, sermon 57, no. 2, p. 97.

21 Catherine of Siena, *The Dialogue*, chap. 41, p. 85.

22 Bernard of Clairvaux, *On the Song of Songs*, vol. I, sermon 20, no. 1, p. 147.

23 John of the Cross, *The Collected Works of St. John of the Cross*, trans. Kieran Kavanaugh, OCD, and Otilio Rodriguez, OCD (Washington, D.C.: ICS Publications, 1991), introduction, p. 22.

24 Bernard of Clairvaux, *On the Song of Songs*, vol. I, sermon 20, no. 2, p. 148.

25 John of the Cross, *The Collected Works of St. John of the Cross*, introduction, p. 28.

26 John of the Cross, *The Spiritual Canticle*, *The Collected Works of St. John of the Cross*, stanza 1, no. 1, pp. 477–78.

27 Bernard of Clairvaux, *On the Song of Songs*, vol. III, sermon 55, nos. 2–4, pp. 84–86.

28 Teresa of Avila, *The Way of Perfection*, chap. 3, no. 6, p. 50; ibid., chap. 13, no. 3, p. 86.

29 Ibid., chap. 6, no. 3, p. 62.

30 Ibid., chap. 6, no. 8, p. 65.

31 Ibid., chap. 8, no 1, p. 71.

32 Ibid., chap. 12, no. 2, p. 82.

33 Bernard of Clairvaux, *On the Song of Songs*, vol. IV, sermon 72, no. 9, p. 71.

Chapter Five

1 Thérèse of Lisieux, *Story of a Soul*, chap. I, p. 34.

2 Ibid., chap. I, p. 30.

3 Ibid., chap. I, p. 17.

4 Ibid., chap. II, p. 37.

5 Ibid., chap. II, p. 48.

6 Ibid., chap. II, p. 49.

7 Ibid., chap. I, p. 29.
8 Ibid., chap. V, p. 113.
9 Ibid., chap. VI, p. 125.
10 Ibid., chap. VII, p. 154.
11 Ibid., chap. VI, p 141.
12 Ibid., chap. IV, p. 75.
13 Ibid., chap. II, pp. 44; chap. I, pp. 24–25.
14 Ibid., chap. II, p. 43.
15 Ibid., chap. VII, pp. 152–53.
16 Ibid., chap. VII, p. 153.
17 Ibid., chap. II, p. 42.
18 Ibid., chap. VII, p. 147.
19 Ibid., chap. VI, pp. 132–33.
20 Ibid., chap. I, p. 25; chap. VI, p. 132–133.
21 Ibid., chap. V, p. 103.
22 John of the Cross, *The Spiritual Canticle*, stanza 25, no. 1, p. 569.
23 Thérèse of Lisieux, *Story of a Soul*, chap. IV, p. 91.
24 Ibid., chap. IV, p. 78.
25 Ibid., chap. VII, p. 157.
26 Ibid., chap. X, p. 216.
27 See Catherine of Siena, *The Dialogue*, chap. 41, p. 83.
28 Thérèse of Lisieux, *Story of a Soul*, chap. III, p. 64.
29 The Grail, *The Psalms: A New Translation,* (Hammersmith, England: HarperCollins, 1963).
30 Ibid., chap. IV, p. 72.
31 Teresa of Avila, *Her Life*, chap. 19, no. 15, p. 171.
32 Thérèse of Lisieux, *Story of a Soul*, chap. IV, p. 73.
33 Ibid., chap. VI, pp. 121–22.
34 Ibid., chap. VI, p. 137.
35 Ibid., chap. VIII, p. 168.
36 Ibid., chap. VII, p. 161; chap. VIII, p. 167.
37 Ibid., chap. VII, p. 151.
38 Ibid., chap. VII, pp. 150–51.
39 Ibid., chap. IV, p. 76.
40 Ibid., chap. IV, p. 77.
41 Ibid., chap. IV, p. 78.
42 Ibid.
43 Ibid., chap. IV, p. 93.
44 Ibid., chap. IV, p. 80.
45 Ibid., chap. VI, p. 121.
46 Ibid., chap. VI, p. 129.
47 Ibid., chap. VI, pp. 130–31.
48 Ibid., chap. II, p. 41.
49 Ibid., chap. II, pp. 44–45.
50 Ibid., chap. II, p. 40.
51 Ibid., chap. IV, p. 74.
52 Ibid. chap. IV, pp. 74–75.
53 Ibid., chap. V, p. 97.
54 Ibid., chap. V, p. 98.
55 Ibid., chap. V, pp. 98–99.
56 Ibid., chap. V, p. 102.

57 John of the Cross, *The Ascent of Mount Carmel*, *The Collected Works of St. John of the Cross*, bk. III, chaps. 16–35, pp. 291–333.

58 Ibid., bk. III, chap. 18, no. 1, p. 295.

59 Ibid., bk. III, chap. 18, nos. 3, 4, 6, pp. 296–97.

60 Ibid., bk. III, chap. 19, no. 3, p. 298.

61 Ibid., bk. III, chap. 19, nos. 5–6. p. 299.

62 Ibid., bk. III, chap. 19, no. 7, pp. 299–300.

63 Ibid., bk. III, chap. 20, no. 1, p. 301.

64 Ibid., bk. III, chap. 20, nos. 2–3, pp. 302–3.

65 John of the Cross, *The Spiritual Canticle*, stanza 26, nos. 18–19, p. 580.

Chapter Six

1 Bernard of Clairvaux, *On the Song of Songs*, vol. IV, sermon 83, no. 1, pp. 180–81.

2 Francis de Sales, *Introduction to the Devout Life*, trans. John K. Ryan (New York: Image Books, 1989), preface, p. 33.

3 Ibid., pt. I, chap. 1, pp. 39–40.

4 Bernard of Clairvaux, *On the Song of Songs*, vol. I, sermon 16, nos. 9–10, pp. 120–21.

5 Francis de Sales, *Introduction to the Devout Life*, dedicatory prayer, p. 31.

6 Ibid., pt. I, chap. 1, pp. 40–41.

7 Ibid., pt. V, chap. 4, p. 263.

8 Ibid., pt. I, chap. 7, pp. 49–50.

9 Ibid., pt. II, chap. 19, p. 112.

10 Ibid., pt. II, chap. 19, p. 112.

11 Ibid., pt. I, chap. 7, p. 50.

12 Bernard of Clairvaux, *On the Song of Songs*, vol. III, sermon 49, no. 8, pp. 28–29.

13 Francis de Sales, *Introduction to the Devout Life*, pt. I, chaps. 8–18, pp. 51–71.

14 Teresa of Avila, *The Way of Perfection*, chap. 10, no. 2, p. 76.

15 Bernard of Clairvaux, *On the Song of Songs*, vol. III, sermon 62, no. 7, p. 158.

16 Ibid., vol. II, sermon 35, no. 1, pp. 166-167.

17 Ibid., vol. I, sermon 12, no. 11, p. 86.

18 See footnotes 2–4 in chapter 3 for references to Teresa of Avila's comments on venial sin.

19 Francis de Sales, *Introduction to the Devout Life*, pt. I, chap. 22, p. 76.

20 Bernard of Clairvaux, *On the Song of Songs*, vol. II sermon 29, no. 5, p. 106.

21 Ibid., vol. II, sermon 29, no. 5, p. 107.

22 Francis de Sales, *Introduction to the Devout Life*, pt. I, chap. 22, pp. 76–77.

23 Ibid., pt. I, chap. 5, p. 48.

24 Thérèse of Lisieux, *Story of a Soul*, chap. VII, p. 158.

25 Ibid., chap. VII, p. 158.

26 Ibid., epilogue, p. 267.

27 Francis de Sales, *Introduction to the Devout Life*, pt. I, chap. 5, p. 49.

28 Bernard of Clairvaux, *On the Song of Songs*, vol. IV, sermon 85, nos. 1, 4, pp. 196–97, 200.

29 Ibid., vol. IV, sermon 85, no. 5, pp. 200–1.

Chapter Seven

1 John of the Cross, *The Ascent of Mount Carmel*, bk. I, chap. 14, no. 2, pp. 151–52.

2 Bernard of Clairvaux, *On the Song of Songs*, vol. III, sermon 52, no. 4, pp. 52–53.

3 Ibid., vol. III, sermon 52, no. 5, p. 53.

4 Thérèse of Lisieux, *Story of a Soul*, chap. XI, p. 242.

5 Francis de Sales, *Introduction to the Devout Life*, pt. II, chap. 1, nos. 1–2, p. 81.

[6] Bernard of Clairvaux, *On the Song of Songs*, vol. IV, sermon 82, no. 7, p. 178.

[7] Ibid., vol. III, sermon 47, no. 8, pp. 9–10.

[8] Francis de Sales, *Introduction to the Devout Life*, pt. II, chap. 1, no. 5, p. 82.

[9] Ibid., pt. II, chap. 8, p. 90.

[10] Ibid., pt. II, chap. 8, p. 91.

[11] Ibid., pt. II, chap. 1, p. 83.

[12] Teresa of Avila, *The Way of Perfection*, chap. 25, no. 1, p. 131.

[13] Francis de Sales, *Introduction to the Devout Life*, pt. II, chap. 1, no. 6, p. 82.

[14] Teresa of Avila, *The Way of Perfection*, chap. 16, no. 3, p. 94; chap. 17, no. 3, p. 99; chap. 19, no. 2, p. 107.

[15] Bernard of Clairvaux, *On the Song of Songs*, vol. II, sermon 32, nos. 4–7; pp. 137–40.

[16] Teresa of Avila, *Her Life*, chap. 8, no. 5, p. 96.

[17] Teresa of Avila, *The Way of Perfection*, chap. 28, nos. 3, 4, p. 141.

[18] Ibid., chap. 22, no. 1, p. 121; chap. 24, no. 2, p. 129; chap. 24, no. 6, p. 130; chap. 29, no. 5, p. 147.

[19] Ibid., chap. 16, no. 11, p. 97; chap. 26, nos. 1–4, pp. 133–34.

[20] Teresa of Avila, *Her Life*, chap. 12, no. 2, p. 120.

[21] Teresa of Avila, *The Way of Perfection*, chap. 24, no. 4, p. 129.

[22] Ibid., chap. 24, no. 5, pp. 129–30.

[23] Francis de Sales, *Introduction to the Devout Life*, pt. II, chap. 1, no. 3, p. 82.

[24] Bernard of Clairvaux, *On the Song of Songs*, vol. IV, sermon 86, no. 3, pp. 213–14.

[25] The full Liturgy of the Hours is difficult for many to say. A wonderful shortened form of this daily prayer of the Church called *Magnificat*, which many people are finding helpful, is now available. Originally published in France, it consists of daily morning, evening, and night prayers, the readings for the Mass of the day, and short meditations and sketches of saints of the day, in an easy to use and shortened format. More information or a subscription is available by contacting *Magnificat*, PO Box 822, Yonkers, NY 10702, 1-866-273-5215, www.magnificat.net.

[26] Francis de Sales, *Introduction to the Devout Life*, pt. II, chap. 12, p. 97.

[27] Bernard of Clairvaux, *On the Song of Songs*, vol. II, sermon 40, nos. 4–5, pp. 202–3.

[28] Francis de Sales, *Introduction to the Devout Life*, pt. V, chap. 17, p. 277.

[29] Ibid., pt. II, chap. 13, p. 103.

[30] Bernard of Clairvaux, *On the Song of Songs*, vol. I, sermon 15, no. 6, pp. 110–11.

Chapter Eight

[1] Teresa of Avila, *The Interior Castle*, sect. I, chap. 2, no. 16, p. 295.

[2] Ibid., sect. I, chap. 2, no. 17, p. 296.

[3] Bernard of Clairvaux, *On the Song of Songs*, vol. I, sermon 19, no. 7, p. 145.

[4] Ibid., vol. II, sermon 33, no. 10, p. 153.

[5] Ibid., vol. II, sermon 33, no. 10, p. 154.

[6] Ibid., vol. III, sermon 64, no. 4, p. 172.

[7] Teresa of Avila, *The Interior Castle*, sect. II, chap.1, no. 2, p. 298.

[8] Ibid., sect. I, chap. II, no. 14, p. 294.

[9] Ibid., sect. II, chap. I, no. 5, p. 300.

[10] Ibid., sect. II, chap. I, no. 3, p. 298.

[11] Bernard of Clairvaux, *On the Song of Songs*, vol. II, sermon 33, no. 11, pp. 154–55.

[12] Teresa of Avila, *The Interior Castle*, sect. II, chap. 1, no. 4, p. 299.

[13] Francis de Sales, *Introduction to the Devout Life*, pt. IV, chap. 2, p. 225.

[14] Teresa of Avila, *The Interior Castle*, sect. II, chap. 1, no. 6, p. 300.

[15] Thérèse of Lisieux, *Story of a Soul*, chap. VI, p. 143.

[16] Ibid., chap. VII, p. 158.

[17] Ibid., chap. VI, p. 143.

[18] Ibid., chap. VI, pp. 143–44.

[19] Ibid., chap. VII, p. 159.

[20] Ibid.

[21] Ibid.

[22] Ibid., chap. VII, p. 160.

[23] Ibid., chap. XI, pp. 247-252, 239.

[24] Ibid., chap. IX, p. 196.

[25] Ibid., chap. X, p. 224.

[26] Ibid., chap. X, pp. 222–23.

[27] Ibid., chap. X, p. 222.

[28] Ibid., chap. X, p. 223.

[29] Ibid., chap. X, pp. 220–21.

[30] Teresa of Avila, *The Interior Castle*, sect. II, chap. 1, no. 7, p. 301.

[31] John of the Cross, *The Dark Night, The Collected Works of St. John of the Cross*, bk. I, chap. 6, no. 6, p. 373.

[32] Francis de Sales, *Introduction to the Devout Life*, pt. IV, chap. 13, no. 1, p. 244.

[33] Ibid., pt. IV, chap. 13, no. 1, p. 245.

[34] Thérèse of Lisieux, *Story of a Soul*, chap. XI, p. 234.

[35] Teresa of Avila, *The Interior Castle*, sect. II, chap. 1, no. 8, p. 301.

[36] Ibid.

[37] Thérèse of Lisieux, *Story of a Soul*, chap. VII, p. 151.

[38] Ibid., chap. IX, p. 196.

[39] Francis de Sales, *Introduction to the Devout Life*, pt. IV, chap. 3, p. 239.

[40] See also Ps. 45:8; Sir. 17:21.

[41] Francis de Sales, *Introduction to the Devout Life*, pt. IV, chap. 6, pp. 244–45.

[42] Ibid., pt. IV, chap. 3, pp. 240–41.

[43] Bernard of Clairvaux, *On the Song of Songs*, vol. II, sermon 30, no. 9, p. 120.

[44] Francis de Sales, *Introduction to the Devout Life*, pt. IV, chap. 6, pp. 245–46.

[45] Ibid., pt. IV, chap. 3, p. 239.

[46] Ibid., pt. IV, chap. 5, p. 243.

[47] Thérèse of Lisieux, *Story of a Soul*, chap. VIII, p. 166.

[48] Raymond of Capua, *The Life of St. Catherine of Siena*, pt. I, chap. XL, pp. 90–95; pt. III, chap. IV, p. 334.

[49] John of the Cross, *The Dark Night*, bk. I, chap. 14, nos. 1–4, pp. 392–93.

[50] Ibid., bk. I, chap. 14, no. 5, p. 394.

[51] John of the Cross, *Living Flame of Love, The Collected Works of St. John of the Cross*, stanza 2, no. 27, p. 667.

[52] Francis de Sales, *Introduction to the Devout Life*, pt. IV, chap. 8, p. 248.

[53] Ibid., pt. IV, chap. 7, p. 247.

[54] Ibid., pt. IV, chap. 7, p. 246.

[55] Ibid., pt. IV, chap. 7, p. 247.

[56] Ibid., pt. IV, chap. 9, p. 249.

[57] Bernard of Clairvaux, *On the Song of Songs*, vol. I, sermon 15, no. 6, pp. 110–11.

[58] Francis de Sales, *Introduction to the Devout Life*, pt. IV, chap. 14, p. 249.

[59] John of the Cross, *Dark Night*, bk. I, chap. 3, no. 3, pp. 366–67.

[60] Francis de Sales, *Introduction to the Devout Life*, pt. IV, chap. 14, pp. 249–51.

[61] Bernard of Clairvaux, *On the Song of Songs*, vol. III, sermon 63, no. 6, pp. 167–68.

[62] Teresa of Avila, *The Interior Castle*, sect. III, chap. 1, no. 6, p. 307.

[63] Bernard of Clairvaux, *On the Song of Songs*, vol. III, sermon 54, no. 8, pp. 76–77.

64 Ibid., vol. III, sermon 54, no. 9, p. 78.

65 Ibid., vol. III, sermon 54, no. 10, pp. 78–79.

66 Francis de Sales, *Introduction to the Devout Life*, pt. IV, chap. 15, pp. 256–57.

67 Ibid., pt. III, chap. 3, pp. 131–32.

68 Bernard of Clairvaux, *On the Song of Songs,* vol. IV, sermon 76, no. 2, p. 110.

69 John of the Cross, *The Dark Night*, bk. I, chap. 9, nos. 1–9, pp. 377–80.

70 Thérèse of Lisieux, *Story of a Soul*, chap. XI, p. 243.

71 Ibid., chap. IX, p. 198.

72 Ibid.

73 Ibid., chap. IX, p. 199.

74 Ibid., chap. IX, p. 200.

75 Catherine of Siena, *The Dialogue*, chap. 63, p.119.

76 Ibid., chap. 78, p. 147.

77 Bernard of Clairvaux, *On the Song of Songs*, vol. III, sermon 56, no. 4, p. 90.

78 Ibid., vol. I, sermon 14, no. 6, p. 102.

79 Thérèse of Lisieux, *Story of a Soul*, chap. VII, p. 148.

Chapter Nine

1 Teresa of Avila, *The Interior Castle*, sect. III, chap. 1, no. 5, p. 306.

2 Bernard of Clairvaux, *On the Song of Songs,* vol. III, sermon 66, no. 2, p. 131.

3 Ibid., vol. IV, sermon 67, no. 8, p. 12.

4 Ibid., vol. II, sermon 35, nos. 7–9, pp. 170–72.

5 Teresa of Avila, *The Interior Castle*, sect. I, chap. 2, nos. 1–5, pp. 288–89.

6 Bernard of Clairvaux, *On the Song of Songs*, vol. IV, sermon 82, no. 3, pp. 173–74.

7 John of the Cross, *The Spiritual Canticle*, stanza I, no. 7, p. 480.

8 Bernard of Clairvaux, *On the Song of Songs*, vol. II, sermon 27, no. 10, p. 83.

9 Ibid., vol. IV, sermon 83, nos. 1–2, p. 181.

10 Ibid., vol. II, sermon 38, nos. 1–2, pp. 187–88.

11 Teresa of Avila, *The Interior Castle*, sect. I, chap. 2, no. 9, p. 292.

12 Ibid., sect. II, chap. 1, no. 11, p. 303.

13 Bernard of Clairvaux, *On the Song of Songs*, vol. II, sermon 36, nos. 5–7, pp. 178–79.

14 Catherine of Siena, *The Dialogue*, chap. 66, p. 124.

15 Ibid., chap. 66, p. 125.

16 Ibid.

17 Bernard of Clairvaux, *On the Song of Songs*, vol. II, sermon 36, no. 6, p. 179.

18 Teresa of Avila, *Her Life*, chap. 13, no. 2, pp. 123–24.

19 Catherine of Siena, *The Dialogue*, chap. 54, p. 107.

20 Augustine, *Confessions*, bk. I, no. 1, p. 3. See also Augustine, *Commentary on Psalm 42*, available at http://www.newadvent.org/fathers/1801042.htm.

21 Catherine of Siena, *The Dialogue*, chap. 15, p. 54.

22 Bernard of Clairvaux, *On the Song of Songs*, vol. I, sermon 17, no. 1, pp. 126–27.

23 Ibid., vol. III, sermon 51, no. 5, p. 44.

24 Ibid., vol. IV, sermon 74, no. 2, p. 87.

25 John of the Cross, *The Spiritual Canticle*, stanza VI, no. 2, p. 498.

26 Bernard of Clairvaux, *On the Song of Songs*, vol. IV, sermon 74, no. 4, p. 89.

27 Ibid., vol. IV, sermon 84, no. 1, pp. 188–89.

28 Francis De Sales, *Treatise on the Love of God,* trans. Henry Benedict Mackey (Rockford, IL: TAN Publishers, 1997), bk. III, chap. X, pp. 153–54.

29 Bernard of Clairvaux, *On the Song of Songs*, vol. II, sermon 21, no. 1, pp. 3–4.

30 Ibid., vol. III, sermon 58, no. 2, pp. 108–9.

31 Ibid., vol. III, sermon 59, no. 6, pp. 125–26.
32 Ibid., vol. IV, sermon 84, nos. 3–4, pp.190–91.
33 Ibid., vol. I, sermon 14, no. 8, p. 104.
34 Ibid., vol. I, sermon 14, no. 4, p. 101.
35 Ibid., vol. I, sermon 7, no. 8, p. 44.
36 Ibid., vol. I, sermon 8, no. 9, p. 52.
37 Ibid., vol. I, sermon 8, nos. 2–3, pp. 46–47.
38 Ibid., vol. I, sermon 8, no. 5, p. 48.
39 Ibid., vol. I, sermon 8, no. 6, p. 49.
40 Ibid., vol. I, sermon 17, no. 8, p. 132.
41 Ibid., vol. I, sermon 17, nos. 1–2, pp. 126–27.
42 John Paul II, Bull of Indiction of the Great Jubilee Year 2000 *Incarnationis Mysterium* (November 29, 1998), no. 2.
43 John Paul II, "This is the day the Lord has made!" *L'Observatore Romano*, English Language Edition, June 3, 1998, pp. 1–2.

Chapter Ten

1 Bernard of Clairvaux, *On the Song of Songs*, vol. IV, sermon 69, no. 1, pp. 26–27.
2 Catherine of Siena, *The Dialogue*, chap. 48, pp. 98–99.
3 Bernard of Clairvaux, *On the Song of Songs*, vol. II, sermon 24, no. 7, p. 47.
4 Catherine of Siena, *The Dialogue*, chap. 48, pp. 99–100.
5 John of the Cross, *Ascent of Mount Carmel*, bk. I, chap. 3, p. 123.
6 Bernard of Clairvaux, *On the Song of Songs*, vol. II, sermon 21, nos. 7–8, p. 9.
7 Francis de Sales, *Introduction to the Devout Life*, pt. III, chap. 11, pp. 153–54.
8 Ibid., pt. III, chap. 14, pp. 162–63.
9 Ibid.
10 Ibid.
11 Ibid., pt. III, chap. 15, p. 165.
12 Ibid., pt. III, chap. 15, p. 167.
13 Teresa of Avila, *The Way of Perfection*, chap. 12, no. 5, p. 83.
14 Francis de Sales, *Treatise on the Love of God*, bk. VIII, chap I, p. 325.
15 Bernard of Clairvaux, *On the Song of Songs*, vol. III, sermon 56, no. 3, p. 90.
16 Francis de Sales, *Introduction to the Devout Life*, pt. III, chap. 13, pp. 159-60.
17 Francis de Sales, *Introduction to the Devout Life*, pt. III, chap. 12, pp. 156–57.
18 Ibid., pt. III, chap. 12, p. 157.
19 "On the Steps of Humility and Pride," in *Bernard of Clairvaux: Selected Works*, trans. G. R. Evans, The Classics of Western Spirituality (New York: Paulist Press, 1987), X.28, p. 123.
20 Ibid., X.30, p. 125.
21 Francis de Sales, *Treatise on the Love of God*, bk. III, chap. XII, p. 158.
22 Ibid.
23 See chapter 11, "Growing in Love."
24 Many of the saints we are quoting make numerous references to the scriptural basis of their teaching. Meditating on the Scripture references they cite is a valuable exercise.
25 Bernard of Clairvaux, *On the Song of Songs*, vol. II, sermon 37, no. 6, p. 185.
26 Some of the following reflections on pride, grace, and faith appeared in a similar form in a chapter from one of my books, *The Catholic Church at the End of an Age: What is the Spirit Saying?* (San Francisco: Ignatius Press, 1994), pt. 2, chap. 2, pp. 214–26.
27 Bernard of Clairvaux, *On the Song of Songs*, vol. II, sermon 22, no. 8, p. 21.
28 Ibid., vol. II, sermon 44, no. 6, p. 229.
29 Ibid., vol. IV, sermon 73, no. 4, p. 78.

[30] Raniero Cantalamessa, *Life in the Lordship of Christ* (Kansas City: Sheed and Ward, 1990), pp. 45–46.

[31] Yves Congar, "The Pope Also Obeys," *30 DAYS*, no. 3 (1993), p. 29.

[32] Bernard of Clairvaux, *On the Song of Songs*, vol. IV, sermon 67, no. 10, p. 14.

[33] Ibid., vol. I, sermon 13, no. 2, p. 88.

[34] Ibid., vol. IV, sermon 84, no. 2, p. 189.

[35] Ibid., vol. I, sermon 13, no. 3, p. 90.

[36] Ibid., vol. IV, sermon 68, no. 6, p. 23.

[37] Cantalamessa, *Life in the Lordship of Christ*, pp. 146–47.

[38] Bernard of Clairvaux, *On the Song of Songs*, vol. III, sermon 50, no. 2, pp. 31–32.

[39] Benedict J. Groeschel, CFR, *The Reform of Renewal* (San Francisco: Ignatius Press, 1990), p. 44.

[40] Cantalamessa, *Life in the Lordship of Christ*, p. 45.

[41] Ibid., pp.152–53. John Paul II has drawn our attention to the teaching of Saint Ambrose, who makes similar points very vividly. "Contemplating the wounds of Christ by which we have been saved, St. Ambrose said: 'I can revel in none of my deeds, I have nothing to boast about; therefore, I will glory in Christ. I will not glory because I am just, but I will glory because I have been redeemed. I will not glory because I am exempt from sins, but I will glory because my sins have been forgiven. I will not glory because I have been a help nor because someone has helped me, but because Christ is my advocate with the Father, and Christ's blood was poured out for me. My sin has become for me the price of the Redemption, through which Christ came to me. For my sake, Christ tasted death. Sin is more profitable than innocence. Innocence had made me arrogant, sin made me humble' (*Giacobbe e la vita beata*, I, 6, 21: SAEMO III, Milan-Rome, 1982, pp. 251, 253)." (General Audience, *L'Osservatore Romano*, English Edition, January 21, 2004, p. 11).

[42] Bernard of Clairvaux, *On the Song of Songs*, vol. II, sermon 22, no. 11, p. 24.

[43] Ibid., vol. IV, sermon 13, no. 1, p. 87.

[44] Ibid., vol. II, sermon 44, no. 8, p. 230.

[45] Ibid., vol. II, sermon 45, nos. 1–2, pp. 232–33.

[46] Ibid., vol. II, sermon 45, no. 2, p. 233.

[47] Ibid., vol. II, sermon 34, no. 1, pp. 160–61.

[48] Ibid., vol. II, sermon 34, no. 3, p. 162.

[49] Ibid., vol. II, sermon 34, nos. 3–4, pp. 162–63.

[50] Francis de Sales, *Introduction to the Devout Life*, pt. III, chap. 7, pp. 143–44.

[51] Ibid., pt. III, chap. 7, p. 145.

[52] Ibid., pt. III, chap. 3, pp. 129–130.

[53] Ibid., pt. III, chap. 7, p. 145.

[54] Thérèse of Lisieux, *Story of a Soul*, chap. X, pp. 221–22.

[55] Francis de Sales, *Introduction to the Devout Life*, pt. III, chap. 3, p. 131.

[56] Ibid., pt. III, chap. 6, p. 140.

[57] Ibid., pt. III, chap. 6, p. 141.

[58] Teresa of Avila, *The Way of Perfection*, chap. 10, nos. 6–8, pp. 78–79.

[59] Ibid., chap. 11, nos. 1–3, pp. 79–80.

[60] Ibid., chap. 10, no. 5, pp. 77–78.

[61] Bernard of Clairvaux, *On the Song of Songs*, vol. II, sermon 30, nos. 10–11, pp. 120–121.

[62] Ibid., vol. II, sermon 30, nos. 11–12, p. 122.

[63] Teresa of Avila, *Her Life*, chap. 11, no. 4, p. 81.

[64] Ibid., chap. 13, no. 7, p. 126.

[65] Bernard of Clairvaux, *On the Song of Songs*, vol. IV, sermon 82, no. 4, p. 175.

[66] Teresa of Avila, *Her Life*, chap. 11, no. 16, p. 118.

67 Ibid., chap. 10, no. 3, pp. 77–78.

68 Bernard of Clairvaux, *On the Song of Songs*, vol. IV, sermon 70, no. 9, p. 45.

69 Francis de Sales, *Introduction to the Devout Life*, pt. III, chap. 3, p. 128.

70 Ibid., pt. III, chap. 3, p. 128.

71 Catherine of Siena, *The Dialogue*, chap. 5, p. 33.

72 Ibid., chap. 8, p. 38.

73 Ibid., chap. 8, p. 39.

74 Ibid., chap. 45, p. 93.

75 Ibid.

76 Ibid., chap. 154, p. 327.

77 Ibid., chap. 154, p. 328.

78 Francis de Sales, *Introduction to the Devout Life*, pt. III, chap. 11, p. 154.

79 Father Raniero Cantalamessa has an excellent little book on obedience, which clearly illuminates both its necessity and its limits. Raniero Cantalamessa, *Obedience: The Authority of the Word*, trans. Frances Lonergan Villa (New York: Pauline, 1989).

80 Francis de Sales, *Introduction to the Devout Life*, pt. III, chap. 11, pp. 154–55.

81 Ibid., pt. III, chap. 11, p. 155.

82 Bernard of Clairvaux, *On the Song of Songs*, vol. II, sermon 42, no. 9, p. 217.

83 Francis de Sales, *Introduction to the Devout Life*, pt. III, chap. 11, p. 155.

84 Francis de Sales, *Treatise on the Love of God*, bks. VIII and IX, pp. 325–409.

Chapter Eleven

1 The Grail, *The Psalms*.

2 Bernard of Clairvaux, *On the Song of Songs*, vol. II, sermon 27, no. 10, pp. 83–84.

3 Ibid., vol. II, sermon 27, no. 11, p. 84.

4 Ibid.

5 Catherine of Siena, *The Dialogue*, chap. 26, pp. 64–65; chap. 54, pp. 108–9; chap. 56, pp. 110–11; chap. 86, pp. 158–159. Isaac of Stella, a Cistercian abbot who died around 1169, uses a similar "three stage" growth in relationship model for spiritual growth.

6 Ibid., chap. 58, p. 111.

7 Bernard of Clairvaux, *On the Song of Songs*, vol. I, sermon 3, no. 2, pp. 16–17.

8 Ibid., vol. I, sermon 3, no. 3, p. 18.

9 Ibid., vol. IV, sermon 83, nos. 4–5, pp. 183–85. See also vol. III, sermon 51, no. 8, pp. 46–47; vol. II, sermon 40, no. 3, p. 201; vol. IV, sermon 76, no. 8, p. 117.

10 Ibid., vol. IV, sermon 77, no. 1, p. 121.

11 Ibid., vol. I, sermon 3, no. 4, pp. 18–19.

12 Ibid., vol. II, sermon 38, no. 3, p. 189.

13 Ibid., vol. I, sermon 7, nos. 2–3, pp. 38–39. See also vol. IV, sermon 83, nos. 3–5, pp. 183–85.

14 Ibid., vol. IV, sermon 76, no. 8, p. 117.

15 Catherine is not strictly consistent in the terminology she uses. Sometimes she attributes mercenary love to the first stage, at others to the second stage. Certainly mercenary love can be understood as having applicability to both stages. Also, sometimes she attributes the love of friendship to the second stage, at others to the third stage. Again, it can properly be understood of both. These aren't hard and fast divisions but rather a continuum where one or the other of the degrees of purity of love may predominate with others also being present in lesser degrees.

16 Bernard of Clairvaux, *On the Song of Songs*, vol. I, sermon 3, no. 5, p. 19.

17 Ibid., vol. IV, sermon 83, no. 5, p. 185.

18 Ibid., vol. IV, sermon 83, no. 6, p. 186.

19 Ibid., vol. III, sermon 50, no. 8, pp. 36–37.
20 Catherine of Siena, *The Dialogue*, chap. 56, p. 111.
21 Bernard of Clairvaux, *On the Song of Songs*, vol. II, sermon 44, nos. 6–8, pp. 229–30.
22 Teresa of Avila, *The Interior Castle*, sect. I, chap. 2, nos. 17–18, pp. 295–96.
23 Ibid., sect. III, chap. 2, no. 10, p. 313.
24 Catherine of Siena, *The Dialogue*, chaps. 6, 7, pp. 33–36.
25 Bernard of Clairvaux, *On the Song of Songs*, vol. III, sermon 50, nos. 3–4, pp. 32–33.
26 Catherine of Siena, *The Dialogue*, chap. 7, p. 38.
27 Second Vatican Council, Dogmatic Constitution on the Church *Lumen Gentium* (November 21, 1964), no. 12.
28 Bernard of Clairvaux, *On the Song of Songs*, vol. II, sermon 41, nos. 5–6, p. 208.
29 Catherine of Siena, *The Dialogue*, chap. 64, p. 121.
30 Ibid., chap. 64, p. 121.
31 Thérèse of Lisieux, *Story of a Soul*, chap. IV, pp. 82–83.
32 Francis de Sales, *Introduction to the Devout Life*, pt. III, chap. 17, pp. 170–71.
33 Ibid., pt. III, chap. 18, p. 171.
34 Ibid., pt. III, chap. 18, p. 173.
35 Bernard of Clairvaux, *On the Song of Songs*, vol. IV, sermon 65, no. 4, p. 184.
36 Francis de Sales, *Introduction to the Devout Life*, pt. I, chap. 4, p. 45.
37 Bernard of Clairvaux, *On the Song of Songs*, vol. IV, sermon 77, no. 6, pp. 126–27.
38 Francis de Sales, *Introduction to the Devout Life*, pt. III, chap. 19, p. 174.
39 Ibid., pt. III, chap. 19, pp. 175–76.
40 Gregory Nazianzen, Oration XLII, no. 20, as cited in Francis de Sales, *Introduction to the Devout Life*, pt. III, chap. 19, p. 176.
41 Francis de Sales, *Introduction to the Devout Life*, pt. III, chap. 19, p. 177.
42 Bernard of Clairvaux, *On the Song of Songs*, vol. II, sermon 26, nos. 4–8, pp. 62–67.
43 Ibid., vol. II, sermon 26, nos. 9–14, pp. 68–73.
44 Augustine, *The City of God against the Pagans*, trans. R. W. Dyson (Cambridge: Cambridge University Press, 1998), bk. XIV, chap. 9, pp. 599–600.
45 Catherine of Siena, *The Dialogue*, chap. 41, p. 83.
46 Ibid., chap. 41, pp. 83–84.
47 Bernard of Clairvaux, *On the Song of Songs*, vol. IV, sermon 78, no. 1, p. 130.
48 Ibid., vol. IV, sermon 77, no. 4, pp. 124–25.
49 Ibid., vol. II, sermon 27, no. 5, p. 78.
50 Francis de Sales, *Introduction to the Devout Life*, pt. III, chap. 19, pp. 174–75.
51 Thérèse of Lisieux, *Story of a Soul*, chap. V, p. 103.
52 Ibid., chap. V, p. 106.
53 Ibid., chap. V, p. 104. (See Augustine's *Confessions*, bk. IX, nos. 23–26, pp. 170–72.)
54 Ibid., chap. X, p. 216.
55 Francis de Sales, *Introduction to the Devout Life*, pt. III, chap. 38, pp. 219–20.
56 Bernard of Clairvaux, *On the Song of Songs*, vol. III, sermon 66, nos. 2–3, p. 193. See also sermon 66, nos. 4–7, pp. 194–98.
57 Ibid., vol. III, sermon 66, no. 5, p. 196.
58 Francis de Sales, *Introduction to the Devout Life*, pt. III, no. 38, p. 220.
59 Pope Benedict XVI, On Christian Love *Deus Caritas Est* (December 25, 2005), pt. 1, no. 5. Available at http://www.vatican.va/holy_father/benedict_xvi/encyclicals/index_en.htm.
60 Francis de Sales, *Introduction to the Devout Life*, pt. III, chap. 38, p. 220.
61 Ibid., pt. III, chap. 17, p. 170.
62 Ibid., pt. III, chap. 38, p. 221.
63 Ibid., pt. III, chap. 38, p. 223.
64 Ibid., pt. III, chap. 39, pp. 226–27.

65 Ibid., pt. III, chap. 39, p. 227.

66 Ibid.

67 Ibid., pt. III, chap. 39, pp. 227–28.

68 Ibid., pt. III, chap. 39, pp. 228–29.

69 Ibid., pt. III, chap. 38, pp. 225–26.

70 Pope Benedict XVI, *Deus Caritas Est*, pt. 1, no. 7.

71 Francis de Sales, *Introduction to the Devout Life*, pt. I, chap. 18, pp. 69–70.

Chapter Twelve

1 Teresa of Avila, *Her Life*, chap. 18, no. 12, p. 162. Since Teresa wrote over a long period of time and treated issues connected with prayer over many works and many years, there is not complete consistency in terminology or classification in her writings; yet there is a substantially clear teaching that can be understood and communicated. While drawing on Teresa's teaching on prayer in several of her works, we will tend to favor the last book she wrote and, presumably, the most mature expression of her thought, *The Interior Castle*.

2 Ibid., chap. 11, no. 5, p. 112.

3 Ibid., chap. 8, no. 7, pp. 97–98.

4 Thérèse of Lisieux, *Story of a Soul*, chap. VIII, p. 165.

5 Bernard of Clairvaux, *On the Song of Songs*, vol. II, sermon 36, no. 7, p. 179–80.

6 Teresa of Avila, *Her Life,* chap. 8, no. 7, p. 98.

7 Ibid., chap. 8, no. 6, p. 97.

8 Ibid., chap. 11, no. 15, p. 117.

9 Ibid., chap. 11, no. 9–10, pp. 114–15.

10 Ibid., chap. 11, no. 10, pp. 114–15.

11 Ibid., chap. 11, no. 11, p. 115.

12 Teresa of Avila, *The Way of Perfection*, chap. 29, no. 8, p. 149.

13 Teresa of Avila, *The Interior Castle*, sect. IV, chap. 3, no. 1, p. 327.

14 Ibid., sect. IV, chap. 3, no. 2, p. 328.

15 Ibid., sect. IV, chap. 3, no. 3, p. 328.

16 Bernard of Clairvaux, *Song of Songs*, vol. II, sermon 45, nos. 7–8, p. 238.

17 Teresa of Avila, *The Interior Castle*, sect. IV, chap. 3, no. 3, pp. 328–29.

18 Bernard of Clairvaux, *On the Song of Songs*, vol. II, sermon 46, nos. 5–9, pp. 243–47.

19 Teresa of Avila, *Her Life*, chap. 14, no. 1–2, pp. 133–34. In her last work, *The Interior Castle*, Teresa uses a slightly different water analogy to describe the prayer of quiet. She explains that she now understands the prayer of quiet to be like a spring welling up nearby, noiseless and overflowing, rather than like water being brought from a distance through aqueducts.

20 Ibid., chap. 15, no. 1, pp. 139–40.

21 Ibid., chap. 10, no. 1, p. 105.

22 Ibid., chap. 15, no. 7, p. 142.

23 Ibid., chap. 15, no. 8, p. 143.

24 Teresa of Avila, *The Way of Perfection*, chap. 30, nos. 6–7, pp. 151–52.

25 Teresa of Avila, *Spiritual Testimonies, The Collected Works of St. Teresa of Avila,* trans. Kieran Kavanaugh and Otilio Rodriguez, OCD, 2nd ed., vol. 1 (Washington, D.C.: ICS Publications, 1987), pt. 59, no. 5, p. 426.

26 Teresa of Avila, *The Way of Perfection*, chap. 30, no. 7, p. 152.

27 Ibid.

28 Bernard of Clairvaux, *On the Song of Songs*, vol. II, sermon 45, nos. 7–8, pp. 238–39.

29 Teresa of Avila, *Her Life*, chap. 15, no. 2–5, pp. 140–41.

30 Bernard of Clairvaux, *On the Song of Songs*, vol. II, sermon 32, no. 1, p. 134.

31 Ibid., vol. IV, sermon 74, nos. 5–7, pp. 89–92.

32 Ibid., vol. II, sermon 31, nos. 4–5, pp. 127–28.

33 Thérèse of Lisieux, *Story of a Soul*, chap. V, p. 105.

34 Ibid., chap. VII, p. 150.

35 Ibid., chap. V, p. 105, citing stanza 3–4 of *Dark Night*.

36 Ibid., chap. VIII, p. 179. See also chap. IX, pp. 187–88.

37 See Jer. 31:33–34; Ezek. 34:15; Mt. 23:8; 1 Jn. 2:20, 26–27.

38 Teresa of Avila, *The Interior Castle*, sect. V, chap. 1, no. 4, pp. 336–37.

39 Teresa of Avila, *Spiritual Testimonies*, pt. 59, no. 6, pp. 426–27.

40 Bernard of Clairvaux, *On the Song of Songs*, vol. III, sermon 51, no. 2, p. 41.

41 Ibid., vol. II, sermon 23, no. 15, p. 38.

42 Teresa of Avila, *The Interior Castle*, sect. V, chap. 1, no. 9, p. 339.

43 Ibid., sect. V, chap. 2, no. 1, p. 341.

44 Teresa of Avila, *Her Life*, chap. 18, no. 12, p. 162.

45 Teresa of Avila, *The Interior Castle*, sect. V, chap. 2, nos. 3–6, pp. 341–43.

46 Ibid., sect. V, chap. 2, no. 7, p. 343.

47 Ibid., sect. V, chap. 3, nos. 3–4; pp. 349–50.

48 Ibid., sect. V, chap. 3, no. 5, p. 350.

49 Ibid.

50 Ibid., sect. V, chap. 3, no. 6, p. 350.

51 Ibid., sect. V, chap. 3, no. 11–12, pp. 352–53.

52 Bernard of Clairvaux, *On the Song of Songs*, vol. III, sermon 60, no. 9, p. 138.

53 Teresa of Avila, *The Interior Castle*, sect. 5, chap. 3, no. 12, p. 353.

54 Thérèse of Lisieux, *Story of a Soul*, chap. X, pp. 207–8, emphasis in original.

55 Bernard of Clairvaux, *On the Song of Songs*, vol. III, sermon 52, no. 2, pp. 50–51.

56 Ibid., vol. III, sermon 61, no. 4, p. 143.

Chapter Thirteen

1 Bernard of Clairvaux, *On the Song of Songs*, vol. I, sermon 9, nos. 1–2, pp. 53–55.

2 Teresa of Avila, *The Interior Castle*, sect. VI, chap. 1, no. 1, p. 359.

3 Bernard of Clairvaux, *On the Song of Songs*, vol. II, sermon 40, nos. 4–5, pp. 202–3.

4 Teresa of Avila, *The Interior Castle*, sect. VI, chap. 1, no. 1, p. 359.

5 Ibid., sect. VI, chap. 2, no.1–3, pp. 366–67.

6 Bernard of Clairvaux, *On the Song of Songs*, vol. II, sermon 29, no. 8, pp. 109–10.

7 Thérèse of Lisieux, *Story of a Soul*, chap. V, p. 112.

8 Teresa of Avila, *The Interior Castle*, sect. VI, chap. 2, no. 4, p. 368.

9 Ibid., sect. VI, chap. 2, no. 6, p. 369.

10 Francis de Sales, *Introduction to the Devout Life*, pt. IV, chap. 13, no. 3, p. 247.

11 Ibid., pt. IV, chap. 13, no. 4, p. 248.

12 Ibid., pt. IV, chap. 13, no. 4, pp. 248–49.

13 Teresa of Avila, *The Interior Castle*, sect. VI, chap. 2, no. 5, p. 369.

14 John of the Cross, *The Ascent of Mount Carmel*, bk. II, chap. 29, nos. 4–5, p. 257.

15 Ibid., bk. II, chap. 29, nos. 7–9, pp. 258–59.

16 Ibid., bk. II, chap. 30, nos. 1–4, pp. 260–61.

17 Ibid., bk. II, chap. 30, no. 7, p. 262.

18 Ibid., bk. II, chap. 31, no. 1, p. 263.

19 Bernard of Clairvaux, *On the Song of Songs*, vol. II, sermon 45, no. 8, p. 238.

20 John of the Cross, *The Ascent of Mount Carmel*, bk. II, chap. 31, no. 2, p. 263.

21 Ibid., bk. II, chap. 31, nos. 1–2, pp. 263–64.

22 Bernard of Clairvaux, *On the Song of Songs*, vol. II, sermon 41, no. 3, p. 206.

23 Ibid., vol. II, sermon 41, no. 3, pp. 206–7.

24 John of the Cross, *The Ascent of Mount Carmel*, bk. II, chap. 11, no. 4, pp. 180–81.

25 Catherine of Siena, *The Dialogue*, chap. 72, pp. 134–35.

26 John of the Cross, *The Ascent of Mount Carmel*, bk. II, chap. 11, no. 5, p. 181.

27 Ibid., bk. II, chap. 11, no. 5, p. 181.

28 Ibid., bk. II, chap. 11, nos. 5–6, p. 181.

29 Ibid., bk. II, chap. 16, no. 10, p. 202.

30 Ibid., bk. II, chap. 17, no. 4, p. 206.

31 Ibid., bk. II, chap. 17, no. 5, pp. 206–7.

32 Ibid., bk. II, chap. 6, no. 7, p. 168.

33 Ibid., bk. II, chap. 16, no. 3, p. 200.

34 Ibid., bk. II, chap. 11, no. 13, p. 184.

35 Ibid., bk. II, chap. 22, nos. 9, 11, pp. 233–34.

36 Ibid., bk. II, chap. 22, no. 19, pp. 237–38.

37 Ibid., bk. II, chap. 24, nos. 1–5, pp. 240–42.

38 Ibid., bk. II, chap. 24, no. 6, p. 242.

39 Ibid., bk. II, chap. 24, no. 7, p. 243.

40 Ibid., bk. II, chap. 26, nos. 5–7, pp. 246–47.

41 Ibid., bk. II, chap. 26, nos. 8–9, pp. 247–48.

42 Ibid., bk. II, chap. 26, no. 10, p. 248.

43 Ibid., bk. II, chap. 24, no. 2, p. 240.

44 Ibid., bk. II, chap. 24, no. 3, p. 241.

45 Bernard of Clairvaux, *On the Song of Songs*, vol. II, sermon 31, no. 2, p. 125.

46 Ibid., vol. II, sermon 31, no. 6, p. 129.

47 Ibid., vol. IV, sermon 70, no. 2, p. 38.

48 I delivered a paper on the topic of John of the Cross and the charisms at a theological conference in Sacramento in 2005. It is available on the Renewal Ministries Web site, www.renewalministries.net.

49 John's treatment of this important subject is primarily contained in *The Ascent of Mount Carmel*, bk. II, chaps. 19–20, pp. 213–223.

50 John of the Cross, *The Ascent of Mount Carmel*, bk. II, chap. 20, no. 3, pp. 220–21.

51 Ibid., bk. II, chap. 19, no. 13, pp. 218–19.

52 Ibid., bk. II, chap. 22, no. 5, pp. 230–31.

53 Ibid., bk. II, chap. 22, nos. 13–15, pp. 235–36.

54 Teresa of Avila, *Her Life*, chap. 16, no. 7; p. 151.

55 Bernard of Clairvaux, *On the Song of Songs*, vol. III, sermon 57, no. 6, p. 101.

56 Ibid., vol. IV, sermon 76, no. 6, p. 115.

57 Ibid., See also vol. II, sermon 30, no. 6, p. 117; vol. II, sermon 31, nos. 8–9, pp. 131–32.

58 Ibid., vol. II, sermon 41, no. 2, p. 205. See also vol. II, sermon 45, no. 5, p. 235; vol. III, sermon 53, no. 2, pp. 59–60.

59 Ibid., vol. III, sermon 48, no. 7, p. 18.

60 Ibid., vol. III, sermon 59, no. 9, p. 127.

61 Ibid., vol. IV, sermon 84, no 7, p. 194.

62 "Do not send me any more messengers, they cannot tell me what I must hear." (John of the Cross, *The Spiritual Canticle*, stanza 1, no. 1, pp. 497–99.

63 Bernard of Clairvaux, *On the Song of Songs*, vol. I, sermon 2, no. 2, pp. 8–9.

Chapter Fourteen

[1] John of the Cross, *The Dark Night*, bk. I, chap. 2, nos. 1–5, pp. 362–64.

[2] Bernard of Clairvaux, *On the Song of Songs*, vol. IV, sermon 71, no. 14, p. 60.

[3] John of the Cross, *The Dark Night*, bk. I, chap. 3, no. 1, p. 365–66.

[4] Bernard of Clairvaux, *On the Song of Songs*, vol. IV, sermon 74, no. 10, p. 95.

[5] John of the Cross, *The Dark Night*, bk. I, chap. 4, no. 1, p. 367.

[6] John Cassian, in his accounts of conversations with monks in the Egyptian desert, devotes an entire "conference" (conference 12) to the question of what level of mastery over even "involuntary" sexual stirrings can be achieved in this life. The monk he interviews is of the opinion that a very high level of mastery over even "involuntary" sexual stirrings is possible. See John Cassian, *The Conferences*, trans. Boniface Ramsey, OP, The Ancient Christian Writers (New York: Newman Press, 1997), pp. 429–54.

[7] John of the Cross, *The Dark Night*, bk. I, chap. 4, no. 3, p. 368.

[8] Ibid., bk. I, chap. 4, no. 6, p. 369.

[9] Ibid., bk. I, chap. 4, no. 7, p. 369.

[10] Ibid., bk. I, chap. 5, no. 2, p. 370.

[11] Ibid., bk. I, chap. 5, no. 3, pp. 370–71.

[12] Ibid., bk. I, chap. 5, no. 3, p. 371.

[13] Ibid., bk. I, chap. 5, no. 1, p. 370.

[14] Ibid., bk. I, chap. 6, no. 3, p. 372.

[15] Francis de Sales, *Introduction to the Devout Life*, pt. III, chaps. 1–2, pp. 121–28.

[16] John of the Cross, *The Dark Night*, bk. I, chap. 6, no. 5, p. 372.

[17] Ibid., bk. I, chap. 6, nos. 6–8, p. 373.

[18] Teresa of Avila, *The Interior Castle*, sect. II, chap. 1, no. 7, p. 301.

[19] John of the Cross, *The Dark Night*, bk. I, chap. 7, no. 1, p. 374.

[20] Ibid., bk. I, chap. 7, nos. 2–4, pp. 374–75.

[21] Ibid., bk. I, chap. 3, no. 6, p. 364.

[22] Bernard of Clairvaux, *On the Song of Songs*, vol. IV, sermon 80, nos. 3–4, pp. 148–49.

[23] John of the Cross, *The Dark Night*, bk. I, chap. 4, no. 8, p. 370.

[24] Ibid., bk. II, chap. 3, no. 1, pp. 398–99.

[25] Ibid., bk. I, chap. 1, no. 1, p. 395.

[26] Ibid., bk. II, chap. 2, nos. 1–2, pp. 396–97.

[27] Ibid., bk. II, chap. 2, no. 3, p. 397.

[28] John of the Cross, *The Living Flame of Love*, stanza 2, nos. 24–25, p. 666.

[29] Ibid.

[30] John of the Cross, *The Dark Night*, bk. II, chap. 10, nos. 1–2, pp. 416–417.

[31] Bernard of Clairvaux, *On the Song of Songs*, vol. III, sermon 57, nos. 7–8, pp. 102–3.

[32] John of the Cross, *The Dark Night*, bk. II, chap. 7, no. 2, p. 406. Some of the many passages that John cites to illumine what he means by the "dark night" are: Job 16:12–16; Lam. 3:1–20; Ps. 139:12; Ps. 143:304; Ps. 55:15; Ps. 18:5–6; Jon. 2:1–3; Ps. 88:8; Ps. 69:1–3.

[33] Teresa of Avila, *The Interior Castle*, sect. VI, chap.1, nos. 2–9, pp. 360–64.

[34] Thérèse of Lisieux, *Story of a Soul*, chap. V, p. 109.

[35] Ibid., chap. VII, pp. 156–57.

[36] Teresa of Avila, *The Interior Castle*, sect. VI, chap. 1, no. 6, p. 362.

[37] Ibid.

[38] Ibid., sect. VI, chap. 1, no. 7, p. 362.

[39] Ibid., sect. VI, chap. 1, no. 9, p. 364.

[40] Ibid., sect. VI, chap. 1, no. 11, pp. 364–65.

[41] Ibid., sect. VI, chap. 1, no. 13, p. 365.

[42] Ibid., sect. VI, chap. 1, no. 12, p. 365.

43 Ibid., sect. VI, chap. 1, no. 10, 13, pp. 364–65.

44 Ibid., sect. VI, chap. 1, no. 10, 15, pp. 364, 366.

45 John of the Cross, *The Dark Night*, bk. II, chap. 3, no. 3, p. 399.

46 It's remarkable to read some of these references in light of John's interpretation: Job 7:20, 12:22, 16:12–16, 23:6; Jon. 2:1–7; Ps. 18:5–6, 55:15, 69: 1–3, 88:4–8, 139:12, 142:3–4; Lam. 3:1–20; Ezek. 24:10–11.

47 John of the Cross, *The Dark Night*, bk. II, chap. 6, no. 3, p. 404.

48 See also Psalm 6 and Psalm 38 for particularly vivid descriptions that speak of the dark night.

49 John of the Cross, *The Dark Night*, bk. II, chap. 5, nos. 5–6, pp. 402–3.

50 Ibid., bk. II, chap. 6, no. 5, p. 405.

51 Bernard of Clairvaux, *On the Song of Songs*, vol. III, sermon 57, nos. 7–8, p. 102.

52 Catherine of Siena, *The Dialogue*, chap. 144, p. 301.

53 John of the Cross, *The Dark Night*, bk. II, chap. 6, no. 6, pp. 405–6.

54 Ibid., bk. II, chap. 6, no. 6, p. 406.

55 John of the Cross, *The Living Flame of Love*, stanza 1, no. 24, p. 651.

56 Francis de Sales, *Introduction to the Devout Life*, pt. IV, chap. 15, pp. 269–70.

57 Francis de Sales, *Treatise on the Love of God*, bk. IX, chap. V; pp. 376–377.

58 Thérèse of Lisieux, *Story of a Soul*, chap. VIII, p. 167.

59 John of the Cross, *The Dark Night*, bk. II, chap. 4, nos. 1–5.

60 Thérèse of Lisieux, *Story of a Soul*, chap. I, p. 15. See also chap. III, p. 59.

61 Ibid., chap. VII, p. 149.

62 Ibid., chap. VII, pp. 149, 158; chap. I, pp. 12, 28; chap. II, p. 39; chap. I, p. 24; chap. IV, pp. 86–87.

63 Ibid., chap. IV, p. 91.

64 John of the Cross, *The Dark Night*, bk. II, chap. 9, no. 1, p. 412.

65 John of the Cross, *The Living Flame of Love*, stanza 2, no. 16, pp. 663-64.

Chapter Fifteen

1 Bernard of Clairvaux, *On the Song of Songs*, vol. III, sermon 61, no. 1, p. 140.

2 Ibid., vol. IV, sermon 85, no. 12, p. 208. See also sermon 85, nos. 10–11, pp. 206–8.

3 John of the Cross, *The Spiritual Canticle*, stanza 22, no. 4, p. 561.

4 Ibid., stanzas 14 and 15, no. 30, p. 537.

5 Ibid., stanza 26, nos. 18–19, p. 580.

6 Thérèse of Lisieux, *Story of a Soul*, chap. VII, p. 159–60; chap. X, pp. 220–29.

7 John of the Cross, *The Spiritual Canticle*, stanza 26, nos. 18–19, p. 580.

8 Ibid., stanza 28, no. 7, p. 585.

9 Thérèse of Lisieux, *Story of a Soul*, chap. VIII, pp. 178–79.

10 Bernard of Clairvaux, *On the Song of Songs*, vol. II, sermon 40, no. 3, p. 201.

11 John of the Cross, *The Spiritual Canticle*, stanzas 14 and 15, no. 30, p. 537.

12 Bernard of Clairvaux, *On the Song of Songs*, vol. IV, sermon 85, no. 12, pp. 208–9.

13 Pope Benedict XVI, *Deus Caritas Est*, conclusion, no. 41.

14 John of the Cross, *The Spiritual Canticle*, stanza 23, no. 6, p. 564.

15 Ibid., stanza 12, no. 8, p. 518.

16 Bernard of Clairvaux, *On the Song of Songs*, vol. IV, sermon 83, no. 3, pp. 182–83.

17 Ibid., vol. II, sermon 23, no. 16, p. 40.

18 Ibid., vol. IV, sermon 71, nos. 5–6, pp. 52–53.

19 Ibid., vol. III, sermon 52, no. 2, p. 51.

20 John of the Cross, *The Spiritual Canticle*, stanza 12, no. 8, p. 518.

21 Bernard of Clairvaux, *On the Song of Songs*, vol. II, sermon 31, nos. 1–2, p. 125.

22 John of the Cross, *The Dark Night*, bk. I, chap. 13, nos. 3, 15, pp. 389–90, 392; John of the Cross, *The Spiritual Canticle*, stanza 21, no. 7, p. 554.

23 Bernard of Clairvaux, *On the Song of Songs*, vol. III, sermon 58, no. 10, p. 117.

24 John of the Cross, *The Spiritual Canticle*, stanza 27, no. 1, pp. 580–81.

25 Catherine of Siena, *The Dialogue*, chap. 96, p. 181.

26 Bernard of Clairvaux, *On the Song of Songs*, vol. IV, sermon 79, no. 5, p. 141.

27 John of the Cross, *The Spiritual Canticle*, stanza 23, no. 1, p. 563.

Chapter Sixteen

1 John of the Cross, *The Spiritual Canticle*, stanza 27, no. 6, p. 582.

2 Ibid., stanza 29, no. 8, pp. 589–90.

3 Bernard of Clairvaux, *On the Song of Songs*, vol. IV, sermon 68, no. 2, p. 18.

4 Ibid., vol. II, sermon 32, no. 8, p. 141.

5 John of the Cross, *The Spiritual Canticle*, stanza 27, no. 8; stanza 28, no. 1, p. 583.

6 Catherine of Siena, *The Dialogue,* chap. 96, p. 181.

7 Bernard of Clairvaux, *On the Song of Songs*, vol. I, sermon 10, no. 2, p. 62.

8 Ibid., vol. II, sermon 27, nos. 10–11, pp. 83–84.

9 Ibid., vol. III, sermon 52, no. 7, p. 56.

10 Ibid., vol. III, sermon 50, no. 5, p. 34.

11 Ibid., vol. IV, sermon 85, no. 13, p. 209.

12 Ibid., vol. III, sermon 57, no. 9, p. 103.

13 Ibid., vol III, sermon 57, no. 9, pp. 103-04

14 John of the Cross, *The Spiritual Canticle*, stanza 27, no. 7. pp. 582-83

15 Ibid., stanza 28, no. 4, p. 585.

16 Ibid., stanza 28, no. 5, p. 585.

17 Ibid., stanza 29, nos. 2–3, pp. 587–88.

18 Ibid., stanza 29, no. 3, p. 588.

19 Bernard of Clairvaux, *On the Song of Songs*, vol. II, sermon 23, no. 7, p. 31.

20 Catherine of Siena, *The Dialogue*, chap. 72, p. 134.

21 John of the Cross, *The Spiritual Canticle*, stanza 29, nos. 10–11, p. 590.

22 Ibid., stanza 25, no. 4, p. 570.

23 Catherine of Siena, *The Dialogue*, chap. 100, pp. 189–190.

24 John of the Cross, *The Spiritual Canticle*, stanzas 4–15, nos. 25–27, pp. 535–36.

25 Bernard of Clairvaux, *On the Song of Songs*, vol. III, sermon 59, nos. 1–2, pp. 120–22.

26 Thérèse of Lisieux, *Story of a Soul*, chap. II, p. 48.

27 Ibid., chap. VI, pp. 124–25.

28 Ibid., chap. VI, p.139.

29 Ibid., chap. VI, p. 141.

30 Ibid., chap. XI, p. 239.

31 Bernard of Clairvaux, *On the Song of Songs*, vol. III, sermon 51, no. 5, p. 44.

32 John of the Cross, *The Living Flame of Love*, stanza 4, nos. 4–7, pp. 709–710.

33 John of the Cross, *The Spiritual Canticle*, stanza 22, nos. 5–7, pp. 562–63.

34 Catherine of Siena, *The Dialogue*, chap. 100, pp. 187, 189.

35 John of the Cross, *The Spiritual Canticle*, stanzas 20–21, nos. 14–15, pp. 555–58.

36 Bernard of Clairvaux, *On the Song of Songs*, vol. IV, sermon 69, no. 7, p. 34.

37 Catherine of Siena, *The Dialogue*, chap. 77, p. 142.

38 Ibid., chap. 100, p. 187; ibid., chap. 96, p. 180.

39 John of the Cross, *The Spiritual Canticle*, stanza 24, no. 4, p. 566.

40 Catherine of Siena, *The Dialogue*, chap. 78, p. 146.

41 Teresa of Avila, *The Interior Castle,* sect. V, chap. 1, no. 5, pp. 337–38.

[42] Bernard of Clairvaux, *On the Song of Songs*, vol. II, sermon 39, no. 5, p. 195.

[43] Ibid., vol. II, sermon 31, no. 7, p. 129.

[44] John of the Cross, *The Spiritual Canticle,* stanza 2, nos. 4, 6, p. 567; ibid., stanza 25, no. 11, p. 577.

[45] Catherine of Siena, *The Dialogue*, chap. 78, pp. 145–47.

[46] John of the Cross, *The Spiritual Canticle,* stanza 24, no. 5, p. 567.

[47] John of the Cross, *The Living Flame of Love*, stanza 2, no. 36, p. 672.

[48] John of the Cross, *The Spiritual Canticle*, stanza 39, no. 9, p. 625.

[49] Bernard of Clairvaux, *On the Song of Songs*, vol. I, sermon 11, no. 1, p. 69.

[50] Ibid., vol. IV, sermon 71, nos. 3–4, pp. 50–51.

[51] Ibid., vol. I, sermon 13, no. 7, pp. 94–95.

[52] Ibid., vol. III, sermon 56, no. 7, pp. 93–94.

[53] Ibid., vol. II, sermon 15, no. 8, p. 112.

[54] Teresa of Avila, *The Interior Castle*, sect. VI, chap. 6, no. 10, p. 395.

[55] Ibid., sect. VI, chap. 6, no. 11, pp. 395–96.

[56] Ibid., sect. VI, chap. 6, nos. 12–13, pp. 396–97.

[57] John Paul II, Apostolic Letter on Preparation for the Jubilee of the Year 2000 *Tertio Millennio Adveniente* (November 10, 1994), no. 16 (emphasis in original). See www.vatican.va/holy_father/john_paul_ii/apost_letters/.

[58] Bernard of Clairvaux, *On the Song of Songs*, vol. III, sermon 49, nos. 1–2, pp. 21–23.

[59] Ibid., vol. III, sermon 49, no. 4, pp. 24–25.

[60] Ibid., vol. I, sermon 7, no. 3, p. 40.

[61] John of the Cross, *The Spiritual Canticle*, stanza 25, nos. 7–8, p. 572.

[62] Ibid., stanza 26, no. 1, p. 574.

[63] Ibid., stanza 26, no. 13, pp. 577–78.

[64] Thérèse of Lisieux, *Story of a Soul,* chap. V, p. 101.

[65] John of the Cross, *The Spiritual Canticle*, stanza 26, no. 16, p. 579.

Chapter Seventeen

[1] Catherine of Siena, *The Dialogue*, chap. 89, p. 166.

[2] Ibid., chap. 145, pp. 303–4.

[3] Ibid., chap. 145, pp. 305–6.

[4] Ibid., chap. 145, p. 306.

[5] Father Frederick Miller has written an insightful study of the particular "trial of faith" that Thérèse experienced in the last year and a half of her life, *The Trial of Faith of St. Thérèse of Lisieux*, (New York: Alba House, 1998).

[6] Thérèse of Lisieux, *Story of a Soul*, chap. IV, p. 79.

[7] Ibid., chap. X, pp. 211–12.

[8] Ibid., chap. X, p. 213.

[9] Ibid., chap. X, pp. 213–14.

[10] Ibid., chap. X, p. 214.

[11] John of the Cross, *Living Flame of Love*, stanza 1, nos. 30, 34, pp. 653–54, 656.

[12] Ibid., stanza 1, no. 36; p. 657.

[13] Thérèse of Lisieux, *Story of a Soul,* epilogue, p. 267.

[14] Ibid.

[15] Ibid., p. 269.

[16] Ibid., p. 264.

[17] Ibid.

[18] Ibid., p. 265.

[19] Ibid., p. 264.

20 Ibid., p. 265.

21 Ibid., p. 269.

22 Ibid., p. 268.

23 Ibid., p. 266.

24 Ibid., p. 263.

25 Ibid., p. 267.

26 Ibid., pp. 268, 266.

27 Ibid., p. 267.

28 Ibid., p. 268.

29 Ibid., p. 269.

30 Ibid., p. 271.

31 Catherine of Siena, *The Dialogue*, chap. 137, p. 283.

32 John of the Cross, *The Spiritual Canticle*, stanza 36, nos. 1–2, p. 610.

33 Ibid., stanza 36, no. 5, pp. 611–12.

34 Bernard of Clairvaux, *On the Song of Songs*, vol. II, sermon 33, no. 2, pp. 145–46.

35 Ibid., vol. II, sermon 33, nos. 3–4, pp. 146–47.

36 John of the Cross, *The Spiritual Canticle*, stanza 36, nos. 11–13, pp. 613–14.

37 Ibid., stanza 37, no. 1, p. 614.

38 Ibid., stanza 37, no. 4, pp. 615–16; see also stanza 38, no. 3, pp. 618–19.

39 Ibid., stanza 38, no. 3, pp. 618–19.

40 Bernard of Clairvaux, *On the Song of Songs*, vol. II, sermon 38, no. 5, pp. 190–91.

41 John of the Cross, *The Spiritual Canticle*, stanza 39, nos. 3–4, pp. 622–23.

42 Bernard of Clairvaux, *On the Song of Songs*, vol. IV, sermon 82, no. 8, p. 179.

43 John of the Cross, *The Spiritual Canticle,* stanza 39, no. 6, p. 624.

44 Ibid., stanza 39, no. 7, p. 624.

45 Ibid., stanza 40, no. 7, p. 630.

Final Encouragement

1 John of the Cross, *The Living Flame of Love*, stanza 3, no. 38, p. 684.

2 Bernard of Clairvaux, *On the Song of Songs*, vol. IV, sermon 84, no. 3, p. 190.

3 Idid., vol. 1, sermon 3, no. 5, p.19.

4 Ibid., vol. IV, sermon 83, no. 1, pp. 180–81.

5 Teresa of Avila, *The Interior Castle*, sect. III, chap. 1, no. 5, p. 306.

6 John of the Cross, *The Spiritual Canticle*, stanza 40, no. 7, p. 630.

7 Thérèse of Lisieux, *Story of a Soul,* chap. IX, p. 200.

INDEX

Index

Eucharist. *See* sacraments, Eucharist
evangelical counsels, 249. *See also* chastity;
    obedience; poverty
excuses, 147, 238
exercise, 132, 167. *See also* recreation

face
    of the Father, 8, 196
    of God, 425
    of the Son, 8-9, 56, 60, 129, 183, 255, 427
    -to-face encounters, 381, 433, 436-7
faculties of the soul, 178, 366, 390. *See also*
    intellect; memory; will
    Doctors and, 401-2
    and prayer, 290-1, 296-7, 299
fallen nature. *See* sin, original
false spirituality, 104, 339. *See also* non-christian
    spirituality
faith, 170, 190, 221
    Doctors and, 334, 386, 419, 421
    and works, 106, 227-31
family, 72, 247, 388. *See also* Martin family;
    sacraments, matrimony
fasting, 138-9, 182, 339
Father, 27-9. *See also* Catherine of Siena; God
    beauty of, 207
    "breast" of, 196-7, 304
    debt to, 223, 251, 261
    fairness of, 58, 142-6
    goodness of, 181
    heart of, 394
    incorrect image of, 28-9
    as Lawgiver, 229
    "lover's games" of, 176, 403
    "possessing," 171
    providence of. *See* divine providence
    and Thérèse, 84
fatigue, 168-70
faults. *See* imperfections
fear
    of the devil, 401
    of death, 428
    of the Lord, 54-6, 61, 67, 190
    "slavish," 13, 253-4, 393
    transformation of, 93-4
feelings. *See* emotions
"filial" love, 13, 255. *See also* unitive way
finances. *See* possessions
firm purpose of amendment, 108. *See also*
    sacraments, confession
flesh, 159, 168, 185, 240, 362, 417
flirting, 264. *See also* sexuality

foolishness, 143
    Bernard and, 55-6, 61, 293
    Catherine and, 58
    Francis and, 165, 264
    Teresa and, 187
    Thérèse and, 82, 377-8
forgiveness of sins. *See* Father, mercy of
Francis de Sales, Saint. *See also specific subjects
    and writings*
    biography, 102-4
    "devout life," the, 105-117
    slogan of, 106
Francis of Assisi, Saint, 24-5, 102, 158, 355-6,
    407
fraternal correction, 332-3
friendship, 120-1, 127, 164, 433
    Bernard and, 113, 381, 395
    Catherine and, 256
    defined, 266-9
    other Doctors and, 262-93
    John and, 342
    for laity, 267. *See also* laity
    "particular," 293
    as a virtue, 267. *See also* virtues
fruitfulness
    physical. *See* procreation; sacraments,
        matrimony
    spiritual, 385-413

God. *See also* Father; Jesus Christ; Spirit
    "abandonment" by, 356, 366, 422, 432
    arms of, 426
    beauty of, 434
    "breathing" of, 398
    dependence on, 364
    glory of, 57, 75, 81, 226, 272
    image of, 186
    kingdom of, 291, 351, 357, 362
    knowledge of. *See* knowledge
    mercy of, 51, 114, 144, 188, 211
    presence of, 403-4
    providence of. *See* divine providence
    "touches" of, 325, 370. *See also* grace
    visits of, 293-6, 379
    will of, 107, 145-6, 153-4, 178, 300, 356,
        379
    "words" from, 312-331
"good Catholics," 182, 193. *See also* laity
good works, 338-40, 391-3, 401, 431. *See also*
    effort; love, acts of; meriting
government. *See* state
grace, 13, 17, 36, 164, 225, 312.

467

Index

"mercenary" love, 13, 254-5, 317, 418. *See also* illuminative way
mercy. *See* God, mercy of
meriting, 225, 227, 300, 322, 391, 429. *See also* effort; grace, response to; self-reliance
mind. *See* intellect
miracles, 334
money. *See* possessions
Monica, Saint, 27, 29-30, 40, 273
mortification. *See* self-denial
Mother Teresa of Calcutta, 341-2
mystics. *See* contemplatives

"narrow gate." *See* spiritual journey, metaphors for
nature, 75-7, 331-3, 394-8
    divine, 439
    human. *See* personhood, soul
    knowledge of. *See* science
nature, fallen. *See* sin, original
near occasions of sin. *See* sin, near occasions of
New Testament, 224, 251, 296, 323, 393, 438.
    See also biblical worldview; Old Testament; Scripture
    figures, 41, 267, 269
    kerygma, 231, 331
    parables, 33, 215, 226, 229, 351, 440
    Pentecost, 409
    Sermon on the Mount, 2, 251, 339
non-Christian spirituality, 360

obedience, 227, 246-9, 310, 360, 375
occasions of sin. *See* sin, near occasions of
old age, 424, 426
Old Testament, 8, 109, 224, 358-9. *See also* Song of Songs; biblical worldview; Scripture
    David, 51, 135, 152, 208, 214, 269, 409-11
    figures, 86, 176, 327, 329-30, 359
    Job, 357, 359, 366, 426
orders. *See* religious orders
ordinary people. *See* laity
"Our Father," 125-6, 128, 174, 292

paganism, 32, 275. *See also* Augustine, and pagan philosophy; *specific individuals and writings*
pain, 244-5, 310, 355, 373, 433. *See also* illness; suffering
paradise. *See* beatific vision; heaven
passion of Christ. *See* Jesus Christ, passion of
passions. *See* emotions

Paul, Saint, 34, 235, 267, 327, 332, 417
Penance. *See* sacraments, confession
penance. *See* almsgiving; fasting; prayer; self-denial
"people pleasing," 377
perfection. *See* spiritual journey
persecution, 289, 433. *See also* martyrs
perseverance. *See* spiritual journey, perseverance during
personhood, 157, 206, 222, 439. *See also* soul
perspective, eternal. *See* "light of eternity"
Peter, Saint, 332, 409-10
pets. *See* animals
pitfalls. *See* spiritual journey, obstacles
Plato, 28, 31-2,
pleasure, 215-220
poetry, 295, 354, 394, 397, 421
popes, 48-9, 103, 106, 193, 236
possessions, 95-9, 208-215, 305, 347, 440
poverty, 164, 208-10, 213, 431-2
praise. *See* jubilation
prayer, 4, 25, 110, 119-136, 148, 151-2, 182.
    See also aridity; contemplation; Divine Office
    continual, 133-6, 387
    defined, 281-2
    distractions during, 126, 128, 130, 291
    fruit of, 215
    goal of, 123
    growing in, 281-304
    meditation, 173, 282, 285
    mental v. vocal, 90, 121-3, 125, 127-8, 288, 291-2, 357
    metaphors for, 410
    methods of, 123-5
    negligence of, 165
    perseverance in, 169
    "schools of," 3, 87, 392
    solitude and, 134, 306-7
    time and place for, 131-3, 242, 248-9, 261, 306, 389, 404
    types of, 135-6, 260-92, 296-9, 309, 387
pride, 54, 145, 219-27, 338-9. *See also* original sin
    Bernard and, 46, 54, 167, 232
    Catherine and, 189
priorities, 140-2, 203, 389, 440
procreation, 27, 57, 273, 276. *See also* contraception; sacraments, matrimony; sexuality
"proficients," *13*, 139, 349-51, 358. *See also* illuminative way
property. *See* possessions
prophecy, 313, 315, 319, 329-31